CONTROLS for OUTER SPACE

NUMBER 1. COLUMBIA UNIVERSITY STUDIES

IN INTERNATIONAL ORGANIZATION

EDITORS: LELAND M. GOODRICH AND PHILIP C. JESSUP

CONTROLS

for OUTER SPACE

AND THE ANTARCTIC ANALOGY

By PHILIP C. JESSUP

and HOWARD J. TAUBENFELD

NEW YORK 1959

COLUMBIA UNIVERSITY PRESS

PUBLISHED IN GREAT BRITAIN, CANADA, INDIA, AND PAKISTAN
BY THE OXFORD UNIVERSITY PRESS
LONDON, TORONTO, BOMBAY, AND KARACHI

Library of Congress Catalog Card Number: 59-14681
MANUFACTURED IN THE UNITED STATES OF AMERICA

To L.K.J. and R.F.T.

The present volume is one of the Columbia University Studies in International Organization, a series conceived and initiated in the belief that encouragement should be given to serious scholarly research in the field of international organization. By virtue of grants from the Rockefeller Foundation, Columbia University is able to offer to a limited number of scholars the opportunity to devote uninterrupted time to research in this field. The initiation of this series of monographs, also made possible by Foundation support, is a further development of this program, based on the premise that it is important not only to encourage research in the field but also to have the more significant results thereof made available in printed form.

This series of monographs is not intended to provide a systematic coverage of the field of international organization nor is it anticipated that volumes will appear with any set regularity. The value of the contribution which the monograph makes to knowledge and understanding of the role of international organization and its functioning in the world in which we live will be the dominant consideration in determining inclusion. The series is published under the joint editorship of Leland M. Goodrich and Philip C. Jessup, with William T. R. Fox and Schuyler C. Wallace acting in an advisory capacity.

Acknowledgments

This study owes its origin and its completion to a generous grant from the Rockefeller Foundation for which the authors are deeply grateful. Through its personnel and otherwise, the Carnegie Endowment for International Peace was also very helpful. Not only in the joint authorship but in many other respects this book can fairly be called a cooperative enterprise since the authors have had indispensable help from a great many different people. It would have been quite impossible for them to venture into many of the scientific questions which are inextricably combined with the legal and political problems of the Antarctic and of outer space without the assistance of persons skilled in the exact sciences who have been most patient and generous of their time and in consultation.

The Council for Atomic Age Studies of Columbia University has furnished aid throughout; our thanks are due its Co-Chairman, Professor I. Rabi, and particularly its Associate Director, Mr. Christopher Wright, who, among many other services, read the manuscript of Parts II and III and made valuable suggestions. Professor Oliver J. Lissitzyn of Columbia University made available his expert knowledge of air law and other subjects and painstakingly read the entire manuscript. Mr. Oscar Schachter and Mr. Sanford Schwarz of the United Nations Secretariat assisted in consultations and in making documents available. Among the many United States government officials who in their personal capacities also helped us to verify facts and to avoid errors are: the United States Antarctic Projects Officer, Rear Admiral David M. Tyree,

USN, his Deputy, Dr. James E. Mooney, and his Chief of Staff, Captain John Cadwalader, USNR; from the Department of State, Mr. Francis Colt de Wolf, Chief, Telecommunications Division, Dr. Arthur L. Lebel, and Mrs. Florence T. Dowling; from the National Aeronautics and Space Administration, Dr. T. Keith Glennan, Administrator, Dr. Hugh Dryden, Deputy Administrator, and Mr. John Johnson, General Counsel; from the United States Weather Bureau, Dr. Harry Wexler and Dr. Gordon Cartwright.

Many of the international scientific activities with which we had to deal have involved both governmental and nongovernmental institutions, and we wish to express our appreciation for the general and detailed help given by George Clement, Joseph Goldsen, Fred Iklé, and William W. Kellogg of the RAND Corporation. Dr. Lloyd Berkner, president of Associated Universities, who, during his tenure as president of the International Council of Scientific Unions, was largely responsible for promoting the International Geophysical Year, was able and willing to give invaluable insights. We are similarly grateful to Laurence M. Gould, president of Carleton College and Chairman of the Antarctic Committee of the United States National Committee for the IGY; to Dr. Hugh Odishaw, Executive Director of the United States National Committee for the IGY; and to Dr. Albert P. Crary, deputy chief scientist for the U.S. Antarctica program during the IGY; to Professors Bernard Barber, Menelaos D. Hassialis, Robert Hayton, Lloyd Motz, W. Albert Noyes, Jr., Bruno Rossi, and Warner Schilling; as well as to Lawrence S. Finkelstein, John C. Honey, James A. Perkins, Walter Sullivan, Rita F. Taubenfeld, and Kenneth Thompson.

Mrs. May Antich assisted throughout with the manuscript and other arrangements, and Mrs. Rose Fenton and Miss Sara Stalder carried the burden of final typing under an exacting timetable. Miss Khurshid Hasan and Mr. Martin Goldman checked all the notes with meticulous care, and Mr. David Padwa assisted both as a conference rapporteur and with United Nations documentation. The staffs of the libraries of the University of California at Berkeley and of the School of Law of Columbia University were of great assistance, particularly Mrs. Florence Zagayko of the latter institution. Finally, we acknowledge the expert and courteous services of the staff of the Columbia University Press who expedited the book to publication.

The book includes, with some modifications, portions of articles which appeared in the *American Journal of International Law* and in *International Organization;* we are grateful to those journals for their permission to use this material. We also acknowledge similar permission from Stevens and Sons Ltd. for permission to quote from C. Wilfred Jenks, *The Common Law of Mankind* (1958); from the Carnegie Endowment for International Peace for permission to quote from Walter Sullivan, "The International Geophysical Year" in *International Conciliation,* No. 521 (1959); from Oxford University Press for permission to quote from F. P. Walters, *A History of the League of Nations* (1952); from the United States Navy Hydrographic Office for permission to use information from some of their maps of the Antarctic, and from the National Aeronautics and Space Administration for permission to use some of their diagrams of proposed space activities. We should also like to express our appreciation to Mr. Douglas Waugh of the American Geographical Society for the care and willing cooperation which he gave in preparing the maps of Antarctica for this book.

It is understood that the authors alone remain responsible for the views expressed and for any errors of fact or judgment.

PHILIP C. JESSUP
HOWARD J. TAUBENFELD

New York, New York
July 1, 1959

Contents

Illustrations

CONTROLS for OUTER SPACE

Introduction

The relative rapidity with which man is surmounting the difficulties in the way of utilizing outer space force one to write with hesitation lest the bare possibility—or seeming impossibility—of the moment of writing turn out to be the reported reality on the day of publication. It is equally necessary to guard against being carried away by alluring prophecies which suggest the necessity of discussing with a sense of urgency imaginary problems of a whole universe infected with the rivalries of powers which are still actually earth-bound. Yet, even though the problems themselves are not imminent, consideration of them may be urgent, either to prevent their seeds from sprouting or to provide the proper climate in which they are to develop.

When this study was projected just a short time ago, it seemed necessary to adduce all fragments of evidence which tended to show that responsible statesmen and reputable scientists recognized that it was not too soon to study the problems which would certainly arise when man began to utilize outer space. At this writing, satellites are in orbit and a committee set up by the General Assembly of the United Nations has adopted a report on the nature of the scientific, legal, and organizational problems man faces in assuring that outer space will be used for only peaceful purposes. Some at least of the actual problems can indeed now be identified and, accordingly, human experience and ingenuity can be mustered to analyze them and—though still tentatively—suggest ways and means for coping with them.

It is clear on a moment's reflection that now, and probably for some time to come, many of the problems connected with outer space are more closely connected with earth and with man on earth. Earth is still the launching site and the base for sending and receiving communications. The needs or desires which inspire the exploration of outer space are earth-born and earth-centered. The use or misuse of outer space of which we speak is man's use or misuse. In speaking of "controls for outer space" we are thinking of man-made and man-applied controls; of controls not *of* space, but of man-made objects and also of men *in* space, and ultimately of men on planets in space. We shall not avoid discussing issues which may arise when contact has been made, through instruments or through human beings, with the surface of the moon or of the planets, but we shall not try to anticipate every eventuality. This study will have served its purpose if it proves to be useful in the times that lie close ahead. They may be fateful times. They may be times in which governments will make decisions which could irrevocably pour our known world into the mold of eventual destruction. If wise decisions are made, there is every reason to anticipate ever more extensive uses of outer space, and to the control of these uses for the maximum convenience, safety, and well-being of man, the ideas discussed here should still be relevant.

It also seems clear to us that the nature of what we may now for convenience call space problems suggests that effective controls must be international in the sense that no rival national controls would be able to cope with them adequately. As we shall remind the reader, there are a very large number of terrestrial activities to which it has been found advantageous to apply international measures—telecommunications, aviation, sanitation, and the production of food, for example. We recognize that as in the case of all the international organizations and administrations with which man has had experience, any system of international controls depends upon the actions of national governments; the world has so far experimented with only limited examples of supranational institutions. Nevertheless, we must examine the possibility that technology may soon or may already have made such conservatism politically or strategically obsolescent, and we may have to suggest that some fresh and vital approach to general international cooperation seems essential for outer space. No real attempt can be made here to blueprint even portions of the tasks which might be shouldered by a world or cosmic government if one were to come into being.

This then is not a brief for the United Nations, nor indeed is it a brief for any particular institutional or organizational device. This is a time of exploration, and the explorations need not be confined to the realms of the natural sciences. Just as technical scientific studies usefully preceded political negotiations for agreement on banning the testing of nuclear weapons, technical legal and political studies may clarify the potentials and limitations of the various alternative types of international agreements which could be negotiated to serve the purpose expressed in the United Nations resolution: namely, to confine the use of outer space to peaceful purposes.

All the parts of this book are related to the ultimate problem of controls for outer space, although the detailed exposition of that subject is reserved for Part III. In that part various future alternatives with their respective prospects and costs are analyzed. It is recognized that the space problem is novel and that it can be quite misleading to apply indiscriminatingly to its solution precedents of international experience on earth. It would be equally unwise to shrug off all such experience as irrelevant. Of rather special relevance is the situation in the Antarctic, where man confronts the last great empty continent; this is dealt with in Part II.

While—in contrast (at the moment) to the situation in outer space—various governments have advanced claims to sovereignty over portions of Antarctica, most of that area is still in a very real sense empty. Unlike the African continent, where budding rivalries and conflicts led the powers in 1885 to seek some measure of international agreement and cooperation, the Antarctic continent is largely uninhabited. Several governmental proposals for an international solution of the potential problems of Antarctica have been advanced. Effective cooperation among various national groups was attained under the program of the International Geophysical Year. As many as ten thousand persons living in Antarctica have been engaged in or have provided support services needed for scientific exploration in a single year. On islands adjacent to the continent there are some small permanent settlements. Governments anxious to substantiate territorial claims have been groping for and finding opportunities for various acts of political administration. Just as scientists and engineers have envisaged whole towns in the tropics enclosed in an air-conditioned shell, so necessity or advantage may lead to facilities for more regular habitation of the polar region. Without reaching any conclusion at this point on the likelihood of such a development, and despite current gaps in our knowledge of Antarctica, our information is sufficient to make it feasible to consider concretely the utilization of various forms of international cooperation which have been previously utilized in other situations. The testing of these forms or devices in those polar surroundings may make it easier to consider which among them might be useful in establishing international controls for outer space.

Even though some forms of international cooperation have already been practiced in Antarctica, the experiment is still on the threshold. Depending on the basic political decisions which governments may make, there are numerous other experiences with international administration and organization which might be pertinent in that they could be adapted to the solution of the Antarctic problem. It is not practicable and it would hardly be useful to recapitulate in this study the whole history of international organization, but in Part I the most relevant portions of that history have been recalled. Although it appears that the immediate and proximate pattern of cooperation in the Antarctic will be along technical or functional lines, the first chapter, which now follows, begins with a summary review of various types of political cooperation which sovereign states have utilized in the past, including the condominium, joint belligerent occupations, the novel case of Spitsbergen, trusteeships, and others. In Chapter 2 the additional examples of international cooperation in administration or government described are principally those established or projected in connection with the League of Nations or with the United Nations—Danzig, the Saar, Leticia, Trieste, Jerusalem, and the like. The numerous instances of functional organizations which have been established on an international scale to deal with communications, health, commodities, transport, welfare, and almost every other aspect of human activities, are brought to mind in Chapter 3, and it is to many of those precedents that we shall have particular occasion to refer in the later discussions of Antarctica and outer space. In the fourth and last chapter of Part I we point out why and how all these precedents may prove suggestive as the newer and still more challenging problems are faced by the international community.

Part I

INTERNATIONAL CONTROLS IN RETROSPECT

1. Shared Controls of Political Administration

THE CONDOMINIUM

The political device most frequently used for sharing between two or three states the governing powers over a particular area is the condominium. Generally, the device has not proved successful in practice.[1]

As applied to the Sudan, it was described by Lord Cromer as a "hybrid State eminently calculated to shock the susceptibilities of international jurists."[2] The principal examples of the use of the condominium device reveal certain useful similarities and differences. They are similar in that they avoid any decision or commitment as to the location of that supreme power known as sovereignty. Certain cases are similar in that the states between or among whom the political administration is shared are by and large political equals on the international scene. Those cases may be sharply differentiated from others in which the "partners" are more nearly comparable to the lion and the lamb. It is to be noted that when the indigenous government, even though primitive, is well-developed but weak, the superimposed condominium is sure to create frictions and inefficiencies; a condominium of an area lacking a preexisting established administration has more chance of success. Instructive lessons are also to be learned by distinguishing between areas in Europe and other areas involving a non-European population. It is a safe generalization that a condominium has never been utilized because it was considered to be desirable *per se*, but rather *faute de mieux* because the states involved were unable to settle a disagreement in any more definitive way.

There are also historical examples of situations other than condominiums in which rivalries between great powers have been resolved by permitting one power a free hand in some area of international concern, sometimes subject to some international supervision. Thus in 1815 Russia, Prussia, and Austria gave England a "mandate" to control the Ionian Islands. In 1898 the separation of Crete from Turkey was sugar-coated by the establishment of an autonomous regime under Prince George of Greece supported by England, France, Italy, and Russia. By the Act of Algeciras in 1906 the major European powers permitted France and Spain to act on their behalf in Morocco, and although France assumed unilateral control six years later, remnants of the international arrangement lingered. The mandate system established by the Covenant of the League of Nations was in part an attempted solution to the usual haggling over colonial territories from which a defeated enemy was excluded, but it also reflected a Wilsonian concern for the inhabitants of the mandated areas. We shall have more to say about the mandate and trusteeship systems later.

The case of Memel at the end of the First World War is an interesting example of delegation of authority by several powers to one of their number. In the face of conflicting German, Polish, and Lithuanian claims, Article 99 of the Treaty of Versailles required the Germans to surrender this Baltic port to the Allied and Associated Powers. After allowing the Reich *Oberkommissar* to continue in charge as their agent for a month, a French force under General Odry took over the territory and administered it for the Allies. He utilized the existing local governmental bodies and interfered little with them. From 1921 to 1923 a French civil servant, succeeding General Odry, administered Memel with the same mandate and with the same use of the local administration.

The regime was an economic and political success but was brought to an end in 1923 by a Lithuanian armed coup in which both the Powers and the League of Nations Council acquiesced. The Memel case is distinctive if one accepts the plausible argument that sovereignty over the territory was vested in the Allies, who authorized France to act as trustee until the signing of the 1923 Convention by which they yielded the territory to Lithuania.[3]

Samoa offers an example of a condominium of three "enlightened" and, roughly speaking, politically co-equal powers unable to create an effective joint rule of a relatively small, backward area. By way of background, it should be noted that by 1850 American, German, and British commercial agents had all established themselves in Apia on Samoa and begun maneuvering to secure superior treatment for themselves and their co-nationals. The Samoans lived under loose patriarchal "governmental" arrangements; each community or clan had its own hereditary "royal" family, but there was little in common between this "rule" and that of a modern, centralized government. Faced with mounting German pressure toward annexation, the Samoan native ruler in 1872 gave the United States "the privilege of entering and using the port of Pago Pago [on Tutuila] and establishing therein and on the shores thereof a station for coal and other naval supplies," and the United States was to use its "good offices" if disputes arose with other governments. This arrangement was confirmed by treaty in January, 1878. Commercial and consular provisions were also included, and Great Britain and Germany obtained similar privileges at this time.

However, aggressive rivalry between foreign traders of the three nationalities and between representatives of the three Powers persisted, and frequently they led to active and far-reaching interventions in Samoan domestic politics. On May 14, 1878, for example, United States Consul Greenebaume, at the request of King Malietoa, raised the United States flag and proclaimed an American protectorate. News of this action caused consternation in the

State Department and, in response to foreign protests, Secretary Bayard disclaimed the act and suggested to the German and English ministers a conference at Washington. Meanwhile, from 1878 to 1885, there were repeated naval interventions by the several Powers to "keep order." In 1885, local German interests seized Apia, declared "war" on Samoa, seized the supreme chief, King Malietoa, deported him, placed high chief Tamasee on the throne, and appointed a German to be his adviser. United States interests promptly fostered a rebellion against Tamasee and replaced him with one Mata'afa, while Congress voted $500,000 to protect United States interests and American warships were sent to the scene.

By the summer of 1886, an investigating commission sent out by the United States, British, and German governments concluded that "the natives were wholly incapable of maintaining a stable or efficient government"; but a conference which met at Washington in June, 1887, to consider the commission's report "failed to come to a conclusion" and closed "with the understanding that the political affairs of the islands should remain in *status quo* until the commission could meet again after having consulted further with their home governments."

After two more years of disorders, the United States, Germany, and England agreed by the Treaty of Berlin that the islands of Samoa were to be "neutral" territory under tripartite protection, though nominally independent. The Treaty provided for a Supreme Court to be appointed by the Samoan government on the nominations of the three Powers, and this Court was to be given extensive powers beyond the judicial. For example, it was empowered to enforce the conduct of governmental affairs in general, and to decide all questions arising under the Treaty of Berlin relating to the kingship, the king's powers, and the rights of the three Powers *vis-à-vis* Samoa. The Court was also to "recommend" legislation to the native ruler. The local government of Apia, the chief city and capital of Samoa, was reorganized under the treaty, and local laws were made subject to joint consular approval with the new Supreme Court also empowered to settle all disputes arising from these provisions.

The arrangement for tripartite control over Samoan affairs is generally considered to have been unsatisfactory and a failure from the start. According to President Cleveland in 1894, "the present Government [of Samoa] has failed to correct, if indeed it has not aggravated, the very evils it was intended to prevent." Rival Samoan chieftains secured support from rival foreign traders who were sometimes backed by naval forces but always inspired more by opportunism than by principle or consistency. Indeed, political conditions in the islands deteriorated so dramatically that the three Powers felt obliged to send another joint commission, which, although offering ameliorative suggestions, reported that no satisfactory solution could be found while all three Powers remained in the islands together, and that "the only system that can assure permanent prosperity and tranquility is a government by one power." This conclusion was acted on by a treaty signed on November 7, 1899, which divided the islands among the three Powers, the three respective sovereignties being mutually recognized in the three separate areas.[4]

Another group of Pacific islands, the New Hebrides, is about double the size of Samoa in area and in the 1880s had about the same population, although the local tribal government was less highly organized. Rival foreign traders strove for predominant influence and control. France and Great Britain were the European powers chiefly interested, but the general balance of political convenience restrained both governments from forcing the issue by unilateral acts of annexation and, at the same time, prevented each from deferring to the claim of the other. In an attempt to meet the problem, a Joint Naval Commission, consisting of equal numbers of French and British naval officers, was formed in 1887 and charged with the protection of life and the maintenance of order. The Commission proved unable to carry out the duties assigned to it—in part, at least, because of the vague nature of its mission and the division of authority. In 1906 France and Britain entered into a Convention establishing a condominium over the New Hebrides, an effort to establish a regularized regime under which each Power would have identical rights and duties.

The Convention provided that, in order to secure the exercise of the "paramount rights" of the two Powers, the islands would "form a region of joint influence" in which the subjects and citizens of each would have "equal rights of residence, personal protection, and trade, each of the two Powers retaining sovereignty" over its subjects or citizens and "neither exercising a separate authority over the Group." It was personal and not territorial sovereignty which was recognized. There were to be two High Commissioners, one appointed by each Power, who were to rule by means of Regulations issued jointly. Such public services as police, post and telegraph, public works, ports and harbors, buoys and lighthouses, public health, and finance were to be joint undertakings. Each Power was to defray the costs of its own administration, while a Joint Court and public services undertaken in common were to be supported by local taxes imposed by the High Commissioners. No native was to acquire the status of subject or citizen of either Power.[5]

The effect of the condominium has been uniformly reported as having "increased discord." Some of the details provide useful warnings against duplicating the arrangements made in this case. There is an excessive amount of administrative machinery. There are three separate administrations, French, British, and Condominium; three tax regimes; two sets of laws; two currencies, French and Australian (even though they are freely interchangeable); entirely separate French and British school systems. Furthermore, in the Joint Court, French and English law are equally valid and applicable, although there is no guarantee that any of the three judges—one French, one English, and one "neutral" (appointed originally by the king of Spain)—would be familiar with any system of law other than his own.[6] In addition, each of the administrations has its own financial structure: the French Resident Commissioner's office receives about half its budgetary needs from the French government and half locally from fees for certificates of origin and registration fees; the British Resident Commissioner's office receives almost all of its funds locally from income tax, fines, fees, and licenses; and the Condominium administration, which maintains hospitals, an agricultural service (since 1952) and other local services, receives its funds almost exclusively from local sources of which about 90 percent comes from duties and fees on imports and exports.[7]

The difficulties presented for economic development by the lack of a unified fiscal administration obviously are enormous, and the Condominium administrators have consistently noted the continuing economic problem as major and unsolved in their annual reports to the United Nations. The existence of separate school systems, too, has occasioned much discussion between the "joint tenants" since it leads to unnecessary expense, but each has been unwilling to give up the merits of its own techniques and, probably, the possible advantages accruing from having the residents acclimated to its own culture and language.

Viewed as an experiment in the political administration of an area and a population, the New Hebrides Condominium is a failure. Indeed, as one writer has acidly remarked, the principal achievement of the Condominium seems to have been the reduction of the native population by about 90 percent in some thirty years.[8]

There is little convincing evidence that economic or strategic interests prevent France and the United Kingdom from surrendering the doubtful advantages of the present regime. If this be so, these two countries might share in the general utility of an experiment in international administration. "Since the number of natives involved is only around 40,000 and because of the unusually bad record of the Condominium, it would appear that whatever risks might be involved in direct international administration, they could not result in a worse situation for the natives than has been the case for the past forty years."[9]

Equally instructive, and more encouraging for the success of programs of shared controls of political administration, is the history of the condominium in the islands of Canton and Enderbury of the Phoenix group, lying north of Samoa. Canton is a coral atoll fifty to five hundred yards wide, completely enclosing a lagoon about eight miles in diameter, while Enderbury is about three miles long by one and three-quarter miles wide. Neither island was inhabited, except perhaps occasionally, until recent years. American companies took guano for fertilizer from the islands intermittently in the 1850s, and both islands were "possessed" by the United States in the mid-nineteenth century under the terms of the Guano Act of 1856. Under that act American laws were extended to over a hundred islands, rocks, and keys in the Caribbean and Pacific. This exercise of authority was not specifically based on a claim to sovereignty; to fall within the purview of the act an American citizen had to take "peaceable possession" and "occupy" an island which was legally *terra nullius*. He had to be the discoverer not of the island but of a "deposit of guano" on it. He could then file a statement with the Department of State and post a bond for the proper operation of his guano claim, after which the Secretary of State certified that the island was registered under the Guano Act and United States laws became applicable to the area. "Nothing in the Act [obliges] the United States to retain possession . . . after the guano shall have been removed. . . ." Enderbury's registration under the Act was proclaimed in 1859 and Canton's in 1860. The islands' guano deposits were worked by a London company in the 1880s as well, and Britain "annexed" Canton in 1889–92, apparently with the thought that any American claim had lapsed through lack of occupation.[10]

The islands went relatively unnoticed for another considerable period, but when air clippers began to span the Pacific they took on a new importance as a potential air base. United Kingdom landing parties from *H.M.S. Leith* went ashore briefly at Canton on August 6, 1936, and in 1937 both American and New Zealand parties used Canton to observe the eclipse of the sun on June 8. In a pattern somewhat comparable to that of the International Geophysical Year in Antarctica, the American party represented both the United States Navy and the National Geographic Society, but it raised the American flag on uninhabited Canton. The New Zealand group, landing from *H.M.S. Wellington* on June 3, 1937, apparently did not "dispute" sovereignty with the Americans but did assert the United Kingdom claim, and a representative of the British government established a residence on Canton in August, 1937. On March 3, 1938, President Roosevelt, in the face of the British claim, issued an executive order placing both islands under the jurisdiction of the United States Department of the Interior. Seven American "colonists" from Hawaii were landed at Canton and four at Enderbury, and these "colonists" remained on the islands for several years.

Following negotiations between the British and American governments an agreement was embodied in an exchange of notes dated April 6, 1939, for the "joint control" of Canton and Enderbury.[11] The arrangement was to last for fifty years, or longer if no agreement was reached on permanent disposition within that period. The question of sovereignty was expressly left open, and facilities for administration and communications were to be shared equally. No detailed plan for government was set up—it was agreed that one official of each nation would form the administration. Most important, provision was also made for the construction of an airport by an American company which, in return for an agreed fee, would make the facilities available to British civil aviation companies. Disputes as to fee, use, and the like were to be arbitrated. Airlines of other countries were to be barred.

After the agreement was concluded Pan American World Airways built a hotel and other facilities on Canton, which became a valuable link in the trans-Pacific air crossing. There were apparently no substantial difficulties in the condominium until the outbreak of war in 1941, when commercial air service to New Zealand was discontinued and American armed forces occupied Canton. The American "colonists" were removed from the islands in 1942, and the armed forces remained in control until after the war ended. After the armed forces withdrew, the condominium was reestablished, and Pan American and a British air line resumed operations. The Civil Aeronautics Administration's station manager was named United States administrator in 1947, and a British administrator was also named. However, "colonies" have apparently not been reestablished on Enderbury, and the population of Canton in 1950 was 263—almost all persons concerned with the maintenance of the island as an air facility.[12]

This "regime," which has had to deal with technical facilities rather than populations, has apparently been adequate to its task, an indication perhaps of the type of situation in which a condominium may exist and yet avoid the disappointing results of such a joint enterprise as that in the New Hebrides. Here the area in question is very small, and there is no indigenous population. The inhabitants are those concerned with operating the air and related facilities.[13] The international political background is one conducive to common effort in the maintenance of an air link in which both states are interested.[14]

The case of the Sudan is usually referred to as another example of a condominium, but the inequality of the co-administrators, England and Egypt, was so great and the relationship between them so complex as to rob the case of much interest in any consideration of the foreseeable future of Antarctica or of outer space. The Sudanese experience was preceded by three years of Franco-British control in Egypt, which is also referred to as a condominium and as an experience in international administration. Whatever its proper label, it was a failure which did no credit to its architects. Beginning in 1876, France, Italy, and Austria intervened in Egypt on behalf of their bondholders, and an International Commission of the Public Debt, including a British member, was established. For three years the powers interfered with the Khedive and with one another. The Khedive was required to appoint an advisory cabinet of Europeans and to pay extravagant salaries to various Europeans who "managed" the railroads, the telegraph, the port of Alexandria, and so on. The wisdom of the West met the benighted inefficiency of the Khedival government by setting up a fiscal control in which a Britisher was in charge of collecting revenues and a Frenchman controlled expenditures. The Egyptians naturally played off one foreign group against the other, which led the Powers in 1879 to "persuade" the Sultan to replace the Khedive with a more amenable successor, who functioned under a strict system of Franco-British control for three years. In 1882, in the face of another Egyptian revolt, Great Britain took the initiative and its armed forces occupied Egypt and established a single British control. Perhaps it was a retrospective justification for the British action which had led Lord Cromer in 1916 to remark that the Egyptian experience proved "that international institutions possess admirable negative qualities. They are formidable checks to all action. . . ." [15]

When British predominance over Egypt was attained in 1882, the tribes of the Sudan were considered semi-barbarous and were held in uneasy check by Egyptian garrisons. Open rebellion against Egyptian rule broke out in this same period, and the zeal of the rebellious Mahdi forces, combined with Egyptian and English mismanagement of military affairs, led to the evacuation of their forces. It was not until 1898 that Kitchener, commanding the Anglo-Egyptian forces, subdued the Sudan and raised both the Egyptian flag and the Union Jack at Khartoum. The real nature of the ensuing joint regime in the Sudan is indicated by Lord Salisbury's instructions to Lord Cromer. He was told to "explain to the Khedive and his Ministers that the procedure I have indicated is intended to emphasize the fact that Her Majesty's Government consider that they have a predominant voice in all matters connected with the Sudan, and that they expect that any advice which they may think fit to tender the Egyptian Government in respect to Sudan affairs will be followed." [16] The ensuing regime established by a treaty of 1899 [17] is the one which Lord Cromer described as "a hybrid state of a nature eminently calculated to shock the susceptibilities of international jurists." The treaty provided that "the British and Egyptian flags shall be used together, both on land and water, throughout the Sudan"; that supreme military and civil command in the Sudan would be lodged in a governor-general, appointed by the Khedive on British recommendation and removable only with British consent; and that full legislative power was in the governor-general. Kitchener became the first governor-general and all high posts in the new administration and army went to the British, the highest post allocated to an Egyptian being that of *mamur*, or under-assistant district commissioner. But Egypt was permitted to meet five-sixths of all military expenditures and all budget deficits of the new regime. Egyptian feeling ran strongly against this treaty, and the Foreign Minister who signed it was later assassinated, but it remained the basic document concerning control of the Sudan, at least in British eyes, until Sudanese independence was established.

Britain solidified her position with respect to the Sudan through agreements with other powers, such as that with France on March 21, 1899, and British dominance remained unquestioned by the European powers.

Good cooperation reportedly existed between low-level British and Egyptian administrators until the First World War, despite the facts that, during this period, the governor-general was practically independent of Egyptian control, and that British policy had assured that "no responsible share in the administration of the country would devolve upon Egyptians." Indeed, the British had even controlled and limited Egyptian migration into the Sudan.[18] Then, in the period from 1919 to 1924, the "condominium" became "unworkable" in practice even at these low levels. A tremendous Egyptian propaganda campaign was launched, forming part of the over-all awakening of Egyptian nationalism stimulated by the changes wrought by the First World War. The campaign was aimed at making the Sudan wholly Egyptian, and it culminated in the assassination of the British governor-general of the Sudan, Sir Lee Stack, on November 19, 1924. The British responded with notice that they were "trustee for the people of the Sudan," and that they would continue to discharge this obligation. They promptly ordered the expulsion of all Egyptian officials and troops from the Sudan while demanding an apology, a thorough enquiry, the prohibition and suppression of all political demonstrations, a £500,000 indemnity, the permanent withdrawal of Egyptian troops, and the creation of a separate Sudanese army.[19]

While the direct aftereffects of Stack's death demonstrated clearly the true source of control in the Sudan, the Anglo-Egyptian rivalry over the ultimate disposition of the area continued openly from this time, and Egyptian propaganda became increasingly strident over the years. The probably predictable long-run effect of this rivalry, as a Sudanese source has put it, was that "it tempted Sudanese politicians to toy with the idea of playing off the disputing co-domini against each other in order to extract from them the widest possible concessions."[20] A concomitant result was the proliferation of political squabbling and splits among the Sudanese, and, in general, the Sudanese political climate deteriorated; charges and counter-charges were constantly being made, and all this contributed to a "lack of trust between the Sudanese and the co-domini and between the Sudanese themselves."[21] Egypt rejected a new treaty covering the Sudan in 1946 and charged in the United Nations Security Council, on July 8, 1947, that the United Kingdom was pursuing a "hostile" policy in the Sudan. The United Kingdom in turn, relied on an Anglo-Egyptian Treaty of 1936, which, while permitting Egyptian troops and officials to return for the first time since 1924, left the question of sovereignty open and provided for the continuation of the administrative system created for the Sudan by the 1899 Agreement.[22] In any event, the Sudan achieved independence in January, 1956, having enjoyed a fair amount of economic development under the legally hybrid regime, but this was largely due to British investment and direction in local enterprise.[23]

The whole experience is hardly an example of a true joint administration. For, as has been suggested, the Sudan was run more as if it were a British colony. The relative efficiency of the conduct of affairs in the Sudan before its independence appears to be attributable to the actual location of power in the hands of only one of the "joint" administrators.

Various European situations deserve mention. There are two examples of shared controls of political administration which have endured for a century or more. The diminutive autonomous principality of Andorra in the Pyrenees is an area of 191 square miles with a population of less than five and a half thousand. Under a regime established in 1278, which has survived numerous international wars, there are co-princes, now the President of the French Republic and the Bishop of Urgel (Spain), who act through deputies. There is an elected council of 24 members which appoints one of its number as the general administrative officer (*syndic général des vallées*). There are no income taxes; budgetary needs are minimal. Revenue is derived from duties on imported goods and from tourists. One hardly knows whether to style it Utopia or *opera bouffe;* one could scarcely hope to imitate it.

On the border of Belgium and Germany lies a district of one and a half square miles, inhabited by some 400 people, called Moresnet.[24] From the Treaty of Vienna in 1815 to the Treaty of Versailles in 1919 Moresnet was ruled jointly, first by Prussia and the Netherlands and then by their successors, Germany and Belgium. Legislative and executive powers were shared in common by the two governments, who jointly appointed a chief magistrate. There was, however, both a German and a Belgium tribunal within the territory and litigants were free to resort to either one. There was a local police force, but the police of either country were privileged to pursue a criminal into the area. The inhabitants were exempt from the military service of both governments. By Article 32 of the Treaty of Versailles Germany recognized "the full sovereignty of Belgium over the whole of the disputed territory of Moresnet." *

While generally accepted doctrines of law are to the effect that rivers and other bodies of water are "owned" in separate portions by nations which touch on the waters (though with various limitations on the right of exclusive use), two examples can be noted of a *joint* ownership over waters of a type leading to joint rather than exclusive jurisdiction.[25] In the Treaty of Aix-la-Chapelle, of June 26, 1816, for example, a joint ownership over "the frontier streams" was established between the Netherlands and Prussia. This arrangement was recognized and confirmed as late as November 24, 1932, by the German Supreme Administrative Court, which ruled that neither state (or its successor) had the right to legislate unilaterally concerning the "streams" in a way which would have been possible if either had exclusive ownership.[26] Similarly, the Gulf of Fonseca, which in a real sense forms part of the "territorial" waters of three states, El Salvador, Honduras, and Nicaragua, was found by the Central American Court of Justice to be held in co-ownership by all three states. The Court ruled that Nicaragua, which in the Bryan-Chamorro Treaty of August 5, 1914, permitted the establishment of a United States naval base in its part of the

* The early arrangement for Oregon is also interesting. By the United States–British Treaty of 1818 Oregon was open to the nationals of both countries, with no agreed territorial division, each having access to the whole for ten years without prejudice to the claims of the other—a situation perpetuated by agreements until the definitive Treaty of 1846. As it worked out, however, a war was almost fought over this territory. Ownership of the Island of San Juan in the Strait between Vancouver and Washington remained in dispute for much longer and was, in fact, subjected to a joint military occupation in 1859 and for some years thereafter. The history is recounted in 1 MOORE, INTERNATIONAL ARBITRATIONS 196–236 (1898).

Bay, had violated El Salvador's "right of joint ownership in the Gulf." [27] While these instances shed little light on the usefulness of the form of condominium for the administration of territories, it is interesting, nevertheless, to observe that the concept of condominium as applied to waters as well as to land areas has already been recognized in international law.

JOINT BELLIGERENT OCCUPATIONS

War waged by an alliance requires measures of cooperation and of distribution or delegation of authority which would be unthinkable in time of peace. A unified military command may be seen as an essential of victory. The cessation of fighting often ushers in an interlude during which the ex-enemy authority is not restored and governmental power is exercised by the victors through some form of military government or belligerent occupation. The relation between the administrator and the population is abnormal even in cases where the victorious army is looked upon as liberator rather than conqueror. For this reason the experience of joint belligerent occupations is more apt to hold interest for us here as revealing patterns of coordination and cooperation between those who share the controls of political administration, than as suggesting any model for the relation between the administering authority and the people or the area administered. A few sample cases have been selected.

Following the Armistice in Europe in November, 1918, the Rhineland was occupied for some ten years by troops of the Allied and Associated Powers.[28]

The Inter-Allied Rhineland High Commission was designated in accordance with Article 432 of the Versailles Treaty as the agency for regulating "all matters relating to the occupation" not otherwise provided for by the Treaty. It was a civilian body composed of representatives of Belgium, France, Great Britain and the United States. It dealt directly with the German authorities, which were in part subordinated to its supervision. Within its assigned sphere of activity it was superior to the commanders of the occupying troops, who had the duty of executing its decisions when necessary. Both the Allied military and civil regimes were directly responsible to the governments they represented. Reconciliation of national and international functions was left to the governments represented, and differences in governmental policies were adjusted within the High Commission by the governments in conference or by individual negotiations rather than by vote.

The four regular members of the High Commission sat at Coblenz. On routine matters, decisions were taken by majority vote with the French President having the deciding vote in case of a tie. The Commission flew the national flags of the four High Commissioners, and the Commissioners and their staffs received diplomatic immunities. A German Commissioner represented the Reich Government at the Commission, serving to channel information to Germany. Relations with American forces, after the Versailles Treaty became effective, were worked out by special agreement and the United States maintained for three years an "unofficial observer" on the Commission.[29]

In general, the Commission governed under a program of six basic ordinances and seven instructions. Initially, German laws which were designed to cover occupied territory had to be registered with the High Commission, which had a veto power. Later, such laws automatically applied unless the Commission questioned them in advance. German courts retained civil and criminal jurisdiction, though not over the occupants, and general civil authority in the German governments was acknowledged. The Commission maintained relations with the Central Rhine Commission as well as with the German states.

During the occupation of the Ruhr, a much more complicated task was undertaken by certain of the governments represented on the Rhineland High Commission; the British did not participate. French and Belgian troops moved into the Ruhr, and an Inter-

Allied Commission for the Control of Works and Mines took over operation of the coal mines. The High Commission, augmented by an Italian delegate, was called on to pass ordinances necessitated by the situation caused by the extension of the occupation. Regular ordinances were based on the High Commission's general authority, but a series of "special" ordinances was declared to be "in pursuance of instructions received by certain of the High Commissioners." To meet the needs of the occupiers, the Commission took over several administrative functions and sequestered considerable property. It constituted five special committees to insure the execution of its decisions on: Customs Managing, Import and Export License Managing, Forest Managing, Special Coal and Mines, and Special Accounting. The Commission sought to control trade over the whole area and also undertook to seize certain material, goods, and property assigned to reparations. Administration of the railways in the occupied zones also was taken over by a Belgo-French *régie* as of March, 1923, but was returned under the Dawes Plan in November, 1924. Disputes relating to the civil responsibility of the *régie* were heard by a Mixed Judicial Commission for the Rhineland Railways which was established at Mainz in February, 1924, under its own rules of procedure. The Commission also controlled transactions in foreign currencies in the area and regulated local currency as well in different degrees at different times. The Ruhr occupation and special agencies constituted to help with it were liquidated in October, 1924, except for the railroad *régie*, which continued into November.

In general, and with the partial exception of the Ruhr occupation, the joint Allied regime was one of supervision of treaty terms rather than of government and was carried out largely on an occupant-zone basis with some coordination from the top through the Inter-Allied Rhineland High Commission. The aims of the participants in enforcing the Peace Treaty, with the probable exception of the French interest in promoting separatist feelings and again with the exception of the Ruhr, were substantially similar and each was relatively free to carry out the terms of the occupation in its own zone—these were undoubtedly factors in minimizing friction between the Allies.

During the Second World War, the Allied campaign against Italy and against the German forces in Italy brought forth a different, relatively unified Anglo-American control over occupied areas.[30] At all times this governmental control was in the hands of the military, though civilian employees frequently filled important posts. Four months after the first landings an Allied Control Commission was established to enforce the terms of the armistice and this in turn became the Allied Commission. Allied direction in that part of the Italian nation which had been freed from German armed forces ran through various stages, from virtually absolute government to the mildest of supervisions: initial military government, control under armistice terms, supervision of co-belligerency, and, finally, "guidance" of a nation restored to near sovereignty. These stages often ran concurrently of course, but in each, to the extent possible, the Allied control was joint.

The Allied commander-in-chief of military operations in Italy was named military governor, and a staff was set up for a military government consisting of both British and American officers. After the Italian surrender the Allied Control Commission replaced the simpler governmental organization which had existed, and the commander-in-chief sat as president ex officio. Commissioners were drawn from both armies. Four sections were set up to handle political, economic, administrative, and military governmental problems, and their various subcommissions, as well as the military government units in the field, were made up as nearly as possible of equal numbers of Britons and Americans. By mid-1944 civilian personnel drawn primarily from the United States Foreign Economic Administration began to appear in numbers in the Control Commission, particularly in the economic section, but the occupation was still run as a part of the military operation.

In 1944 several provinces were handed back to the Italian government; the Commission dropped the word "Control" from its title, and the Allied governments announced exchanges of diplomatic representatives with the Italian government, which became fully autonomous in the following year.

The problem in Germany in 1945 was quite different, for here the apparatus of the Reich government and even of local government was largely destroyed. In addition, signs of stress had already begun to appear in the relations of the four victors involved. After the unconditional surrender of the German forces on May 7 and 8, 1945, and the abolition of the "German government" then in existence, Great Britain, the United States, the Soviet Union, and France, in a Joint Declaration issued on June 5, 1945, assumed supreme authority over Germany, including all the powers possessed by the German government and "any state, municipal, or local government or authority." It was expressly stated that Germany was not annexed and that her future boundaries and status would be determined later. However, the international personality of Germany appears to have been suspended until an "independent German Government should be set up exercising with relative freedom the right to conclude treaties and to maintain diplomatic relations." [31] Whether "sovereignty" was actually transferred to the Allies was warmly debated but never officially settled.

Following the Declaration of June 5, 1945, it has been suggested that authority over Germany was "vested in three bodies; (a) in the British, United States, Russian and French Commanders-in-Chief, each with respect to his own zone of occupation; (b) in the Control Council, composed of the four Commanders-in-Chief, in matters affecting Germany as a whole; (c) in an Inter-Allied Governing Authority for the area of 'Greater Berlin' operating under the general direction of the Control Council and consisting of four Commandants each of whom serves in turn as Chief Commandant." [32] In any case, supreme authority was to be wielded unilaterally by the commanders-in-chief in their respective zones of occupation, but jointly "in matters affecting Germany as a whole" by the Allied Control Authority for Germany (ACA) located in Berlin and made up of the Allied Control Council and various subordinate agencies. The Potsdam Agreement of August 2, 1945, reiterated the principle of political decentralization, provided for the restoration of local self-government, and stipulated that Germany should be treated as a single economic unit.

At first the occupation authorities provided almost all governmental services in Germany. During 1945–46 German local and Land governments were established, but it never became possible to implement the Potsdam provision for treating Germany as a single economic unit. In 1947, as a consequence, combined Anglo-American arrangements and machinery and an integrated organization were established, the only truly fused control and "governmental" arrangement in the course of the entire occupation. Three years later the trizonal High Commission period followed. During the bizonal period (1947–49), parallel Allied and German governmental units were set up, with decision-making bodies of Allied officials heading the Allied mechanism, while most of the actual work was increasingly left to German agencies. The German interzonal machinery pointed the way to an eventual central German government for West Germany and the East-West split widened.[33] In Berlin itself the combined system effectively ceased to function after the Russians withdrew from the Allied Kommandatura in June, 1948, as the blockade began to be established. Thereafter the Western sector continued to be administered on a tripartite basis while the Soviets controlled the Eastern sector.[34]

From the fall of 1949 all governmental powers in West Germany were subject to an Occupation Statute which enumerated the authority and functions of the Allies, all other governmental responsibilities being returned to the German authorities. The Occupation Statute was finally superseded by contractual arrangements signed by the Western Allies and the West German Republic on May 26, 1952, which, as ratified, transformed West Germany from an occupied area to a free sovereign state.

From 1949 to 1952 the Allied High Commission, "for the exercise of supreme Allied authority in the Federal Republic of Germany," was composed of one High Commissioner from each of the three Western nations.[35] In general, the rule of unanimity in voting which had been used in the Four Power Control Council and in meetings of the three military governors gave way to a majority vote formula; the principal exception was to amendments to the German Basic Law which required unanimous consent. In matters involving American financial assistance, however, a weighted vote was used with voting strength made proportionate to the funds made available to Germany by the governments concerned. No weighted vote was ever cast, but its existence clearly strengthened the American position. Appeals could be made in some instances to home governments from an adverse vote, but such appeals only suspended the action for stated periods. In fact, matters were rarely put to a formal vote, since committees were small and compromise was expedited by knowledge that effective adverse decisions might be made and by the desire to present a united front to the Germans. In some three years only sixteen non-unanimous decisions were taken; in only four of these cases was a suspensory appeal taken to the home government.[36]

The High Commission's work was of course largely carried out through a large number of committees and other sub-units concerned with various aspects of German life and German-Allied relations. These generally were made up of an equal number of representatives from each national element, each representing his nation's point of view—a system which at least occasionally led to different representatives of the same nation taking divergent positions in different committees on what was essentially a single problem.[37]

The High Commission was served by an Allied General Secretariat, but this too was tripartite, consisting of three separate elements working together but not integrated.[38] Each nation appointed a national secretary, and the office of Secretary-General to the Commission rotated among them as did the chairmanship of the Allied Council. Through daily meetings of the secretaries coordination was obtained. Again, committees and working groups of the Secretariat were made up of equal numbers of representatives from the national elements.

The reasons for the complexity of the Allied controls of political administration in Germany after the Second World War were partly the product of the international impasse. They included the splitting away of the Soviet government from the alliance, the resulting delay in the negotiation of a peace treaty, and reluctance on the part of France to restore Germany as a European power. In Japan the situation was far simpler, because the United States insisted on retaining the dominant position which it had held during the actual fighting. Relatively little control was exercised by the inter-allied Far Eastern Commission over the administration of General Douglas MacArthur.

In Austria, which was acknowledged by the Allies to be a liberated and not a conquered country, the Soviet Union blocked the conclusion of the State Treaty until May, 1955. During the long interval the pattern was not unlike that in Germany, although the smallness of the country and the existence of adequate Austrian governmental authority simplified the arrangements. The Four Power Control Agreement of June 28, 1946, recognized the Austrian government which had already been formed but reserved certain questions to the Control Authority. The Allied Commission for Austria, established under these arrangements, was charged with completing the separation of Austria from Germany, assisting the Austrian government, and preserving the rights of the Allies. It consisted of an Allied Council of the four High Commissioners for Austria, an Executive Committee on which all four were represented, and four separate staffs. In Vienna, in contrast to Berlin, the quadripartite Commission functioned with fair success.

THE SPITSBERGEN CASE

One very interesting regime was designed to solve problems similar to those which arise in Antarctica. The proposed regime was designed before the First World War, but it never functioned. Its framers did not take into account the possibility of utilizing a general international political organization, yet their plan is perhaps more comparable to the international regimes described in subsequent chapters than to the joint administrations already discussed.

The archipelago of Spitsbergen, an area lying between northern Greenland and Franz Joseph Land, totally lacking in indigenous population and relatively unsuited for permanent habitation due to its arctic climate,[39] was claimed from time to time, with varying degrees of exclusiveness, by several European nations.[40] The islands were discovered in 1596 by the Dutch navigator Barents, but first formal possession was not taken until 1614 when an English group landed. The Danes claimed the area in 1615 as well. Of these three, the Dutch did not claim exclusive sovereignty but only asserted that, under the doctrine of the freedom of the seas, their nationals had the right to visit Spitsbergen at will. The French made a similar claim to the right to use. The Dano-Norwegian claim was based on the theory that all polar lands were part of or belonged to Greenland, and also that Denmark and Norway had sovereignty over the northern sea. While these disagreements were never formally resolved, they were not crucial since agreements were worked out to regulate whaling, which was the primary economic interest. Further, the problem of sovereignty became even less important in the mid-seventeenth century as the whale fishery declined. For most of the eighteenth and nineteenth centuries the islands were largely ignored in international affairs, though they were visited by commercial and scientific parties.

In 1871, however, Sweden, inspired by a national company's desire to settle a colony of Finns in the islands to mine phosphates, sent a note to the Powers asking whether any had claims to Spitsbergen and proposing, if no objection was made, to annex the area. France and Germany, occupied with war, and Great Britain agreed, providing their fishing rights were protected, but Russia objected, and her objections, based largely on consideration of the strategic position of the archipelago, proved insuperable. As a consequence, Sweden and Russia agreed in 1872 to regard Spitsbergen as *terra nullius*, to allow free right to establish scientific and industrial enterprises there and, so far as their nationals were concerned, to notify the Powers of such establishments and of the area of their occupation.

The islands were still visited for whaling, fishing, and hunting through the nineteenth century, but it was the discovery of the availability of important coal and iron beds near the end of the century that made them important to many nations.[41] Within the following decade, for example, companies formed in Sweden, Norway, the United States, and Britain began to mine coal or staked out claims, and a Russian company also bought an option on some Norwegian claims. Further, in 1910, a German expedition visited Spitsbergen to check its usefulness for air (and perhaps sea) bases. Norway maintained a wireless station and Germany a meteorological post on the islands as well. Faced with the influx into the area of men of many nationalities, and the increased economic and strategic potential of the islands, the Norwegian government [42] addressed a circular note to all governments which had made claims of any sort, including mere freedom to use, suggesting a conference to consider the problem.[43] As a result, a preliminary meeting was held in 1910, and, in conformity with its decisions, delegates from Norway, Sweden, and Russia met again in 1912 and drew up a protocol of 77 articles. This protocol was designed to meet the need for (1) obviating the disadvantages arising from the lack of any legal order there;[44] (2) the protection of the exploitation of natural resources; (3) the preservation of the status of *terra nullius;* and (4) the recognition, due to their share in the discovery, their territorial proximity, their investments or their scientific explorations, of the special concern of Russia, Sweden and Norway in the legal organization of Spitsbergen. A new conference of interested powers met in 1914 but was unable because of the outbreak of war to take final action on the draft prepared by the three nations. This program for internationalization did not survive the war either, for, by a treaty of February 9, 1920, signed by representatives of the United States, the United Kingdom, Denmark, Sweden, Norway, the Netherlands, Japan, Italy, and France, with Russia temporarily in eclipse, Norwegian sovereignty was recognized, though her sovereignty was restricted as to military use and as to equality of access.[45] While, therefore, the 1912 proposal for an international regime was never applied, it is interesting both for its own features and because it deals with an Arctic area comparable in several respects to Antarctica.

Under the draft convention prepared in 1912, Spitsbergen's neutrality was formally provided for and its status as *terra nullius* was preserved—that is, no state was to be permitted to annex it in whole or in part nor could it be subjected, in any form, to the sovereignty of any Power. Natural and juristic persons while at Spitsbergen retained their own nationality.

The government of the area was to be entrusted to an International Commission of one member each from Norway, Russia, and Sweden. The members were to receive six-year appointments. The presidency of the Commission was to rotate annually, and the Commission was to meet at least once a year, in the country to which the President belonged. All decisions, except in cases appealed from local courts, had to be unanimous. This Commission was charged with all the tasks of government, from decreeing needed regulations for order and security to the provision of postal, telegraphic, and public utility services, for which taxes and charges could be levied. No explicit provision was made for the representation of Spitsbergen's interests in international affairs, presumably because they were not expected to be important. Any state could establish "scientific" and "humanitarian" institutions and occupy property for the purpose, but the Commission designated the property to be used.

Persons sojourning or domiciled in Spitsbergen were to be subjected generally to the civil jurisdiction of their national courts; if the case involved two nationals of one state there was no problem, but if the nationalities were divergent, the defendant's courts were competent. For all cases involving possession or rights of occupation of real estate in Spitsbergen, or between workers and employers there, or in cases of contract or tort up to fixed amounts in which the obligation was to be discharged in Spitsbergen or if the wrong occurred there, or if there was no other competent jurisdiction, a special international functionary, a "justice of the peace," was to have competence to hear and decide, subject to appeal to the Commission. The justice could apply rules of private international law, the articles of the Convention and, in some cases, "general" principles of law in deciding cases. The states parties to the Convention were to assure that these civil decisions were assimilated to "foreign decisions in general." This justice of the peace was to be appointed by the Commission for a six-year term and was to sit in whatever city was designated by the Commission.

Most criminal acts committed in Spitsbergen were to be tried by the competent tribunals of the criminal's national state and the contracting Powers were to establish the appropriate jurisdiction at home for trying such acts. For infringement of local Spitsbergen laws and regulations, however, the Commission could provide penalties up to three months in jail and limited fines. Extradition arrangements were contemplated. These cases were to be tried before another international official, a commissioner of police, and appeal again lay to the Commission as a court of last resort. The police commissioner was also appointed by the Commission for a six-year term, but in this case the appointment was to be based on the nationality of the majority of persons living or working in Spitsbergen. The commissioner had charge of an "international police force" as well.

Since Spitsbergen was to remain a public domain in perpetuity, only rights of occupation and exploitation could be acquired, and several provisions dealt with the requirements for asserting claims. No state could occupy or acquire real estate except, as noted above, for scientific, humanitarian, and religious purposes. Further, only those "under the jurisdiction" of the contracting Powers could assert claims, though rights acquired before the entry into force of the convention were to be protected. Areas could also be reserved by the Commission if they were of special scientific interest, and all harbors were reserved for use by all. An elaborate system for registration and proof of claims was also provided. Regulation of hunting, fishing, and preservation of wildlife were also reserved to the Commission.

On the financial side, the members of the Commission were to be paid by their own states while other expenses of administration and of the judiciary were to be met by local fees, taxes on production and other taxes and rates levied by the Commission. If revenues failed to cover expenses, Norway, Sweden, and Russia were to meet the deficit.

Transitional provisions were included, and all disputes relating to the Convention were to be arbitrated. Nonsignatory Powers were to be free to join. The Convention was to run for eighteen years and be renewed, unless denounced, for successive eighteen-year periods. Thus, detailed provision was made for a rather clumsy regime which was, in some respects, similar to a multiple condominium but which had many "internationalized" features as well. It was certainly not clear, however, that the three members of the Commission, who were to be nationals of the states most directly concerned in the area, were expected to govern in the purely "international" interest rather than being national "watch-dogs." Indeed, if questions affecting conflicting important economic or strategic interests, at least of those three nations, arose, it is hard to believe that the unanimity required for all decisions would have been found. Nor was there any superior body which could resolve such a difference.

OTHER ARRANGEMENTS

There have been many instances in which national territories have been subjected to international obligations or "servitudes" of some sort on behalf of another or several other states. Such, for example, is the case for neutralized and demilitarized areas and for those subject to foreign "leases" or other military base arrangements.[46]

As one illustration of the first-mentioned type, the Aaland Islands in the Baltic have been under the control of a single Power but, at least since 1856, subject to an international regime of a sort due to their strategic location. By a Convention entered into in that year, Russia agreed with Great Britain and France that she would not fortify these Islands, which were under her sovereignty, and some sixty-four years later a Committee of Jurists, appointed by the Council of the League of Nations, took the view that this Convention, embodying "a settlement regulating European interests . . . constituted a special international status . . . for the Aaland Islands" and that "every State interested has the right to insist upon compliance with them." [47]

After the First World War the islanders, in the face of Finnish insistence that the area rightfully belonged to Finland, indicated a preference for Swedish sovereignty. Notwithstanding this, a Convention signed at Geneva on October 20, 1921, and ratified by Denmark, Estonia, Finland, France, Germany, Italy, Latvia, Poland, Sweden, and the United Kingdom—but not Russia—provided for Finnish sovereignty. Finnish rule was to be subject to several provisos, however, including the permanent demilitarization of the Islands, the prohibition of the manufacture, transit, importation, exportation, or re-exportation of arms and munitions, and the grant of the right of innocent passage to warships, subject to international rules and usage. In the event of war the Islands were to be neutral, and no military activities were to be conducted on them. Further, authority was given to the Council of the League to take measures necessary to safeguard the provisions of the Convention.[48]

When, in 1939, the governments of Sweden and Finland proposed a temporary relaxation in the demilitarization regulations due to "the weakening of the security system of the League of Nations and the political and military difficulties which at present stand in the way of the application of the guarantee system provided in the 1921 Convention," Soviet opposition prevented the Council of the League from taking a decision on the merits of the case.[49] On October 11, 1940, Finland and the Soviet Union reached an agreement on demilitarization of the Islands, and the Peace Treaty with Finland of February 10, 1947, provides in Article 5 that "the Aaland Islands shall remain demilitarized in accordance with the situation at present existing." [50]

After the First World War the Bosporus and Dardanelles were also demilitarized and, under the Treaty of Lausanne of 1923, a Straits Commission was established.[51] The Commission was made up of representatives of Turkey and nine other Powers. It had no operational role but served rather to supervise transit. It was responsible for assuring that warships would pass through the waterway without hindrance, and for reporting on the number and types of warships using the Straits and the Black Sea. Turkish desire to reassert its sovereignty over the waterway, combined with the need for more effective measures of defense, led to the termination of the Commission by the Montreux Convention of 1936.

An agreement to demilitarize an area may put a state in a position where it must rely for military defense on the observance of a treaty which, in turn, may have only as much strength as the international community interest gives it. On the other hand, if the state which agrees to demilitarize is strong and aggressive some international supervision is essential to avoid such evasion as Japan's fortification of her mandated Pacific islands.

In other instances nations have, on occasion, both under duress and willingly, "leased" areas to other states. During the opening and exploitation of China, for example, a series of leases was extorted by the European powers to give them commercial, judicial, and even "territorial" rights to such cities as Kiaochow (to Germany), Port Arthur (to Russia), and Kuang-chow Wan (to France). Kiaochow passed from German to Japanese hands under Article 156 of the Versailles Treaty, and it and Kuang-chow Wan were returned to full Chinese authority in 1922. By a Sino-Soviet Agreement of August 14, 1945, Port Arthur was to be used jointly for thirty years, but under the terms of the Treaty of Moscow of February 14, 1950, it was to be fully restored to the Communist Chinese government by 1952.[52] Other instances of forced territorial arrangements may be found in the course of the relations of the European powers with Turkey[53] in the nineteenth century, but all of these situations, so long as the "tenant" has the power to impose its will, represent a shared sovereignty largely in the sense that the lessor retains nominal ownership while the lessee administers the area as if it were its own. The form of the control would differ with the purposes to be served.

In a different category are arrangements arrived at voluntarily in which a sovereign gives up only limited rights in an area, as exemplified by the leases of naval and air bases by the United Kingdom to the United States in 1941.[54] Ninety-nine-year leases were obtained to sites in Newfoundland, Bermuda, Jamaica, St. Lucia, Antigua, Trinidad, and British Guiana, which involved a limited concession of jurisdictional rights but "no surrender of sovereignty or of the exercise thereof." The limited concessions include the jurisdiction of United States courts with regard to treason, sabotage, espionage and similar offenses committed within the leased area (Art. 4), and the provision that no arrest shall be made and no process served within the leased area without the permission of United States authorities (Art. 6). However, in case of refusal of permission, they must, except for the offenses referred to in Article 4, surrender to the authorities of the territory the person whose arrest is sought.

In 1950 the conditions under which jurisdiction can be exercised by the United States were modified. Thus the United States has exclusive jurisdiction, if a state of war exists, where the accused is a member of a United States force. It also has exclusive jurisdiction, even if a state of war does not exist, if the accused is a member of the United States forces in respect to security offenses wherever committed and offenses against the interests of the United States committed inside the leased area. It has concurrent jurisdiction over all other offenses wherever committed. It also has exclusive jurisdiction with respect to security offenses over non-United States citizens wherever a civil court of the United States is sitting in the leased territory. The government of the territory in question remains responsible for enacting legislation necessary to ensure the safety and security of the American naval and air bases.[55] American courts have held that the United States does not possess sovereignty over such a base.[56]

While a lease arrangement with a friendly power may work well when the goals are the same and the purposes limited, long-term arrangements in emerging colonial areas will probably not, as with American bases in former French-controlled areas of North Africa, stand up over the years. Presumably, "leases" to an international organization, involving extensive governmental control, would also prove objectionable today in populated areas. Nevertheless, short-term leases or concession rights remain possibilities where only some limited function is to be performed and perhaps also where a nation in control of an area, particularly if the area is uninhabited, lacks the ability to open it up.

Status of forces agreements involve relinquishments of jurisdiction similar to those in voluntary leases. It is interesting to note that an agreement relating to the status of the United Nations forces in Japan was entered into in connection with the Korean conflict. Thus, at least in the eyes of many members, the United Nations has already been a party to an arrangement limiting a nation's sovereignty to this extent.

THE CONCEPT OF AN INTERNATIONAL INTEREST FORMALIZED

The concept that a nation or individual obtaining control over a savage or previously "uncivilized" people or area must use its power for the advancement of the interests of the inhabitants and of civilization generally was, as several investigators have shown, developed at least as early as the sixteenth century.[57] Perhaps the most famous instance remains Burke's opening speech in the House of Commons on February 15, 1788, indicting Warren Hastings for violating a "sacred trust" to the world and particularly to the natives of India.[58] In any event, by the nineteenth century, when the European powers were dealing with Turkish and, later, with African affairs, the idea of the "sacred trust," whatever its meaning in practice, had already been a familiar concept for many years.

One instance of international concern with an area warrants consideration because it was directly in the minds of those who constructed the Mandates System of the League of Nations. The General Act of the Berlin Conference on Africa of 1885 explicitly "marked the acceptance by the powers of the principle of national trusteeship" and attempted, at least, to substitute "peaceful negotiation for dangerous competition between the powers." [59] The Conference marked an attempt to avoid international disputes over colonies by insuring equal economic access for all purposes of trade and navigation. Thus it attempted to treat the affairs of an extensive area on a collective basis for a collective gain and, at the same time, to protect the local peoples. A direct "mandate" was given for the administration of the area to a legal entity which was not a state but rather a company, the International Association of the Congo, the "cover" for King Leopold.[60] While the mandatory's rule was to be "subject to the limiting conditions of the Berlin Congo Act," no international supervisory machinery was provided and no sanction existed save the "force of public opinion." The infamous history of what amounted to a personal mandate is well known. Leopold's regime shortly became a scandal and the "Association" was obliged to give up control to the Belgian state, which assumed the rule of the general area in 1908. While Belgium termed its control a national trusteeship, unilateral rule of the Belgian Congo became a fact, though other aspects of the Berlin settlement were kept alive through additional conferences and conventions which established a lasting pattern of limited colonial power cooperation and implied or explicit responsibility in Africa.[61] The earlier arrangements, which included provisions for the economist's perennial substitute for colonial rivalry and imperialism, the "open door" for trade, proved in practice unacceptable; these were not complied with, and, in time, were officially dropped.[62] Nevertheless, international bureaus were established at Zanzibar and Brussels, though only to exchange documents, data, reports of law enacted, judicial decisions, and statistics concerning trade in slaves, firearms, and liquor. The International Commission proposed by the Berlin Act of 1885 to observe conditions in the area never functioned, because the signatories failed to nominate representatives.

It is not our purpose to repeat in any detail the story of the development of the Mandates System. Many proposals looking toward an internationalized treatment for colonial areas were made while the First World War was still in progress, particularly by the anti-imperialists, socialists, Fabians, and others in Allied countries.[63] Most important of all, Woodrow Wilson pressed for a substantial degree of internationalization for the areas to be taken from the defeated powers: "He thought that the German colonies should be declared the common property of the League of Nations and administered by small nations. The resources of each colony should be available to all members of the League." [64]

In his second draft for the Covenant, Wilson proposed a genuine and powerful international control over the former enemy territories. The League was named the "residuary trustee" of those areas, "with sovereign right of ultimate disposal or of continued administration." [65] All necessary authority and control was vested in the League, which was, however, permitted to delegate its "authority, control or administration" to a "State or organized agency."

The idea of direct international administration in particular was subjected to a barrage of criticism not only from those who favored the closest possible approach to national annexation, but also from "students" of joint international administrations of the past who emphasized the failures--as some still do today. Marshal Smuts, though not rejecting an eventual program involving use of international personnel, argued in his very influential *The League of Nations: A Practical Suggestion* that past experience was applicable to conditions in 1919, that only states were strong and experienced enough to be mandatories, initially at least, and that, while limited "international business arrangements" such as the postal arrangements and the Danube Commission had worked fairly well, an international political administration could only result in "paralysis tempered by intrigue" where applied to "territories or peoples." [66] Wilson's own expert on colonial affairs, G. L. Beer, after a study of "international protectorates" and "administrative internationalism" which he identified substantially with the regimes in Samoa, the New Hebrides, and Egypt, also indicated a preference for "concentration of responsibility" in one state to avoid "intrigues and rivalries among the governors who have never been able to forget the special interests of their own states." [67]

At the Peace Conference proper neither Wilson nor anyone else argued for direct League administration even of the former German colonies, the observations of British, American, and other "colonial experts" being of considerable influence in reenforcing the conferees' belief that "the economic or political interests of the partners [in joint or international administration] would be likely to pull in different directions and so reproduce the characteristic defects of the *condominiums* of the past" [68] and produce "confusion of authority." Lloyd George, in the Council of Ten, without bothering to indicate the oft-stated objections, summarily dismissed the question with the comment that "it was generally agreed" that the former enemy colonies could not be directly administered internationally.[69]

Thus, the idea of international administration was abandoned rather quickly by all concerned, chiefly because the major powers concerned wanted no part of it but also in part because analogies from the past were misunderstood in relation to the League's theoretical possibilities and because the idea of a truly international, impartial governmental regime was too new and revolutionary.

Article 22 of the Covenant as ratified provided for "tutelage" of the former enemy areas in each case by an "advanced" nation. A permanent Commission was, however, "to receive and examine the annual reports of the Mandatories and to advise the Council on all matters relating to the observance of the mandates." [70] While the Commission was relatively impartial and competent, and was useful in bringing public and parliamentary attention to bear on conditions in the mandated areas, its interest in promoting good relations between itself and the only sources of power, the mandatories, limited its effectiveness. "Its task of attempting to introduce international supervision was a difficult pioneering assignment, for the execution of which powers and machinery were alike inadequate. At best it suffered from the fundamental defect that, while it might prevent a relapse in colonial policy, it would not stimulate advance." [71] It lacked the ability to compel mandatories to do anything, and even its sources of information were limited, for it could not make independent investigations or receive communications directly from the territories—they had first to pass the mandatory's review. No real international administration was involved—control remained in the mandatories throughout.

During the Second World War, President Roosevelt, who shared Wilson's opposition to the perpetuation of the colonial system, was nevertheless finally dissuaded from pressing for the "dissolution of the British Empire" or of any other Allied "empire." As plans for the post-war organization developed, the notion of international administration of all subject areas was advocated and opposed both in the United States and elsewhere. No provisions on the subject were included in the draft Charter prepared at Dumbarton Oaks. At San Francisco, idealism found expression in the Declaration Regarding Non-Self-Governing Territories, while military interests were protected by provision for "strategic" trusteeships. The Declaration contains no enforcement provisions and strategic trusteeships are under the jurisdiction of the Security Council where the great powers have a veto.

The trusteeship system of the United Nations [72] is administered by the Trusteeship Council, which is a political rather than an expert group, made up of representatives of all states which are Administering Authorities, all other permanent members of the Security Council, and enough other states which are not Administering Authorities to balance those which are, on a one-state-one-vote basis. The system has certain features which insure that international attention can be focused on the problems of the Trust Territories to a greater degree than was possible under the League of Nations. The Charter contains no provisions forbidding the fortification of the territories, however, and no limit was placed on the incorporation of the territories into customs, administrative, or other unions. No time limit was set for the life of a trusteeship, though, in the case of Somaliland, a limit was set in the Trust Agreement, and the United Nations flag flies, except in Somaliland and in the United States Trust Territory where it is regularly displayed, only on "appropriate occasions," as determined by the Administering Authorities, lest the natives be "confused" and think that the UN flag is the "official" one for the area.[73]

On the affirmative side, the Trusteeship Council can visit the Trust Territories and has regularly sent missions to do so. Inhabitants of the Territories may petition the United Nations directly, and in practice petitioners are given oral hearings in New York. The weakness of what remains essentially a voluntary system is, however, shown by the case of Southwest Africa which was under League mandate to the Union of South Africa but which, despite constant UN pressure, that country has declined to place under the trusteeship system.[74] On the other hand the pattern of the times is making rapid inroads on all colonial regimes, and by 1961 at least four former trust territories will have become independent states. This result of the general nationalist revolution is not confined to Trust Territories but the trusteeship system has played a role by no means insignificant.

The United Nations Charter also embodies, in Article 81, one interesting and potentially significant new concept. It provides that the United Nations might itself serve as an Administering Authority, thus making possible actual international administration of areas by a general international organization. No area has as yet been placed under direct United Nations administration, though this possibility has been suggested at various times for the ex-Italian colonies, Jerusalem, Trieste, and other troubled areas. It was considered and rejected by the Powers in control of such former mandates as Samoa.[75] Many technical problems exist in connection with the United Nations' becoming an Administering Authority. For example: Who are the "states directly concerned?" Who would represent it on the Trusteeship Council? Could there be an "agreement" between the Organization and itself? How could the Organization examine petitions to itself? Who would supervise the Organization's administration? Can the Organization use the Trusteeship Council to exercise administration? Can the General Assembly create, under Article 22 of the Charter, a needed "subsidiary organ" to meet these needs even though the Trusteeship Council is not specifically authorized to do so? [76] In the few instances in which direct United Nations control has been suggested none of these technicalities has prevented the preparation of a program. It seems clear that, considering the extensive powers of recommendation available to the UN, if there is substantial agreement among the members, a method involving UN administration through an agent, a subsidiary body or even an existing organ could be made effective. In two of the instances in which a United Nations trusteeship has been proposed, that is for Eritrea and for Korea, the proposal was not abortive because of any technical or theoretical difficulties; in the case of Eritrea another solution was preferred, and in Korea the Soviet Union was insistent upon establishing and maintaining Communist control.[77] Moreover, in neither Eritrea nor Korea did the local population want a trusteeship. Since the trusteeship system has its origin and purpose in the international concern for people who need assistance in progressing toward independence or self-government, some other form of United Nations action will probably be designed for use in Antarctica or in outer space if the states concerned decide to favor internationalization.

2. *The Role of International Organizations*

This chapter draws attention particularly to situations subsequent to the establishment of the League of Nations after the First World War and to administrative institutions functioning under a world-wide political organization. The League and its successor, the United Nations, represent a stage of development in international organization so far beyond earlier achievements as to contribute a new element in the establishment and operation of international controls of administration. Nevertheless, it is utterly erroneous to think of the League institutions as unprecedented and this chapter begins with one of their interesting predecessors, the international regime of Tangier.

TANGIER

The city of Tangier, occupying a strategic position on the coast of North Africa at the entrance to the Mediterranean Sea, was for many hundreds of years a point of conflict, being controlled at various times by the Arabs, Berbers, Spaniards, Portuguese, and the English.[1] Even after the British abandoned Tangier to the Berbers in 1684 they successfully prevented all other European powers from seizing the city, thus protecting Britain's control over the entry into the Mediterranean. Over the years, though Rabat was officially the seat of the Moroccan government, Tangier became the "diplomatic capital" of Morocco, as the diplomatic representatives of foreign powers made their residence in this more modern and better located city. These diplomats, in turn, had an important influence on the city's local government through their direct connection with the Moroccan government.

Even before actual internationalization of Tangier was considered in the early twentieth century, the interests of various foreign nations in Tangier had led to joint international action with respect to certain internal problems of the city. Thus, a Sanitary Council began to function as early as 1793 and very quickly made its weight felt in matters of health and quarantine to control outbreaks of plague. In 1840 the Sultan issued a decree formally turning over to "the representatives of the Christian Powers" the mission "of maintaining the public health upon the coast of this Empire, to make all rules and to take all measures to reach this end." Each consul in turn acted as president of this Sanitary Council for one month (later three months), and a small tonnage tax on all ships entering the port supported the operation. The Council functioned by majority vote. By 1892 it had expanded its functions to include the provision of water, the construction of a major slaughterhouse, and the cleaning of streets and control of sewage. In 1893 a Health Commission was created, consisting of twenty-six members. Of these ten were named by the legations, one Moroccan by the Sultan, two Mohammedans by the local administration, one Jew by the chief rabbi of Tangier, and twelve others were chosen by a local electorate of natives and foreign residents. The French and Spanish consuls alternated as president of the Commission, which soon extended its jurisdiction to include lighting the streets, inspecting the markets, establishing clinics, drawing fish and game laws—in fact, it ran the whole gamut of health and welfare regulation. The Commission obtained its funds from a small subvention from the Moroccan government, small grants from various governments, and several small taxes assessed locally.[2]

A great weakness of the sanitary regime, however, was the

lack of an effective sanction. The establishment of a native police force was frequently suggested, but, even with officers being drawn from various countries, no plan could be devised which would effectively set to rest the fear that some Power would gain a special advantage; no action was ever taken along this line. The Health Commission ceased to exist in 1925 when the International Statute of Tangier came into effect.[3]

While the Sanitary Council and Health Commission had given Tangier a form of international control since the late eighteenth century, there was no effective approach to the formal internationalization of the area until the twentieth century. Without going into the complex political maneuvers of the Powers in the late 1800s and early 1900s as they attempted to gain control over sections of northern Africa, by 1906 affairs had reached a state in which a general settlement of the North African problem seemed necessary to avoid war. Largely at German insistence, a conference was held at Algeciras, beginning on January 16, 1906. After three months of acrimonious debate, a plan for the reorganization of Morocco was pounded out. It was not really implemented, however, for native banditry, war, and rebellion continued in Morocco, and it was not until 1909–12 that French accords, first with Germany and then with Spain followed by a French military intervention "at the Sultan's request," turned Morocco into a French protectorate. Nonetheless, a special regime was to be provided for Tangier, taking into account the long-established interests of several Powers there.

The Conference of Algeciras had relatively little to do with Tangier directly. In 1913 and 1914 negotiations were carried on by France, Morocco, Spain, and Britain, in particular, with respect to the city's status. On November 5, 1914, an agreement was finally reached.[4] It provided for a Municipal Assembly of thirty-five members. Eleven represented the Powers and one the Sultan; of the twenty-three other members three were selected by the Mohammedans, three by the Jews, and seventeen by the Europeans, who made up at most a quarter of the population. The Assembly was to have legislative powers, but the Committee of Control, consisting of twelve members—eleven representing the Powers and one the Sultan—was to supervise its work in the interests of the Powers with, in effect, the right of veto. Each state had one vote. A Spaniard was to head the military police force and a Frenchman the civil police. In addition to ordinary courts, a Mixed Court consisting of seven judges—two French, two English, two Spanish, and one German—was established to have supreme power over questions of law and fact. To avoid rivalries, the proportion of each country's nationals in the municipal services was fixed according to a scale based on the number of its nationals in Tangier and its economic importance in the city.[5] Because of the outbreak of the First World War this plan was never put into effect.

The question of Tangier's status was discussed repeatedly at the diplomatic level during and after the War, and a Statute for the city was drafted, with much labor, in 1923.[6] It came into operation on June 1, 1925, although the United States and Italy did not become parties to the Statute at that time. Under the 1925 Statute the Tangier Zone was neutralized and given substantial autonomy, although the sovereignty and authority of the Moroccan ruler were recognized. Because it actually functioned for some thirty years, this "international" government of Tangier will be described in some detail.

Legislative power under the Statute was vested in the Legislative Assembly, consisting of four French, three British, four Spanish, two Italian, one American, one Belgian, one Dutch, and one Portuguese member, all appointed by their respective consulates, plus six Mohammedans and three Jewish subjects of the Sultan, appointed by the Mendoub, the Sultan's representative at Tangier. Since the native Moroccans in Tangier constituted more than three-fourths of the city's total population, their representatives in the Assembly were thus disproportionately outnumbered, and the native group did not even elect these representatives. An administrator was provided to carry out the Assembly's decisions and to direct the international administration of the Zone. For the first six years, the office was to be held by a Frenchman. Under him were a Spanish assistant administrator in charge of health, a British assistant administrator in charge of financial services, a French engineer for state public works, and a Spanish engineer for municipal works. Public security was to be assured by a force of native police commanded by a Belgian with French and Spanish subordinate officers. The diplomatic agencies at Tangier were to be replaced by commercial consulates, and all existing commissions and committees were to end. The consuls, in turn, were to form a Committee of Control to insure the observance of the regime of economic equality and other provisions of the Statute. A Mixed Court with French, British, and Spanish magistrates was to handle questions concerning foreign nationals. Arabic, French, and Spanish were all official languages, and laws and regulations had to be printed in all three. The native population was to be subject to an administration by Moroccans appointed by the Sultan, whose representative, the Mendoub, headed that administration and presided over the Assembly as well, though without vote. The provision for control of the natives by the Sultan represented a victory for the French, who controlled Morocco, and was quite in contrast to the provisions of the 1914 project which had placed full control and "sovereignty" in the international administration.[7]

Neither Italy nor the United States agreed to the terms of this Convention, which was nevertheless put into force on July 1, 1924. The absence of the United States and Italy caused various irritations and inconveniences and even prevented the Assembly from having a legal quorum. This difficulty was resolved by the simple expedient of considering the two countries' representatives present on all occasions.

In its initial years the Tangier regime was beset by many less readily solvable problems, however, including local business protests against economic clauses in the agreement and heavy payments to Morocco; the weakness of the local police force; the complexities of the postal service, with three post offices at Tangier (British, Moroccan, and Spanish) issuing some sixty-one denominations of stamps; the difficulties of the Mixed Court representing several systems of law and using juries of varied nationalities, tongues, and religions; and the refusal of American and Italian nationals and ships, with the support of their Governments, to recognize the new regime's taxes, port dues, and other regulations.[8] In 1928 the Statute was revised in order to obtain Italian adherence, but the new provisions left the basic form of government, with all its defects, exactly the same. It merely added another Italian to the Assembly and appointed an Italian assistant administrator as director of judicial services and an Italian magistrate in the Mixed Court. A new gendarmerie of four hundred men was also provided for, to be commanded by a Spaniard, though residents of Tangier protested the added costs since this force apparently was designed primarily to support French and Spanish interests in other parts of Morocco. While the "internationalization" was thus made more complete by the addition of Italy to the participating states, such changes as were made in the Statute were primarily intended to satisfy Italy and evidenced no concern for the welfare of the area itself and no interest in making the complicated administration more workable or the government more democratic.

As the administration of Tangier worked out in practice over the next twelve years, the Sultan of Morocco, through his local representatives, absolutely controlled three-fourths of the city's population (the Mohammedans and the Jews), which meant that this group was subject to French control, inasmuch as Morocco was a protectorate of France. The Legislative Assembly was quite international in composition, as noted, with foreign representation allocated roughly in accordance with a country's economic interests in Tangier, modified by such politically based demands as it could get satisfied.[9] The Assembly apparently performed its tasks with adequate skill, providing both a reasonably sound financial regime for the government and regulation of the city's health, welfare, and economic affairs. The Committee of Control, consisting of the consuls representing Belgium, France, Great Britain, Holland, Italy, Portugal, and Spain, met about twice a month and examined all laws and regulations the Assembly voted, with the right to veto any which violated existing laws or treaties, or were outside the powers of the Assembly, or in which any member of the Assembly was directly, personally interested. Assembly-inspired changes in salary schedules, post, telegraph or telephone services, and certain other arrangements required a three-fourths or unanimous approval by the Committee, and it had power over the use of taxes and the budget as prepared by the Assembly. The administrator, appointed by the Sultan on the nomination of the Committee of Control, was aided by three assistant administrators, who watched over public health, public finance, and judicial services, and by two engineers. The administrator could be removed at the instance of the Committee of Control on a three-fourths vote, and he, in turn, could request the removal of his assistants, of various nationalities, by that Committee on grounds of non-collaboration. Any person removed had to be replaced by one of like nationality, though these "civil servants" were not representatives of their countries of national origin and were supposed to be concerned with Tangier rather than with national interests. The administrator carried out the Assembly's instructions but was far more important than this implies, for he also determined, in part, the Assembly's agenda and participated in its sessions as an adviser. He also actually prepared the budget, which, "in spite of maintaining a governmental machinery extensive enough to run a small state instead of a very small city" [10] was always balanced from local sources until after the Second World War. The civilian police force, composed of Europeans and natives, was under his control, as was the Zone's small armed force or gendarmerie. In short, most usual public services were provided by the international administration, even to the provision of an international jail, though in some instances, as with hospitals, there were also French, British, Italian and other national facilities. No public education was provided, however; the Powers and private agencies maintained their own schools, though many natives attended them. On the judicial side, a full-fledged court system was set up in 1923, including both civil and criminal parts and with a series of appellate tribunals; and, despite the difficulties of language, law systems, and the like referred to earlier, by 1929 over 4,500 cases were being heard annually. Codes of law were also eventually prepared, based largely on French and Spanish sources, and were generally considered a "marked" improvement over those of either French or Spanish Morocco.

Tangier was occupied by Spain during the Second World War, but this unilateral control terminated in 1945. A new and more truly internationalized regime was proposed by experts of Britain, France, and the United States in 1945, but the Soviet Union agreed to only a temporary regime, insisting that Franco Spain be barred from effective participation. While various plans were put forth in the next few years, only a limited set of changes could be agreed to; these, involving chiefly a revision of the Mixed Court system into a more fully international jurisdiction and clarification of the powers and function of the governor, became effective in 1952 and 1953.[11] The tide of nationalism had meanwhile swept over Morocco, however, and with Moroccan independence, the Statute was abrogated and arrangements were made for the termination of all special rights and privileges in Tangier in the Final Declaration and annexed protocol of the Tangier Conference of October, 1956.[12]

In evaluating the Tangier experience, the leading American student of the city's development, Graham H. Stuart, has struck a familiar note in concluding that, on the whole "the primary purpose of providing a satisfactory and effective international machinery for the administration of the city was constantly sacrificed to selfish political ends . . . [for] the Powers were much less interested in effective administration than they were in political advantages." Furthermore, both France and Spain, who were the main participants, were not "really interested in obtaining a successful international administration" because each "felt that the Zone rightly belonged within its sphere of influence" and each expected this result to follow on the joint control's failure. According to Stuart:

> An unbiased observer after carefully studying its government would not be able to cite it as an example of outstanding success in international administration. He might even be inclined to question whether in fact it is an international city. The various states participating are not equally represented nor are they represented in proportion to their interests. Neither is the ultimate authority vested in a truly international body, as was the case of Danzig [*sic*] and the Saar under the League of Nations. The arrangement is a sort of condominium between the Sultan and the Powers, or perhaps it might more accurately be termed an international protectorate.[18]

Regardless of its classification, Tangier does represent an example of multinational administration which functioned, in some technical fields at least, for a hundred and fifty years. What it achieved in longevity it failed to achieve in efficiency and humanity, in its expanded form, during the last thirty years of its existence. There was no element of trusteeship—the interests which the "international regime" was primarily designed to protect were the interests of the Powers and their nationals, not those of the natives. Like the New Hebrides and other basically similar regimes which lack the pseudo-international trappings of Tangier, it was in practice weakest in matters such as education, in which the welfare of the native population conflicted with the self-interest or aroused the interminable jealousies of the several participating national states.

DANZIG

The Paris Peace Conference at the end of the First World War was confronted by the difficult problem of giving Poland access to the sea. The solution backed by Polish representatives was simple—Poland as constituted would include the port city of Danzig and surrounding territory. While Wilson had "promised" to assure Poland of "a direct outlet to the great highways of the sea," the issue of handing a population of one nationality to another to rule was also raised, and neither he nor the British were willing to give Danzig, which had a German population, to Poland outright. A compromise solution was evolved, therefore, which separated Danzig from Germany and gave it the status of a free city while recognizing Poland's right to control and develop the port and to make sure that communications between Danzig and Poland were not under foreign control.[14]

The regime as developed by a treaty between Danzig and Poland of November 9, 1920, and extended by a treaty of October 24, 1921,[15] provided for the conduct of Danzig's foreign relations and her representation abroad by Poland. Ships of Danzig and Poland were to receive the same treatment at the port; Poland and the Free City of Danzig became a single customs area under the Polish customs legislation and tariff; Poland acquired the right to establish postal, telegraph, and telephone services in the port; a joint waterways board of five members representing both parties was established; and a free zone in the port of Danzig was retained.[16]

Article 102 of the Treaty of Versailles placed Danzig "under the protection of the League of Nations," and Article 103 placed its Constitution under the League's "guarantee." A resident representative of the League, to be called the "High Commissioner," was to be appointed by the Council and charged with the delicate task of "dealing in the first instance with all differences arising between Poland and . . . Danzig in regard to this Treaty or any arrangements or agreements made thereunder" and with the important duty of supervising the creation of a constitution for Danzig. A representative of the High Commissioner did in fact assist a Constituent Assembly of Danzig residents in drafting a Constitution, though primarily in an advisory capacity; the Council of the League accepted the draft on November 17, 1920, subject to minor amendments, which were not fully worked out until May, 1922, when the League's formal consent was announced and the Constitution entered into force.

The Constitution provided for full self-government for the citizens of the free city and took into account the new and distinct Danzig nationality. Article 5, however, placed upon the League, as the Council had previously provided, the responsibility of granting or denying permission to Danzig to "(1) serve as a military or naval base; (2) erect fortifications; and (3) manufacture munitions or war material on its territory," and thus neutralized the area. Article 42 also set forth that "the Senate of the Free City shall furnish to the League of Nations at any time upon the request of the latter official information regarding the public affairs of the Free City" while Article 72 required the League's assent to laws concerning Danzig nationality. The Convention of Paris of November 9, 1920, further involved the League with the free city, particularly in placing limits on Polish maneuvers with respect to the city. Article 6 of that Convention, for example, provided that:

> Poland shall conclude no treaty or international agreement affecting the Free City without previous consultation with the Free City; the High Commissioner of the League of Nations shall be informed of the result of this consultation.
>
> The High Commissioner shall in all cases have the right to veto any treaty or international agreement, in so far as it applies to the Free City of Danzig, which, in the opinion of the Council of the League of Nations, is inconsistent with the provisions of the present Treaty or with the status of the Free City.

Further, in the event of disagreement between the Polish and Danzig governments the League was charged with the appointment of the President of the Danzig Port and Waterways Board, an important post from the point of view of what Poland considered her vital interests. In addition, Poland and Danzig were required to submit certain specified disputes to arbitration by the High Commissioner while other differences were to be submitted to the High Commissioner for his decision or, if he deemed it necessary or if the parties could not get together after negotiation under his auspices, to the League Council. Thus, while it was often argued that Danzig was not a "protectorate" of the League, the League undertook to guarantee its Constitution and offered collective protection to its territorial integrity and political independence from both Germany and Poland.[17] In return, Poland was to be guaranteed free access to the sea.

Having neutralized Danzig and placed the city under League protection, the Council had to concern itself, in the field of discussion at least, with the theoretical problem of defense of Danzig, though no universally satisfactory solution was found to this problem.[18] The High Commissioner, for example, was made responsible to the League for defense of the free city, but had only the right to call on Poland to furnish troops, and had no instructions at all if the attacker was Poland. Indeed, the League was actually active in Danzig substantially only in the supervisory and mediatory spheres, carried out largely through this office of the High Commissioner.

The difficult role played by that official has been described by Sir John Fischer Williams in a statement before the Permanent Court on November 9, 1931, as follows:

> The High Commissioner is not a person who is a sort of Viceroy of Danzig; he has no direct executive authority in Danzig; he is not a person who can make rules or regulations for Danzig. He is there to help the League. He is there—at any rate for certain special purposes—as

the watch-dog of the League to assist it in carrying out its duties, and he has a certain judicial function, subject to an appeal to the Council of the League, in regard to the settlement of differences which arise between the Free City and Poland in regard to the carrying out of their mutual obligations.[19]

Thus, he was a limited League "watch-dog" but with real functions within restricted though vital political and military areas—without, however, the means to enforce his judgments. In addition to the military dilemma, for example, he was made responsible for "the maintenance of order on the territory of the Free City" if local forces proved insufficient, but he had no right to issue orders to the chief of police or to the Danzig police force. On the "judicial" side, too, all of the High Commissioner's decisions were appealable to the League, where decisions were inevitably political, to some extent at least. A unanimous vote was necessary in the Council for any decision there, and, since both Germany and Poland were Council Members from 1926 on, the judicial merits of appeals gave way to political jockeying to avoid a veto.

The pay and allowances of the High Commissioner were fixed by a resolution of the Council on November 17, 1920. His salary and the funds for his upkeep were obtained from Danzig (about 90 percent) and Poland until 1937, when the League paid him. The dependence on local funds had subjected him before this change to attacks and abuse from both parties. Appointments were for a three-year term though the Council, to which he was solely responsible, retained the right to dismiss him at any time. His staff was international in character, and he and his staff enjoyed diplomatic privileges and immunities as representatives of the League. Annual and special reports were made to keep the League informed.[20] With the rise of the Nazis, the Commissioner used his influence to keep the German government of Danzig in line and succeeded in protecting the non-Nazi elements in the city for three years or so. The collapse of the world situation, of course, terminated the role and the legal existence of the Office of the High

Commissioner, the last Commissioner leaving the city in December, 1939, after it was in Nazi hands.[21]

THE SAAR (1920–34)

"The only important example of international government in the history of the League is that of the Saar Territory; and this, in spite of early difficulties and mistakes, was remarkably successful." [22] While reservations must be made to this statement, its overall conclusions are not too far off the mark.

With the close of the First World War, France was insistent on the annexation of the Saar Territory, or, at least, on the creation of a French mandate there, the main argument employed being that only through Saar coal could France recover from the damage inflicted by the Germans in the coal fields of northern France. Faced with the opposition of her Allies to the seizure of this German-peopled area France agreed to a form of direct League "trusteeship" for a fifteen-year period. This arrangement had several unique features. To begin with, Germany, in Article 49 of the Versailles Treaty, renounced her rule in favor of the League "in the capacity of a Trustee." [23] Next, the Council of the League constituted, for a limited duration, the Saar Governing Commission, an organ totally distinct from the Permanent Mandates Commission, and the Council appointed to one-year terms—and retained the right to remove—the Commission's five members, including a Frenchman, a Saarlander, and three other members who could not be citizens of France or Germany. Members of the Commission did not represent their governments as such, and the Commission was to act for the benefit of the area as a whole while recognizing France's special interests. The officials in the Saar made a declaration of loyalty to the Commission as a representative of the League of Nations. This Commission was, in fact, the government of the Saar; for, while the Commission organized and consulted a local representative group, the Advisory Council, it needed no approval for its action, though in a few instances decrees were withdrawn because of Advisory Council opposition. The Commission alone was empowered to govern, to maintain order (for which it could rely both on local police and, for several years, a small number of French troops stationed in the Saar), and to interpret the relevant sections of the Treaty of Versailles.[24]

At the first session, the Commission (January–May, 1920) encountered its first controversy. The Council of the League appointed Victor Rault, the French member, chairman on the strength of the French argument that the Saar's close economic ties with France (it was included in the French customs area) required the appointment of one familiar with French administrative techniques. While there was considerable "neutral" support for German opposition to this appointment, which certainly undermined the international non-political nature of the Commission's administration, the Secretariat supported the French view.

The League Council committed itself to the Commission by promising, in March, 1922, to reappoint Rault and the others year-by-year for the succeeding three years, thus assuring a continuity of office. The French continued to attempt to ignore the international nature of the regime. For example, Rault was the only member with whom they would discuss problems concerning mines, customs, and the like, and this, together with his "ability," "force of character," and command of two of the other four votes on the Commission, permitted him to make decisions as he thought best and without paying much attention to the protests of the Canadian member or the Saarlander. While these decisions were apparently not by any means determined solely on the basis of French interest, these first stages of this administration can hardly be termed democratic or perhaps even international.

Faced on February 5, 1923, with a strike of miners, who had relatively few complaints of their own but had gone out following strikes in the Ruhr, Rault feared general disorders. He doubled the French garrison of 2,000 men stationed in the Saar and decreed restrictions on liberties, stipulating prison terms for criticism of the Commission, the League, any Member of the League, or any signatory of the Versailles Treaty. World public opinion was "shocked" at such an approach in territory "governed" by the League. Though no arrests were made and the decree was withdrawn in July, after the strike ended, the Saar Commission was examined at Geneva by the Council, which showed its dissatisfaction, stressing the international character of the obligations of the Commissioners and warning that the Commission was individually and collectively responsible to the Council alone and not to any of the member governments. Rault agreed to consult his colleagues more regularly in the future, and he actually did so.

Although he may not have always understood the international character of his assignment, Rault proved to be an efficient administrator and, despite the contretemps just described, an efficient and loyal civil service was developed under the Commission. The Saar prospered and the government obtained its revenues principally from ordinary taxes and levies on products exported. Salaries of the Commission's members were charged to local revenues. Canadian and British chairmen succeeded Rault, and the French garrison was withdrawn in 1927. Reports were made by the Commission to the Council at three-month intervals, in which it set out the grievances presented to it, the problems it faced, and details of its success in administering the area. Saarlanders could petition the Commission directly and, of course, were represented on it through the required appointment of one citizen of the area to its membership.[25] Despite the inevitably "undemocratic" nature of rule by an appointed Commission, no German complaints about the Commission's activities were heard after 1927.

The Commission was reasonably successful in maintaining order even after the Nazis took control of Germany, but the regime was subjected to constant abuse from across the "border." In accordance with the original provision calling for a fifteen-year trusteeship, a plebiscite was to be held in January, 1935; and, following the proposal of Anthony Eden on December 5, 1934, another "first" was achieved with the dispatch to the Saar of an international military force, sponsored by the Council, to police the plebiscite.[26] While the Saar overwhelmingly voted to return to Germany (by 477,119 votes, compared with 2,124 favoring French annexation), some 46,513 Saarlanders were sufficiently impressed by past experience to vote for a continued League trusteeship although the League did not conduct an active campaign for the *status quo*.[27] The Commission then ceased to be the government of the Saar after January 10, 1935, having paid its own way and left the territory free of public debt.[28] The League's principal historian, F. P. Walters, has rather sanguinely summed up the experience as follows:

> The fifteen year record of the Saar Governing Commission is a standing proof of the practical possibilities of international administration. After some bad mistakes in its early years, it had shown that even under the most unfavourable circumstances a group of men from five different countries can work together loyally and efficiently. Although two of its five members, the Saarlander and the Frenchman, were appointed to watch over the special interests of their respective countries, the Commission as a whole had grown more and more conscious of itself as a unit responsible only to the League of Nations. . . . And the period of international government had been closed by the best-managed of all plebiscites, and the unprecedented and successful experiment of the International Force.[29]

LETICIA

Another interesting, if limited, example of direct international administration is found in the "government" established in 1933 by a Commission of the League of Nations for about a year in an area of Colombia. In brief, a dispute had arisen over the area of Leticia, which consisted chiefly of a port of that name giving access to the Amazon and having a population of about 600 persons. Peruvian troops entered the area, which had generally been considered Colombian territory, and remained there. On Peru's proving intransigent, the matter was brought to the attention of the League Council. A Committee of Three, composed of representatives of Ireland, Spain, and Guatemala, was asked to look into the dispute; the United States had a representative present at the Committee's meetings. In March, 1933, the Council adopted a Report under Article 15 which generally supported Colombia's rights and recommended "the complete evacuation by the Peruvians and their forces of the territory contained in the Leticia Trapezium and the withdrawal of all support from the Peruvians who have occupied that area." However, the Report suggested that Peru hand over Leticia not to Colombia but to a Commission of the League which would administer the area for one year "in the name of the Government of Colombia," using some Colombian troops which were, however, to be regarded as an international force. After the year, Leticia was to revert to Colombia if there was no other agreed settlement.

The murder of the Peruvian dictator, Sanchez Cerro, led to the installation of a new president who, fortuitously, was willing to accept the League's proposal. On May 25, 1933, representatives of Peru and Colombia agreed to a procedure recommended by the Council for effectuating the March Report. The important part of the Council's program provided that:

> The Council shall appoint a Commission to be in Leticia within a period of not more than thirty days. The Peruvian forces in that area shall withdraw immediately upon the Commission's arrival, and the Commission, in the name of the Government of Colombia, shall take charge of the administrative organization of the territory evacuated by these forces.
>
> For the purpose of maintaining order in the territory in which it is to administer, the Commission shall call upon military forces of its own selection, and may attach to itself any other elements it may deem necessary.
>
> The Commission shall have the right to decide all questions relating to the performance of its mandate.

By the end of June, 1933, the League Commission, composed of representatives of Brazil, Spain, and the United States, reached Leticia. A League of Nation's flag was hoisted, and the Commission embarked on a year's rule. During this time the population quadrupled; a hospital, three schools, and other buildings were erected, property damaged during the Peruvian occupation was repaired, and there were no reported cases of violence.[30] On May 24, 1934, the League Commission turned Leticia over to the Colombian government. The experience demonstrated in a minor way the technical possibility of simple forms of direct international rule by commission, at least over a small area with simple administrative demands and an appreciative population, and in which none of the internationally appointed "governors" had any interest.[31]

THE ITALIAN COLONIES

The Italian peace treaty at the end of the Second World War contained stipulations for the disposal of the Italian colonies in North Africa, which at the time were occupied by British and French forces. By Article 23 Italy renounced all right and title to those possessions and in a separate Annex it was agreed that if the Big Four could not agree upon the final disposal of the colonies, the matter would be referred to the General Assembly, whose recommendation they agreed would be binding. It is the only instance in which the General Assembly has been given such power. No new patterns of international administration were in the end adopted, but some of the proposals considered in the course of the negotiations are of interest as indicating types of solutions which certain governments have advocated.

At the meeting of the Council of Foreign Ministers held in London in September, 1945, the United States submitted a plan calling for direct international administration for periods of ten years for Libya and Eritrea and indefinitely for Somaliland. There was to be a "neutral" administration, appointed by and responsible to the Trusteeship Council, with an advisory committee of seven, including one representative each from the Big Four, one from Italy, and two from the former colonies, to assist it.[32] France opposed internationalization, and the Soviet Union dismissed the

American proposal for a seven-member advisory board with a Russian proverb to the effect that "a child which has seven nurses does not get nursed at all." The Soviet Union argued in turn for trusteeship under the Big Three with, as suggested earlier at Potsdam, Russia administering Tripolitania for ten years to compensate for losses caused her by Italy and to give her merchant fleet needed bases on the Mediterranean.[33] To help set aside certain fears, Molotov reportedly gave the interesting but somewhat ambiguous assurance that "We do not propose to introduce the Soviet system into this territory apart the democratic order that is desired by the people." [34] The Western powers indeed had no intention of placing Russia on the Mediterranean—Britain in particular opposed Russia's plan as a threat to her life line—but Britain's representatives followed the American lead only in a qualified manner due to the nature of this "great, new and untried experiment," probably reflecting Britain's lack of enthusiasm for developing forms of international tutelage for colonial areas.[35] When the Soviet Union at a subsequent meeting of the Council of Foreign Ministers in 1948 suddenly accepted the original United States plan, the United States declared that it no longer believed the plan was workable. With no agreement in sight, the Four Powers at that same meeting announced that, in accordance with the treaty, the question was submitted to the General Assembly.

Discussion during the Third Session of the General Assembly failed to lead to a decision. At the Fourth Session the Soviet Union proposed immediate independence for Libya and direct international administration under the Trusteeship Council for Eritrea and Somaliland for five years.[36] An Indian draft plan proposed direct UN trusteeship for Libya and Somaliland for ten to twenty years; Liberia suggested a direct UN trusteeship for Somaliland; and Guatemala and Pakistan asked a direct UN trusteeship for Eritrea.[37] A variety of other related proposals was considered, but in the end the General Assembly decided that: (1) Libya should become an independent sovereign state not later than January 1, 1952; (2) Somaliland should become an independent sovereign State after ten years of Italian trusteeship;[38] and (3) Eritrea should be federated with Ethiopia.[39]

In each of the territories, however, the United Nations had a role to play. In Somaliland, a quite special trusteeship was arranged; in Libya and Eritrea, the Organization was to be midwife at the birth of a new political entity. Each role exemplifies some phase of international administration or, rather, of supervision.

In accordance with the terms of the General Assembly's Resolution, Adrian Pelt was elected United Nations Commissioner in Libya on December 10, 1949, and went to Libya with something less than two years to effectuate Libyan independence. The Commissioner reported directly to the Assembly, as did Britain and France, which were still in occupation and were named as the administering authorities.

Aided by the Council of Libya, the Commissioner drew plans for the future government of Libya and successfully assisted in the progressive transfer of power from the administering authorities to the federal government of Libya.[40] On December 24, 1951, Libya was proclaimed an independent and sovereign state by Idris El-Senussi, its new king.[41]

It appears that this technical job of transfer of power at least may well be satisfactorily and expeditiously accomplished, when all parties are in agreement, by international civil servants, even with small staffs and limited powers. The more long-range problem, the creation of a viable new state, stable and independent economically and politically democratic, is far more complex. Perhaps this rapid creation of a state, accompanied by extensive technical and financial assistance for extended periods, is a new alternative to international trusteeship and even to direct international administration for backward areas, for it emphasizes the nationalistic desires of the people of an area rather than the international claims on that area (to free access, for example) and yet provides the territory with the tutelage and support it in fact needs. Where there is no population, however, the needs of the international community for equality of economic access or for the maintenance of stability in strategic areas, or both, may more appropriately lead to an internationally imposed regime or control of some sort.[42]

Despite the skepticism shown by many representatives at the United Nations both as to the possibility of preparing Somaliland economically and otherwise for independence in a brief period and as to the propriety of Italy's being the Administering Authority,[43] the General Assembly's Resolution of November 21, 1949, provided that Somaliland should become an independent sovereign state ten years from the date of the Assembly's approval of a trusteeship agreement for the territory with Italy as Administering Authority. Unlike all other territories which became trusteeships, Somaliland was not then under the control of the prospective Administering Authority; further, for the first time the Trusteeship Council and not the Administering Authority prepared the draft Trusteeship Agreement, though this was modeled on Italian and Philippine drafts, plus Dominican Republic "suggestions."[44] The Agreement as negotiated, in addition to limiting the term of the trusteeship to ten years, also imposed certain unique safeguards indicative of the international community's interest in the area. As approved by the General Assembly on December 2, 1950, the Agreement and its annex specified that the "sovereignty of the Trust Territory is vested in its people"; it created an Advisory Council, composed of representatives of Colombia, Egypt, and the Philippines to "aid and advise" Italy; it provided that the judiciary should be absolutely independent; and it set forth the fundamental rights and liberties of the people. Furthermore, it stressed periodic UN review of the country's administration and progress towards independence.

As permitted by the General Assembly, Italy relieved the British of the administration of the territory on April 1, 1950, even before the Trusteeship Agreement was ratified, and the Advisory Council began to function a few days earlier, on March 27, 1950.

The Council soon complained that it was being ignored, but after six months it reported that the situation had improved and that it was being consulted on important questions.[45] Despite early agreements, however, the Council has had a stormy career for several reasons. The Council, for instance, which was to aid and advise the Administering Authority and, in a sense, serve as a channel to the Trusteeship Council, soon split internally over its role with respect to petitions from the Territory. Differences of opinion on this issue and on others reportedly grew "violent," and "personal animosities" also appeared which hampered the Council's work. Its relations with the Administering Authority also became tense, principally because of the confusion over the Council's proper relations with the inhabitants. It has also been very difficult, apparently, to keep the Council's members in the Territory long enough to establish a quorum for needed business—a quorum of two members existed for only twenty-three days in the year from April 1, 1953, to March 31, 1954.[46] The Council, with its headquarters at Mogadishu, has, nevertheless, been useful in giving the Trusteeship Council first-hand progress reports and information on the problems faced by the administration in leading Somaliland to independence by 1960.[47] The Council has not been a great success. This has been due in part to its own difficulties—to the fact that its role as intermediary was inadequately defined and it was left without any clearly marked area of competence or source of special authority. It was also due in part to unfortunate problems in personnel, linked probably to the fact that the members were representatives of states rather than international civil servants, a sort of powerless "condominium" of advisers who were also busy with other matters of their own. And Somaliland has not been developed toward independence as rapidly as the Trusteeship Council has indicated might be appropriate.[48]

Somaliland is then an interesting hybrid case. While the regime of international supervision is more developed than for other trust territories, the Administering Authority has retained almost complete control of the area. The time limit on the length of the trusteeship, on the other hand, is an extremely important device, since the Authority knows the results of its "tutelage" will be on public display in a few years and the population is assured of its political independence.

Under the terms of the General Assembly's Resolution of November 21, 1949, a Commission was to ascertain more fully the wishes of the Eritreans. This approach was adopted after the rejection of various proposals: for immediate independence, for a Trusteeship under Italy, for a three-year direct United Nations Trusteeship (suggested by Poland), and for outright annexation by Ethiopia.[49] A Commission consisting of representatives of Burma, Guatemala, Norway, Pakistan, and the Union of South Africa visited the area but did not reach agreement, since the delegations of Burma and the Union of South Africa favored a federation of Eritrea and Ethiopia, the Norwegians suggested the full unification of the two, and, interestingly, the Guatemalans and Pakistanis suggested a direct UN trusteeship for up to ten years, at the end of which Eritrea would become independent. Under this plan there was to be an administrator appointed by the General Assembly and advised by a council consisting of representatives of the United States, Italy, Ethiopia, a Moslem country, and a Latin American country, and representatives of the Coptic Christians, the Moslems, and the minorities. Economic agreements were to be concluded with Ethiopia, looking toward an economic union; free zones at the ports of Massawa and Asaba would be established; and the United Nations was to help plan the economic development of Eritrea.[50]

The General Assembly rejected the suggestion of direct administration in December, 1950, as the usual arguments against this type of regime were again brought forth and, more important, as Ethiopia's special situation was accorded weight. It provided instead for the federation of Eritrea as an autonomous unit under the Ethiopian Crown.[51] The Resolution set forth a detailed plan for Eritrea's future, and a United Nations Commissioner, assisted by experts appointed by the Secretary-General, was provided to try to unite the geographically scattered and politically unorganized Eritreans, to assist in the creation of an Eritrean assembly, and to prepare a draft constitution. On September 15, 1952, as provided by the General Assembly's Resolution, Eritrea became an autonomous unit federated with Ethiopia under a local government created with the aid of the United Nations representative.[52]

While, despite several proposals to the contrary, the Libyan and Eritrean cases did not ultimately require any direct United Nations administration or control, the Organization and its representatives played a direct part in the creation of these entities in their current form and thus contributed to and learned from the governmental solutions involved. The Somaliland trusteeship as worked out also placed the government of the area under a single state; but here the potentially useful techniques of the Organization's preparation of the agreement, of supervision—or at least of obtaining information—through committees in permanent residence, and of time limitations were put to use. While in no sense involving international administration as it might be practiced, the trusteeship system has in this instance been made more responsive to the need for control over an Administering Authority.

TRIESTE

With the end of the Second World War the problem of Trieste, which had for many years been a bone of contention between Italy and Yugoslavia, remained for solution. While the city of Trieste was largely populated by Italians, the southern hinterland was Yugoslav in character, and both countries insisted on the need for Trieste as a port.

Since the Allies were unwilling or unable to reconcile divergent views and pick Italy or Yugoslavia, Trieste, which was in fact occupied at the time in part by Anglo-American forces and in part by Yugoslav troops, was made a Free Territory under the terms of the treaty of peace with Italy.[58] The treaty provided for assurance by the Security Council of the Territory's integrity and independence and for that body to set a date for the coming into force of a Permanent Statute, the text of which is contained in Annex VI to the treaty.

The Permanent Statute declared that the Territory would be demilitarized and made neutral, and that only at the Security Council's direction could armed forces be allowed in the Territory. Citizens were to be guaranteed civil, political, and human rights by the Territory's Constitution, and Italian and Slovene were to be the official languages.

The government of Trieste was to be in the hands of a governor, a Council of Government, a popular assembly, and a judiciary under the Constitution. The governor was to be appointed by the UN Security Council "after consultation with the Governments of Yugoslavia and Italy." He could not be a citizen of either country or of the Free Territory of Trieste. He was to serve a five-year term and could be reappointed or suspended or dismissed after a hearing by the Security Council. His salary and allowances were to be borne by the United Nations; he was to report annually to the Security Council; and he was charged "as the representative of the Security Council [with responsibility] for supervising the observance of the present Statute including the protection of the basic human rights of the inhabitants and for ensuring that public order and security are maintained by the Government of the Free Territory in accordance with the Statute, the Constitution and laws of the Free Territory." He had the right to veto laws passed by the popular assembly and to reject the administrative measures of the government if they conflicted with the Statute or the governor's responsibilities thereunder, but his actions were subject to review by the Security Council. Where the Territory's independence or security were threatened, the governor could directly order the Territory's government to take action as he directed, but review by the Security Council, on petition by the assembly, was again provided for. He was also given authority to reject treaties and other international agreements made by the Trieste government if they conflicted with the Statute, the Constitution, or laws of the Territory. The international character of the office of governor and of his staff was expressly set forth in Article 25:

> In the performance of their duties, the Governor and his staff shall not seek or receive instructions from any Government or from any other authority except the Security Council. They shall refrain from any act which might reflect on their position as international officials responsible only to the Security Council.

A powerful new international "overseer" would thus have been created, backed by the might of the United Nations Security Council.

Normal legislative authority in Trieste was to be in a popular assembly, elected by all citizens of the territory on the basis of proportional representation. The governor could suggest legislation to this body. The Council of Government, formed by the assembly, was, however, to be the Territory's executive authority, subject to the rights of the governor. There was to be also a free and independent judiciary. The Territory was to have an independent police force and monetary system. Freedom of transit for neighboring states, without discrimination, was established. The basic Statute could be amended by the Security Council, and the assembly was permitted by a two-thirds vote to petition for an amendment. The inhabitants of the Territory were not, of course, consulted on their preference as to form of government, but they were given the option to choose Italian citizenship and to leave the area, if necessary, if they preferred.

An instrument was included in another annex to the treaty governing the provisional regime to be established in Trieste by the governor, once appointed. Further, and of more permanent importance, another annex contained provision for a free port in Trieste, and an international regime for the port was outlined. The port was to be technically a state corporation of Trieste, with a director selected by the governor from a list prepared by the Council of Government. This director, too, could not be a citizen of Italy or Yugoslavia. He was to report annually both to the governor and to the Council of Government.

While Yugoslavia and Italy were given limited special privileges in the port, all nations were to be treated equally with respect to transit facilities, harbor dues, and charges. The port was to have an "autonomous budget." An "International Commission," with its seat in the free port, was also established to "investigate and consider all matters relating to the operation, use, and administration of the free port," and to recommend needed changes to the port director, the Free Territory, or any state concerned. Disputes were to be settled by arbitration if necessary. The Security Council was again charged with amending the instrument, if appropriate, at the suggestion of the Council of Government or of three or more states represented on the International Commission.

Thus, in these several instruments, the major Powers provided for a regime designed to meet many of the criticisms leveled at the Danzig and Memel "solutions" of the First World War, and they succeeded, on paper, in creating a pattern of true international supervision and, to a limited extent, of partial international administration. The viability of the proposals was never put to the test.

The Council of Foreign Ministers referred the various documents relating to Trieste to the Security Council, where they were approved in January, 1947.[54] In the debate, the Australian representative argued forcefully that nowhere in the Charter was the Security Council given sufficient power to discharge the duties proposed in the Trieste arrangements or to give general guarantees of the integrity and independence of particular territories. The Syrian representative also raised this question, with respect at least to "international administration." The representatives of the Soviet Union, the United Kingdom, the United States, France, and Colombia and the Secretary-General of the United Nations made it clear, however, that in their opinion Article 24 of the

Charter in particular was sufficiently broad to permit the Council to discharge its proposed obligations. The British representative stressed the point that under these proposals the Council could not be said to be administering Trieste but rather was to have "general control over the administration, and, in any difficulties that arise, appeal can be made to it; but it is not actually being asked . . . to undertake any direct absolute administration. . . ." [55]

Subsequently, however, the Trieste problem became entangled in the broader issues of the "cold war," and agreement was never reached in the Security Council on the selection of a governor. The area accordingly remained under military government until a solution by partition was negotiated with Italy and Yugoslavia in 1954. The acquiescence of the Soviet Union wrote *finis* to this promising experiment in international administration.[56]

JERUSALEM

At one stage of the still unended United Nations discussions of a solution for the problem of Palestine, serious consideration was given to the establishment of an international regime for Jerusalem and the Holy Places. Like other proposals this one was not put into effect but elaborate preparations were made.

The Palestine question was first considered by the United Nations General Assembly in a special session in the spring of 1947. It adopted a resolution creating an eleven-nation investigative board known as the United Nations Special Committee on Palestine (UNSCOP), with the permanent members of the Security Council barred from membership.[57] UNSCOP spent many weeks in Palestine and Lebanon, and then retired to Geneva to prepare a report which was concluded on August 31, 1947. While a number of general principles were agreed to unanimously, including an ending of the British mandate at the earliest practical date, the Committee split on a suggested solution. A majority (Canada, Czechoslovakia, Guatemala, Netherlands, Peru, Sweden, Uruguay) recommended partition with economic union, while a minority

(India, Iran, Yugoslavia) favored a federal state after a three-year period, with the city of Jerusalem as capital. Australia abstained. The majority plan proposed that Jerusalem, Bethlehem, and their rural subdivisions form the city of Jerusalem, to be administered by the United Nations as a permanent trusteeship. All of Palestine was to be administered for a two-year probationary period starting September 1, 1947, by the United Kingdom, either alone or jointly with one or more other members under United Nations auspices.[58]

At the General Assembly session in the fall of 1947, the Palestine problem was referred to a Special Committee on the Palestine question, composed of all members. UNSCOP's majority proposal was modified, but only in details, and the revised plan calling for partition with economic union was accepted by the General Assembly on November 29, 1947, by a vote of 33 to 13, with ten abstentions. The mandate was to terminate by August 1, 1948, and the independent states and a special regime for the city of Jerusalem were to come into existence two months after the British military evacuation but not later than October 1, 1948. A Special Commission composed of representatives of Bolivia, Czechoslovakia, Denmark, Panama, and the Philippines was to supervise the implementation of partition, and the Security Council was requested to support the settlement. The Trusteeship Council was asked to draft a statute for the international regime for Jerusalem along indicated lines.[59]

Much to the consternation of the representatives of most of the nations seeking a peaceful solution to the crisis, the British, who had themselves placed the matter before the United Nations, now refused to permit the Special Commission to enter Palestine in order to carry out its mission. The Arabs and Jews who had been arming as effectively as they could in view of the prospective departure of the British, stepped up their activities at this time, and between November 30, 1947, and April 1, 1948, some three thousand persons are estimated to have been killed on each side.

By early 1948, following the British announcement on December 11, 1947, that the mandate would be unilaterally terminated on May 15, 1948—thus in fact scuttling any real possibility of introducing the United Nations' plan—the General Assembly felt obliged to ask the Trusteeship Council "to study . . . suitable measures for the protection of the city [Jerusalem] and its inhabitants," for which the United Nations had a special responsibility under its plan. By mid-spring the Palestine Commission was forced to conclude that it would be impossible to implement the United Nations' plan due to "the armed hostility of both Palestinian and non-Palestinian Arab elements, the lack of cooperation from the Mandatory Power, the disintegrating security situation in Palestine, and the fact that the Security Council did not furnish the Commission with the necessary armed assistance. . . ."[60]

While events made it impossible to put the plan into effect, since the major powers were unwilling to impose it and the mandatory was in the end hostile to it, the proposal for the creation of a separate entity under direct United Nations administration was an interesting one.* Briefly, the Draft Statute[61] prepared by the Trusteeship Council followed the General Assembly's suggestions

* Somewhat similarly, in 1937, a Committee of Experts of the League of Nations drafted a Statute and Fundamental Law for the territory of Alexandretta, a part of Turkey until the end of the First World War and, in 1937, a part of French-mandated Syria. The League's Council approved this plan which provided that the area was to remain within the Mandates system as long as Syria did. After Syrian independence, Syria was to handle Alexandretta's foreign relations; France and Turkey were charged jointly with its defense; and the League, through a Commission, was to supervise the conduct of affairs under the Statute with the right to veto laws contrary to the Statute or the Fundamental Law. Local affairs were to be handled by an elected assembly, and the area was to have its own budget. A sort of collective protectorate was thus to be established. In fact, however, the program was not effectuated due to Turkish opposition and French support of the Turkish position, and, despite protests by Syria and the Mandates Commission, a Franco-Turkish Treaty of June 23, 1939, "ceded" this portion of the French mandate to Turkey without further international commitments. See generally, M. Khadduri, *The Alexandretta Dispute*, 39 AM. J. INT'L L. 406–425 (1945).

and established the city of Jerusalem as a *corpus separatum* under a special international regime, administered by the United Nations with the Trusteeship Council designated to discharge the responsibilities of the Administering Authority on behalf of the United Nations (as per Article 81 of the Charter). The objectives of the Administering Authority, including free access to all of the Holy Places, were set out; provision was made for local autonomy and protection of all faiths within the city; and residents were to become citizens of the city, unless they decided otherwise, with the right to consular protection elsewhere—the governor and, if necessary, the Trusteeship Council being charged with making appropriate arrangements. The Council was to appoint a governor who was not to be a citizen of either state in Palestine, and was to serve for a fixed term. He was to represent the United Nations and exercise all powers of administration on their behalf, aided by a staff of "international officers." The governor was charged with keeping peace in the city, and a special police force, with members recruited outside Palestine, was to be at his disposal. A separate judiciary and legislative council (subject to certain veto powers in the governor) were to be established, and the freedom of the city's citizens and the techniques of protection and preservation of the Holy Places were also spelled out. Even the sources of revenue were specified. Funds were to come from local taxes and rates, and a preference was expressed that the United Nations itself be called on, at most, for loans.

The Statute was to remain in force for ten years, unless the Trusteeship Council determined earlier that revision was needed, and then the Council was to reexamine the entire program, in consultation with the city's residents, to determine the future of the special regime. Thus, a truly "international" if not very democratic regime was to be created, though linked economically to the new Jewish and Arab states. The provision of Charter Article 81, providing that the United Nations might itself be an Administering Authority, would have been employed for the first time.[62]

The current "solution" to the Palestine crisis was achieved by force of arms after the withdrawal of British forces. Israel proclaimed herself a state on May 14, 1948, and was duly recognized as such by the non-Arab world and occupied an area, after her defeat of the combined Arab armies, roughly similar to that established in the United Nations partition plan. Jerusalem, however, was occupied by and in fact divided between Israel and Jordan and remains so divided today.

The United Nations, however, continued to be concerned, at least with this Jerusalem area. By the Resolution of December 11, 1948, for example, the Assembly called upon the United Nations Conciliation Commission to make detailed proposals for a permanent international regime for Jerusalem, and, in December 1949, the Assembly again adopted, by vote of thirty-eight to fourteen, with seven abstentions, a Resolution providing that

> The City of Jerusalem shall be established as a *corpus separatum* under a special international regime and shall be administered by the United Nations. The Trusteeship Council shall be designated to discharge the responsibilities of the Administering Authority. . . .[63]

The Trusteeship Council duly redrafted its Statute for an internationalized Jerusalem in 1950, taking into account the existence of a recognized Jewish state, the position of Jordan, and the Assembly's call for democratizing the administration. Few substantial changes were made. The Statute provided again for a governor to be appointed by and to be responsible to the Trusteeship Council for a three-year term, and for a Legislative Council of twenty-five members to assist the governor, the members to be elected by an electoral college: eight by the Moslems, eight by the Christians, and eight by the Jews.[64] Both Israel and Jordan, however, have formally incorporated the parts of Jerusalem occupied by them into their own territories. Israel has been subjected to criticism by the Arab states for "violating" the "international status" of Jerusalem by erecting buildings there for governmental and university purposes and for receiving foreign diplomatic representatives there rather than in Tel Aviv, but at the same time the old part of the city remains under exclusive Jordanian occupation.

UNITED NATIONS AREAS

The features of one more form of sharing responsibility between an international organization and a state must also be noted briefly. In the Agreement between the United Nations and the United States Regarding the Headquarters of the United Nations, effective November 21, 1947,[65] for example, no mention is made of a transfer of sovereignty over the rather limited geographic area occupied by the United Nations as its headquarters district. The United States is charged with assuring that the United Nations not be dispossessed of its property, however, and, even more important, it is provided that "the headquarters district shall be inviolable" and American authorities can enter it only with the consent of and under conditions imposed by the Secretary-General.[66] Further, the district "shall be under the control and jurisdiction of the United Nations," and the Organization has the power to make all needed regulations within the district for carrying out its functions. No inconsistent law of the United States is applicable within that area. Except for these instances, however, American laws apply within the district and United States courts have jurisdiction over acts done and transactions occurring within the area. The Organization also relies, normally, on New York's facilities for water, light, and other public utilities, fire protection, and the like, and for external police protection and even internal, if requested, though it now maintains its own security force.

Provisions also cover transit to and from the district; exclusions from United States immigration, entry, and related laws; privileges and immunities of representatives and others; and arbitration of disputes. The United Nations was expressly authorized to establish and operate telecommunications systems, and the United States was to arrange, if requested, for premises located elsewhere (which would then become part of the district) if needed for operation of such equipment and, in fact, for an airport as well. In the event that the seat of the United Nations were removed from the district, it was also provided that "all right, title and interest" of the organization in real property there would be conveyed to the United States or a subdivision thereof. Thus, an arrangement the primary purpose of which was stated to be "to enable the United Nations at its headquarters in the United States, fully and efficiently to discharge its responsibilities and fulfill its purposes" came into being. Full control and jurisdiction to the extent needed were made available to the United Nations and the district was made inviolable, subject in certain particulars to American law and jurisdiction as well. The Agreement concentrated on the functions to be performed in the area and sought to assure that they could be carried out with a minimum of interference. Roughly similar arrangements were also worked out between the United Nations and the Swiss Federal Council for use of the Ariana site at Geneva, the former headquarters of the League of Nations.[67]

Whatever name is given to the form of the arrangement, one patterned on those in New York and Geneva involving inviolability of the area and personnel and providing for transit, technical facilities, and the like, might well be essential to any future permanent program of control or supervision by an international organization of a location within the recognized territory of a state.

3. *Functional Organizations*

In addition to situations in which two or more nations have planned for and, more rarely, carried out joint political controls over populated or unpopulated areas, there is an ever growing number of instances in which several nations have found it useful and possible to coordinate their activities through an international functional organization. A number of studies of such organizations exist.[1] This chapter is focused on the potential applicability of this type of international cooperation to the Antarctic and outer space, although to give an adequate picture it is necessary to include both general comments and specific details which are not directly relevant to that theme. Considered first are those international functional organizations and arrangements which would or could, as currently constituted, be utilized to play a part in the Antarctic or outer space. A second group includes a closely related category of current organizations which presently perform functions elsewhere in situations that are analogous to those which can be expected to arise in the Antarctic or outer space. Thus, the consideration of both groups of organizations involves at least a preliminary identification of problems which may be created by man's penetration into the Antarctic and outer space, including such immediately identifiable areas for investigation as scientific research, weather forecasting, telecommunications problems, preservation and exploitation of natural resources, navigation, transportation, and financing of exploration or development.

A listing of fields in which international governmental organizations exist today is impressive; organizations have been created to parallel most of those in which national and local governments function.[2] They include arrangements dealing with agriculture, animals, atomic energy, banking, money and finance, coal and steel, commodities such as cotton, rice, sugar, rubber, tin and wheat, customs, defense,[3] social and economic development both generally and of limited areas, drugs, education, exhibitions, food and nutrition, forestry, geography, health, navigation, the resources of the seas, safety, transportation and transport facilities on land, sea and air, immigration, the protection of women and children, labor and refugees, traffic in women, slaves, liquor and arms, protection of patents, trademarks, industrial, artistic and literary properties, meteorology, postal service, sanitation, care of the sick and wounded, police work, statistical techniques, technical cooperation, telecommunications, and weights and measures.

The mere recital of subjects is perhaps misleading in a very important sense, however, for in most fields in which these arrangements exist, the organization commonly has the limited functions of collecting and disseminating information, preparing for meetings and "coordinating" and "stimulating" activities which are carried out, if at all, by national groups. These limited functions are useful and at times highly important, but they do not involve the delegation of any national power to the international organization and do not arouse apprehensions of infringements on national sovereignty. In a limited number of instances, however, the organization itself or some directing unit of it has been given, directly or indirectly, operational, police, or supervisory powers which can only be described as "supranational," to some extent, at least.[4] Instances of "derogations" from national sovereignty occur or have occurred in connection with the recent economic integrations in Western Europe—in the Coal and Steel Community and the newer Euratom and the European Economic Community—in connection with river navigation, in the protection of the resources of the sea, in certain aspects of control of the traffic in slaves and drugs and, potentially, in the control of the use of atomic energy even under the Statute of the International Atomic Energy Agency.

ORGANIZATIONS POSSIBLY RELEVANT TO THE ANTARCTIC OR OUTER SPACE

While the history of many existing functional organizations offers much that is potentially of interest here, only a limited number of agencies now operating could, even by stretching their existing constitutional arrangements, be expected to play a direct role in the problems of the Antarctic or of outer space. Eliminating from consideration both the United Nations itself and all groupings which are essentially military, most other organizations are limited to specified geographic areas or to action with respect to resources, facilities or commodities which are irrelevant, for the foreseeable future, to our considerations. Among those which function in relevant fields, however, and which, as a consequence, require closer scrutiny are the International Civil Aviation Organization (ICAO), the International Telecommunications Union (ITU), the World Meteorological Organization (WMO), UNESCO, and the International Whaling Commission.[5] Conceivably, the International Bank for Reconstruction and Development (IBRD) or another of the international financial institutions might be utilized to provide funds for projects in new areas but it seems more probable that, since the IBRD is limited to use of funds for development purposes on behalf of its members, it might only be called on for aid in such matters as technical surveys.

ICAO is limited in a technical sense to problems involving the use of airspace, air transportation, air navigation, and the like. Routes and facilities over or in the Antarctic would present problems not vastly different from those faced today in other parts of the globe. If the Soviet Union were willing to participate actively in ICAO,*

* The important political problems, even for the Antarctic, of participation by all major Powers are apparent.

and if there were general ratification of a new treaty, then ICAO might discharge new responsibilities beyond airspace.[6] This would seem appropriate since ICAO's general purposes, including the development of standards, practices and procedures for flight, the insurance of the safe and orderly growth of international civil "aviation," the development of principles of navigation, the prevention of economic waste due to unreasonable competition and the avoidance of discrimination between nations and their carriers,[7] are just as pertinent to the ultimate peaceful, commercial use of outer space as they are to flight at lower levels. Further, the Council of ICAO is already authorized to conduct research into aspects of "air" transportation and navigation.[8] Obviously, changes would be necessary to adapt ICAO to a broader role when extra-terrestrial commercial transport becomes practical economically. The existing organization is not designed to undertake or to be capable of undertaking direct exploration, exploitation or control of new areas; it is, rather, a device for the orderly regulation of existing opportunities in a commercial field.[9] While this is important, it presents no crucial political or economic problems or difficulties where extensive collaboration exists between the commercial participants in any event, and where the adoption of standard practical practices tends to benefit all. Even today, its decisions on standards, practices, and procedures are not binding on a State which finds it impracticable to comply with the international standard and so notifies the organization.[10] However, under Article 12 of the Convention, decisions are binding while aircraft of Parties are over the high seas.

Another function sponsored by ICAO might be relevant to other areas terrestrial or extra-terrestrial. Under a 1954 joint support agreement nine sea stations are maintained by twenty-one ships, of which the United States supplies ten, for weather-reporting.[11] In addition, there are jointly supported meteorological, communications, traffic control, and LORAN services maintained in Iceland, Greenland, and the Faroes. Further communication facilities for

ICAO members are afforded by Atlantic cable. The cooperative basis for the cable provides that the United States takes one-half for its own use and pays half the cost; Canada takes and pays one quarter; the final quarter goes to all ICAO members participating, and the cost is shared among thirteen Atlantic countries including the United States and Canada. ICAO has also divided the world into eight geographical regions, in each of which it holds meetings to help determine the requirements for air navigation and the facilities, services, and procedures needed in each. ICAO then attempts to secure implementation of the plans by the states in the region and to help the interested governments establish and provide the needed services.[12]

The International Telecommunications Union (ITU), with almost a hundred members, is charged generally with the allocation by agreement of the limited number of available frequencies among the participating nations, the registration of frequencies used, the facilitating of cooperation between nations, the making of studies and collection of pertinent information, and the formulation of recommendations for change.[13] It has an already demonstrable interest in some of the uses of outer space and perhaps of the Antarctic too. Interference with broadcasts on earth due to the passage of Soviet and American satellites and the use of the Atlas "talking satellite" has indicated both the potential use of such objects in the communications field and the problems of allocation that will arise due to the physically limited number of frequencies available to man for such purposes (see Chapter 8).

The ITU functions through Plenipotentiary Conferences meeting generally every five years, Administrative Conferences also meeting every five years, a standing Administrative Council of eighteen nation-members representing all parts of the world, a Secretariat, and Consultative Committees in the fields of telegraphy, telephone, and radio (on which private companies as well as national administrations may serve), and the International Radio Frequency Board, whose members "shall serve, not as representatives of their respective countries, or of a region, but as custodians of an international public trust." [14]

The ITU is actually an arrangement for allocating a scarce commodity by agreement and for promoting cooperation between states with respect to highly important national industries which are regulated or nationalized in most states.[15] It is in no sense an operating agency as constituted and does not itself provide communications facilities at all.* It is further limited in that there is no effective international sanction at its disposal to prevent non-compliance with agreed arrangements, the pirating of channels, and the like—self-interest in maintaining a cooperative relationship is again the basis for compliance; and this, as has been demonstrated, is not always enough where national power is disparate.

Another agency with, at least theoretically, a great interest in the Antarctic and the use of outer space, both from the scientific and technological points of view, is the World Meteorological Organization (WMO), whose membership included seventy-seven states and twenty-three territories in April, 1959.[16] Here too, however, the organization is charged basically with promoting and improving standards, encouraging research and exchange of information, facilitating cooperation in making observations, and providing technical assistance rather than performing any operating functions of its own. Organized on the basis of a World Congress, an Executive Committee, Regional Associations, and Technical Committees which can study problems in the science and make recommendations "on any subject within the purposes of the Organization," the WMO serves to encourage cooperation between national bureaus and has no facilities at all for research or the maintenance of stations or services of its own. It might perhaps serve to coordinate national weather studies undertaken in or with respect to the Antarctic or outer space. In fact, the WMO already has a special Antarctic func-

* Other telecommunications organizations, such as the African Telecommunications Union, are similarly constituted and limited.

tion, one which has the characteristic, rare for an international organization, of providing for the custody of secret information. Whaling factory ships in Antarctic waters can supply important weather information but whalers do not like to disclose their locations to their competitors. To meet this situation the following procedure has been set up by the Executive Committee of WMO: Cape Town and Sydney are designated as the two centers for collecting weather messages from whaling ships. The South African Union Weather Bureau prepares individual cyphers for issue to each of the whaling factory ships operating in the Antarctic, copies of the cyphers to be held by the ship and each of the two collecting centers "and by no one else." The two centers make daily broadcasts of the reports from the whaling factory ships excluding the names and positions of the ships, but this latter information is encoded in another cypher held only by national meteorological services requiring the broadcasts and *not* by any of the whaling factory ships. In return for the reports from the ships, the two centers broadcast daily weather bulletins for the express use of the ships.[17] On the other hand, by apparent intent of the parties, WMO is in no position to develop a world weather service, whatever the usefulness of such an undertaking, particularly since weather information is considered highly important for security purposes by the major powers.*

UNESCO's functions are so many and varied that only a small part of its activities in stimulating and aiding research and distributing information could be useful in the Antarctic or space situations. UNESCO's General Conference in 1958 authorized the Director-General to cooperate in stimulating research to help solve problems involved in "exploration of extra-terrestrial space." As will be mentioned in the later discussion of the International Geophysical Year (IGY), UNESCO played an important part in help-

* The argument that "weather" is primarily of local or regional concern, whether valid or not, would not itself detract from the usefulness of a service which provided local information and also operated on a world-wide basis.

ing to finance international scientific cooperation. UNESCO's role has normally been limited to drawing up proposals to be implemented by member states. Certain UNESCO projects, such as the establishment in 1957–58 of the Provisional International Computation Center at Rome, may serve very useful functions in facilitating international cooperation, particularly in space research.

The International Whaling Commission, while not limited to the southern seas, has existing responsibilities with respect to, at least, one important resource of the Antarctic region. The Commission, consisting of one representative of each Party to the treaty, was established pursuant to the International Convention for the Regulation of Whaling which entered into force in 1948. It is charged both with encouraging studies and assembling statistics regarding whales and whaling and with amending, by a three-fourths vote, within the purposes of the Convention, the schedule of regulations which form an integral part of the Convention. This again is an organization which regulates the preservation and sharing out of a limited resource, the supply of whales, in an area which belongs to no one—the open seas.

The Convention's regulations relate to protected and unprotected species, size limits, open and closed waters and seasons, types of permissible gear, maximum catch, and so on, and they are of substantial economic importance to the whaling nations. A member which objects to an amendment may, however, both delay the entry into force of the amendment for all members and totally prevent its application to itself.[18] An inspection system is called for, too, but only to the extent that inspectors, appointed and paid by the governments having jurisdiction over a ship or installation, are stationed on factory ships and at land stations. A protocol proposed in 1956 provided for inspectors appointed by and responsible to the Commission itself, but this has not been acted on.[19] There is no central supervisory agency—each government is required to take "appropriate measures to ensure the application of the provisions of this Convention and the punishment of infractions . . . by persons or by vessels under its jurisdiction."[20] The ultimate sanction is identical with the motive which led to the conclusion of the Convention, namely the threat to the supply of whales and thus to the industry dependent upon that supply. The investment in the large new factory ships, for example, is very heavy. But long-range wisdom in planning conservation often fights a losing battle with immediate commercial or profit interest of companies or individual crew members. While the closed season has been generally respected, there has been a tendency to exceed quotas in the final days of the open seasons. The concern over the diminishing supply which first led to the negotiation of the whaling conventions is again being keenly felt.[21] Whatever its limitations, the international arrangements for the conservation of whales constitute a functioning cooperative system in the Antarctic which is all the more important now that modern methods and equipment have made shore stations unnecessary.

Certain other techniques of regulation evolved in international agreements for the sharing of aquatic resources are also of potential interest for Antarctica. The Convention of 1911 for the Preservation and Protection of Fur Seals,[22] between the United States, Russia, Great Britain (on behalf of Canada), and Japan, not only prohibited the killing, capturing, or pursuit of seals at sea ("pelagic sealing") in wide areas of the Pacific, but also bound the Parties to keep any ship violating these rules, whatever its nationality, from using their ports and to prohibit importation of sealskins taken in violation of the rules. Cruisers of the four Powers provided a policing force at sea, and skins properly taken were stamped so that they could gain entrance into markets of those nations. The United States, Russia, and Japan each accounted in annual percentages fixed by the treaty to the other Parties for skins taken on the islands over which they respectively exercised jurisdiction. This provision, which in effect delegated to the territorial states the function of reaping the harvest subject to an obligation to share, is of special interest. The 1911 Convention was denounced by Japan in 1941, but a new treaty along the original lines and among the same four states was concluded in 1957. This treaty established the North Pacific Seal Commission with one member from each state. It acts by unanimity, and its expenses are shared equally. Each party turns over to the Commission an amount equivalent to the value of the sealskins it confiscates for violations of the Convention.[23]

The halibut fisheries received special attention in the United States–Canadian Convention of 1937 for the Preservation of the Halibut Fishery of the Northern Pacific Ocean and the Bering Sea,[24] which provided for similar enforcement techniques and an International Fisheries Commission, which can suspend or change closed seasons, limit catches in various areas, and control fishing vessels and the manner of fishing. Further, Canada, Japan, and the United States, in the International Convention for the High Seas Fisheries of the North Pacific Ocean, of May 9, 1952, provided for more extensive conservation measures, limitations on fishing by nationals of the Contracting Powers, and the establishment of an International North Pacific Fisheries Commission to regulate activities under the Convention. Where stocks of fish are listed by one nation as subject to its conservation program and the others on the Commission agree, the nationals of all others are barred from fishing those stocks.[25] A violator of the rules who is a national of one of the Parties may be arrested by any one of them but will be tried in the courts of his own country. This is a familiar provision in fishery treaties. Interference by nationals of nonmembers leads initially, at least, only to a conference among the Parties under the terms of the Convention. A similar Commission exists under the International Convention of February 8, 1949, for the North West Atlantic Fisheries.[26] Here too, the Commission's prime concern is conservation and adverse activities by nationals of nonmembers are to be called directly to the nonmember's attention.

Other related groups include the General Fisheries Council for the Mediterranean and the Indo-Pacific Fisheries Council, both of which are subsidiary bodies of the Food and Agriculture Organization, though their activities are limited to recommending and coordinating research, formulating problems for solution, and studying national legislation,[27] and the Inter-American Tropical Tuna Commission, which is empowered to make investigations, collect and analyze information, and propose joint action for conservation.[28]

ORGANIZATIONS IN RELATED OR ANALOGOUS FIELDS

The Antarctic and outer space present obvious opportunities, even now, for joint or coordinated scientific undertakings by the nations of the world and, indeed, the International Geophysical Year (IGY), which will be considered in Part II, indicated the real benefits which could be expected from this type of effort. There are a number of examples of current international arrangements functioning in the field of joint or coordinated scientific work, using the term broadly; but, with the possible exception of the International Hydrographic Bureau, there seem to be no existing governmental organizations able to play an immediate role in either of our special areas.

The International Hydrographic Bureau, of which more than thirty maritime states are members, has a direct interest in all matters relating to this science and has, therefore, a special interest in relatively unexplored areas of the seas. It is expressly limited, however, to a consultative capacity, with no authority over its members' hydrographic services, and is not to "be concerned with matters involving questions of international policy." It confines its work largely to coordinating surveys made by members, studying methods and techniques to be used in surveying the oceans, and, in general, serving as a coordinating and information agency. While thus not in a position to play any political role in the Antarctic, the Bureau does employ technical assistants of its own and can, under its statutes, conduct "research on any other matters relating to Hydrography." [29] If funds were made available in substantial amounts, it would, therefore, be technically possible for the Bureau to conduct at least one portion of the research work needed in that area.

Among the existing intergovernmental organizations which, at least, set a pattern for international cooperation in scientific effort, several may be listed. There are, for example, the organizations to coordinate the exploration of all phases of the Mediterranean Sea and to carry out scientific and technical studies, through use of qualified reporters [30] and others, to encourage investigations and coordination of research in the eastern North Atlantic Ocean; [31] the International Bureau of Weights and Measures, which keeps the international prototypes of the meter and kilogram and makes comparison and verifications of new prototypes and national standards; [32] the International Institute of Refrigeration, which coordinates research and can do studies in that field; the Permanent International Bureau of Analytical Chemistry of Human and Animal Foods, which maintains laboratories and archives and is charged with developing techniques of analysis useful in this pursuit; the Scientific Council for Africa South of the Sahara, which plans research programs and encourages national participation in cooperative efforts in the fields of science, health, and the like; and the Inter-American Statistical Institute, to which both governments and private persons belong, which was formed to stimulate methodology, improve techniques, and formulate projects to be carried out nationally.[33] An example of the way in which international technical cooperation sometimes succeeds in surmounting political barriers (as it has notably in the Antarctic) is provided by an international committee for the limnological study of the Danube, formed in 1958 and now carrying out a prearranged program. Its members are West Germany, Austria, Czechoslovakia, Hungary, Rumania, Bulgaria, and the Soviet Union.[34]

A substantial amount of scientific cooperation exists in the field of agriculture, as well as in food and nutrition, though many of the cooperating organizations also have other purposes.[35] There are, for example, the Inter-American Institute of Agricultural Sciences, which can carry out experiments and research; the International

Commission of Agricultural Industries, which, among other jobs, coordinates research activities; the International Seed Testing Association (made up of individuals as accredited by governments), designed to further accurate and uniform methods of testing and evaluating seeds; the Commonwealth Agricultural Bureau, and the Institute of Nutrition of Central America and Panama. Related too to the problem of international scientific collaboration are those agencies promoting, stimulating, and coordinating research in the field of disease and medicine, including the International Scientific Committee for Trypanosomiasis Research, the International Office of Epizootics, the International Red Locust Control Service, and, particularly, the World Health Organization, although this is only one of its multiple functions.

Attention has already been paid to air transportation and the possible development of the role of ICAO in Antarctica and in space. It is pertinent to note other international agencies which are concerned with transportation either by land or water.

The newest of the United Nations specialized agencies is the Intergovernmental Maritime Consultative Organization (IMCO), which is strictly limited to a consultative and advisory role [36] with respect to international cooperation in making uniform the regulations and practices of governments in international maritime trade and shipping. IMCO is also designed to facilitate the ending of discriminatory practices and unnecessary restrictions, and to aid in establishing standards for safety at sea and for maritime navigation; [37] its Convention does not provide for any rule-making or enforcement powers.

Other transportation organizations, all of them limited to the collection and publication of information, assistance to members in settling disputes, the achievement of uniform standards and rules through national action, and other non-operating tasks which call for no intrusions into the realms of national sovereignty, include the Central Office for International Transport by Rail, dealing essentially with European problems arising under the Conventions of 1952 for the transportation of merchandise and passengers' baggage;[38] the International Conference for Promoting Technical Uniformity in Railways, another European organization which functions through sporadic conferences of government experts and a central office at Berne;[39] and various motor traffic conventions which deal with uniform danger signals, necessary equipment, international certificates and permits, and the like, all in an effort to ease the transit of motor traffic between the nations of the world.[40] The railroad agreements in particular are numerous in Europe because Europe is a developed area cut up by nationally oriented transport facilities which can be and have often been used for national ends. Once a new divided land area becomes developed, or once a new medium for transportation becomes available, some form of cooperation, if not indeed of general regulation, is an essential in this politically and economically divided world.

Another field in which the movement into space will bring problems of a type already familiar is that of control of and assistance to navigation and the operation of navigation facilities. In this area we find the oldest joint ventures on the international scene, including some which, within their own spheres of activity, have enjoyed both substantial autonomy and certain supranational powers. We also find expressions of principles of general equal economic access and freedom of navigation which are very reminiscent of instances discussed in our earlier section on "governmental" administrations, though neither these principles nor the autonomy of the agencies to be described have withstood wartime and even cold war tensions and pressures.

The oft-cited instances of the Commission for the Control of Navigation on the Rhine and of the European Danube Commission come readily to mind.* Control of the Rhine began as early

* There are certain modern parallels, such as the quasi-independent government bureaus exercising "legislative," "executive," and "judicial" authority, and even joint development organs such as the Port of New York Authority, so that these commissions are not as alien to "normal governmental" procedures today as they must have appeared a hundred or more years ago.

as 1803, and the Congress of Vienna in 1815 formulated general principles for keeping the Rhine free for navigation and for assuring equal treatment for the nationals of many states.[41] The Commission initially and in more recent years made general regulations with respect to navigation and served as an appeals court in both civil and criminal matters involving navigation. The Commission, made up generally of officials of the riparian states, drafted rules which were then submitted to the riparians for adoption. The riparian states also set up the Rhine Navigation Courts, which applied the same regulations and recognized each other's decrees, and all riparians issued common regulations for their sections of the Waterways Police. Again, inspectors who assured that the Rhine agreements were effectuated were paid and appointed by the riparian states but were subordinate to the Commission.[42]

The European Danube Commission, established by the Treaty of Paris of 1856, was essentially a "regime" imposed on Turkey and its weak riparian vassal, Rumania. The Commission included representatives of England, France, Austria, Prussia, Russia, Turkey, and Sardinia.[43] The Commission was initially charged with engineering duties—the design, construction, and deepening of channels. It, too, levied dues for passage with rates set by a majority vote, made and enforced regulations through fines imposed by its own officials, licensed tugs, lighters and pilots, ran hospitals and a rescue service, dredged channels, and did related work to make the river ever more usable. All flags were to be accorded equal treatment.

The channel and port work completed by the Commission were "neutralized," as were the administrative and technical personnel by 1891. The Commission floated loans on its own credit backed by tolls and on occasion with joint guarantees by the Powers. In the Treaty of Berlin of 1878, its jurisdiction was extended upriver "in a complete independence of territorial authority" (Article 53). A special flag was designed for the Commission in 1882, and its employees wore a distinctive armband. It was essentially self-supporting, its principal income coming from tolls. In all ordinary matters and in fixing tolls, a majority vote of the Commission sufficed, but unanimity was required for a change in operating principles. While the Convention Regarding the Regime of Navigation of the Danube signed in Belgrade on August 18, 1948, nominally preserved the principle of "free and open navigation" for all states and of equal charges and conditions for use, participation in the Commission was limited to "riparian" states and Britain and France lost their role.[44] At present the Convention appears to be effective only for the Soviet bloc and Yugoslavia, though Austria and Germany may presumably participate.[45]

Along similar lines, a group of nations with interests in shipping banded together to maintain a lighthouse at Cape Spartel in Morocco on the North African coast about eight miles from Tangier at the entrance to the Mediterranean Sea. The lighthouse was actually built by the Moroccan government in 1861–64, the construction being supervised by a French engineer, and the "sovereign" rights of the Sultan have at all times been formally recognized. Because of the potential usefulness of the light for signaling purposes in time of war, the major Powers were insistent on its permanent neutrality, and, in return for a suitable arrangement, the Sultan insisted that the Powers pay for keeping up the light. Pursuant to a treaty signed by the Sultan and representatives of ten Powers—Austria, Belgium, France, Great Britain, Italy, the Netherlands, Portugal, Spain, Norway, and the United States—on May 31, 1865, the upkeep and maintenance of the light were undertaken by these Powers with expenses to be shared equally and not in proportion to local commerce; the neutrality of the light was guaranteed. Germany and Russia later adhered to the treaty.

The role of the Powers was carried out through the International Commission of the Cape Spartel Light, made up of the diplomatic representatives of the Powers resident at Tangier.[46] The Commission was established in 1865 and performed its largely technical and nonpolitical function with "most satisfactory" results until the full independence of Morocco was achieved in 1956. The facilities of the lighthouse were improved from time to time and its "neutrality" and internationally supported operation were maintained with the important exception of the World War periods. In 1914, for instance, French authorities took over the technical direction of the lighthouse, ousting its keeper, Herr Gumpert, an Austrian subject whose family had tended the light since its establishment. The International Commission was not consulted, but after the War the French withdrew.[47] Spain unilaterally took over the light during the Second World War and retained control until 1945 when Allied pressure forced her out and the International Commission was reestablished. With these exceptions, the Commission functioned steadily for almost a century in a narrowly circumscribed operating capacity in this important, though essentially technical, field of navigation.[48]

Another type of cooperatively sponsored aid to navigation is the ice patrol service managed and maintained by the United States on behalf of some fourteen nations in the North Atlantic. States contribute to the costs of this service in accordance with the total gross tonnage of ships of their nationality passing through that area, though for convenience billings are arranged on a unit basis with Britain and the United States bearing the heaviest cost burden.[49] A limited number of North Atlantic Ocean Weather Stations are jointly supported as well.[50]

There are several organizations in various parts of the world charged, in various ways, with promoting the broad development of or cooperation in an entire area. Cooperation of this type may prove useful in the Antarctic and outer space. Some of these regional agencies perform essentially a research and advisory role only. The Agreement of October 30, 1946, for the Establishment of the Caribbean Commission between the United States, Britain, France and the Netherlands,[51] for example, notes that the Signatories

Being desirous of promoting scientific, technological and economic development in the Caribbean area and facilitating the use of resources and concerted treatment of mutual problems, avoiding duplication in the work of existing research agencies, surveying needs, ascertaining what research has been done, facilitating research on a co-operative basis, and recommending further research . . .

establish the Commission as a research and advisory body on social and economic matters of regional interest with all administration of the areas remaining in national hands. The Commission and its auxiliary bodies, the Caribbean Research Council and the West Indian Conference have, however, been quite active, having completed surveys of existing and potential industries, transport and communications facilities, and tourism in the area, conducting weekly multilingual radio programs and publishing an information bulletin.[52]

A roughly similar organization exists for the Southwest Pacific area—the South Pacific Commission—formed by Australia, New Zealand, the United States, France, England, and the Netherlands in 1947.[53] This too is an advisory and consultative body, dealing with the economic and social problems of the area, designed to study and recommend measures for coordinated services and to furnish such technical assistance as is needed. There is a research council, too, and the Commission actually appears to supervise a health study center and medical facility in Fiji though, as in the Caribbean, each area is subject solely to the territorial sovereign. Also similar is the Commission for Technical Cooperation in Africa South of the Sahara, which is designed to assure joint study of pressing African problems, to make recommendations, to advise member governments, and to supervise the work of several technical subsidiary bodies which in turn make studies and recommendations.[54] Again, mutual cooperation is the aim and the organization has no independent powers. Other entities studying common economic and social problems in the Americas and limited to fostering cooperation in the approach to their solution include, of course, the Organization of American States (OAS) [55] and the

Organization of Central American States (OCAS).[56] In a different way, the Council for Technical Cooperation in South and South East Asia (the "Colombo Plan") seeks to promote the economic growth of an extensive area, though in this case the organization's role is essentially that of coordinating bilateral and joint programs of technical assistance.

In Western Europe, several arrangements in recent years have gone far in treating regional problems collectively. The Council of Europe, for example, is authorized to discuss questions of common concern in the economic, social, cultural, scientific, legal, and administrative fields; but, as would be anticipated with such broad coverage, neither the Consultative Assembly nor the Council of Ministers may do more than deliberate and present recommendations to the Governments involved.[57] On the economic side, the Organization for European Economic Cooperation (OEEC),[58] which was originally set up in 1948 to provide a "European" approach to Western European recovery and to allocate rationally Marshall Plan assistance to the area, remains an important organ of general Western European economic cooperation, through consultation, today. Further, the "OEEC method" of cooperation retains staunch supporters, particularly Great Britain, as an alternative to more drastic economic integration.

There have also been developed in Western Europe in recent years a number of institutions involving not only cooperation between sovereign equals but actual mergers of economies, or of sectors of economies, which are especially interesting due to their concept of area development, to the powers assigned them, and to this general approach to international controls. They lead directly, for example, to the question whether functional union and, really, functional international government is possible without political power and, therefore, without a political merger too. A brief mention must, however, suffice here.

Quite narrowly based but by now functioning reasonably successfully, for example, is the economic amalgamation of the Netherlands and the Belgo-Luxembourg Union markets into Benelux.[59] One of the few instances of an intergovernmental organization with certain supranational powers is the European Coal and Steel Community, formed by Belgium, France, Italy, the Netherlands, Luxembourg, and the German Federal Republic to promote the development of this critical sector of the economy of Western Europe. Although limited to a particular segment of the Western European economy, one of the distinct goals of the "Schuman Plan," which launched the Community in 1952, was broader economic unity and, eventually, some form of political unity. Without these, it was fully recognized, the preliminary venture with coal and steel could not in the long run succeed. The fifty-year treaty [60] establishing the Community expressly sets out the supranational character of its functions, which include the collecting of information, defining of objectives, providing of financial means for investment by and with the readaptation of enterprises, the assurance of stability in these fields, the maintenance and observation of conditions of competition, and, when absolutely necessary, the taking of direct action with respect to production and the operation of the market. Duties and restrictions on the movement of coal and steel as well as discriminations, subsidies, restrictive practices, and the like are forbidden.

The Coal and Steel Community is operated by a nine-man High Authority, which is likewise expected to rise above nationalities. Its members serve for six-year terms; they are nationals of the member states, but not more than two can be of any one nationality; all must give up any interests in the industries with which they deal and agree to refrain from business or professional activities in these fields for three years after leaving the Authority. Though appointed by agreement of the members, they are independent in action. With respect to many things, including programs, fines and penalties, encouraging research, investments, production, prices, agreements and concentrations, transport problems and rates, wages and conditions of competition, the Authority can, by majority vote, make decisions which are binding in detail on members, make recommendations which are binding as to objectives, or give opinions which are not binding. The High Authority is aided by a Consultative Committee of producers, consumers, and workers and is responsible to the Assembly of delegates chosen by the parliaments of the members. The Assembly can censure it and in a sense can control it; for it can force the resignation of the entire membership of the High Authority by a two-thirds vote. To round out the picture, the Community has both a Council of member governments and an impartial Court to which members, legal entities, and the Council can appeal decisions of the High Authority and whose decision is final and binding. The Community is self-supporting through "taxes" levied on coal and steel production; it can acquire property, sue and be sued, borrow money, and so on. It is, in other words, a well-developed institution controlling, to a considerable extent, the conduct of major industries across national borders, and, aided by the general post-war prosperity, it has been relatively successful in achieving many of its objectives without grave dislocations, at least through 1958.

More recently, the Treaty creating the European Economic Community came into force, establishing the foundation for an over-all common market among the six members of the Coal and Steel Community.[61] The Treaty proper sets forth the tariff steps and related economic arrangements and provides for an eventual organization in agriculture with power to regulate prices, subsidize production, ensure stocks and stabilize exports and imports, and for an investment bank for economic development within the Community. The European Commission, appointed by a Council of Ministers of the participating states, is the executive organ. It is composed of nine members serving four-year terms and is the permanent body responsible for securing implementation of the Treaty. The Council of Ministers not only appoints the Commission but makes decisions with respect to the extent of the common market. An advisory 101-member Economic and Social Committee has also been appointed by the Council. The European Parliamentary Assembly, elected by the parliaments of the participating nations, and a Court of Justice common to all three European Communities have also been established—the Court is superseding that of the Coal and Steel Community. (The third Community, Euratom, is considered below.)

It is premature to discuss here any application of such devices to Antarctica and outer space. (The proximate problems of those areas will be considered in Parts II and III.) But it is not irrelevant to remind the reader of the great variety of cooperative devices which governments have already utilized for purposes both small and large.

In addition to arrangements for area cooperation and area integration, there have also been several international attempts at general economic or financial cooperation.[62] Among the oldest of such institutions still extant is the Bank for International Settlements, established in 1930 to promote cooperation between the central banks, provide facilities for international financial operations, and act as trustee in regard to financial settlements entrusted to it. It has the power to buy and sell gold, make advances to central banks, discount and rediscount, deal in exchange, and generally to perform the functions of a banker's bank.

Its administering board is composed of the governors of certain central banks, of seven representatives of finance, industry, or commerce appointed by these same governors, and up to nine men selected by the board from lists submitted by the central banks of other countries. It is incorporated in Switzerland, but the treaty, to which Switzerland is also a party, provides that the charter of the corporation could not be abrogated or amended. The Bank is immune from taxes and also from suit in the courts. Disputes among the governments are to be submitted to arbitration.[63]

The planning for the period after the close of the Second World War included UNRRA for immediate relief needs, and the International Bank for Reconstruction and Development (IBRD) and the International Monetary Fund (IMF) to provide financial stability and the restoration of economic prosperity over the long pull. Despite the generally satisfactory operations of both the latter institutions, their resources and functions are now found to be inadequate and it is proposed to increase their capital funds. They have already been supplemented by the International Finance Corporation (IFC) and the Special United Nations Fund (SUNFED). A new international bank for the Americas is also under consideration, as is an International Development Association.[64]

One further field, that of atomic energy, is discussed at this point as an illustration of current cooperative "peaceful" ventures in an area which is intertwined with problems of defense and major national interests. There is, first, the International Atomic Energy Agency (IAEA), created by a treaty signed in October, 1956, and thus far still badly plagued by indecision as to its proper role, by extravagant small-nation demands, and by lack of support. It is not a "specialized agency" of the United Nations but an "autonomous international organization under the aegis of the United Nations." It is particularly interesting for its stipulated powers of inspection and sanction, even though these have not yet been used.

The IAEA has a General Conference made up of representatives of all members, a Board of Governors of ten members representing the five nations most advanced in the "technology of atomic energy, including the production of source materials" and five other nations advanced in the art or producers of source materials, and a "minimum" internationalized staff including scientific personnel. Members are to exchange information and to supply the IAEA with raw materials, services, and facilities. The IAEA is both to assist members in working out and obtaining materials for their projects and to undertake to provide services, equipment, and materials itself. Either function requires approval by the Board of Governors plus a formal agreement between the IAEA and the member or group of members involved in the project. In any IAEA project, or in others if requested by the parties, the Agency is to apply safeguards as to health, safety, and prevention of diversion to military uses. Using its own staff of inspectors, it is:

> To send into the territory of the recipient state or states inspectors, designated by the agency after consultation with the state or states concerned, who shall have access at all times to all places and data and to any person who by reason of his occupation deals with materials, equipment, or facilities which are required by this statute to be safeguarded, as necessary to account for source and special fissionable materials supplied and fissionable products and to determine whether there is compliance with the undertaking against use in furtherance of any military purpose . . . , with health and safety measures, and with any other conditions prescribed in the agreement between the agency and the state or states concerned. Inspectors designated by the agency shall be accompanied by representatives of the authorities of the state concerned, if that state so requests, provided that the inspectors shall not thereby be delayed or otherwise impeded in the exercise of their functions; [and] in the event of non-compliance and failure by the recipient state or states to take requested corrective steps within a reasonable time, to suspend or terminate assistance and withdraw any materials and equipment made available by the agency or a member in furtherance of the project.

Further, if a recipient fails to account for materials furnished, the Board of Governors, after a continued non-compliance, shall:

> report the non-compliance to all members and to the Security Council and General Assembly of the United Nations. In the event of failure of the recipient state or states to take fully corrective action within a reasonable time, the board may take one or both of the following measures: direct curtailment or suspension of assistance being provided by the Agency or by a Member, and call for the return of materials and equipment made available to the recipient Member or group of Members. The Agency may also, in accordance with Article XIX, suspend any non-complying Member from the exercise of the privileges and rights of membership.[65]

The IAEA apportions its administrative expenses to members "guided" by the principles used for the United Nations budget and is also expected to earn an income from charges made for its services. Disputes are to be referred to the International Court of Justice.

In Europe there have been several organizations established in this same field. The six members of the European Economic Community and the Coal and Steel Community have also established the European Atomic Community (Euratom), using the same Assembly and Court. With the development of a generally integrated economy it was deemed necessary to share the peaceful potentials of the atom as well and to avoid duplication of facilities. The executive organ is again a Commission whose members, within the terms of the treaty, function as international civil servants rather than as national representatives. The Commission is responsible to the Council of Ministers and, less directly, to the common parliamentary Assembly. A number of consultative committees have also been established. Initial programs called for the development of 15 million kilowatts of electricity from nuclear plants by 1967, but the goal has now been scaled down to 4–5 million kilowatts.[66]

Of wider membership is the European Organization for Nuclear Research (CERN), established by a Convention which entered into force in 1954 between Belgium, Denmark, France, Germany, Greece, Italy, the Netherlands, Norway, Sweden, Switzerland, the United Kingdom, and Yugoslavia. The preparatory work for its creation, involving scientific, administrative, and legal studies, was undertaken by UNESCO while the actual implementation and financing of the project was taken over by the states involved. Its purpose is collaboration by individual scientists in nuclear research "of a pure scientific and fundamental character," and its basic program included the construction in Switzerland of an international laboratory and related facilities and the sponsoring of general cooperation.[67]

More recently the European Nuclear Energy Agency (ENEA) was established, effective February 1, 1958, under the OEEC, which had previously established a Steering Committee for Nuclear Energy. Its area of interest is like that of Euratom, but it is generally a research and advisory body concerned with applied research and technology.[68] Studies are as a rule to be carried out by *ad hoc* expert groups. Earlier, in December, 1957, twelve members of the OEEC signed a Convention on the Constitution of the European Company for the Chemical Processing of Irradiated Fuels (Eurochemic).[69] This latter device is an international company, established by international agreement, but designed to have states, public and semi-public bodies, and private groups as shareholders. Its purposes include the construction and operation of needed plants and facilities for fuel processing and the first plant and its laboratories are scheduled for Mal, Belgium. In management and control it is linked with ENEA and Euratom.[70]

THE INTERNATIONAL GEOPHYSICAL YEAR

One of the most interesting experiences in recent years, and one which we shall deal with again more specifically in the chapters on Antarctica and outer space, is that of the world-wide scientific cooperation in investigating the mysteries of the earth and the universe during the period from July 1, 1957, through December 31, 1958—the International Geophysical Year.[71] While not a government program, the IGY was carried out with government backing.[72] While not a military program, it received extensive support from the armed services. While not an "international program," it was collaborated in by nationals of sixty-six countries,[73] each country carrying out its own program with coordination achieved through a small core of unpaid officials.

By 1950 the geophysical sciences had reached a point where it was felt that progress was being hampered by lack of world-wide joint effort. New research tools—radiosonde balloons, rockets, radar, cosmic ray research, computers, new types of spectroscopes, and many others—had both revealed new problems and brought the solution of others close to hand. "The tools available . . . made it possible, for the first time, for man to escape from this environment and look directly into naked space."[74] To achieve world-wide simultaneous or related observations and to coordinate a program of interrelated studies, a program was developed between 1950 and 1952 under which the International Council of Scientific Unions (ICSU), a federation of thirteen general and specialized unions of the various sciences,[75] created the Comité Spécial pour l'Année Géophysique Internationale (CSAGI) to run the IGY.

ICSU is itself essentially a nongovernmental body, though some of the national academies of science or comparable national bodies are governmental or quasi-governmental.[76] It is considered a nongovernmental body by UNESCO, which provides a parallel organ at the intergovernmental level. A formal agreement was made between ICSU and UNESCO in 1947 which defined their areas of operation. UNESCO annually grants about $200,000 to the thirteen adhering Unions, this sum being allocated by ICSU to its programs of conferences, publications, and permanent services. ICSU in turn offers expert advice to UNESCO upon request.[77]

National committees to formulate programs were established in more than twenty nations by mid-1953, and by the fall of 1954, when CSAGI met in Rome, participation was assured by the Soviet bloc; and many of the international scientific unions and other organizations, including WMO, had developed coordinated plans for projects. The Rome conference defined includable plans as those involving "specific planetary problems of the earth," which meant (a) problems requiring concurrent synoptic observations at many points, involving cooperative observations by many stations; (b) problems of branches of the geophysical sciences whose solutions will be aided by the availability of synoptic or other concentrated work during the International Geophysical Year in other geophysical sciences; (c) observation of all major geophysical phenomena in relatively inaccessible regions of the earth that can be occupied during the International Geophysical Year because of the extraordinary effort during that interval, in order to augment our basic knowledge of the earth and the solar and other influences acting upon it; (d) epochal observations of slowly varying terrestrial phenomena, to establish basic information for subsequent comparison at later epochs.[78]

Six regions were singled out for special attention, including, as we have seen, the Antarctic and the Arctic, the equatorial region, and three pole-to-pole meridians for making a maximum number of observations. In addition to the Antarctic, the exploration of outer space ranked as a major objective of the IGY.

The core of the IGY administration was the Bureau of CSAGI, eventually a five-man body including citizens of Great Britain, the United States, the Soviet Union, France, and Belgium. The international administrative outlay was only about $100,000 a year, derived principally from UNESCO, ICSU, and the United States and Soviet Academies of Science, though national programs ran to "hundreds of millions of dollars." [79] To avoid involving CSAGI in political controversy, arrangements for assistance between nations as to funds, personnel, and the like were worked out bilaterally. A series of international conferences was held in the months preceding the start of the IGY, which was set for July 1, 1957, to set the final programs for the following eighteen months. Most of the projects were worked out on lines generally satisfactory to the scientists involved, but at least one suggested program, that for aerial photographic traverses of the Arctic, was dropped because of varying degrees of Soviet and United States opposition; another, a study of fallout, was severely limited due to Soviet objection.[80] Additionally, the bitter conflict between Nationalist and Communist China flared up to mar the general spirit of cooperation.

In September, 1955, the Chinese Communists announced to CSAGI that they had begun to form an IGY committee but conditioned their participation on nonacceptance of the Chinese Nationalists as participants. This did not appear to be an obstacle at the time, since nothing had been heard from Taiwan in the three years following an initial invitation to participate in the IGY. By early 1957, the Chinese People's Republic indicated plans for some 27

IGY stations, and its scientific representatives participated in a regional conference at Moscow from August 20 to 25, 1956, and in Spain in September, 1956. In November, 1956, however, a Chinese Nationalist scientist in a letter to CSAGI stated that Taiwan was a member of ICSU and protested the presence of Chinese Communists at meetings. He demanded the deletion of the People's Republic from the IGY list of participants.

The Secretary-General of CSAGI reminded Taiwan that it could not "deal with governmental problems" or base participation on political considerations. The Nationalists then requested an invitation to a regional meeting to be held at Tokyo in February, 1957, and made no reference to barring delegates from Peiping. It was then proposed by CSAGI that both Taiwan and Peking pledge themselves to send only scientists and not to raise political issues involving the barring of scientists from the other. Only Peking attended the Tokyo meeting, but the Chinese Communists continued to insist that there be only one "National Committee" recognized for China. The Bureau of CSAGI was faced with Taiwan's continued insistence on recognition, supported by the National Academy of Sciences of the United States. In June, 1957, it made one more attempt to resolve the problem by quietly accepting Taiwan but, at the same time, dropping the term "national" in its reference to committees, so that, for Chinese participation, the entries would read:

Chinese IGY Committee: Peking
Chinese IGY Committee: Taipei

On June 29, 1957, Peking announced its withdrawal from CSAGI until acceptance of Taiwan was revoked. Yet, informally, the People's Republic appears to have carried out its IGY program, including the development of tracking stations and weather observatories. Some information resulting from this program, particularly weather reports, was broadcast by the radio stations of the People's Republic and picked up in Japan and hence, eventually, found its way into the IGY program. But when the IGY came to an end, the Chinese

People's Republic, the third largest nation in area, was still not a member—a major case in which the IGY was significantly affected by political considerations.[81]

World Data Centers were established for the IGY in the United States and the Soviet Union, and a third was shared between Western Europe, Japan, and Australia to receive and retain complete sets of all IGY data. Some thirty thousand scientists at four thousand stations participated in making observations—the space research program alone used stations scattered throughout the world. That program, too, illustrated both the decided usefulness of international cooperation and the limitations to be anticipated in any noninternationalized endeavor.

In all, with the exception of the few problems discussed above, the IGY was a remarkable example of international cooperation through a maze of bilateral agreements and multinational understandings, using the form of international, scientific, nongovernmental arrangements. The work of the IGY in the Antarctic and in space research is left for consideration in later chapters.

Even before the end of the IGY, however, it was generally felt that in many fields the work begun should be continued. The Western countries leaned to less ambitious programs in specific fields or areas and, in fact, a Special Committee on Antarctic Research (SCAR) was formed in March, 1958, and a Special Committee on Oceanic Research (SCOR) met for the first time in August, 1958. The Soviet delegations seemed to favor continuing the IGY itself, perhaps, as Walter Sullivan suggests, because [82]

> it was more difficult, in Moscow, to get a new policy decision than to get more money for research, whereas in Washington the reverse was true. The Soviet scientists in 1954 had "sold" the IGY to the Kremlin and the results had been gratifying, not only scientifically but personally. After years of comparative isolation, the Soviet scientists had regained contact with the Western world and found that their work was accepted and valued. Like their Western colleagues, they had also discovered that, at least in the world of science, peaceful co-existence and competition were practical realities. But, once the IGY policy de-

cision had been made, it was easier to extend it than to obtain a decision on new proposals such as the creation of a special organ to coordinate space research.

The United States scientists, on the other hand, had obtained some $40,000,000 from Congress for what was to be a one-time expenditure. It was evident that far more than that had been spent in support from the Department of Defense, especially in the Antarctic (where aircraft losses alone ran into millions of dollars) and in the launching of earth satellites. Rather than ask for more money to extend the program, it might be more politic to ask for lesser sums for individual research projects.

In the end, "International Geophysical Cooperation 1959" was agreed to and the Committee on Space Research (COSPAR) was established. Thus, to an even more limited extent, joint work goes on, though under increasing political pressures, as we shall see.

As has already been pointed out, the foregoing brief description of many forms of international cooperation through functional organizations is not intended to suggest that the international community or part of it is prepared to take comparable measures now in regard to the Antarctic or to outer space. Existing international organizations have been created in response to felt needs and to serve specific purposes. Those organizations considered in this chapter have been generally responses to situations in which the tasks to be accomplished cannot satisfactorily be performed within national limits or through the resources of any single nation. Economy through a sharing of cost and manpower has also been a motivating factor. Attention has been called to those situations in which existing international organizations could actually be utilized to meet some of the problems which have already been identified in Antarctica and in outer space, but more detailed consideration of these possibilities will be given in Parts II and III.

In many cases there are apparent conflicts between considerations of national sovereignty and practical interests of governmental or nongovernmental groups which are more interested in some practical situation than in abstract questions of precedent or prestige. A factor to be considered is the disparate practice among nations in the assumption of functions by government, even quite outside the Communist states. Postal services are universally governmental and no problem of mixed public and private interest enters into the operations of the Universal Postal Union. On the other hand, while telegraph and telephone are commonly part of the postal service in many countries, they remain private enterprises in the United States. When the problem of railway coordination arose in Europe, some of the roads were privately owned and operated while others were state enterprises; today they are almost entirely state owned and operated. In the newer field of atomic power one sees in the United States some movement from government monopoly to private enterprise; in Europe it is still chiefly in the hands of government.

So too, in the IGY, the extent to which an academy of sciences is identified with a government may vary from country to country. It is possible to debate whether or not the IGY was an example of nongovernmental cooperation. The fact remains that there was government participation from all quarters, and yet political differences were not allowed to block substantial achievement. This is why the Director of the Office of International Relations of the United States National Academy of Sciences–National Research Council is led to hope "that the United Nations and its specialized agencies, when they contemplate the initiation of international scientific activities, will call upon organizations such as ICSU for advice and assistance. If this should happen, the IGY, in addition to making a significant contribution to science and human welfare, will have brought to the United Nations a valuable tool for the conduct of international scientific relations." [83]

Regardless of the nature of the activity involved, the record makes it clear that some form of international organization may readily be created and utilized when there is a conviction that it would serve a useful purpose. This is the central point which must be kept in mind as one comes to look at the future of Antarctica and of outer space.

4. *Patterns for the Future*

In the preceding chapters we have examined some situations in which governments have acted together in groups large or small to accomplish certain ends. Why did they not act alone in these cases? Is not individual, independent, "sovereign" action generally assumed to be or to have been the dominant objective of all states strong enough to indulge in it? As suggested at the outset, the answers to such questions, even in so far as they can be hazarded, may suggest how man can most profitably explore and exploit the new frontiers of the Antarctic and of outer space. In the descriptive parts which precede, some attention has been paid to the occasion for each joint or multiple action and to the organizational device utilized. This summarizing chapter seeks to indicate more comprehensively those forces which have been operating in the international community during the last hundred years, the increasing momentum of which may mark the decades ahead.

The Charter of the United Nations recognizes that there is an "inherent right" of self-defense. Such an inherent right exists because of the universal instinct for self-preservation, felt not only by individuals on their own behalf but also by persons acting responsibly in governments of states. In our tendency to personify the state we are likely to attribute this feeling of government officials to the collectivity itself, to the extent that usage has made it permissible to speak in terms of the state as the actor. The response of states then to this self-protective urge has, paradoxically enough, contributed to both the solitary and the cooperative courses of action.

The contribution to the solitary course of action is so amply illustrated in day-to-day experience that it scarcely needs historical illustration. We are apt to catalogue the flow of examples under the labels "defense" and "security." Thus the Soviet refusal to subordinate its freedom of action in maintaining armaments to any system of inspection which inevitably represents a collective or cooperative approach. Thus, too, the emphasis in the United States upon the military aspects of the still uncertain uses of space and of the satellites or missiles which man may control in space. If the scholar suggests that all national claims to the moon should be foresworn in favor of the United Nations, the military strategist is bound to ask what potential military advantage he is being asked to deny himself. If one talks about an international regime in the Antarctic, one is reminded of the German naval activities in its waters during the Second World War and the strategic importance of Palmer Peninsula if the Suez and Panama Canals were blocked. In face of the impossibility, or at least difficulty, of proving in advance the specific gains to the national interest, including the guarantees of security which would flow from international cooperation, the official who believes his state possesses the means for self-defense is apt to choose the solitary in preference to the cooperative course of action.

On the other hand, it is rare indeed to find a situation in which a state is so confident of its military superiority over any possible enemy or combination of enemies that it is uninterested in the support which other states may give it. So throughout modern history the search for security has led to alliances which may be identified as cooperative courses of action to serve a protective function.* Some of the cases of cooperative action we have examined were

* The story of military alliances, theories of balance of power, and the like has often been told and has not been recapitulated here, although the possibility that either space or Antarctic problems may find a solution which is neither bipolar nor universal cannot be excluded.

inspired, at least in part, by defense considerations, where those interests have been served by denying a potential strategic advantage to an adversary through placing some bit of territory under an agreed international regime. The Aaland Islands, Crete, Tangier, and others are cases in which this element appears. Although an alliance in the conduct of war is recognized as a thing of necessity and not of preference, the aftermath of a war in which the great identified danger of the moment has been eliminated by joint victory may lead to temporary joint belligerent occupations and to efforts to broaden and perpetuate the alliance. Or, on the contrary, it may result in suspicion, friction, and a return to separateness. The system of collective security which the framers of the League of Nations and the United Nations sought to establish was obviously designed to substitute for unilateral defense a cooperative course of action which would in turn facilitate other measures of international cooperation. While collective security has not been secured, many of the attendant measures of cooperation have become firmly established.

These other measures of cooperation are various and much older than the two organizations established during the aftermaths of World Wars. Short of intense concern for self-defense where the strategic interest is most apparent, it has been noted that some cooperative solutions have been inspired by the need to effect a compromise between conflicting claims when the states involved felt disinclined to settle the issue by actual armed conflict. The condominiums in Samoa, Egypt, and the New Hebrides are examples, as is the proposed solution for Spitsbergen. In other instances, where the political elements are still dominant, collective decisions have been reached to prevent individual and lesser states from initiating a conflict which might spread. In this context one thinks of Memel, Leticia, and Danzig. The historical fact that from time to time throughout the modern period states have joined in some common solution of a territorial problem as an escape from conflict is quite pertinent to a consideration of Antarctica, where eight states have already, with more or less insistence, asserted claims to sovereignty. Some of those claims overlap and conflict; all of them are rejected by the two great powers, the United States and the Soviet Union. If it were not for the considerations of self-defense which have just been discussed, it would seem that every consideration of logic would impel toward an international agreement to adopt a cooperative course rather than several solitary courses of action before some new discovery suggests an immediate short-range advantage to the discoverer or to whatever state is in a position to capitalize on the discovery. Unhappily, it is the very prospect of the possibility of such a discovery which makes defense-conscious states refrain from tying their own hands, at least when the mores of their community dictate the binding force of a promise.

Although the interests of defense are primary, they are obviously not the only national interests. It will be noted later that in the Antarctic the prospect that the national economic interest may be served by territorial claims plays a significant part. In the age of discovery it was the economic motive which first led states to send explorers across the oceans. Sometimes trading stations sufficed at first to tap the economic wealth of newly discovered lands. In other circumstances, or as time passed, it seemed desirable to claim sovereignty of an area and on that base to erect the system of colonial monopoly which was characteristic of the colonial period. As it then became necessary to guard the far-flung empire and its wealth, the emphasis shifted to defense. The English interest in Egypt reflected both Lancashire's demand for cotton and the Admiralty's concern with the protection of the "lifeline" of the Empire through Suez. England for a time had to share with France control of the Suez Canal through stock ownership and the political control of Egypt through a condominium.

In spite of our ability to point to traces of a "trusteeship" concept as early as the sixteenth century, it is an inescapable fact that during long stretches of modern history (and of ancient history, for that matter) the inhabitants of a desired territory, especially if they were of a different culture or were militarily weak, were regarded merely as indigenous resources to be used (e.g. as slaves) or as natural obstacles to be overcome, as one might hack a path through a jungle or forest. Against the background of a century of development of the philosophy of the rights of man, Woodrow Wilson's conception of self-determination heralded a more effective acceptance of a political principle of responsibility for the welfare and wishes of people. As applied to the tangled ethnographic puzzles of post-war Europe this Wilsonian principle was largely inapplicable, although it found valid reflection in the protection of some minorities. In the colonial world of less-developed peoples, the resulting League of Nations mandate system did provide a precedent which, in the general stream of inclination toward the development of international organization, led to the trusteeship system of the United Nations and has now blended with a willing or reluctant yielding to the irresistible currents of contemporary nationalism. Earlier manifestations of this sensitivity to the rights of rather primitive peoples were reflected in the nineteenth-century collective approach to some of the problems of Africa, which at the same time was being carved up into colonial domains. It is these domains which are now emerging into nationhood. One can not forebear to ponder the impact on international relations of this new force, but we must note that it is not one which will in the short run influence definitively decisions about the polar and the cosmic spaces which are at present unpeopled. This is not to deny that any agreed international settlement of these two problems can be strongly influenced by the newly developed power and interests of anti-colonial voting blocs in the General Assembly of the UN. Futile to speculate at this juncture about the "inhabitants" of other planets and whether—if they exist—it is we or they who will need to be reminded of the right of self-determination.

The preceding chapters have also—without any pretense to novelty—called attention to the fact that there are many aspects of international relations which are important in themselves but which are not inextricably enmeshed in considerations of national interests, political or strategic. Even though political or other so-called vital interests are involved, they are considered separable in some manner or to some degree. They may be separable in the sense that governments are prepared to accept a temporary solution which avoids the final issue and provides a tolerable compromise for the time being. The United States proposal of May 2, 1958, for the Antarctic seems to be of this type, as will be noted later. Separability may also be found along functional lines, as where international cooperation may be accepted in the regulation and maintenance of the navigational facilities of the Danube without affecting the politics of the river basin. Communications are of vital interest to the military strategist, but various aspects of telecommunications can be entrusted to an International Telecommunications Union; one waits to see whether telecommunications with satellites are among those aspects. Although the sovereign control of a nation's superjacent airspace is jealously guarded as essential to the national safety, seventy-four states are members of ICAO, which can set certain standards in the interest of safe flight, and the Chicago Conventions contain agreements on certain reciprocal rights of overflight and landing. The economic welfare of an important segment of the population is a matter of great national interest, but it has been found possible to enter into international cooperative measures for the conservation of the resources of the sea and thus to regulate and control short-range commercial profits. Atomic energy might be selected as a prime example of a subject of the most intense importance to the national interest, but some aspects are covered by the treaties establishing the International Atomic Energy Agency, Euratom, and the European Nuclear Energy Agency. And perhaps as important as the discovery of the splitting of the atom is the political realization at which many governments have at long last arrived, that sovereignty itself can be divided, as witness the supranational institutions of the European Community and, indeed, many provisions of the Charter of the United Nations.

The institutions of the European Community have actually been given executive and judicial functions comparable to those normally possessed by national states. It is probably too soon to say whether they are successful. Judgment can be passed on some of the earlier types of dual or multipartite action, even though one cannot be dogmatic in saying that success or failure was in each case the result of the type of arrangement used. The condominium, in which two or more states by agreement divide between them the functions of government, has failed when used to govern people. A mixed administration with local participation, where background rivalries kept the powers in balance, functioned reasonably well in Tangier. In a small community like Leticia, a governing commission appointed by a world-wide international organization has succeeded, and the same may be said of the more ambitious League administration of the Saar. A similarly appointed League administrator with limited powers served a useful purpose in Danzig. In general, the case studies would seem to indicate that a crucial factor in the success of a multinational administration is the effective internationalization of the administrative personnel.

These may appear to be cases in which states are dealing with peoples or places which, like outer space, are not already under their sovereignty and that it is different when states are asked to surrender bits of preexisting sovereignty as, exceptionally indeed, has been done in the European community. But the amount of sovereignty restricted or surrendered may be minimal. One may look at a series of cases starting with those where the "surrender" to the international organization could scarcely frighten the most cautious guardian of the national interest.

One of the conclusions of Sayre in his early survey of functional organizations, published in 1919, in accounting for the relatively unimportant and disappointing work accomplished by such agencies was the unwillingness of states to delegate any real power to them. They were virtually impotent because of the "impossible" conditions attached to any grants of authority and the lack of real control in their administrative organs. As the preceding chapters have shown, a substantial number of these international functional organizations are limited to the collection and exchange of information. Some are charged with the effort to coordinate national activities through those means. Some, in addition, have their own research staffs or laboratories and may publish the results of their studies. Others, like FAO, may through their experts play an important advisory role in technical assistance, which is, of course, furnished only on request. A number of organizations have the power to set standards, as does ICAO. WHO's powers go somewhat further in that the Health Assembly, in addition to setting purity and related standards, may adopt regulations on sanitary and quarantine requirements, nomenclature of drugs, and on labeling of items moving in international commerce. Under the stipulations of the narcotics treaties the Drug Supervisory Body may in certain circumstances prepare estimates of national narcotic drug requirements. "This is important because the maximum of narcotics which may be imported into any country or territory is computed on the basis of these estimates and an embargo on the importation of narcotics is imposed to enforce this provision." [1] Moreover, the treaties also provide certain sanctions for the violation of some other rules of international narcotics control. The International Red Locust Control Service has men and machines at its disposal and, with local government cooperation, conducts operations to control outbreak areas in Africa and destroy the pest.

In many instances an organ which does not include all the membership, or which votes by majority, is given power to alter technical rules or standards which may for that reason be incorporated in separate annexes. The Board of Governors—or by delegation the Executive Directors—of the International Monetary Fund can prescribe a margin above and below par value for transactions in gold; members are bound by such a prescription. In the case of the International Whaling Commission, its regulations are binding on member states unless they object within ninety days.

One of the earlier examples of an agency with certain substantial independent powers and a limited right of direct "interference" in the conduct of national activities was the Permanent Sugar Commission, established in 1902. The Sugar Commission, made up of one delegate from each member, was authorized to decide whether bounties were being used in non-signatory countries and, if they were, member states were bound to apply stated countervailing duties on imports from such countries. A majority vote was sufficient to require the increased surtaxes, and there was no appeal from a second decision by the Commission. The decisions were apparently usually complied with during the decade in which the Commission flourished.[2] The existing International Sugar Council is quite different, consisting of representatives of both exporting and importing states, in which votes are weighted according to tonnage. By majority vote the Council can assign export quotas to producers, establish price limits, and assure that importers limit their intake from nonparticipants. Non-compliance with an established quota or failure to take agreed quantities may lead to the offender's treatment as a nonparticipant or expulsion from the organization.

Among other organizations which have had at least limited powers in the commodity field are the International Wheat Council, the International Tin Council, the Inter-American Coffee Board, and the International Tea Committee, the latter in effect a cartel arrangement of producers only.[3] The Wheat Council functions through its Executive Committee, in which exporting and importing states have weighted votes. It sets export quotas, and its decisions are binding on all members if no review is requested. A member can lose or forfeit its votes through its own actions and can be deprived of its vote, or be expelled, for breach of the Agreement.[4] The Coffee Board could, by a 95-percent vote, in "grave" situations set quotas for the exports of coffee to the United States.[5] The sole major importer, the United States, had one-third of the votes.

Once it has been realized that the long-range national interest will be served by following a cooperative course of action, and the political decision has been made that this course can be tried without immediate prejudice to the needs of self-defense and national economic well-being, the devices which may be utilized are clearly numerous. If so-called "surrenders of sovereignty" (meaning even the slightest impairment of absolutely unfettered freedom of national action) could be measured in units, one could almost order ready-made a type of international organization to fit any number of units. Consider first the modifications in practice of what was once thought to be the sacrosanct principle of unanimity in voting in international organizations.

To a substantial degree, it can be said that existing functional organizations have replaced the rule of unanimity with that of "majoritarianism." Since a large number of these groups cannot take action which in any sense binds the members to act in particular ways, this is of course less important than its mere statement would indicate. Nevertheless, as we have seen, a number of organizations, or their organs, can make findings, rulings, or regulations, or set standards and practices, or establish quotas, which have a persuasive or even a binding effect; and it is interesting to see that the principle of unanimity has, even in these instances, generally been abandoned.

A few organizations still require unanimous agreement to effect binding changes as does, for some changes, the Postal Union. The Inter-American Coffee Board required a 95-percent majority to set quotas, which, in its system of weighted voting, gave the United States, the principal importer, and Brazil and Colombia, the chief exporters, a veto. In some instances a three-fourths or two-thirds vote is required,[6] but by far the most common practice today calls for a majority decision in most circumstances combined with a two-thirds requirement for certain "important" or otherwise specified questions or for decisions by certain bodies.[7]

The picture evoked by this pattern of majority decision is, of course, misleading in the sense that, with a few exceptions, the more important a state's interest the greater its reluctance to entrust decisions to international organizations operating by majority rule. Even where no outright veto exists, where an organization has in fact been given limited powers, as in the commodity arrangements, the IBRD and the IMF, and others, systems of weighted voting have been introduced which give extra votes to nations individually or as a class in accordance with their contributions, or apparent interests and roles in the fields in which decisions are made. This has been particularly true in dealing with economic matters and serves to "resolve disputes which are not too 'political' or 'important' to foreclose any method except diplomacy, but are important enough that nations prefer to avoid their decision by impartial judges or arbitrators" or by an unweighted majority of the international community.[8]

Votes have in some instances been assigned solely on the basis of the financial contribution made by a party to the organization, usually by permitting the state to choose one of a number of "classes" of membership.[9] European railroad agreements have assigned votes in proportion to length of lines, and the International Hydrographic Bureau proportions some votes to merchant tonnage. As already noted, both the IBRD and the IMF allot votes on their Boards of Governors, in part equally (250 votes per state) and in part in accordance with financial obligations undertaken, giving the United States about one-third of the total.

On both the Wheat Council and the Sugar Council, total votes assigned exporters equal the total votes assigned importers providing a veto by class if needed, but within each class votes are apportioned in accordance with a nation's guaranteed purchase or sale of wheat for a given year or average imports and exports of sugar.[10] In other instances, numbers of votes are fixed and assigned by the constitutional arrangement—the Coal and Steel Community, for example, permits Germany, France, and Italy eighteen representatives (and hence votes) each in the Assembly while giving the Netherlands and Belgium ten each and Luxembourg four. In the Council of the Economic Community, which is made up of national representatives and can make some decisions by majority vote, Germany, France, and Italy each have four votes, the Netherlands and Belgium two each, and Luxembourg one—in some cases, the majority must not only amount to twelve but it must also include the votes of any four states.

In general, to the extent that weighted votes give effect to the realities of important disparities of wealth, power, interest, and the like, and permit "necessary" states to join with some assurance of available protection, the technique will undoubtedly be used in the creation of international institutions.

Voting weighted according to financial contributions is, of course, similar to voting by shares of stock in a corporation, and governments have used the corporate device in various forms to achieve similar purposes. They could also use it for operations in space and the Antarctic. Stock has been issued in exchange for cash contributions and for noncash contributions as well. One example is the European Company for the Financing of Railway Rolling Stock (Eurofima), which came into existence as a result of the need felt to integrate the financing of railway rolling stock in Western Europe. In 1955, the railway administrations of Austria, Belgium, Denmark, France, Germany, Italy, Luxembourg, the Netherlands, Norway, Portugal, Spain, Sweden, Switzerland, and Yugoslavia signed the Basic Agreement and, on October 20, 1955, the governments of these countries signed the Convention, to which was annexed the Statute of the Company. The Company is governed primarily by both the Convention and the Statute, and secondarily by Swiss law, in so far as the Convention does not provide to the contrary. It is registered in accordance with Swiss law but, under an Additional Protocol is exempt from stated local taxes. The capital is fixed at 50 million Swiss francs and is apportioned as follows: France and Germany, 26 percent each; Italy, 14 percent; Belgium, 11 percent; Switzerland, 8 percent; Netherlands, 6 percent; Sweden, Yugoslavia, and Luxembourg, 2 percent each; the remaining 3 percent is split up among Spain, Portugal, Norway, Austria, Denmark,

Greece, and Turkey. Shares are either Class A, obtained for cash and potentially subject to receipt of dividends, and Class B, for the contribution of freight cars. Class B may be converted to Class A. Each shareholder's vote is proportional to the nominal value of all shares held, and voting in the General Assembly is by majority except on certain important questions, when a seven-tenths vote of the registered capital is needed. The Administrative Council serves as the board of directors—each railway administration having at least 2 percent of the capital is entitled to two directors who serve for three-year terms. Majority vote carries in the Council except on the question of a loan, when a three-fourths vote is needed.[11]

Like Eurofima, the International Company of the Moselle is registered under the laws of a state, in this case Germany. The Company came into existence on January 28, 1957, and is charged with the development of the Moselle River for navigation and power purposes. The Contracting Parties—France, Germany, and Luxembourg—put some DM 370 million at the Company's disposal in varying proportions. Tolls are to be collected to pay the costs of the Company and to repay loans. Actual work on the project is done by the waterway department of each territorial state on a reimbursable basis.

The Company has the status of a limited company in German law and is governed as to organization by the Convention and annexed Statute and, subsidiarily, by German law. It has special exemptions, including tax relief, under the laws of Germany and of the other participating states as well. Its General Assembly is charged with approving an annual budget, distributing profits, and amending the Charter. Decisions are taken by two-thirds majority of the registered capital except where the Convention or German law require more and except for a three-fourths majority for decisions on the auditors' report and unanimity for amendment of the Charter. There are two Managing Directors, one French and one German, who, by joint decision, direct the Company's management. If agreement is impossible, either can request a decision by the Council of Supervision, composed of fourteen members—six German, six French, and two Luxembourg—appointed by the states involved for four-year terms. Decisions are by two-thirds majority. A special protection is afforded Luxembourg in that any decision directly affecting Luxembourg's territory, taken by any organ of the Company, must be concurred in by her representatives.[12]

Eurochemic owes a good deal to the precedent of Eurofima but differs in some respects. After extensive work by committees of the OEEC, a corporate form was devised to handle the construction and operation of needed plants and facilities for processing irradiated fuels. Eurochemic, then, is an international company established by treaty and derives its legal form and status solely from the International Convention. Only where the Convention and the Statute of the Company are silent may recourse be had to the law of Belgium, the state in which the Company's plant and laboratories are located.

The Convention signed by twelve governments established the constitution of the Company while a Statute, annexed to the Convention and needing unanimous consent of the member governments for major changes, set out the allotment of the Company's capital and the Company's organization. Shares in the Company may be held by governments, public or semi-public institutions, and even private groups. The initial allotment of 400 shares, with an authorized value of 20 million E.P.U. units of account, went to West Germany, Austria, Belgium, Denmark, France, Italy, Norway, the Netherlands, Portugal, Sweden, Switzerland, and Turkey. Of this group France, Italy, Portugal, and Sweden designated agencies to act as shareholders in the Company—all are strictly government agencies except for the Swedish group, which is three-sevenths privately owned. All the shareholders constitute a General Assembly. The Assembly's approval is required for a transfer of shares except where the transfer is between persons of the same nationality and is approved by the government having jurisdiction over the persons involved. All transfers to persons of different nationality also require the approval of a Special Group of the Steering Committee of the European Nuclear Energy Agency, a body made up of government representatives. That Group may also consider and propose measures of common interest raised by the Company's operations—its decisions bind the Company. Amendments to the Statute must be approved by the Group, which also hears disputes between participating governments concerning interpretation and application of the Statute. Majorities needed on votes in the Group vary with the matter in question. The governments thus keep a direct hand in the Company's affairs.

The Company itself is made up of a General Assembly including all shareholders plus a representative of ENEA and one of Euratom in an advisory capacity, and a Board of Directors of fifteen plus representatives from ENEA and Euratom as advisors. Each shareholder with at least 5 percent of the shares is entitled to a seat on the Board. As usual, the Board does the actual managing of the Company.[13]

Operations by states through such corporate forms escape entirely the application of another international legal principle which used to be considered sacrosanct—the principle of equality of states. Indeed it was this principle which was invoked to justify the demand for unanimity. So firmly rooted was this principle of equality that it was necessary to include in the Charter of the United Nations a statement that the Organization is based on it. This is not the place to reopen the long argument on the definition of equality, but, at least as international practice has developed, it does not mean parity in all aspects of participation in international organization. The analysis of voting arrangements has already illustrated this. Actual provisions regulating participation in various organs are additional examples.

While many of the existing international governmental organizations are set up on the strict basis of the "sovereign equality" of the members, a significant number have recognized and given special treatment to factors which are considered especially important from the point of view of the successful (and equitable) functioning of the organization. The Security Council of the United Nations, even more emphatically than did the Council of the League, for example, gives weight to the importance of the major powers in peace preservation activities. The Trusteeship Council, too, consists of the powers administering Trust Territories plus non-administering permanent members of the Security Council plus enough other members to balance the administrators. In the make-up of the recently convened Intergovernmental Maritime Consultative Organization (IMCO), for example, the directing Council of sixteen is to be made up of representatives of six nations "with the largest interest in providing international shipping services," six "with the largest interest in international seaborne trade," and four others elected by the Assembly, two on the basis of interest in shipping services and two on the basis of interest in seaborne trade. The Convention establishing the IMCO did not come into effect until ratified by "21 States of which seven shall each have a total tonnage of not less than 1,000,000 gross tons of shipping. . . ." Further, the IMCO Maritime Safety Committee of fourteen members is to include at least the eight "largest ship-owning nations." [14]

Similarly, the Assembly of the ICAO is required in electing its Council of twenty-one states to give adequate representation to states of chief importance in air transportation, to states making the largest contribution in providing facilities, and to states representing all sections of the world. The Executive and Liaison Committee of the Postal Union, too, is required to be representative of widespread geographic areas, as is the Executive Board of WHO. The International Labour Organization must include among the sixteen governmental representatives on its Governing Body eight appointed by the members "of chief industrial importance," and six of the sixteen must be from non-European states. For changes in its Constitution the ILO requires approval of two-thirds of the members, including ratification by at least five of these same important states. The Governing Board of the International Atomic Energy Agency consists of the five Agency members "most advanced in the technology of atomic energy including the production of source materials" plus five others well advanced in the art or producers of needed raw materials, with geographical distribution of importance in the selection of this group. The UN Commission on Narcotic Drugs includes fifteen members who are either important producers of raw materials, important manufacturers of narcotics, or have an important social problem in narcotics control. The IMF provides for at least twelve Executive Directors, five appointed by the five nations with the largest "quotas" and seven elected by the Governors, including two from American states and five from non-American states not otherwise included. The IBRD, similarly, gives the five members with the largest number of shares one Executive Director each but provides less specifically for the election of seven others.[15]

Thus, importance in the field to be covered, knowledge and technical ability, previously demonstrated abilities, power in general, geographic representation, and the need to include certain states to avoid important loopholes, have all been accorded weight in different ways—a challenging complex. Later chapters will suggest what special factors might appropriately be given consideration in establishing administrative arrangements in the Antarctic and outer space if new international organizations are utilized. Precedent at least does not require full equality in representation. Nor does precedent call for any particular type of organization, although many ingenious ones have been invented and tried.

If no previous type of organization is considered by governments to be helpful in meeting the problems confronted as man penetrates the frontier areas of the Antarctic and of outer space, new ones will be developed. If man's ingenuity has already met the challenge of astronautics, it may likewise grapple with the technology of international politics. But it is precisely at this point that the contrast between the exact sciences and the humanistic sciences unfortunately destroys the parallel. Even when a technically perfect solution of a problem is found, the mind and the spirit of man may conjure up reasons of pride, spite, hate, prejudice, greed, fear, or inertia which prevent common progress along an agreed road.

Part II

INTERNATIONAL CONTROLS FOR THE ANTARCTIC

5. *The Antarctic*

The Antarctic is defined generally for our purposes as the entire area south of the sixtieth parallel.* It is often taken to include several "sub-Antarctic" islands north of that line.[1] It contains the only polar continent—an almost completely lifeless mass containing about 5½ to 6 million square miles, or roughly the size of the United States and Europe combined.[2] It is the coldest, stormiest and highest of the continents, averaging over a mile above sea level. While all other continents are tied together by isthmian links, or land bridges, or by narrow straits, Antarctica's Palmer Peninsula is some 700 miles of ocean from its nearest neighbor, Cape Horn in South America. "For complete, utter, but magnificent desolation there is no scene on earth comparable to the ice mantle that smothers the Antarctic Continent. The desolation is no illusion."[3]

THE PHYSICAL SETTING

Unlike the Arctic, which is essentially an oceanic basin covered with floating ice and hemmed in by continental and island masses, Antarctica is apparently a continent. East Antarctica, lying in the Eastern Hemisphere, is a vast ice plateau rising to over 13,000 feet in height, while West Antarctica, is dominated topographically by

* A common scientific but infrequent political delimitation of the Antarctic is in terms of "the Antarctic Convergence," a circumpolar zone of more or less sharp temperature gradient, which varies in position between about 47° and 63° S. Its mean position is shown on the inset to the map facing page 144. It is distinguished by a sharp change of temperature within a short distance at the surface, sometimes as much as 7°F., as the cold Antarctic waters sink beneath warmer waters moving south.

a series of folded ice-covered mountains which appear to be continuations of the Andes of South America. The ice cover is at least 10,000 feet thick in places, and there is indeed continuing speculation that Antarctica may be an archipelago rather than a continent, with the seas between land masses frozen solid.[4] Lying almost entirely within the Antarctic Circle (66°30′ S.), the continent is entirely dark at midwinter (about June 22) and entirely in sunlight at midsummer (about December 22). Average temperatures for the warmest months are below freezing even at the coasts, and on a yearly basis they average well below zero. The lowest reading yet recorded is minus 125.3° F., reported by a Soviet group at Vostok, at the South Geomagnetic Pole, in 1958. Winds of high velocity are frequent. There is little actual precipitation; the annual amount has been reported at about six or seven inches of water. There are a limited number of ice-free valleys, amounting to perhaps 200,000 square miles; there the temperature range is not unlike that of Minneapolis.[5]

Antarctica is a desert. It does not appear that man has ever lived in the region proper, though coal and other organic deposits and fossil records indicate that Antarctica was not always a frozen waste. On some of the rock exposures there are lichens and mosses, and occasionally an arthropod or other primitive animal forms are found in moist places among the mosses in summer. "The largest land animal known is a wingless mosquito."[6] The waters around the continent teem with life however, ranging from floating microscopic plants and animals to the largest creature ever to inhabit the earth, the great blue whale. Penguins, gulls, petrels, and fulmers all are found as well. Only a tiny part of the continent has been explored geologically, but thus far no mineral sources of commercial value have been found. There are apparently vast coal deposits, but those found thus far are of low-grade lignite which would not be commercially usable even if extraction and transportation were not a problem. There are traces of some 174 minerals thus far reported—including manganese, copper, lead, nickel, and even uranium.[7] Geographically and geologically, there is no reason to suppose that the mineral resources of Antarctica are very different from those of other continents.

Building airbases in Antarctica involves obvious difficulties. During the winter months good runways have been built in McMurdo Sound on the ice which seasonally breaks up and goes to sea. A relatively small strip has been utilized at Marble Point on the edge of McMurdo Sound in territory claimed by New Zealand.[8] A suitable location for a ten-thousand-foot strip at Cape Bernacche in the same area has been surveyed, and consideration has also been given to locations in the Bunger Hills and on Deception Island.

THE POLITICAL SETTING

Early History. While the actual existence of Antarctica was unknown to the ancient and even to the medieval worlds, the existence of a southern continent was one of the assumptions of such early geographers as Hipparclus and Ptolemy. The earliest known map bearing the name "Terra Australis" appeared in 1531, but all areas south of the known world were included as part of that land. Vasco da Gama's voyage around the Cape of Good Hope and Magellan's expedition cut down the size of this hypothetical mass, but it was not until the voyages of James Cook in 1772–75 that the continent was circumnavigated, though Cook never saw the continent itself. His report on the coldness and inhospitable nature of the southern seas led to the abandonment of the search for an inhabited southern land area.[9]

There is little actual evidence of any discovery of the Antarctic continent itself until the nineteenth century. The first probable sighting of the South Shetland Islands has been credited to the English Captain William Smith on October 17, 1819,[10] while the sighting of the continent is variously attributed to a Briton, Captain Edward Bransfield, in 1820; to an American sealing captain, Nathanial Brown Palmer, in 1820; and, by the Soviet Union since 1949, to Admiral Bellingshausen, who circumnavigated the continent in 1819–21 in Tsar Alexander I's service (though he appears not to have recorded an actual sighting). All of these claims are based on a modern reading of old and imperfect records, while the "first person to sight the continent and to record it as such with conviction was a Nantucket whaling captain named Christopher Burdick, whose landfall was not far from the point in dispute by the supporters of Palmer and Bransfield. Burdick recorded in his log the sighting of the southern continent on February 15, 1821." [11]

Interest in problems of terrestrial magnetism led to a sizable expedition from 1838 to 1843 and to the discovery of the Ross Sea in 1841. Other occasional voyages were made in the next fifty years, but the first confirmed evidence of a landing on the continent proper dates only from 1898. In 1895 the Sixth International Geographical Congress noted that "exploration of the Antarctic regions is the greatest piece of geographical exploration still to be undertaken," a comment which, despite the numerous explorations of the twentieth century, could still be made today.

National Claims in the Antarctic. National claims to portions of the Antarctic have thus far been based on discovery, on occupation, on performance of administrative acts including issuing decrees or orders, printing postage stamps, and setting up post offices, on prior claims even without discovery, or on continuity, contiguity, or the so-called "sector principle," or on some combination of these bases. The meaning of "discovery," of "occupation" and of the "sector" doctrine requires certain initial comment with respect to Antarctica.[12]

Discovery has been advanced as one explicit basis for English legal claims in the Antarctic and it is at least implied in the Australian, French, and Norwegian claims and in Russian expressions of interest. Even before the nineteenth century, mere discovery by sighting, without taking possession at least by symbolic annexation, did not result in acquisition of sovereignty over the territory sighted.[13] Possession was more important than prior discovery, and even discovery was limited in that the act of discovery had to have the character of state action, though this could be conferred retroactively. It now appears, too, that the need for an occupation to be an "effective" one was recognized by the end of the eighteenth century.[14] More recently Secretary of State Hughes, speaking for the United States in 1924, asserted that it was "the opinion of the Department that the discovery of lands unknown to civilization, even when coupled with a formal taking of possession, does not support a valid claim of sovereignty unless the discovery is followed by an actual settlement of the discovered country." [15] The United States has, in fact, despite the activities of United States whalers and sealers and of scientific expeditions, refrained from making public claims to the Antarctic while thus far also refusing to recognize claims by any other nation.[16]

Obviously, the need for "effective occupation" is tempered by the difficulties of settlement in polar regions, and less exacting standards have been held applicable. Inability to perfect title at all in polar regions was a tenet of several writers on international law, but in more recent years the intermittent presence of official personnel or licensed commercial enterprises has been deemed of significance. Huber, in the Island of Palmas case, pointed out that "sovereignty cannot be exercised in fact at every moment on every point of a territory. The intermittence and discontinuity compatible with the maintenance of rights necessarily differ." [17] Very infrequent "administration" was upheld as sufficient for a small, desolate island in the Clipperton Island Award,[18] and "effective occupation" was interpreted by Secretary of State Olney to be such as is "reasonable under all the circumstances in view of the extent of the territory claimed, its nature, and the uses to which it is adapted and is put. . . ." [19] Of prime legal importance is the Eastern Greenland Case decided by the Permanent Court of International Justice in 1933. While basing its decision on additional factors, the Court held that Norway's claim to have discovered the area was insufficient to confer sovereignty. In upholding Denmark's claim the Court pointed out that a "continued display of authority," involving the intent and will to act as sovereign (*animus occupandi*) plus some actual exercise or display of authority (*corpus occupandi*) were needed, but that in thinly populated and uninhabited areas very little actual exercise of sovereign rights is needed in the absence of competition. Authority did have to be exercised "as and when occasion demands," but Denmark's administrative acts even without effective occupation of the whole or even annual visits, together with coastal settlements, were enough.[20]

In more recent times, as technology has progressed, the Antarctic has actually been "settled" to a limited extent. Indeed, in recent years the summer "population" of the Antarctic has reached ten thousand, including scientists, support personnel, whalers, and the like. By 1952, at least seventeen permanent (year-round) military, weather or scientific stations were being maintained by Chile, Argentina, and Britain in the "American" quadrant of the Antarctic, and the question of the possibility of permanent establishments has thus been answered.[21]

The sector theory seems to have first been suggested for the Arctic but appears to have first been used by the British with respect to their claims to the Falkland Island Dependencies in the Antarctic.[22] In the Arctic, the theory uses the doctrines of continuity and contiguity. The sovereignty of a nation whose territory already reaches into the Arctic circle is extended to the Pole itself, in the sense, at least, of laying claim to all continental territory and islands lying within a region delimited by drawing extensions from the easternmost and westernmost extremities of the country to the Pole.[23] The doctrine has been vigorously pushed for the Arctic by the Soviet Union and Canada, which have obvious and extensive interests in the regions continuous with or contiguous to the mainland, though any claim to control over at least the areas of the Arctic which are clearly ice-covered seas has inevitably run into opposition.[24]

Present claimants in the Antarctic have apparently invoked the aid of the sector principle in different ways. Unlike the geographical situation in the Arctic, no nation's territory on another continent projects into the Antarctic proper, that is, below the sixtieth parallel. There are some islands between the sixtieth parallel and the Antarctic Circle which might be considered to fall into a special category apart from the generally contested claims on the continent of Antarctica. Sectors whose apexes are at the South Pole spread back to base points which may in some cases be continental or island land masses but in others are rather arbitrarily designated points along the sixtieth parallel. These points are sometimes alleged to correspond with areas explored on the shores of the continent of Antarctica, but often they actually have only a tenuous connection with such activities.[25] Argentina and Chile add to their claims that they are closest to the Antarctic continent, though some 700 miles away, that the Palmer Peninsula is a continuation of the South American continent, and that a continental shelf, in fact, joins the two continents. The sector theory has not as yet been tested before an international tribunal, but, even though it ignores the problem of "effective occupation," there is evidence of increasing support for the principle.[26] While the United States and the Soviet Union reject all Antarctic claims, every major claimant has an Antarctic sector to defend.[27]

Conflicting Claims. Formal claims to portions of the Antarctic do not appear to have been made by any nation before the twentieth century. On July 21, 1908, however, Great Britain issued Letters Patent which, as amended on March 28, 1917, claimed all islands and territory between 20° and 50° W. below the fiftieth parallel south latitude, and all islands and territory between 50° and 80° W. below the fifty-eighth parallel south latitude.[28] Claim to this territory, known as the Falkland Islands Dependencies, is based on discovery, principally on the voyages of Smith in 1819–20 and Bransfield in 1820, on formal acts of taking possession, on the maintenance of several stations, on the exercise of acts of sovereignty, and on the sector theory.[29] For much longer periods Britain has claimed outside the Antarctic the Falkland Islands proper, as well as several other islands, including South Georgia. For example, Cook landed on and formally annexed South Georgia in 1775.[30]

Towards the end of the nineteenth century, new whaling techniques led to the wholesale destruction of whales to such an extent that the British took steps to try to preserve the whaling industry and also to profit from it by granting leases for shore facilities, issuing whaling licenses and taxing the oil produced—all with reference to the British-claimed area. A Buenos Aires company, the Compañia Argentina de Pesca, began operations in the region in 1904 under British license and apparently is still active.[31] In 1906, a regulation required that applications for whaling licenses be addressed to the Governor of the Falkland Islands; it was made illegal to take whales without a license and the payment of royalties was required.[32] The need of whalers at the time to use convenient land stations for processing made this system reasonably effective and South Georgia became the center of the whaling industry; six companies were licensed to operate there by 1910.

The government of the Falkland Islands Dependencies was provided by the Executive Council of the Falkland Islands.[33] A British magistrate and consular officer accompanied the whaling fleet from 1907 on, though from 1910 to 1930 he was stationed each season at the factory built in 1910 on Deception Island. No challenge to the British license system was received from 1908 to 1931. By 1925–26 factory ships began to reach the area, equipped so that operations on shore became unnecessary; British income from fees dwindled. The capabilities of these ships led to such destruction of whales that governments were induced to conclude the Whaling Convention which has already been discussed.[34]

British state acts in the Dependencies, in addition to the whaling measures, consisted of surveys of the area, promulgation of ordinances regarding their administration by the Falkland Islands' Government, visits by officials, the issuance of postage stamps and the operation of post offices and telegraph and radio stations, protests of the activities in the area of nationals of all other states,

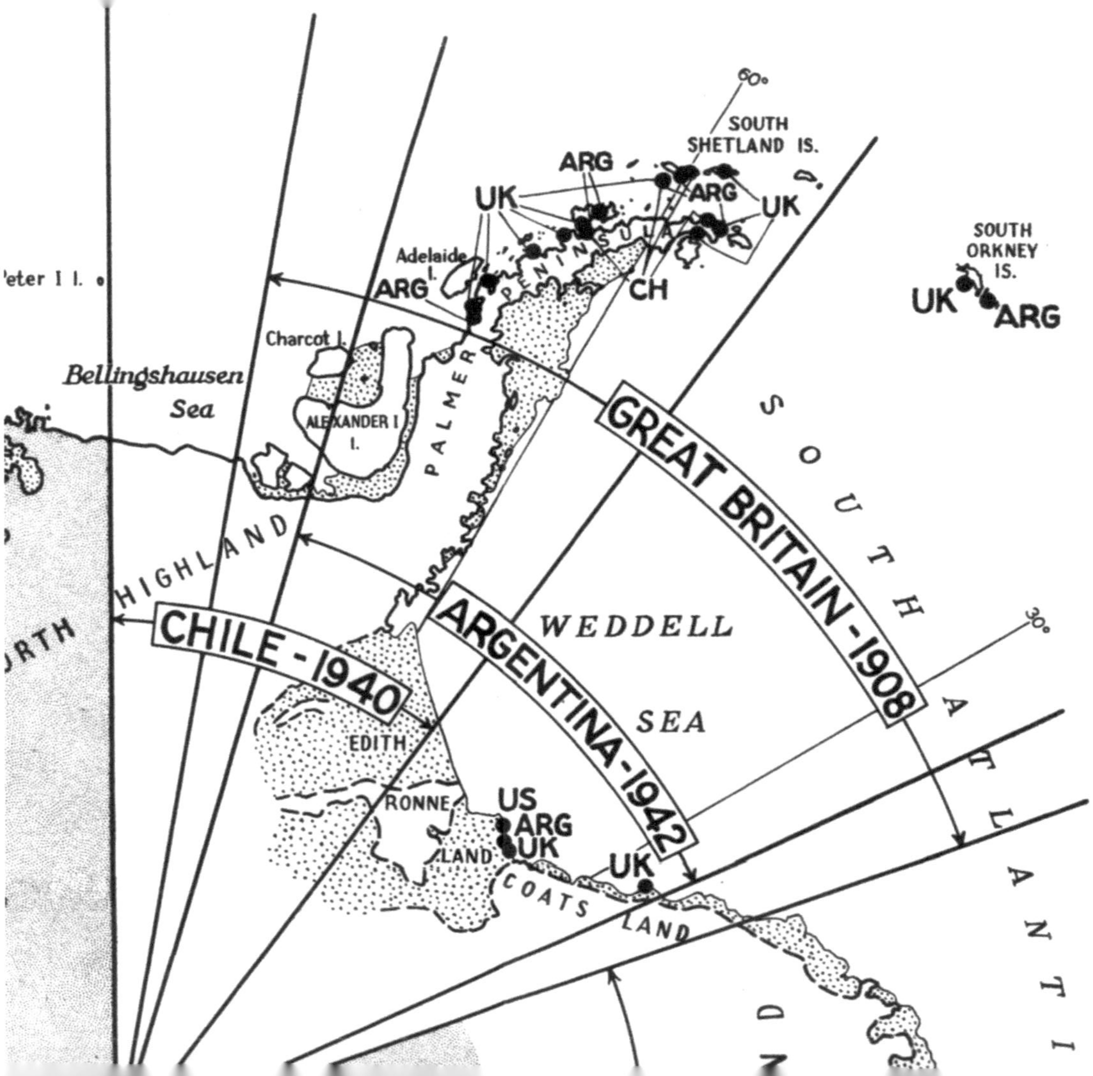

SOUTH SHETLAND IS.
60°
ARG
UK
ARG
UK
CH
PENINSULA
Adelaide I.
ARG
Peter I I.
SOUTH ORKNEY IS.
UK
ARG
Charcot I.
ALEXANDER I I.
PALMER
Bellingshausen Sea
GREAT BRITAIN - 1908
SOUTH ATLANTI
HIGHLAND
ARGENTINA - 1942
CHILE - 1940
WEDDELL SEA
30°
EDITH
RONNE
LAND
US
ARG
UK
UK
COATS LAND

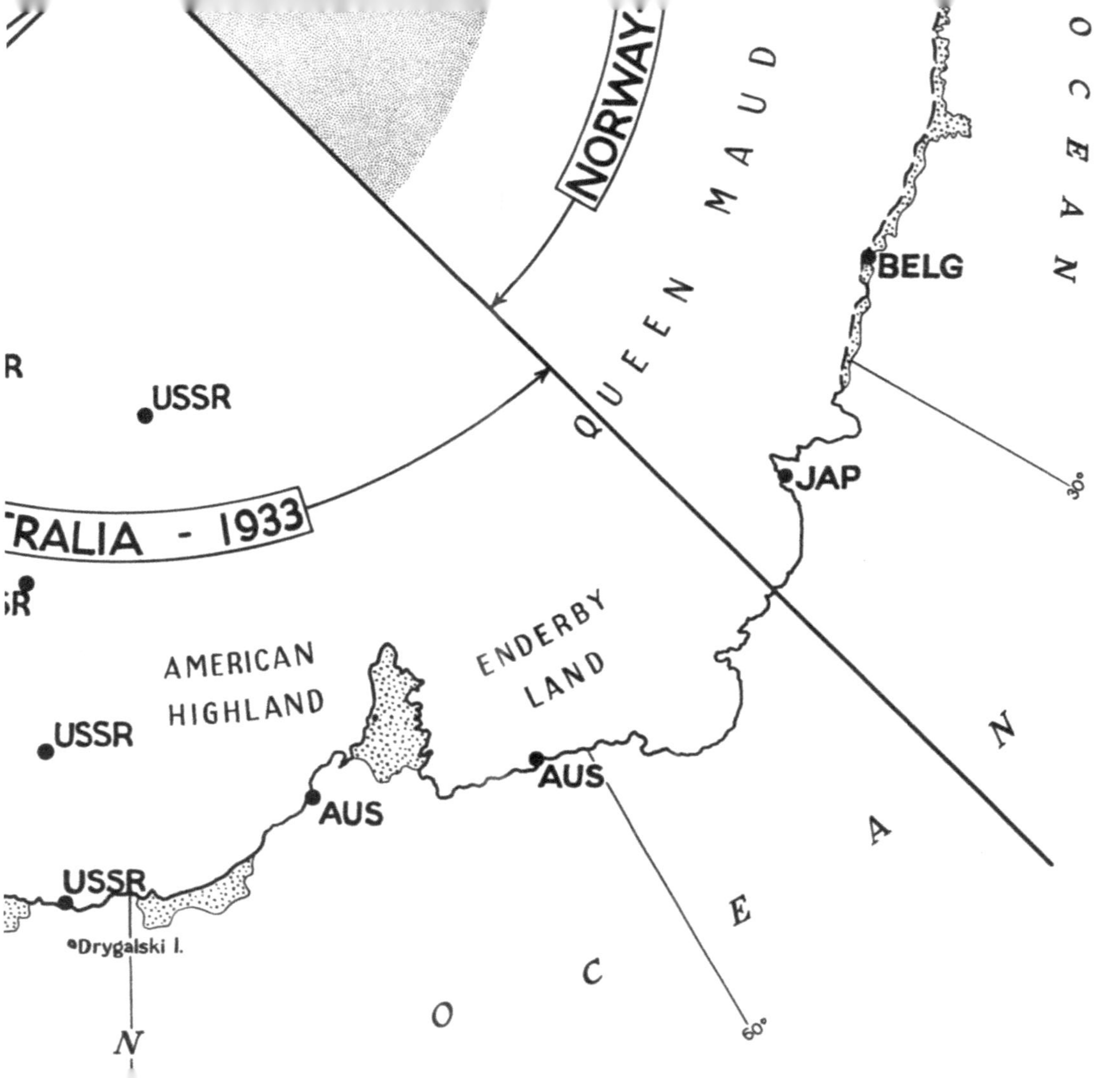
NORWAY
QUEEN MAUD
BELG
JAP
OCEAN
30°
TRALIA - 1933
USSR
ENDERBY LAND
AMERICAN HIGHLAND
USSR
AUS
AUS
USSR
Drygalski I.
OCEAN
60°

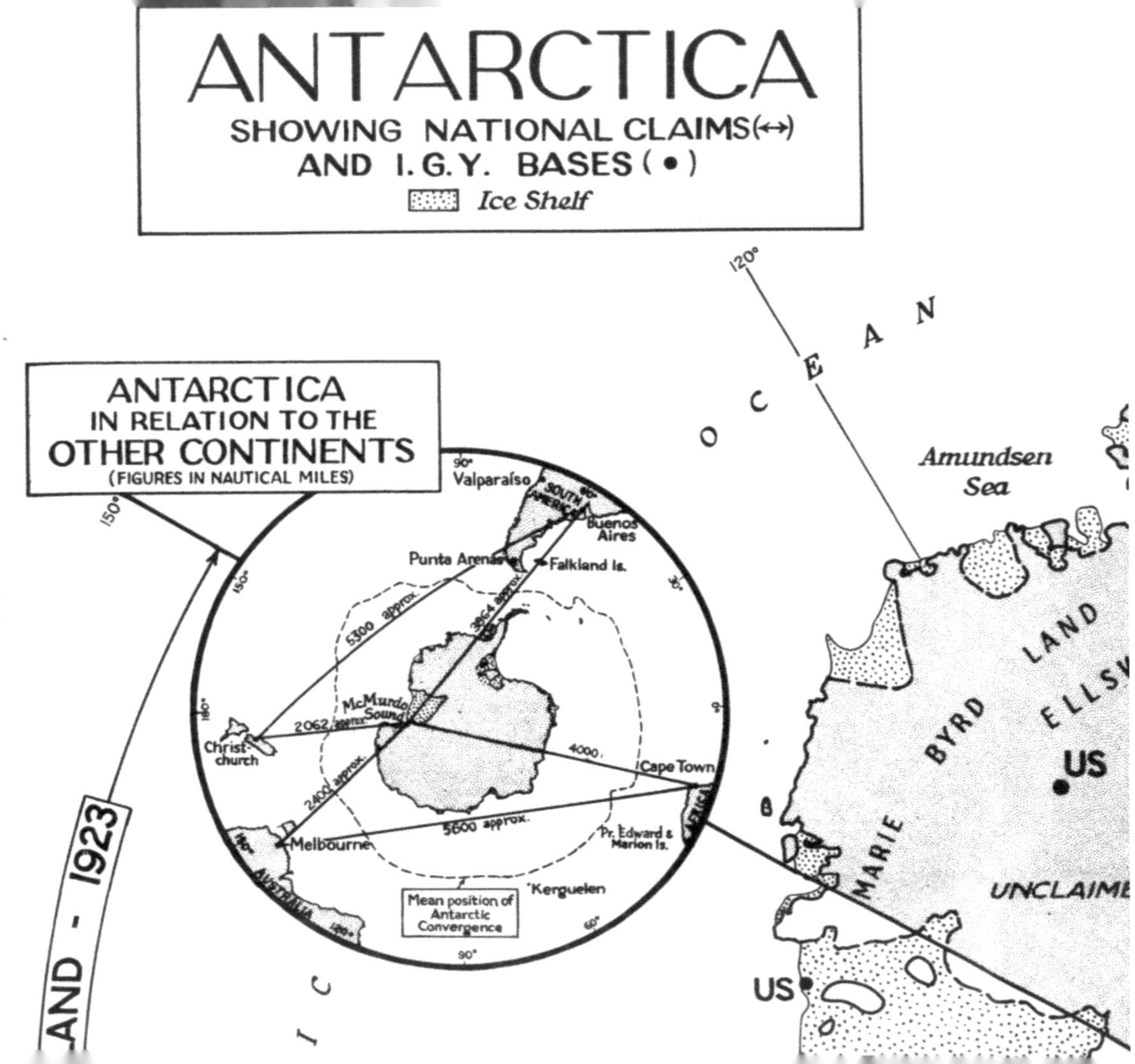
ANTARCTICA
SHOWING NATIONAL CLAIMS(↔)
AND I.G.Y. BASES (•)
Ice Shelf
ANTARCTICA
IN RELATION TO THE
OTHER CONTINENTS
(FIGURES IN NAUTICAL MILES)
Valparaiso
SOUTH AMERICA
Buenos Aires
Punta Arenas
Falkland Is.
5300 approx.
3864 approx.
McMurdo Sound
2062 approx.
Christchurch
2400 approx.
4000
Cape Town
AFRICA
5600 approx.
Melbourne
AUSTRALIA
Pr. Edward & Marion Is.
Kerguelen
Mean position of Antarctic Convergence
90°
30°
0°
60°
150°
180°
120°
O C E A N
Amundsen Sea
MARIE BYRD LAND
ELLSW
US
UNCLAIME
US
AND - 1923
I C

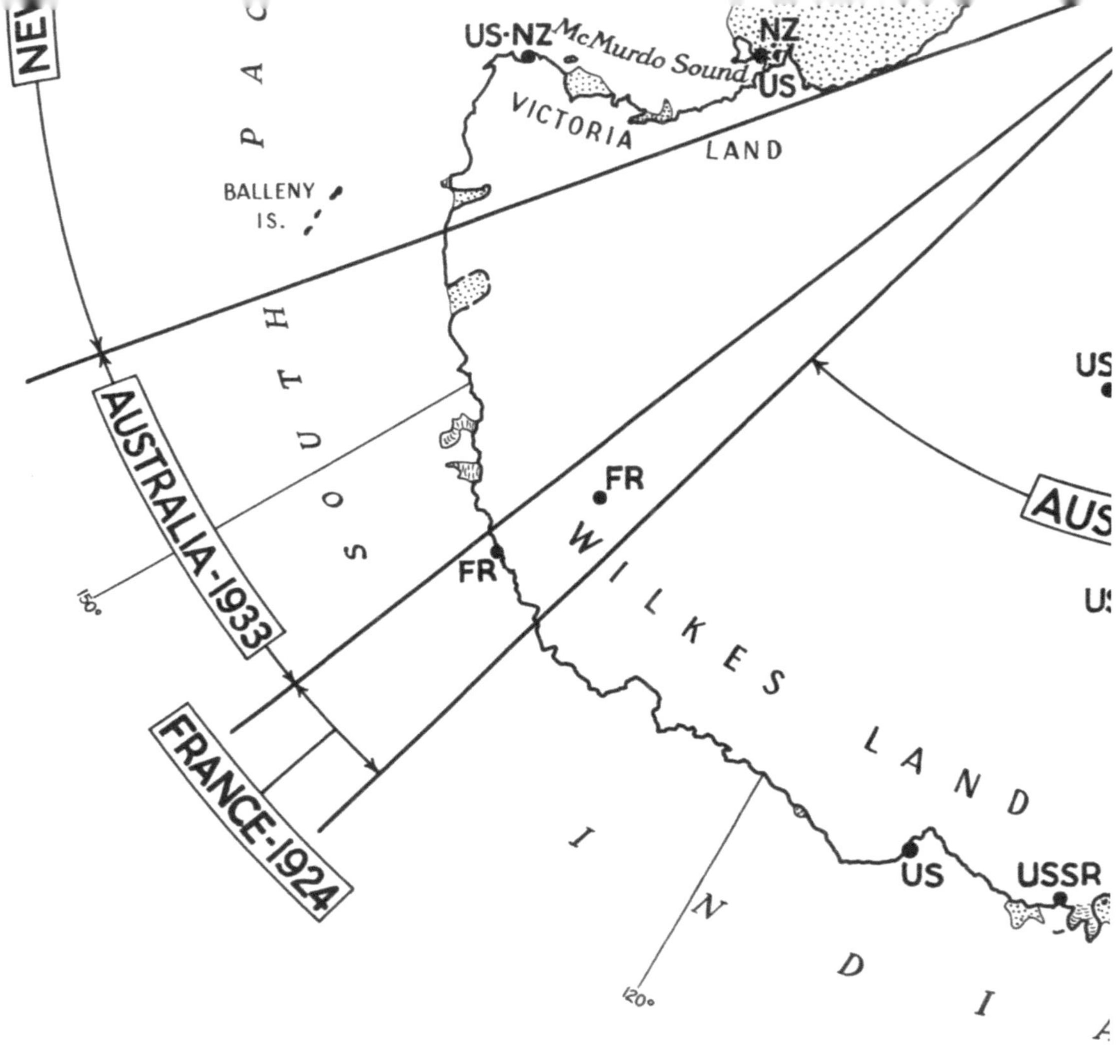
US·NZ
McMurdo Sound
NZ
US
VICTORIA
LAND
BALLENY
IS.
AUSTRALIA-1933
FRANCE-1924
FR
FR
WILKES LAND
US
USSR
150°
120°

issuance of maps defining the claims, and similar activities. Only South Georgia is actually populated, in the common meaning of the term, having several hundred permanent inhabitants.

During the Second World War the British withdrew from their Antarctic stations for a few years, but, faced with Argentine and Chilean claims in the area, and fearful of German inroads, they reestablished several stations in the so-called "Operation Taberin" of 1943–45, being careful to swear in the leader of each small outpost as a magistrate and to establish a post office, telegraph station, or the like as a sign of sovereignty.[35] During this period British forces also removed markers left by other national claimants.

After the war, jurisdiction over the Dependencies was changed from the Admiralty to the Colonial Office, and extensive surveys have been conducted in support of British claims, financed in part by what little comes in from the export tax on the output of the whaling stations on South Georgia. As late as 1956 there was reported to be enough business to require, in exchange, that ten British posts broadcast weather reports to aid the whalers.[36] Activities in recent years in the course of the running conflict with Argentina and Chile are described below after discussion of the claims of those nations in this same area.

Both Argentina and Chile have advanced claims to portions of the "American Antarctic," to which Britain has also laid claim. The Latin American claims both conflict and overlap and there are certain reasons for treating them simultaneously.[37] Both have denied the validity of claims based on discovery alone, insisting that effective occupation is the proper test and that "discovery and scientific expeditions carried out in the Antarctic do not and cannot constitute any title to this region." While these countries reject discovery as a basis for claims, both rely on proximity and contiguity, and both trace their "rights" historically to succession to the "rights" received by Spain under the Papal Bull *Inter Caetera* of May 4, 1493, and the Treaty of Tordesillas to all lands west of the forty-sixth meridian and, presumably, extending to the Pole.[38]

The Spanish claims went undisputed for several hundred years, but the actual existence of Antarctica was then unknown.

Argentina maintains her claim in part on succession to the rights, the *uti possidetis* at the time of the break with Spain, of the Viceroyalty of Río de la Plata. It appears that the claim was first mentioned in a communication to Britain on November 30, 1925, in connection with a dispute over a wireless station built by Argentina at British-claimed Laurie Island, the existence of which had been reported to the International Bureau of the Telegraphic Union at Berne. The British-Argentine dispute over the Antarctic is, however, complicated by Argentine claims to the Falkland Islands proper and certain other islands which are not here considered as part of the Antarctic.[39] In any event, a claim similar to that of 1925 was addressed in 1927 to the Universal Postal Union by Argentina in a protest over British stamps issued by the Falkland Islands' government.

The Argentine claim in the Antarctic proper extends from longitude 25° W. to 74° W. and is bordered on the north by the sixtieth parallel.[40] It has been officially stated:

> Argentine . . . sovereignty is based . . . in the aggregate of the historical antecedents of its titles—maintained firmly in all circumstances by the Argentine Government [and] spiritually identified with the feeling of the nation's entire population; in the insuperable geographical position of the Republic; in the geological continuity of its land with the Antarctic lands; in the climatological influence that the neighboring polar zones exercise over its territories; in the rights of first occupancy; in the pertinent diplomatic measures; and, finally, in its uninterrupted activity in this same Antarctic terrain.[41]

An Argentine Antarctic Commission was established in 1939 and, in 1948, an "Antarctic and Malvinas" division was set up in the Foreign Affairs Ministry. Postage stamps depicting the Argentine Antarctic territory have been issued from time to time, and actual post offices serving her year-round base have been in operation since 1947.[42] An Argentine expedition on board the *Primero de Mayo* in 1942 proclaimed the annexation of all territory within the sector 25° and 68°34′ W., and, while no decree confirmed this claim, commemorative bronze plaques were installed on Deception and Wiencke Islands which, on their later removal by the British, led to an extensive diplomatic controversy.*

Argentina has in recent years used the sector theory, which she originally rejected, though the portion of her claim which extends to 74° W. is slightly farther west than any of her territory on the South American mainland. Her claim to this area was first revealed in an official Argentine map of the Antarctic zone issued in November, 1946, which brought forth a protest from Chile. The Argentine claim has not in general been based on formal annexations and decrees since the area in question is said to be "understood" to have always been Argentine and, hence, no direct incorporation is needed. All maps in Argentina must depict this official Sector.[43]

In 1955, a new law entitled Provincialization of the National Territories converted Patagonia (below the forty-sixth parallel), Tierra del Fuego, the Argentine Antarctic Sector, and the "Islands of the South Atlantic" into one province, apparently in order to show an administrative organization of the territory to bolster the perfection and maintenance of her title.[44] Further, on February 28, 1957, the Argentine Government "reestablished" the "National Territory of Tierra del Fuego, the Antarctic, and the Islands of the South Atlantic" with a capital at Ushuaia and including the British-held Falkland Islands and South Georgia Island, among others.[45]

Intense popular interest in these claims has been reported; the younger generation is apparently educated to assert Argentina's rights "with a dedication verging on fanaticism." [46]

The Chilean claim to a sector between 53° and 90° W. was put forth in Decree No. 1747 on November 6, 1940, by President Aguirre Cerda.[47] It was said to be an attempt "to fix with accuracy the limits of a sovereignty that had existed since the 16th cen-

* This 1942 date is used for the Argentine claim on the map facing page 144 without any reference to the date of origin of the claimed title.

tury," [48] for Chile, too, holds that the Republic succeeded to the colonial rights of the Spanish Captaincy-General in these "southern territories." [49] Chile also claims on the basis of continuity, contiguity, and actual use, and "a sizeable literature has been built up in the last few years defending the Antarctic . . . as an established part of the 'national patrimony.' Special instruction is required in the schools stressing Chilean rights and expeditions. As part of their growing economic and political nationalism Chileans have become extremely conscious of the 'Southland' frontier in general." [50]

Chile maintained a whaling station on Deception Island from 1906 to 1914, and stamps have been issued since 1947 showing the Chilean claim. President Gonzalez Videla personally visited Chilean installations in the Antarctic in 1948, the first Head of State to do so, thus arousing Chilean patriotic emotions.[51] A Maritime Governor and postal officer are maintained on Greenwich Island. Protests have been regularly delivered to any foreign nationals in the area. The Chilean Antarctic Commission now functions directly under the Foreign Minister, with the Minister of National Defense as the alternate president and members of the Chilean Senate and Chamber of Deputies as members.[52]

As we have seen, British, Argentine and Chilean claims overlap with respect to the Palmer Peninsula area, the Antartic region closest to South America. Because of its similarity to the Andes Mountains, this area is believed to be the most likely place for the discovery of mineral resources.[53] The various names of the Peninsula, in fact, reflect the multiple claims which exist to it. The United States calls it Palmer Peninsula, after the early American captain; Britain knew it as Trinity Land and now calls it Graham Land; Chile now terms it Tierra O'Higgins, and Argentina's name is Tierra San Martín.

Late in the Second World War the British and Argentine navies successively removed claim plaques left by the other party, and the issues raised by competing claims have flared up several times in recent years.[54] The 1947 visit of Argentine naval units to the Antarctic was protested by local British officials as a violation of British territory. Argentina refused to accept the protest, which was delivered in the name of the Governor of the Falkland Islands, since Argentina claims sovereignty over these Islands as well. Argentina has gone so far, in defense of her "sovereignty," as to refuse to treat mail franked with Falkland Islands' stamps as carrying necessary postage.[55] While Argentina and Chile have not given up their own quarrel, they united in 1948 in agreeing to act jointly with respect to the "South American Antarctic" (25° to 90° W.), to engage in common efforts to develop the area and, in effect, to work together against non-American claimants.[56] Each has formally protested all "acts of sovereignty" by rival states.

By late 1948, fear of a clash in the area was so great that Chile, Argentina, and Britain agreed to forego sending warships "south of 60° latitude South" except for normal relief expeditions, and this agreement, reached originally for the 1948–49 Antarctic season, has been renewed each November since.[57]

Incidents have continued to occur however. In February, 1952, the Argentine navy forced by gunfire the withdrawal of a British meteorological party from the Hope Bay area, though the matter was later adjusted through diplomatic means and the British were permitted to land.[58] In 1953, a magistrate representing the British Governor of the Falkland Islands, accompanied by two constables and fifteen marines, had huts built by Argentine and Chilean parties in the Deception Islands dismantled. He also arrested two Argentines found there under the Falkland Islands Alien Ordinance.[59]

In 1944 there were no permanent stations on the Peninsula; by 1955 there were seventeen year-round stations supported by the different claimants and with a total population of about 150 men. Gould points out that, with respect to IGY and even pre-IGY scientific efforts in the Palmer Peninsula: "The concentration of stations in this area is a reflection of the multiplicity of claims rather than the desirability of having so many scientific stations so close together." When representatives of participating nations met in Paris in 1955 to decide on locations for IGY stations, Argentina protested a British plan to establish the chief British station near the head of the Weddell Sea, since Argentina already had a base there. The establishment of a United States base in this same contested area apparently served to calm the Argentinians as removing the political connotations from the establishment of bases.[60]

Both Argentina and Chile have adamantly refused to take the multiple claims to the International Court of Justice, insisting that sovereignty is so clear that no "third power" may judge this domestic question.[61] Both also base their modern claims on the hemispheric nature of the Charter of the Organization of American States and the Rio Treaty, and the need for and right to repel acts of an "extracontinental Power" against the "territorial Patrimony." [62] Britain originally tried to get the claims before the ICJ by offering to defend any action brought, and in 1955 made a unilateral application which had to be dropped from the Court's list in 1956 because neither Chile nor Argentina is bound by the "optional clause" and, as indicated, both denied the Court's jurisdiction and neither would appear.[63] It has been suggested that nationalist feelings and local politics combine to explain the refusal to submit to a court or arbitral decision; for a government which lost or which perhaps even appeared to give in to this extent would be in danger of being ousted.[64] No immediate solution to these conflicting claims appears likely—they are not in process of negotiation in any sense.[65]

Other Formal Claims. The second formal claim in point of time was that of New Zealand to the area from 160° E. to 150° W. Administrative authority over this area, known as the Ross Dependency, was assigned by the United Kingdom to the Governor-General of New Zealand by an Order in Council of July 30, 1923.[66] The claim is principally based on discoveries by Ross in 1841 and by Scott and Shackleton between 1901 and 1909. New Zealand maintained an IGY station, Scott Base, on Ross Island and occupied another station jointly with the United States. Regulations of a general nature have been issued by the New Zealand government, and whaling regulations were issued in 1926 and 1929. Postal facilities were provided for the first Shackleton expedition of 1909 and New Zealand "mildly" protested postal facilities and a wireless station established by the first Byrd expedition which had a base in the Ross Dependency.[67] The United States as usual reserved all rights. The New Zealand official appointed to administer the area has the powers of a magistrate and justice of the peace but no holder of the office appears to have visited the territory.[68] The government has also recently appointed a "Superintendent" who also serves as Secretary to the Ross Dependency Research Committee, an organization established in 1958 to coordinate and supervise New Zealand activities in the Ross Dependency.

French expeditions have been active in the Antarctic since 1738–1739 when Bouvet de Lozier discovered Bouvet Island. Essentially, the present French claim rests on the discoveries of Dumont d'Urville in 1840. On March 27, 1924, France claimed Adélie Land, named by d'Urville for his wife.[69] Certain islands have also been claimed as well. The limits of the French claim were defined in a decree by the President of the French Republic on April 1, 1938, which asserted French sovereignty over "the islands and territories situated south of the 60th degree and between 136°–142° E."[70]

The territories claimed by France were originally attached as an administrative dependency to the government of Madagascar, a place as remote from Antarctica as is any apparent French interest there. The first expeditions to land on Adélie Land did not arrive until 1949, although as early as 1938 the French had acceded to a British request for rights to overfly Adélie Land in exchange for reciprocal rights for French aircraft over British Commonwealth territories in the Antarctic.[71] There has been some French exploration in recent years, but no attempt has been made to enforce administrative provisions there in these desolate reaches of Antarctica.[72] On August 6, 1955, however, a new administrative set-up was established for Adélie Land and the Kerguelen group of islands —they were transferred from the control of Madagascar, given "administrative and financial autonomy" and the seat of the new government was "established" in Paris. There are still no inhabitants and permanent, year-round stations have not been established.

Australians participated in many Antarctic expeditions, especially between 1911 and 1931 but made no formal claims until February 7, 1933, when a United Kingdom Order in Council laid claim to the area south of the sixtieth parallel and between 160° E. and 45° E. (except for Adélie Land between 136° E. and 142° E.) and placed it under the Commonwealth of Australia.[73] This wedge amounts to about a third of the continent. The claim was based primarily on the explorations of several Englishmen in the nineteenth century and of the Australian Douglas Mawson in the twentieth century.[74]

The Antarctic generates Australian weather to some extent, and Australia has indicated that "strategic and defense considerations make it desirable that the territory south of Australia shall not be in the hands of another power." [75] Other than the issuance of whaling regulations in 1936, however, Australia did little in the way of performance of acts of state until recent years, when the Australian Antarctic Territory was incorporated into the legal structure of the Australian Capital Territory, "a small enclave which surrounds and includes Canberra. It was as though the District of Columbia had been enlarged to include Alaska, and was further evidence of Australia's determination to maintain her foothold in Antarctica." [76]

Faced with the possibility of German claims to sections of the Antarctic off which Norwegian whaling vessels had long operated and in which Norwegian explorers, including Roald Amundsen, the first man to reach the Pole, had been active, Norway, on January 14, 1939, claimed the wedge between 20° W. and 45° E., naming it Queen Maud Land.[77] They had previously claimed Bouvet Island in 1928 and Peter I Island in 1931, and they enacted laws concerning both these islands.[78] Unlike other claimants, Norway's objective has been primarily to protect the whaling industry, and, despite explorations by several Norwegian expeditions, she has not claimed sovereignty over the territory lying poleward from the coast, at least south of about 81°.[79] On May 28, 1948, these territories were made "dependencies" of Norway,[80] but no administrative acts appear to have taken place.

One other nation, the Union of South Africa, has made a formal claim to islands in this general area. On January 30, 1948, South Africa proclaimed her sovereignty over Marion Island and Prince Edward Island in the sub-Antarctic and has maintained stations there ever since.[81] These claims do not appear to have been challenged.

The Position of Other Governments. Other less formal claims have also been made by or on behalf of several nations. The United States, for example, has thus far not asserted any formal claims to territory in the Antarctic. Voyages of American sealing and whaling ships in the early years of the nineteenth century have already been noted. As early as 1839–40, Admiral Charles Wilkes demonstrated conclusively the existence of the Antarctic land mass in a voyage which took him halfway round that continent. It was not until almost a hundred years later, however, in 1928–29, that Richard E. Byrd led the first Byrd Antarctic Expedition into the area. Before then, in 1924, Secretary of State Hughes had expressed the classic United States position with respect to claims in the southern reaches.[82] The position of the State Department, it will be recalled, involved a reservation of all rights with respect to claims made by all other nations and the refusal to assert any formal claims on behalf of the United States.

Expeditions from the United States were not equally shy about making claims, however, and a large number of unofficial claims exist on behalf of the United States. The first Byrd expedition surveyed the unexplored area beyond 150° W. in 1929 and named it Marie Byrd Land, claiming it for the United States.[83] A flag was raised on Supporting Party Mountain in latitude 85°25′ S. and longitude 147°55′ W. on December 20, 1929, and a cairn of rocks was built to enclose a written claim for the area as a "dependency or possession of the United States." [84] This claim, and others made by other Byrd parties and by the Ellsworth expedition of 1935–36, brought forth reiterations by the State Department of the Hughes policy of 1924 despite pressures from writers [85] and from the Congress of the United States. On July 1, 1930, for example, Senator Tydings introduced a resolution authorizing and directing the President "to lay claim to all areas in the Antarctic which have been discovered, or explored by American citizens." [86] Nothing came of this, but in 1936 Congress voted to award a gold medal to Lincoln Ellsworth for "claiming on behalf of the United States approximately 350,000 square miles of land in Antarctica between the eightieth and one hundred and twentieth meridians west of Greenwich, representing the last unclaimed territory in the world." [87]

By 1938–39 the German threat led President Roosevelt to ask the State Department to make a policy study of the Antarctic problem, and that study suggested a reversal of the Hughes doctrine. Reasons given for a reversal included the need to protect aviation, mineral, strategic, and related "rights" in view of the activities of other nations.[88] On January 7, 1939, therefore, Roosevelt "enthusiastically" approved a plan establishing a United States Antarctic Service in the Department of the Interior, with cooperation to be obtained from the Departments of State, War, and the Navy.[89] The Antarctic Service was formed for the purpose of "organizing, directing, and co-ordinating the conduct of an investigation and survey of the natural resources of the land and sea areas of the Antarctic regions . . . ," and the establishment of a number of permanent or semi-permanent stations was planned in order to open the way for extensive claims. President Roosevelt's Order of November 25, 1939, to the Service noted that "the United States has never recognized any claim of sovereignty in the Antarctic regions by any foreign state" and warned members of the service not to "take any action or make any statements tending to compromise this position." It went on, however, to state that:

Members of the Service may take any appropriate steps such as dropping written claims from airplanes, depositing such writing in cairns, etc. which might assist in supporting a sovereignty claim by the United States Government. Careful record shall be kept of the circumstances surrounding such act. No public announcement of each such act shall, however, be made without specific authority in each case from the Secretary of State.[90]

The Antarctic Service established West Base near the site of Little America, set up earlier by Byrd, and East Base on Stonington Island near the foot of Palmer Peninsula in 1940. Explorations were conducted from both bases, but the Second World War ended the Antarctic Service. Other United States interest in the same period is also shown by Roosevelt's 1939 request to Sumner Welles to investigate the possibilities of a joint claim to the "American Antarctic" "in behalf of, and in trust for, the American Republics as a whole," with, perhaps, an inter-American governing body. In the same year Secretary of State Cordell Hull declared that "considerations of continental defense make it vitally important to keep for the twenty-one American Republics a clearer title to that part of the Antarctic continent south of America than is claimed by any non-American country," a statement currently invoked by Chile and Argentina in their disputes with Britain.[91]

After the end of the Second World War the United States Navy conducted Operation Highjump in 1946, the largest exploratory venture in Antarctic history,[92] and Operation Windmill, a smaller version of the same in 1947.[93] The originally secret directives for both of these expeditions and, indeed, for Operation Deepfreeze I, which headed south in 1955 to prepare bases for the IGY, contained instructions to the effect that one objective was the extension and consolidation of "United States sovereignty over the largest practicable area of the Antarctic continent."[94] Markers and flags were in fact left in many places surveyed.[95] Since this objective was inconsistent with the world-wide "gentleman's agreement" that the IGY should not be burdened with political overtones, reference to political activity of any sort was eliminated from the directive for Operation Deepfreeze II of 1956–57.[96]

In 1946, Under Secretary of State Acheson restated the position of the United States in these terms:

> . . . the United States Government has not recognized any claims of any other nations in the Antarctic and has reserved all rights which it may have over those areas. On the other hand, the United States has never formally asserted any claims, but claims have been asserted in its behalf by American citizens.[97]

Congressional and public interest in the area has continued in the United States however, and a succession of Congressional committees has called for a reevaluation of the traditional policy of avoidance of claims.[98] In January, 1954, for example, a Joint Resolution was introduced before the 83d Congress declaring the "right of sovereignty of the United States . . . from 90° W.–150° W." while reserving all rights elsewhere.[99] More recently, the Report of a Subcommittee of the House Committee on Interstate and Foreign Commerce, issued on February 17, 1958, suggested that:

> While the understanding of the participating nations in IGY is that territorial claims will not be made during IGY, the establishment of permanent scientific stations in the Antarctic, and the facilities for their supply . . . precipitate the need for attention to the various territorial claims, which have been made in Antarctica. . . . We are of the opinion that the time has arrived for a re-evaluation of [the position taken by Secretary Hughes in 1924]. . . . We appreciate the ramifications attending any such re-evaluation.[100]

The more recent United States initiatives in regard to the future of the Antarctic are discussed in Chapter 6.

A Japanese expedition visited the Antarctic in 1911–12, concentrating on the Bay of Whales region, the Ross Ice Shelf, and the Edward VII Peninsula. Vague, nonspecific claims were thereafter made by Japan, but, whatever their validity, they were waived in the Peace Treaty of 1951 wherein Japan renounced, in Chapter II, Article II, "all claim to any right or title or interest in connection with any part of the Antarctic area. . . ." Nazi Germany, too, mounted a ship and seaplane expedition in 1938–39 which resulted in the mapping of some 300,000 square miles and the dropping from the air of vast numbers of steel shafts with the Nazi emblem as a sign of a claim. The markers were dropped every 15 or 20 miles and a flag was also raised.[101] The Federal Republic does not appear to have pressed any claims. No peace treaty with Germany exists as yet.

The Soviet Union has never claimed any Antarctic territory, but the Soviet government has expressed considerable concern with the area in recent years.[102] In the last ten years the discoveries of Bellingshausen and Lazarev, sailing in the Tsar's service in 1819–21, were recalled and celebrated at the All-Soviet Geographical Society.[103] The mere lapse of some 130 years did not, it was argued, cause any loss of rights.[104] When the United States sought tentatively in 1948 to bring together those nations with claims in the Antarctic, in order to consider the political future of the continent,[105] the Soviet Union raised its voice in protest over not receiving an invitation. A Soviet Memorandum of June, 1950, declared in part:

> The Government of the U.S.S.R. cannot agree to such a question as that of the Antarctic regime being settled without its participation. . . . The Soviet Government deems it necessary to state that in accordance with international practice all countries concerned should be invited to take part in discussion of the regime of any sphere of international importance. The Soviet Government holds that this international practice should also be observed in settling the question of the Antarctic. . . .[106]

The United States' suggestion was characterized as a "fig leaf to cover the American imperialists' design to seize the whole of the Antarctic." [107] Soviet whalers and scientific expeditions have been active in the area ever since 1947, and the Soviet Union apparently means to stay and to be reckoned with in any future settlements.[108]

Certain other nations, inspired in part at least by the interest aroused by the IGY, have participated in the scientific work of the IGY or have otherwise indicated a continuing interest in the Antarctic. Thus, Belgium, which has not put forward any formal claim to Antarctic territory, has asserted that, on the basis of the discoveries of an 1897–99 scientific expedition in which Belgium played a leading part, she would expect to be included in any international discussions about the future of the political status of Antarctica.[109]

Three Latin American states which have thus far played no part in the Antarctic have recently begun consideration of claims which might be asserted on the basis of projecting their borders poleward. Simply by dropping a line to the Pole, the following divisions would result: to Brazil, 34°40′ to 53°20′ W.; to Uruguay, 53°20′ to 56°40′ W.; to Argentina, 56°40′ to 66°30′ W.; to Chile, 66°30′ to 75°40′ W.; to Peru, 75°40′ to 81°20′ W., after eliminating potential overlaps. These divisions obviously overlap existing claims, but it seems reasonable to suppose that Brazil, Uruguay, and Peru may all seek to assert their "rights" in order to participate in any solution to the Antarctic problem.

Thus numerous states have already asserted claims in the Antarctic: Britain, France, New Zealand, Australia, Norway, and South Africa recognize each other's claims; the United States and the Soviet Union have, in effect, reserved all rights, but a claim by the United States to the area of Marie Byrd Land and vicinity would be recognized and probably welcomed by the entrenched claimants; Chile and Argentina have made claims which mutually overlap and which also conflict with that of Britain; other nations, including Belgium, Poland, Japan, Uruguay, Brazil, and Peru have all indicated an interest in any settlement. India has pressed for recognition of a broad world interest in the area. Such a recognition might avoid certain difficulties inherent in national ownership of sectors—the problems of who "owns" the Pole and how practically to distinguish separate national territories at or even near their points of convergence; of the strategic importance to many nations of freedom of the southern sea routes if the Suez and Panama canals were closed; of control of this vast "weather factory" which affects the entire world; of general access to and efficient development of such "riches" as may be discovered there.[110]

6. *Cooperation in the Antarctic*

The value of the Antarctic to the nations of the world can be analyzed in terms of those features which are of current interest, those which are likely to be relatively important in the near future, and those which, while conceivable, are for one reason or another highly problematic in the short run. In the first category are: the strategic nature of the area; its significance for enhancing a state's prestige or power position in the world; the riches of Antarctic waters; its importance for weather forecasting especially for South America, Australia, New Zealand, and South Africa; and its unique advantages for further scientific exploration of the earth itself and of outer space. In the near future may lie the development of facilities for transpolar air routes and for a tourist industry. Longer-range possibilities which might be realized after the installation of nuclear reactors for heat and power, and perhaps as a result of new technology, would include the exploitation of mineral resources, if these prove to be significantly rich.

THE POTENTIALS OF THE ANTARCTIC

The strategic importance of Antarctica in time of wars has already been noted. In 1940, it will be recalled, Secretary of State Hull remarked that consideration of continental defense required that the American states maintain a "clearer" title to the quadrant lying below the Americas than was claimed by any non-American state. German raiders actually operated quite successfully in the southern waters during the Second World War, sinking several

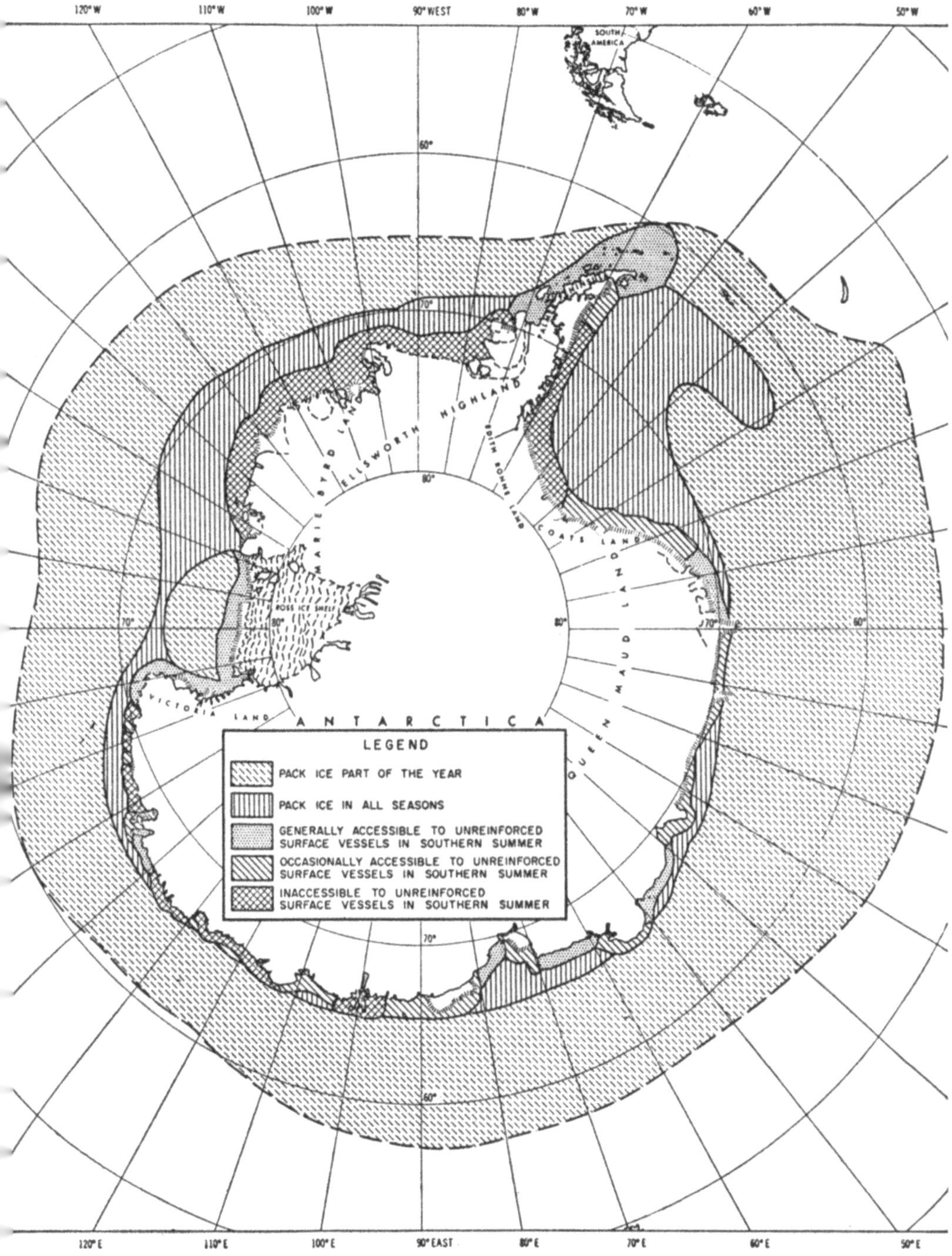

ACCESSIBILITY OF ANTARCTIC COASTS

U.S. Navy Hydrographic Office, H.O. Pub. No. 705 (1957), Fig. 23

hundred thousand tons of shipping, including the Australian cruiser *Sydney* and the first United States ship lost in the War. They also mined the ports of Sydney, Melbourne, Adelaide, and Hobart, and captured a substantial part of the Norwegian whaling fleet. The British squadron based at Port Stanley in the Falkland Islands fought three major fleet actions to keep shipping routes open during the two World Wars—the battles of Coronel, the Falkland Islands, and the River Platte.[1]

While the area does not have the immediate significance of the Arctic for military purposes, the closure of either the Suez Canal or the Panama Canal would force essential shipping into southern waters and the Antarctic might again attract raiders and become a center of operations for long-range submarines. Senator Alexander Wiley of Wisconsin indicated American fears in 1958, pointing out that

> in the event of war, there is always a possibility of the destruction of the Panama Canal by enemy attack. This makes the maintenance of an open waterway around Cape Horn vital to our national security. One Russian submarine base properly located, without deterrent from the United States, might well close this vital route.[2]

The threat of the maintenance of bases by "unfriendly" powers in the Antarctic, even though a thousand miles away, has already caused alarm in other countries as well. This was the case, for instance, with the creation in 1956 of Russian scientific bases in the sector claimed by Australia. This step, which was considered part of the IGY program, led to vigorous editorial protests and indications of apprehension in the Australian press. The raising of the Soviet flag on February 14, 1956, for the Twentieth Congress of the Soviet Communist Party, reportedly caused a "sensation" in Canberra.[3]

One wonders, however, whether such speculations and alarms smack more of refighting the last war than of anticipating the next. Just as modern factory ships in the whaling fleets have eliminated the need for shore bases in time of peace, so the cruising range of nuclear-powered submarines reduces the previous need for refueling or other bases in time of war. Whether in a nuclear war of the future there will be opportunity for long-term naval maneuvers is also open to question. The strategic importance of Antarctica might be found in bomb-testing or missile-launching sites or the unique advantages of the South Pole for contact with satellites on polar orbits. Its role in future air routes is considered later.

It is obvious that Chile and Argentina feel themselves—and quite properly—to be strategically especially closely affected by and interested in Antarctica. The bellicosity of their expressions of interest probably has several closely interrelated causes which, together, make a not unfamiliar pattern. They have real interests to protect, but they are small powers and lack the clear-cut, consistent backing of any large power. The Argentine conflict with Great Britain over the Falkland Islands is over a century old and has long been a matter of local public concern and anger, like the Belize question in Guatemala. If it be said that at least Guatemala is talking about adjoining territory, one may recall that more recently Indonesian excitement over West Irian has been successfully promoted to a national interest of the first order. Argentina and Chile would understandably be afraid of the establishment of a hostile power across 700 miles of water in Palmer Peninsula, but such a fear could be met by some international solution which might well provide safeguards. Even among larger powers which have been styled "imperial" there have been evidences that prestige considerations inspire the acquisition and forbid the surrender of territories which dot a world map with the color of the metropolitan homeland. In such a complex, foreign factors become integral parts of domestic politics, and an opposition party can ride to victory on the denunciation of "surrender of national territory." In the case of Chile and Argentina it has been suggested that "the existence of such [Antarctic] claims has frequently been the excuse for whipping up more intense feeling at home, perhaps for diverting attention from internal problems." [4] In any case, the Antarctic areas have repeatedly been referred to as portions of the national patrimony and have been "incorporated" into mainland political divisions, somewhat as Algeria is considered part of metropolitan France and Portuguese overseas territories are "provinces" and not "colonies." Chilean and Argentine political claims, interests, commitments, and sensibilities in the area raise delicate problems and must be taken into account when any form of international regime is proposed for the whole of Antarctica. The feeling in Australia may be somewhat less intense, but it is sufficiently comparable to demand consideration.

For weather forecasting, both Chile and Argentina maintain several permanent meteorological stations in the Palmer Peninsula. While much of the information and knowledge to be gathered from observation of air movement and other phenomena in the Antarctic regions will presumably be of use to meteorologists all over the world, those two countries are most immediately and directly affected; for them, weather observation in these latitudes is of immediate concern. South African, Australian, and New Zealand weather, too, is in part "made" in the Antarctic, and all of these states will continue to be vitally interested in weather information from this region. Operations designed to change weather patterns would obviously be of concern to all nations.

Among current economic potentials of the Antarctic, whaling has already been discussed at length. Norway is the nation most interested in this industry, but Russia, Britain, the Netherlands, Japan, and other nations are also involved. There have also been proposals for the "farming" of sea-elephants, which are valuable for their oil, and for international cooperation in bringing back the fur seal population.[5] The harvesting of plankton has often been suggested but remains at best a problem for the future when, and if, techniques become available and the pressure of population forces the resort to this new food source. The possibilities for maintaining sheep, rabbits, reindeer, and horses have all been investigated with some success, but only in such sub-Antarctic areas as South Georgia.[6]

On the general scientific side, a Congressional committee has stated the importance of the Antarctic in these terms:

> First, it is a large part of our planet—some 6 million square miles in area—and a largely unknown part, too. Second, it is the largest repository of ice in the world, containing 86 percent of all the world's glacial ice. Third, it is the world's most efficient cold-air factory, far more so than the Arctic. It also contains the pole or hub of the atmospheric circulation in the Southern Hemisphere. Fourth, its melting ice creates vast amounts of cold water, which sinks to the bottom of the ocean and, as the Antarctic Bottom Current moves across the equator, moves into the Northern Hemisphere. Fifth, it enables study to be made of the aurora australis and comparisons with the aurora borealis. Sixth, it contains the South Magnetic Poles and affords the opportunity for extensive geomagnetic studies. Seventh, it presents a stable platform for the study of the thermal and electrical properties of the atmosphere cut off from sunlight for many months, for the study of ionospheric phenomena affecting radio propagation, and for the study of concentrations of cosmic radiation. Eighth, it offers a stable platform for the tracking of earth satellites having the significant north-south orbit.[7]

Many of these matters were investigated during the International Geophysical Year.

Other activities to be anticipated in the near future in the Antarctic may include the development of trans-Antarctic routes for commercial aviation and the building of a tourist industry. The building of additional permanent weather stations, of the new types needed to take advantage of satellites on polar orbits, will lead to an increase in basic knowledge as to what "makes" weather. Conditions in the Antarctic, the "greatest source of cold weather in the world," will be of more concern on a world-wide basis as an aid to general forecasting. Apparently too, weather satellites on polar orbits, reporting to a station in the Antarctic, would provide excellent coverage of the entire earth's surface. Material changes in climactic conditions in the Antarctic, such as a substantial warming, would affect the level of the oceans sufficiently to concern all seaports. It has been estimated that the melting of all the Antarctic ice would cause a rise of 150 to 200 feet in the level of the oceans, submerging all seaports and many densely populated land areas.[8]

The Antarctic does not offer the same potential for air routes as does the Arctic, because most of the world's land mass and population are in the Northern Hemisphere. World traffic will inevitably be largely between the major centers in the north for many years to come, but trans-Antarctic routes would save from three thousand to seven thousand miles and, hence, considerable time.* The cost of an Antarctic base would be out of proportion to the prospective profits of commercial transportation companies at present.[9] In 1957, the United States and Australia specified in an amendment to their commercial aviation agreement that service be authorized along three routes, including one over the Antarctic; other alternate routings appear possible.[10] As the population in the Southern Hemisphere grows, these routes will become more important, but permanent landing facilities and a vast improvement in radio communications are prerequisites to any real use.[11] Under existing circumstances such costly construction could be undertaken only by governments—and only if they believed some strategic or political interest would also be served.

Some recent visitors have sung the praises of the Antarctic as a potential tourist mecca—"the scenery is unsurpassed in the world"—and, eventually, a substantial industry might be developed.[12] In this connection, it may be recalled that Spitsbergen, itself a rather desolate spot, though not as difficult to live in as the Antarctic, has been visited by tourist parties for many years. Chilean and Ar-

* See inset on map opposite page 144. Certain potential "great circle" routes would effect the following savings (all in nautical miles):

Capetown, South Africa, to Christchurch, N.Z., direct, is 5,943 miles; via McMurdo Sound, 6,060 miles. By current commercial routes (via Johannesburg, Mauritius Island, Cocos Island, Darwin, Sydney) it is 9,516 miles.

Buenos Aires or Santiago to Christchurch is about 5,300 miles direct; via Punta Arenas and McMurdo Sound, 5,926 miles. By current commercial routes (via Los Angeles, Honolulu, Canton, Fiji) it is 11,372 miles.

Substantial savings might be effected on routes between South Africa and Australia, and between southern South American cities and Australia. Technological developments in aviation might make these savings unimportant.

gentine cruise ships have already exposed some of the beauties of the Antarctic to tourists, but only at respectful distances. The difficulties and distances and the lack of facilities and transport in the Antarctic make tourism seem only a longer-range possibility.

The prime potential of the Antarctic which must await further exploration or the development of new techniques is the mining of valuable resources. As has been noted, there is no present knowledge of any sufficiently valuable deposits of minerals. The assumption that the mountain ranges which form the spine of the Palmer Peninsula are a continuation of the Andes, which contain rich mines, encourages the expectation that important mineral discoveries will be made. This expectation undoubtedly is a prime factor in keeping up interest in the area.[13] Even with the most modern techniques, exploitation of such resources would present complex problems and is probably not economically feasible. Ice, for example, is plastic and flows to fill shafts as they are dug. If deposits are found, however, it has been suggested that atomic power may be used to remove the ice cover in places. Some outcroppings are ice-free. New and vastly more powerful atomic ice-breakers, of which the Soviet Union will reportedly have three in operation by the end of 1960, may permit year-round access by ships to Antarctic shores.[14] In any event, it seems likely that nations will be loath to give up claims and rights while the economic value of the area remains unknown, unless they anticipate some off-setting advantage or compensation.

Other uses may, of course, develop in time—perhaps in ways not now even thought of [15]—but, barring a catastrophic shift in climatic conditions, man's ability to use the Antarctic will probably remain fairly restricted. It is not likely that there will be a large permanent resident population.

THE IGY IN ANTARCTICA

Recent years have witnessed a tremendous outburst of cooperative scientific investigation into the mysteries of the Antarctic. The International Geophysical Year (IGY), which was, as we have seen, technically a cooperative, nongovernmental effort by national members of the International Council of Scientific Unions (ICSU), had as one of its major objectives the acquisition of knowledge about Antarctica.[16] The IGY projects were largely scientist-designed, though government supported. For Antarctic programs, a special subdivision of CSAGI was created which met in four preparatory conferences in 1955, 1956, and 1957. The continuing Working Group on Radio Transmissions was organized to establish an internationally coordinated Antarctic communications network. As part of the IGY arrangement there existed a "gentleman's agreement" that all activities undertaken were to be regarded as nonpolitical and, hence, of no value in making future territorial or other claims, an important feature in view of the existing claims to Antarctic territory.[17] Obviously, however, national activities are not apolitical solely because the scientists say they are—especially where many nations are jockeying for position in a place which may have great economic, political, strategic and scientific potentials. Indeed, even science itself is today a political (and military) weapon, and success in scientific endeavor enhances a nation's prestige position. Anything that furthers science furthers strategic techniques—any base that is especially good for the gaining of knowledge is valuable strategically. Further, since whatever is learned about the Antarctic gives a clearer view of what its potentials really are, even the pursuit of "pure" scientific interests clarifies, for better or worse, the political value of the area and may lessen or heighten the conflicts over it. Political results are the inevitable by-products of research—else governments would not be paying the bills.

As part of the search for knowledge coordinated in the IGY, twelve countries established some sixty scientific bases, forty-eight of them on the continent proper. Seven of these were on the inland ice, the first time that bases were established inland on the continent,[18] and some 715 men wintered in the Antarctic in 1958, a record number.[19] The participants were the United States with seven stations; the Soviet Union with three or four; Britain with sixteen, eleven of which are in the Falkland Islands or the Palmer Peninsula; Argentina with ten, six of which are on the Palmer Peninsula; Australia with two; Chile with six to nine, in the Palmer Peninsula; Belgium with one; France with two; Japan with one; New Zealand with two, one of which is shared with the United States; Norway with one; and the Union of South Africa with one. While most nations operated stations in their own claimed areas, the United States had stations in the British, Australian, New Zealand, Argentine, and "open" areas, and the Russians were within the Australian claim. The United States also had a station at the South Pole which, in accordance with "sector" theory, placed it within six different claims. Observations have been made on weather conditions, glaciology, geology, geomagnetism, the ionosphere, and radio propagation problems. One of the joint ventures was quite successful. This was a Weather Central operated by the United States at its Little America base with participation by Soviet, Argentine, Australian, and French scientists and receiving information from various national stations. Scientists of different nationalities serving at each other's stations generally contributed effectively to the scientific work in progress. For example, the Soviet Union and the United States exchanged meteorologists between Mirny and Little America for the two years of the IGY.

Realization of the importance of IGY work in the Antarctic led to several suggestions for a continuation of scientific cooperation past the end of 1958, the termination of the IGY. As early as December 6, 1956, the United States National Committee for the IGY asked the Secretary-General of CSAGI whether it was felt that the Antarctic program should be continued for another year; and, in June, 1957, the United States delegate to the Antarctic meeting in Paris urged that the costly IGY stations be continued. He was supported by delegates from Russia, Belgium, and Argentina. Britain, Australia, Chile, and the Union of South Africa opposed the proposal at that time. By the end of 1957, however, ICSU created a Special Committee on Antarctic Research (SCAR) which first met in February, 1958, to consider post-IGY cooperation.[20] Membership is open to any nation whose scientists winter over in the Antarctic. Budget contributions for years after 1958 were to vary according to the number of personnel from the country assessed who were wintering in the Antarctic.

For SCAR's purposes the Antarctic was defined as "that region bounded approximately by the Antarctic Convergence," which would include most of the sub-Antarctic Islands. Other islands, however, including those occupied by the Union of South Africa, were approved for inclusion in the SCAR program, though lying outside the Convergence.* At the third SCAR meeting in Australia in March, 1959, scientists from all countries engaged in research on the Antarctic (except Chile) agreed that an urgent task was the complete mapping of the continent, since present maps are "only rough sketches" and "there are large areas of Antarctica that have never been seen by the human eye. . . ." Cartography had been omitted from the IGY program because of its possible political implications, but the Soviet Union and perhaps others engaged in extensive mapping activities during the IGY period. A Soviet proposal at the SCAR meeting to divide up the Antarctic for mapping purposes and assign different areas to different states was rejected. Other activities discussed included the need for better radio communications between Antarctica and the rest of the world, the study of the behavior of all forms of life in the Antarctic, and the protection of fauna. At this same meeting Poland's request to adhere to SCAR was accepted "as from the date of the disembarkment of their wintering party on the Antarctic continent." [21]

In January, 1958, the United States announced plans for continuation of scientific observation in 1959, supported by Operation

* The islands are Macquarie, South Georgia, Gough, Tristan da Cunha, Prince Edward, Crozet, Amsterdam, St. Paul, and Kerguelen.

Deep Freeze IV, an operation under naval command. The Antarctic Weather Central was moved from Little America to Australia however. The Soviet Union also announced a continuing program,[22] and Poland, with an established record in scientific cold weather work, planned to take over one of the Russian bases in 1959–60, thus increasing the Communist bloc presence in the Antarctic. An American invitation to the eleven other participating nations to exchange scientific observers was generally accepted by the others in 1959 though the Soviet Union, which exchanged observers during the IGY, declined the invitation without explanation.[23] The Ellsworth Station is operated by Argentina, with one United States scientist present. The joint United States–New Zealand operation of Hallett Station is being continued, and, as noted, personnel from both the United States and Australia are manning the Wilkes Station, the arrangement to have "no effect on the rights or claims asserted by either country in Antarctica." [24]

The first fruits of the IGY operation in Antarctica are vast amounts of new information, still largely unprocessed, made generally available to scientists around the world. The feasibility and advantages of scientific cooperation which disregards political tensions appear to have been demonstrated.

PROPOSALS FOR AN INTERNATIONAL REGIME IN ANTARCTICA

Since the end of the Second World War considerable attention has been focused on the possibility of an international regime for the Antarctic. Suggestions for international consideration of the status of the area and even for direct international administration in the Antarctic have come from private groups and from government officials as well. The Trusteeship Council took no action on petitions presented to it in 1947 by a private organization which urged it to take control and administer Antarctica.[25] The Commission to Study the Organization of Peace in its 1957 Report, entitled *Strengthening the United Nations*, repeated its recommendation of 1947 that in view of the "involved" and "insurmountable" existing claims, an "international regime for the Antarctic continent should be established, with direct administration by the United Nations." [26] The development of resources, it urged, could be handled by a specialized agency or by nations acting under licenses issued by the United Nations, and a small inspection force, using an air patrol, would be maintained.

In 1948 the United States suggested a multilateral conference of all the states concerned, and possible internationalization of the area, but without favorable result. The states invited were Argentina, Australia, Chile, France, New Zealand, Norway, and the United Kingdom. The displeasure of the Soviet Union at not being among those invited has been described earlier.[27] More recently, in part inspired by the success of the IGY, there have been further suggestions from several quarters for scientific or political cooperation and even integration in Antarctica. The Director of the Soviet Antarctic Expedition, Mikhail Somov, reportedly suggested in early 1958 "some sort of permanent international scientific station in the Antarctic." [28] On February 11, 1958, Prime Minister Macmillan, in a switch from the traditional British position on sector claims, called for internationalization and demilitarization of the Antarctic with national claims ruled out, though only nations with a "direct" interest in the area would apparently be included on the international commission.[29] Prime Minister Nash of New Zealand also indicated that he was prepared to raise the question of international control at the United Nations and that any arrangements should have United Nations approval, though an independent administering body might be used.[30] In 1958 the United States seized the initiative. On May 2 of that year President Eisenhower announced that, to avoid the Antarctic's becoming "an object of political conflict," invitations had been issued to the eleven other countries involved in cooperation in Antarctica during the IGY to confer in order to find a way to keep that region "open to all nations to conduct scientific or other peaceful activities" there under "joint administrative arrangements" which would "ensure the successful accomplishment of these and other peaceful purposes." [31] The notes containing the invitation included a strong assertion of American rights:

> The United States for many years has had, and at the present time continues to have, direct and substantial rights and interests in Antarctica. Throughout a period of many years, commencing in the early eighteen-hundreds, many areas of the Antarctic region have been discovered, sighted, explored and claimed on behalf of the United States by nationals of the United States and by expeditions carrying the flag of the United States. During this period, the Government of the United States and its nationals have engaged in well-known and extensive activities in Antarctica.
>
> In view of the activities of the United States and its nationals referred to above, my Government reserves all the rights of the United States with respect to the Antarctic region, including the right to assert a territorial claim or claims.

The note continued, however, to say that the United States Government believed "that the interests of mankind would best be served, in consonance with the high ideals of the Charter of the United Nations," if the countries directly interested in Antarctica were to conclude a treaty providing a continuation of friendly and peaceful scientific cooperation. The note then went on to say:

> It is believed that such a treaty can be concluded without requiring any participating nation to renounce whatever basic historic rights it may have in Antarctica, or whatever claims of sovereignty it may have asserted. It could be specifically provided that such basic rights and such claims would remain unaffected while the treaty is in force, and that no new rights would be acquired and no new claims made by any country during the duration of the treaty. In other words, the legal *status quo* in Antarctica would be frozen for the duration of the treaty, permitting cooperation in scientific and administrative matters to be carried out in a constructive manner without being hampered or affected in any way by political considerations. Provision could likewise be made for such joint administrative arrangements as might be necessary and desirable to ensure the successful accomplishment of the agreed objectives . . . the cooperation of the specialized technical agencies of the United Nations would be sought. . . .

The ensuing negotiations, which were carried on with remarkable respect for their confidential nature, lasted during twelve months. On April 12, 1959, Poland asked to be included in the Conference, but no invitation was issued. Finally, on May 31, 1959, the Department of State announced that the Antarctic Treaty Conference would be held in Washington on October 15, 1959.

An alternative international approach was suggested by Ambassador Lall of India on July 15, 1958, when he requested that "the question of Antarctica" be placed on the Agenda of the Thirteenth Assembly of the United Nations, since "the area is coming to have practical significance to the welfare and progress of all nations" and

> in view of the fact that many countries including India are particularly interested in the meteorological aspects and implications of all that happens in Antarctica, it would be appropriate and timely now for all nations to agree and affirm that the area will be utilized entirely for peaceful purposes and for the welfare of the whole world. . . .
>
> The Government of India believe that this limited purpose can be achieved without any nation renouncing such rights as it may claim in Antarctica, or claims of sovereignty or other rights consistent with the Charter. The Government of India are of the view that the action proposed can only be taken by the world community as a whole, and they accordingly suggest that consideration be given to the question. . . .[32]

A similar proposal had been made by India[33] in 1956 but withdrawn, largely because of opposition from Argentina and Chile. The 1958 suggestion ran into even broader resistance, particularly since the twelve nation conference described above seemed to be in the offing, and India again decided not to press the issue.

All suggestions for the elimination of national claims have met vigorous and even violent opposition from the statesmen of certain nations. Chile's Minister of Foreign Affairs Contreras stated in February, 1958, that there was an "American Antarctic" which was part of the American Security Zone; that Chile's rights were ancient and well established; and that:

For the reasons indicated, the Government of Chile could only reject any proposal which might imply the internationalization of, or condominium over, any part of its National Territory, whether it be in Antarctica, in America, or in its insular possessions in the South Pacific.

Once such proposals for political mergers were eliminated however, Sr. Contreras said that Chile might well be willing to continue scientific collaboration.[34] Similarly, on February 14, 1958, the Argentine Foreign Minister said, with respect to the Macmillan proposal, that Argentina "will maintain its classic position of retaining its rights over the Argentine claimed sector."

Such positions were obviously known to and taken into account by the United States in making its proposals of May, 1958. It is to be anticipated that further negotiations will proceed in the direction of scientific cooperation which leaves aside political issues, as the United States suggested. During such a period of cooperation there would seem to be no reason why, as the United States also indicated, the United Nations and its facilities should not be used. Such a pattern of cooperation if continued for a number of years might lead to some more definitive solution, assuming that the general political complexion of the world remained unchanged. In the meantime, the experience gained with international cooperation through international organizations could be of great value.

ADMINISTRATION IN THE ANTARCTIC

The problems to be coped with in the Antarctic have been suggested in the previous pages. They have also been summarized by Jenks in the following rather broad terms:

(a) the prevention of activities in Antarctica prejudicial to the peace and the political and military security of the southern hemisphere; (b) the maintenance of such measure of law and order as the peaceful development of Antarctica may require; (c) the provision and maintenance of air navigation facilities; (d) the provision and maintenance of meteorological services; (e) the provision and maintenance of such telecommunication services as may be required for the peaceful development of Antarctica; (f) whaling and the utilization of the other resources of the Antarctic Ocean; (g) the exploitation of any mineral resources discovered in the Antarctic which may be capable of utilization; (h) any continental shelf problems which may develop in Antarctica; and (i) general responsibility for the co-ordination of future scientific research in Antarctica.[35]

One might also mention the fact that the three-power technical report of 1958 on establishing sites for monitoring nuclear tests included four locations in Antarctica.[36]

Although it seems probable that a strictly political approach to the management of the Antarctic problems will be avoided, at least for the immediate future, it is obvious that any arrangement will have to take into account a number of different national interests. With this and the record of historical experience in shared enterprises in mind, several possible alternatives may be explored.[37]

First among the possible future political patterns is that which is identical with the current situation, that is, with several nations maintaining, more or less vigorously, their national claims, some of which overlap. Some unclaimed areas remain, and such important nations as the United States and the Soviet Union have, in effect, refused to recognize all other claims to sovereignty while reserving the right to make their own claims. Even at the present time it has been possible to achieve limited scientific cooperation and limited (and rather vulnerable) regulation of a major regional industry, whaling. It has also, on the whole, been possible to avoid armed conflict between the claimants, though enough "incidents" have occurred to make it probable that any considerably increased traffic in the area would lead to numerous international irritations.

A second possible pattern would involve the completion of the present partial division of Antarctica by subjecting the entire continent to mutually recognized claims. This may be called, for convenience, a national solution. As we have seen, Britain, France,

New Zealand, South Africa, Norway, and Australia now recognize each other's claims, and all would undoubtedly welcome a similar United States claim in the presently unclaimed wedge. Such a solution would require a decision by the United States as to whether or not it should make a claim and, if so, how much it should claim; it would also require resolving the British-Argentine-Chilean dispute (which is bound up with the British-Argentine dispute over the Falkland Islands as well) and the Argentine-Chilean disagreement. Of course the Soviet Union would protest and refuse to recognize the arrangement. Whether the existing Soviet bases in what would then be Australian territory would be allowed to remain would no doubt depend on factors of world politics quite unrelated to Antarctica itself. Other states, including those in South America with potential sector claims, might also object to the "settlement" and might agitate the matter in the Organization of American States. The asserted interests of the rest of the world as championed by India would have been ignored, and on this ground the Soviet position might find support in the United Nations from the so-called Asian-Arab-African bloc, again joined by some of the Latin American states. Even though the continent does not have an indigenous population, the arrangement would be denounced as an "imperialist" one. Among the nine contracting states themselves, the converging sector partition might well, as already noted, be quite unsatisfactory.

A third pattern would accept the national divisions but would attempt to ameliorate this solution by imposing various limitations on the sovereigns and placing servitudes on the area. This might be called a limited national solution. Thus the entire area might be subjected to a regime of neutralization and demilitarization in order to remove, in theory, the fear of many nations that the Antarctic might be used in such a way as to jeopardize their security. The world's experience with such regimes—Belgium, the mandates, and others—has not been a happy one; they have not turned out to be "war-proof." At present, it may be recalled, the United

Kingdom–Argentine–Chilean Agreement of 1948 provides that warships shall not be sent south of the sixtieth parallel except on routine matters. This or some such arrangement might be expanded and made applicable to all states.[38] A program involving an inspection system under the aegis of the United Nations, such as that suggested by the United States for the Arctic in 1958, might be agreed upon.[39] Despite wide support for this program for the Arctic, it failed because it was unacceptable to a major Arctic power, the Soviet Union. Comparable opposition would not be expected from what would then be the Antarctic powers, at least providing that other latecomers claiming sectors do not have to be considered. As the negotiations on disarmament and control of nuclear weapons have shown, the world's diplomats are not likely to accept at face value grandiose but empty promises in matters which they feel are of central concern to their own national security.

There remains the problem of the "rights" of the rest of the world in such matters as an economic "open door" policy and sharing in meteorological advantages, although the latter is technical in nature and perhaps, therefore, more amenable to a cooperative functional solution. The principle of free and equal economic access might be pressed, but, as has been pointed out in earlier sections, past attempts at such modified "imperialist" solutions which recognized national claims to sovereignty but attached limitations to national economic autonomy did not prove effective in, for example, nineteenth-century Africa or the League Mandates.[40]

Indeed, in addition to providing unsatisfactory assurances to the rest of the world, such limitations on economic sovereignty might well meet with stiff opposition from the hypothetical Antarctic powers. It seems probable that many of the present claimants would be averse to permitting the free exploitation of an area which, as they may suppose, could prove to contain very valuable deposits. Chile in particular has been a supporter in the United Nations in promoting the adoption of a resolution asserting a state's sovereign right to exploit its own natural resources.[41]

Presumably the extent to which the Antarctic powers would accept any limitations upon their sovereignty in the area would depend on the degree to which they felt it necessary to conciliate or yield to world opinion or segments of it. One can envisage any of these political solutions emerging from secret negotiations among the governments directly concerned, which would then announce to the rest of the world a *fait accompli.* One can also imagine that either before or after the event they might feel it desirable to have United Nations support, which might be of sufficient value to be secured at the price of certain concessions. It is clear that present claimant states which want to have their titles confirmed would need to enlist the support of the United States, and if the United States were willing to cooperate on condition that certain international obligations were assumed for the whole continent, its condition might be met.

A fourth possibility, really only a variant of others, involves a recognition of national claims together with a merger of political administrations into one or more condominiums. Chile and Argentina appear to be conducting some activities in common now, although a condominium is among the international solutions which Chile has expressly rejected. Further, it has been suggested that if the United States does make a claim to the area from 90° to 150° W. it would do well to consider a merger with New Zealand, through whose territory entry into the United States' portion is most readily made. If Australia were brought in (and these nations share common concerns as the ANZUS pact indicates), half of the continent would be a single administrative unit.[42] Despite the deservedly ill repute of condominiums of the past, the United States–United Kingdom arrangement for the shared use of Canton and Enderbury, with national claims put "on the shelf," may justify the hope that where scientific and technical functions are all that need be provided such a condominium of an unpopulated region can prove satisfactory to the parties at least. There might be advance planning for the exploitation of important resources if any are discovered in one sector.

A fifth political variant, on which many changes could be rung, would involve the surrender of national claims to sovereignty to a supranational body representing only those states surrendering claims or interests, or, perhaps more usefully for some purposes, to an international body representing the interests of all nations and peoples. This might be an organ of the United Nations, some body formed under the Trusteeship Council or the General Assembly, or some new entity entirely.[43] The International Court of Justice and the specialized agencies might also be incorporated in such a system. As earlier instances we recall the plans drawn up by the Trusteeship Council at the request of the General Assembly for the administration of Jerusalem as a *corpus separatum*, the proposals for a United Nations trusteeship over one or more of the former Italian colonies in North Africa, and the original plan for Trieste. But all of these regimes had to do with governing people —a significant difference currently favorable to an Antarctic solution.

This is the type of solution favored by the Commission to Study the Organization of Peace, which correctly concluded that there were no legal or other technical obstacles to an assumption of title to Antarctica by the United Nations.[44] Apparently some such plan would have the support of the United Kingdom and of New Zealand.

Such an internationalized solution, it is assumed by many, would most easily assure protection of the security interests of the present claimants as well as of the rest of the world; would avoid such problems as "ownership" of the Pole and transit across "national" boundaries, particularly in the air and especially where the sectors narrow as they converge; would facilitate the rational undertaking of scientific investigations and make their results readily available to all; and could provide for free access for exploration, exploitation, and development of the Antarctic without the hampering effect of national jealousies or barriers.[45] It would still need to meet the problems of a "government"—the choice of a currency, of a legal system, a language or languages, and the like.

Even without the formal surrender of claims to a new body, the same results might well be accomplished by a world-wide agreement based, as was that proposed for Spitsbergen, on a declaration that the area was and would remain *terra nullius*.* The Spitsbergen formula, which has already been described, could be lifted almost bodily for incorporation in a General Assembly resolution asking the interested states to deal with the Antarctic situation. The abortive plan provided for all the trappings of government—a commission to prescribe laws and provide public services, civil and criminal courts, and an "international" police force. In pursuance of the objective of maintaining Spitsbergen as *terra nullius*, it was provided that no *state* could acquire or occupy real property except for scientific, humanitarian, or religious purposes. Private persons could acquire rights of occupation and exploitation but not absolute title. The Commission was to levy rates and taxes to cover the costs of administration, except that the Commissioners were paid by their own governments and the three states represented on the Commission agreed to share equally in meeting any deficits. Other states were free to accede, but control remained in the Commission of three. Although it would be misleading to lay too much stress on similarities between Spitsbergen and Antarctica, the international regime for the former would have been an interesting experiment; its statute remains an interesting prototype.

If one were to appraise the political probabilities that any one of the foregoing lines of action would be followed, one would obviously bear in mind several factors which are almost too commonplace to mention.

It seems reasonable to assume, for example, that the deep division between the West and the Communist world and the concomitant underdeveloped state of general political international organization will continue to form the backdrop for all international negotiations, including those concerning the Antarctic.

* From a legal point of view, the term *terra communis* would seem more appropriate, since the very concept of *terra nullius* implies that sovereignty over it may be acquired by any state.

While this situation persists, any solution which completely froze one of the world's major political contenders out of the Antarctic while aggrandizing the other would not be an agreed solution. The Soviet Union must either be included in an Antarctic settlement or such a settlement must be imposed. Only an imposed settlement could produce a final, unmodified division of the Antarctic between the present sector claimants plus the United States. This situation may incline the West to favor some sort of international approach which would neutralize and make tolerable Soviet participation.

There are also within the Western world conflicts of interest which would tend to limit the scope of any internationalization that would be welcomed. Chile and Argentina are espousing claims for the protection of the "homeland" or the "national patrimony." They will not willingly endure internationalization of "their" sectors, or interference in their "domestic" affairs. Even if they were persuaded, it is by no means clear that either the United States or the Soviet Union is likely to favor any strong solution involving direct international administration by a general international organization like the United Nations. Such a solution, while solving some problems, invites unwelcome political complication. Voting arrangements which would avoid an undesirable veto power, generally give undue political weight to noncontributing states—to blocs of small states. Further, a strong international solution would probably arouse the opposition of those who fear to lend great prestige and provide significant precedent for further experiments in international government, even if fundamental ethical cleavages did not exist and great power conflicts did not have to be considered.

The small states of Asia and Africa and the new and potentially powerful states which are not presently capable of or interested in mounting Antarctic expeditions and establishing claims, and which in general benefit greatly in political power from the present voting arrangements in the United Nations General Assembly, would presumably be the most interested in a relatively strong international solution. They would seem to have nothing to lose and perhaps something to gain. This may be why India has twice raised the Antarctic issue in the United Nations. However, there are several reasons for feeling that this group of states will not be disposed to feel that the Antarctic has much short-run meaning for them. The Antarctic, being unsettled, is unlikely to arouse anti-colonial emotionalism, and the undefined, problematical economic potentials of the Antarctic are at present of only remote importance, especially to nations with a great underdeveloped potential at home.

Present indications are obviously not conducive to sanguine expectations of any broad degree of political internationalization for the Antarctic in the near future. On the other hand, whichever approach involving the retention of claims to sovereignty is the actual one, it is quite possible to envisage the surrender by the claimants of some technical facets of administration and operations to some joint international body or bodies. While claims to basic national territorial "sovereignty" were recognized, frozen, or joined in one or more condominiums, with or without international guarantees of a strategic or economic nature, certain functions—such as scientific research, weather forecasting, construction and maintenance of international air, telecommunications, and navigation facilities—might be coordinated, supervised, regulated, or even conducted by one or more international organizations. The whaling industry is already a partial example. In some instances existing organizations such as ICAO might fill the bill, in others a new body, perhaps on the order of the European river commissions, might be developed. There might be several independent functional organizations operating in the area; there might even be an over-all coordinating body. International conferences have, as in the case of Africa, on occasion been able to settle at least for limited periods the problem of major power conflict in new areas.[46] Despite the fact that the world has become smaller and the number and variety and organization of nation states demanding consideration has grown larger and more varied, perhaps the same may be accomplished for the Antarctic in the near future.

Without any pretense that the following suggestions form anything like a comprehensive survey of the possible institutional forms or indeed of the problems involved, we turn to some of the arrangements which might permit the study and use of the Antarctic without provoking international conflict. A broad objective of any arrangement for sharing the use of an area must be to assure that the arrangement as it develops is compatible with the strategic and security interests of neighbors, other states involved in the Antarctic, and the world community. The second broad objective to be accomplished is the efficient, equitable organization of the desired uses of the Antarctic for immediate scientific and economic research, development, and exploitation, including a wide range of activities such as whaling, prospecting for resources, weather forecasting, and satellite tracking. A longer-run objective would presumably include assurances that developing economic arrangements would remain compatible with the economic interests of neighbors, claimants, and the world community, thus assuring some safeguards for the effect of Antarctic activities on such crucial variables as weather and climate throughout the world, and perhaps also implying some concept of general "equitable" access to the resources, both physical and scientific, of the Antarctic.

Looking at the precedents one is led to suggest that the promotion of the most effective program for research and development in the area might be accomplished through an intergovernmental agreement, the preamble to which might read:

> The Governments of [here would follow presumably the names of the governments now participating in the negotiations initiated by the United States];
>
> Being desirous of promoting scientific, technological, and economic development in the Antarctic area and facilitating the use of resources and concerted treatment of mutual problems, avoiding duplication in the work of existing research agencies,

> surveying needs, ascertaining what research has been done, facilitating research on a cooperative basis, and recommending research. . . .

With the substitution of the word "Antarctic" for "Caribbean," this is the text of the Agreement of October 30, 1946, for the Establishment of the Caribbean Commission between the United States, Great Britain, France, and the Netherlands. The analogy is convenient, but it has its limitations too. The Caribbean Commission, it will be recalled, deals with a peopled area with clear-cut lines of sovereignty, and the governments established the Commission as a research and advisory body on matters of regional interest without impinging at all on the political administration of various parts of the area by the several states. The social problems which have interested the Caribbean Commission—and the comparable South Pacific Commission formed by the same states plus Australia and New Zealand in 1947—would not now concern an Antarctic Commission.

For the time being, it may be assumed that such an Antarctic Commission would likewise not discharge onerous governmental responsibilities but would be in general a coordinating machinery for the activities of the participating governments and organizations. As a purely functional body it would thus avoid, perhaps, political wrangles over a "veto" power. It might not face the complexities of the political international organizations or need to devise a form of weighted voting as in such institutions as the International Bank and the Monetary Fund, the International Wheat Council, and the like. Other organs for exploitation might well have to employ more complex arrangements.

At the outset, it may be noted, we are assuming that only the governments most directly interested by reason of past and present activities in the Antarctic would be parties to the treaty creating the hypothetical Antarctic Commission. The United States' note of May 2, 1958, proposing an Antarctic conference, for example, suggested that states were interested in the area on the basis of claims of sovereignty, "past discovery and exploration, geographic proximity, sea and air transportation routes, and other considerations." Other countries, however, may wish to be included. The Soviet Union may well wish to be joined by other Communist-bloc nations—Poland, for example, whose bid for participation has already been noted. We have also mentioned signs of emerging interest in Brazil, Uruguay, and Peru. Other states, such as India, might also claim a voice on the basis of "economic, cultural, military or other concerns or interests." [47] If it is considered necessary to take account of these and other demands for representation, there are various precedents which could be utilized. For example, there are more than sixty states which are members of the International Atomic Energy Agency and which participate in its General Conferences, but control is exercised by the Board of Governors, composed of ten members advanced to varying degrees in the "technology of atomic energy, including the production of source materials." Similarly, in the newest of the specialized agencies, the Intergovernmental Maritime Consultative Organization (IMCO), the directing Council of sixteen is made up of representatives of six nations "with the largest interest in providing international shipping service," six "with the largest interest in international seaborne trade," and four others selected according to defined criteria which also reflect interest in the subject.[48] It is readily seen that a comparable formula could be used for an Antarctic Commission with a directing Board or Council composed of those states "which maintained stations in Antarctica during the IGY." This category, it will be recalled, includes all the states which have pressed territorial claims, but this fact does not exclude possible demands of other states to participate.

Again, whatever the over-all framework, it may become necessary to regulate the exploitation of the natural resources of the Antarctic. The more efficient an Antarctic Commission is, the sooner this issue will become important. At present, economic questions are largely at the stage of geological and other scientific study, but with the introduction of nuclear reactors for heat and power developments might well be relatively more rapid than they have been. A good case can be made for the use of nuclear reactors in the Antarctic. Because of the enormous transportation costs to and in the Antarctic (now at about $6,000 a ton for supplies delivered at the Pole) nuclear power reactors would have there an economic competitive advantage which they now lack elsewhere. The states establishing an Antarctic Commission could in this detail make use of the International Atomic Energy Agency, which under Article III of its Statute is authorized

> To make provision, in accordance with this Statute, for materials, services, equipment and facilities to meet the needs of research on, and development, and practical application of atomic energy for peaceful purposes, including the production of electric power, with due consideration for the needs of the underdeveloped areas of the world.

The Agency itself may establish the "facilities, plant and equipment," and may operate them with its own staff.[49]

So far as whaling is concerned, the industry is already regulated, though not very successfully, by the International Whaling Commission. This Commission does not have and does not desire any connection with the United Nations. If and when Antarctic mineral resources prove economically attractive however, we may come to a critical period for the successful continuation of a purely functional approach to Antarctica. The sector claims will then acquire a new significance, and the value and international cooperation of purely technical organizations may not survive.[50] But it might be possible to delegate responsibility to certain states particularly interested, just as the 1911 Fur Seal Convention delegated to the United States, Russia, and Japan the taking of seal skins on the islands under their jurisdictions, subject to a duty to share proceeds with other states which surrendered their right to continue pelagic sealing. More applicable would be the interesting device worked out under the auspices of the OEEC for the chemical processing of irradiated fuels in the interest of a group of European countries, the international stock company known as Eurochemic. This company, it may be recalled, derives its legal form and status from the treaty itself, without the intervention of any national legislative act. It is governed by the Convention and its annexed Statute, with the law of the headquarters state, Belgium, as a residuary source. This device of an international stock company created by treaty is to be distinguished from the method used to set up the Bank for International Settlements in 1920, Eurofima in 1955, and the International Company of the Moselle in 1957. These actually were chartered by states, although in each case the chartering state restricted by treaty its freedom to deal with the company as a purely national stock company. One can envisage the eventual establishment by treaty of an international stock Company for the Exploitation of the Minerals of Antarctica (CEMOA), stock being allocated on the basis of the extent of the exploration and development of the continent or parts of it, perhaps weighted by the period of time over which such activities have been carried on. The capital would presumably be contributed proportionately by the shareholders, who would have a vote on the control board and a share in the profits corresponding to their stock holding. Some provision could be made for participation by other states at later dates if they showed adequate reason or exerted sufficient pressure.

In its operations, IAEA might furnish CEMOA with a nuclear power plant. Annual information might be sent to UNESCO or to ECOSOC. Scientific cooperation might be continued under SCAR or some organ of the Antarctic Commission. The Commission's relation to CEMOA would have to be spelled out for other matters as well. Since national claims are presumably not surrendered under these arrangements, the very success of the explorations might in turn lead to the resurrection of old claims and the destruction of the cooperative venture. While the operation might eventually be self-sustaining and even profit-making, initial capital could be raised through issuance of stock, either equally to nations with a tangible interest as of some given date or, in proportion to the amount a state was willing to invest, with special managerial benefits from increased participation, on the expectation of greater profits, or on the basis of anticipated general benefits from all or some of the activities of the development group or one or more of its subsidiaries. All of these and other techniques for raising funds are in use by international organizations today. Generally, where an organization offers special benefits to certain of its members those members make a larger financial contribution. Generally, too, members who pay more expect to have an added say. Consideration has to be given then to several factors: the benefits to be anticipated, plus the ability to pay, plus the need to preserve the truly international character of the operation.

Any general convention concerning administration in the Antarctic might also provide certain guarantees of an economic or scientific nature for the benefit of the international community. These would share the usual difficulties of international guarantees if the political settlement were any but the unlikely one of internationalization of the entire area. To the extent they were purely technical, they might stand a good chance of success. Thus, nonstrategic meteorological and satellite-tracking stations operated on the continent by any of the parties could be operated for the benefit of the world community. WMO would naturally be involved in the reception and distribution of weather information, at least to the extent permitted under existing patterns. We have seen that WMO already has the special Antarctic function of providing for the custody of secret information received from whaling factory ships in Antarctic waters. WMO might also furnish technical assistance or even create a special body to work in the Antarctic. One may recall that during the IGY the United States operated a Weather Central at Little America with scientists from five other countries participating on the staff. In the field of civil aviation, ICAO may provide air navigation facilities under Articles 69, 70, and 71 of its Convention. It may even pay for their development and man them if requested to do so by a member.[51] The text of these articles seems to limit these functions to the territories of member states; their exercise in some parts of Antarctica might therefore be interpreted as a recognition of some state's sovereignty. If this does present a legal obstacle, it is surely not insurmountable. Jointly supported facilities are now provided in Iceland and Greenland. At least in terms of constitutional authority, ICAO might either turn an Antarctic facility over to an air line consortium, operate it itself, or permit one line to operate it but with the requirement that it be open to all on payment of fair charges. If service to the Antarctic becomes important, it might be provided by a chosen air line or by all interested air lines on an equal basis.

So long as the Antarctic remains relatively uninhabited and relatively unimportant strategically, and its potentials lie in scattered fields—scientific study, meteorology, whaling, a few air facilities, and the like—limited functional arrangements with adequate powers might well meet the needs for use of the area. It seems a wasted opportunity not to experiment with a more unified, international governmental approach which might, while favorable conditions last, be installed successfully. Whether progress will be made even along the lines of cooperation alone in all of these fields cannot, of course, be foretold unless one knows the general drift of international politics during the months and years to come. The utility of dealing with the observable problems of Antarctica on an international basis is apparent; the technical nature of the problems to be overcome, the lack of a permanent population, the potential importance of the Antarctic to all the world in matters such as weather observation—all suggest the basis for a successful international sharing. The precedents exist for use, exploitation, and administration on a shared basis, and a number of international agencies already in existence can be utilized with relatively little further ado. Those charged with arriving at political solutions for the future of the Antarctic will have to make their decisions against this backdrop.

Part III

INTERNATIONAL CONTROLS FOR OUTER SPACE

7. Outer Space

THE PHYSICAL SETTING

The Solar System and Beyond. Our earth is the fifth largest of nine planets known to be orbiting about a minor star, the sun, which is, in turn, one of some hundred billion stars comprising a galaxy known as the Milky Way.[1] The sun is itself in orbit—an orbit which takes two hundred million years to complete—about a central point in the galaxy which is some thirty thousand light years, or 176,250 trillion miles [2] away. The galaxy is shaped like a grindstone; it is ten thousand to twenty thousand light years thick at the center, a thousand light years thick at the edge, and some eighty thousand light years across. Astronomers believe they see more than two hundred million other galaxies in the range of a 200-inch telescope, our largest at present, across an expanse of some two billion light years.

Earth is the third closest planet to the sun, its mean distance from that star being about 93 million miles. Closest to the sun is Mercury, at a mean distance of 36 million miles. Mercury is believed to be a small rocky sphere, about half again as large in diameter as Earth's moon, and, as it always keeps the same face to the sun, its temperature is estimated at 750°F. on one side and close to absolute zero on the other. It has no atmosphere.

Even less is known about the surface of Venus, orbiting at a mean distance of 67 million miles from the sun; a dense, opaque cloud surrounds it. Venus's major atmospheric component appears to be carbon dioxide. It is somewhat smaller than Earth. It never comes closer than 25 million miles to Earth, and it is estimated that a voyage to Venus would take about 140 days at speeds now feasible. Mars, fourth from the sun at a mean distance of about 142 million miles, is the best known planet, though most questions about it, too, remain unanswered. In diameter it is about half the size of Earth, has an appreciable atmosphere consisting largely of nitrogen, and has a daily temperature range in the "tropics" ranging from perhaps 70° to 100°F. Plant life, at least, is widely believed to exist, and "although human life could not survive without extensive local environmental modifications, the possibility of a self-sustaining colony is not ruled out."[3] A trip from Earth would take about 260 days.

The four "giant planets," Jupiter, Saturn, Uranus, and Neptune, orbit at mean distances ranging from close to 500 million to 2,800 million miles from the sun. All are massive bodies of low density, which rotate rapidly and are believed to consist of a small, dense, rocky core surrounded by a shell of ice and covered by thousands of miles of compressed hydrogen and helium. Temperatures range from −200°F. to −300°F. Some of their satellites are larger than Earth's moon and may prove more hospitable than their planets. Almost nothing is known about the smaller planet Pluto, except that it is extremely cold, has a small radius and a mass about 80 percent that of the earth, and its mean distance from the sun is over three and a half billion miles.

Earth's moon is only about 239,000 miles away, and, with a diameter of about 2,160 miles, is about one-fourth Earth's size. Earth's mass is over 81 times that of the moon however. The moon has no appreciable atmosphere, and its surface is believed to be dry, dust-covered rock. Its surface is also marked by many large craters and high mountains. Transit time from Earth to the moon at presently attainable speeds would be from one and a half to five days, while it would be about 110 days to Mercury, 2.7 years to Jupiter, 6 years to Saturn, 16 years to Uranus, 31 years to Neptune, and 46 years to Pluto.[4]

Beyond the solar system, and beyond the reach of man using known propulsion systems, lie the stars. The nearest is the star system Alpha Centauri, about four light years or some 25 trillion miles away. Pluto, by way of contrast, is 5½ light *hours* from the sun. Observations of other stars have led to the belief that many

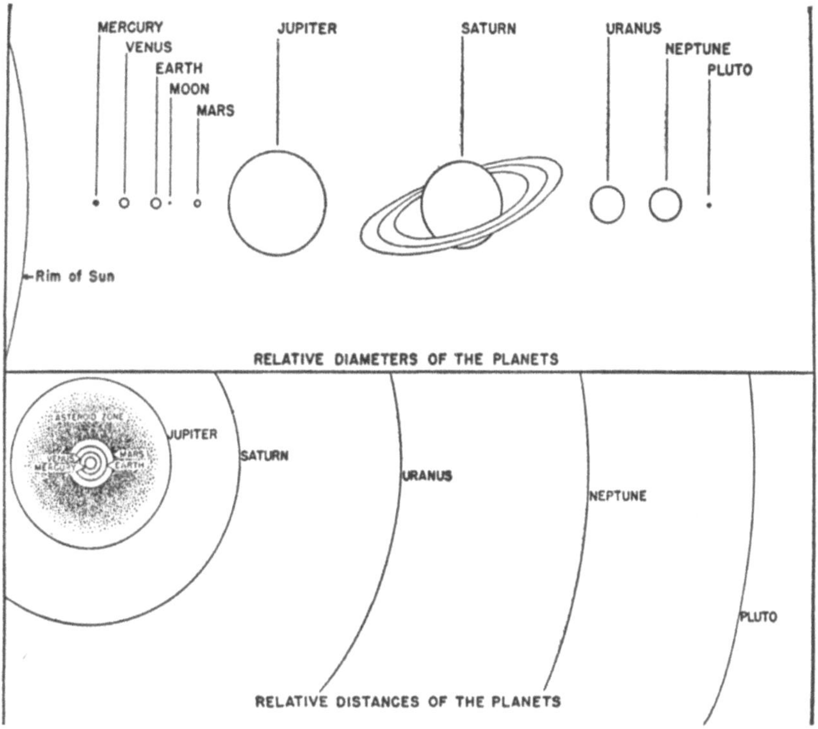

MEMBERS OF THE SOLAR SYSTEM

Courtesy, American Museum of Natural History, Hayden Planetarium, New York

have planetary systems—estimates range as high as 50 percent, but no estimate today is considered really reliable. Even minimum estimates indicate perhaps one to ten billion stars with planetary systems, and hence the possibility of life, in our galaxy alone.[5] For "practical purposes" it has been suggested that man limit his planning to the solar system for generations.[6]

The earth itself is surrounded by an atmosphere usually described in terms of four layers, though a fivefold division is frequently employed by scientists and by some writers.[7] Each layer has its own peculiar characteristics. Each blends into the next, and statements concerning the thickness of the layers vary depending on the characteristics studied. Moreover, the earth's "atmosphere" has in fact no limit, for it gradually grows thinner and thinner, until the trace of air becomes imperceptible. The boundary between the atmosphere and space is "entirely arbitrary" from the scientific viewpoint.[8] One half of the entire mass of the atmosphere is below 3.6 miles, however, and 97 percent of its mass is below 18 miles.[9]

Of the layers, that closest to the earth is usually called the troposphere; it varies roughly from about 10 miles at the equator to 3 to 5 miles at the poles. It contains approximately three-fourths by volume of the air mass surrounding the earth and is marked by a descending temperature gradient as one rises from the earth's surface. This is, of course, the area in which almost all human activity has heretofore been confined.

Most of the remaining air in the atmosphere is in the next layer, the stratosphere, which rises to a height of 50 to 70 miles above the earth. At this outer extremity the aerodynamic force of lift needed to sustain the flight of any currently conceived heavier-than-air winged craft ends, leading to the view held by some that all areas further removed from the earth should be termed "outer" space.

Above the stratosphere is the layer generally called the ionosphere, though it is sometimes divided into the mesosphere and the thermosphere.[10] It extends for several hundred miles, perhaps 400 to 500 miles above the earth.[11] Next is the exosphere, which gradually merges into interplanetary space.[12] It is generally said to extend for 10,000 to 18,000 miles beyond the earth, though traces of atmospheric components as far out as 60,000 miles are reported. For our purposes, it may well be that at least the exosphere should be joined with "interplanetary space" when speaking of "outer" space.*

Regions beyond the atmosphere, too, have names employed by most astronomers—*solar space* refers to the area occupied by the solar system; *galactic space* includes solar space and the area beyond solar space but occupied by our galaxy; and *extragalactic space* refers to all else beyond the Milky Way.[13]

Commercial flight today is carried on almost exclusively in the troposphere, and the highest known flights by aircraft have not gone beyond the lower regions of the stratosphere, being less than twenty miles above the earth. Man-made rockets have for some years penetrated into the exosphere, however, and the recent Russian and American space and lunar probes have penetrated into interplanetary space. Satellites have been placed in orbit from 121 to 26,000 miles from the earth's surface. The flight of the American X-15 is intended to mark the penetration of a "rocket-aircraft" to a height somewhere between one hundred and two hundred miles.[14]

Radio and related waves have long been sent from the earth as far as the ionosphere. In fact, the electrified layers of the ionosphere act as a reflecting mirror for radio waves, which travel in straight lines, and thus make long distance radio possible. Man has for some time been able to bounce radio waves off the moon, the oldest of Earth's satellites, making use of a "window" in the ionosphere which permits passage of radio waves of certain frequencies, and, on February 10 and 12, 1959, waves were bounced off Venus as well. The United States Navy plans a regular Washington–Hawaii radio service using the moon as a reflector. In the spring of 1959 intelligible communications were sent on an experimental basis from Jodrell Bank in England to Cambridge, Massachusetts, via

* To the extent the exosphere forms a true portion of the atmosphere and rotates with the earth, national claims to sovereignty and control which are discussed below, may be on a different footing from claims to "outer" space.

the moon. If artificial satellites do not prove more convenient for the purpose, the moon could also be used for world-wide television.[15] It has also been suggested that the moon can eventually be used to "monitor the face of the earth" and give information on nuclear explosions and other phenomena through use of rebounding waves.[16]

Thus, though the troposphere and the lower stratosphere will continue to serve as the principal area for man's activities for many years to come, the problems raised by human activities in "outer" space are already with us. It is useful, therefore, to examine the extent to which man has or is expected shortly to move into this new arena.

Man's Entry into Space. Even with man-made satellites already in orbit around the earth and apparently about the sun as well, with scientific rockets penetrating the ionosphere almost daily from some point on the globe, and with military missiles attaining heights of 400 to 600 miles above the earth, it is difficult for the human mind to adjust to the even greater exploits expected within a few more short years. By May, 1959, ten satellites had been placed in orbit and four space probes, two of which had escaped earth's gravity, had been launched either by the United States or the Soviet Union.[17] The satellites have already performed significant scientific tasks; they have made possible inferences as to the distribution of the earth's mass and the measurement of atmospheric density and of the size and shape of the earth, as well as allowing estimation of the occurrence of micrometeorites and of ionization, temperatures, cosmic rays, and other radiation in space. In at least one (Explorer III), information has been stored up and its transmission triggered by radio from the earth. Sputnik II carried a dog into flight. Vanguard II was the first crude meteorological satellite and the SCORE project of the United States demonstrated the feasibility of Earth-to-satellite and satellite-to-Earth direct communications and telecommunications relays.[18] Discoverer II, launched on April 13, 1959, on a polar orbit, was designed to test techniques designed to stabilize a satellite in flight so that reconnaissance cameras could function effectively, and to make recovery of a payload possible.[19] Some missile nose cones have been recovered intact. In May, 1959, the United States succeeded in recovering two monkeys alive after a flight into outer space in a missile, indicating the probability of engineering a safe return for human space travelers in the not too distant future.[20]

While the sequence of activities in space will be a function of many variables, including considerations of budgetary policy, priorities and cost, military strategy, and scientific curiosity, it has been estimated that, with the adaptation of present equipment, the achievement of the following by the United States is possible, probably by 1964: [21]

(a) orbit satellite payloads of 10,000 pounds at 300 miles altitude;
(b) orbit satellite payloads of 2,500 pounds at 22,000 miles altitude;
(c) impact 3,000 pounds on the moon;
(d) land, intact, 1,000 pounds of instruments on the moon;
(e) land, intact, more than 1,000 pounds of instruments on Venus or Mars;
(f) probe the atmosphere of Jupiter with 1,000 pounds of instruments.

It should be possible to track these experiments as well, and "communications as far as Mars seems reasonably well in hand. . . ." [22]

On actual timing, the United States, at least since the days when Sputnik I deflated American publicity about the "Vanguard" project, has eschewed a formal timetable.[23] Nevertheless, the National Aeronautics and Space Agency (NASA) outlined a program to Congress in April, 1959 which included:

the launching of eight satellites, two deep-space probes, and 45 to 50 sounding rockets in 1959;

the launching of six satellites, four deep-space probes, and 90 to 100 sounding rockets to heights of 4,000 miles in 1960;

the investigation through these means of the atmosphere of Earth, Mars, and Venus, the ionosphere of Earth, the planets, and the sun, the types of charged particles in space, the gravitational, electrical and magnetic fields in space, the "astronomy . . . of the universe," and the general theory of relativity (through use of precise atomic clocks in two satellites);

the establishment of a system of meteorological satellites within ten years, probably including five on polar and one or more on stationary equatorial orbits to make possible global weather forecasts (including a satellite with TV cameras in 1960 and a pattern of meteorological satellites by 1961–62);[24]

the establishment within ten years of systems of communication and navigational satellites (in fact, perhaps by 1960–61);

sending a man to the moon within ten years and establishing radio stations and telescopes there.[25]

The United States gave much publicity to the selection of a group from which its first "man in space" will be chosen, with estimates on timing favoring 1961 as the probable year for the venture.[26] Other estimates indicate the possibility that, if it is deemed important enough to justify the necessary appropriations, man may reach the moon by 1963 or 1966 and might even send an eight-man rocket to Mars by 1970 or 1980.[27]

Soviet scientists, too, have announced plans to put men on the moon and "to be on the planets by 1965."[28] The president of the Soviet Academy of Sciences, A. N. Nesmeyanov, indicated that these achievements were called for by the current Seven Year Plan, and Professor Katayov announced plans for a television relay station to be placed in a hovering orbit, probably in a location over Indonesia.[29]

Thus, a variety of uses of space are current or imminent, many of them impinging on daily affairs around the earth. Before contemplating the implications of this new set of situations, it will be highly instructive to glance briefly at the existing "regime" in the "airspace" in which man has already operated for many years.

THE POLITICAL-LEGAL SETTING

The Airspace and State Sovereignty. Before the day when controlled movement above the earth's surface became a practical reality, there was a widespread belief that airspace, at least that above what was needed for common activities on the ground, was free for the peaceful use of all. This hypothesis was advanced by Grotius,[30] for example, and, despite recognition by some scholars and statesmen of the potential danger of the use of aircraft in warfare,[31] it was still urged by Fauchille and others in the early years of the twentieth century.[32] As late as 1910 an International Conference on Air Navigation could reach "agreement" on the right of a plane of one nation to fly over another so long as no threat to security was presented,[33] though, unlike Fauchille, the Briton Westlake and his supporters urged a recognition of national sovereignty in the airspace, subject to a right of innocent passage only.

The experiences of the First World War and the post-war wave of economic nationalism led to universal agreement on the full and absolute sovereignty of each state in the airspace above its territories.[34] Its right to exclude foreign aircraft from, and to impose its jurisdiction within, its airspace was expressly recognized in the Convention for the Regulation of Aerial Navigation signed at Paris in 1919, and in its amending Protocols.[35] Limited rights of innocent passage for planes of contracting states were accorded by the Convention however, though, in practice, many states insisted on prior consent to entry.[36]

In the period following the Paris Convention, the doctrine of exclusive national sovereignty in the airspace found widespread expression in the laws of Great Britain, the United States, the Soviet Union, and, indeed, in all those countries legislating on the matter.[37] The Ibero-American Convention signed at Madrid in 1926 and the Pan American Convention signed at Havana in 1928, to which the United States was a party, also recognized an exclusive national sovereignty in the airspace. States vigorously asserted their rights to exclusiveness in this period as well.[38] By 1944 the consensus was that complete and absolute sovereignty was an established principle of international law.

In that year, a conference was called at Chicago to prepare a new civil aviation convention. Despite President Roosevelt's

> hope that you will not dally with the thought of creating great blocs of closed air, thereby tracing in the sky the conditions of future wars and that you will see to it that the air which God gave to everyone shall not become the means of domination over anyone [39]

the Convention as adopted set forth again, in its first Article, that "The Contracting States recognize that every State has complete and exclusive sovereignty over the airspace above its territory." [40] This, as has been suggested, represents the positions of states already vigorously asserted in the inter-war period in national legislation and in public utterances. A right of innocent passage remains, in Article 5, limited to nonscheduled civil aircraft, which can fly over a nation and make non-traffic stops without prior permission.

The Convention neither defines "airspace" nor any equivalent term such as "air," [41] nor does it provide for the situation in other areas of space, nor does it attempt to regulate other than civil aircraft.[42]

As we look forward to problems of administration in outer space, it is interesting to note that at the time of the drafting of the 1944 Chicago Convention the United States pressed for free commercial competition on international routes, Australia and New Zealand proposed full international control and operation of international airlines, and Britain and Canada suggested that frequencies of flights and the like be placed under an international board of directors operating according to a set of agreed principles. The

Chairman of the New Zealand delegation told the Conference, for example, that a joint world monopoly would "spread as widely as possible among all the nations of the world the beneficent effects of this new amenity" and would help prevent war by affording "a very large degree of safety against the misuse of aircraft." [43] These views were rejected, however, and, with respect to civil aviation today, there are only limited rights even to "innocent" passage in the airspace in peacetime except as extended by specific agreements, and free international airways exist only over the oceans.[44]

This insistence on national sovereignty in superjacent airspace has been based both on security factors and, to a considerable extent, on economic factors.[45] States have sought to build and protect their own commercial airlines, and those with established facilities and air transport companies have demanded a *quid pro quo* for entry into their airspace.[46] In the case of military aircraft the dominant factor has been security—a point so obvious that it has been little discussed since the First World War. Considering their capabilities for mass destruction, it is usually assumed that no nation will tolerate the presence over it of uninvited foreign military planes.[47]

As one report sums up these national attitudes:

> Fauchille's main policy argument for freedom of the air was economic. Without undue distortion, it may be described as a free-trade argument. It failed, not only because of growing economic nationalism and the enmities bred by war, but for reasons of national security. The entire territory of a nation is exposed to observation and sudden attack from the air. No one can set an altitude beyond which observation and attacks are impossible.[48]

Obviously, man's penetration of outer space can merely enhance national strategic and economic concerns, though the problem of competition among commercial carriers may well not be a serious one with respect to the use of space for transport purposes for some time to come.

In general, too, states may object to the penetration of their airspace not only by foreign aircraft, but also by Herzian waves used for radio transmissions,[49] though the enforcement of any such "rights" against unfriendly powers presents difficult problems and the delivery of protests and use of jamming techniques represent the limits of current protection of borders against unwelcome onslaught by radio. Nevertheless, the principle of complete national sovereignty is still asserted in these cases.

As to other areas within the atmosphere, and to means of penetrating airspace other than through use of aircraft, it is possible for Lauterpacht to assert: "that the airspace over the open sea and over unoccupied territory is free and in the former case incapable of appropriation may be taken as almost universally accepted."[50] While generally correct, this statement is subject to important caveats which will be discussed later, together with its implications for a regime in outer space.

Airspace and Outer Space. Granting, as we have observed, that there is universal agreement today that a state has "complete and exclusive" sovereignty over the "airspace" above its national territory and national waters, the meaning and extent of "airspace" remain technically undefined.[51] The term "airspace" is found in the vast majority of treaties and national legislation dealing with the "upward" extent of national sovereignty, but, until recent times, no need has been felt for an agreed definition since it simply was not possible for man to perform acts at altitudes above any possible scientifically defined limit of airspace. Rockets and earth satellites have, of course, completely changed this picture.

Consequently there have been in recent years many unofficial efforts to define "airspace," in order to determine more definitely the applicability of existing treaties and legislation and to lay the foundation for a regime for the regions beyond. In general, attempted definitions fall into three groups. One, influenced by considerations of national security, suggests that "airspace" as used in treaties, legislation, and assertions of national rights must be taken to apply to all areas above the earth's surface in which man-made instrumentalities, whether controlled or not, can be in operation at any given time. "Airspace" becomes then, "usable" space in the broadest sense.[52]

Supporters of this approach rely on the fact that from at least the time of the Roman emperors the law has recognized that private property rights and governmental powers extended to the space above the surface of the earth. Thus the law dealt with overhanging trees, projecting eaves, and the height of buildings. The convenient Roman law maxim *cuius est solum eius est usque ad coelum* was often repeated by the courts until the practical consequences of the modern development of the airplane led to the judicial pronouncement that, as a basis for private claims to control all the airspace over an individual's property, the maxim had "no place in the modern world." [53] But the same development aroused fears for the national safety and led, as has been described, to the consolidation of the rule of national sovereignty over the superjacent airspace.

In terms of defining and making "sovereignty" meaningful within this limitless upward extent of national territory, those who maintain that such a posture is necessary for preservation of national interests meet both physical and legal difficulties. On the legal side, an agreement that airspace meant space to the outer limit of all flight would avoid the problem of measuring the upward extension of national boundaries and would avoid the need for a new convention on civil craft, for the Chicago Convention of 1944 would automatically apply and the ICAO would have an extended function.[54] It has also been suggested that, if sovereignty is not extended infinitely outward, it should extend at least "as far into space as it is physically and scientifically possible for any one state to control the regions directly above it." [55] These arguments have been pressed even by some writers who admit the difficulties which would exist in determining national boundaries in the outer areas,[56] a point deserving some clarification.

The technical problem of the extension of sovereignty into space, if that extension is based on some projection upward of national territory, can be approached by projecting the nation's boundaries upward on the basis of perpendicular measurement from the earth's surface, using lines from the earth's center through the boundaries and out to infinity, or by use of lines parallel to a line which would intercept the center of the nation and the center of the earth and run through the nation's borders to infinity. These techniques would give results which could be diagrammed as follows: [57]

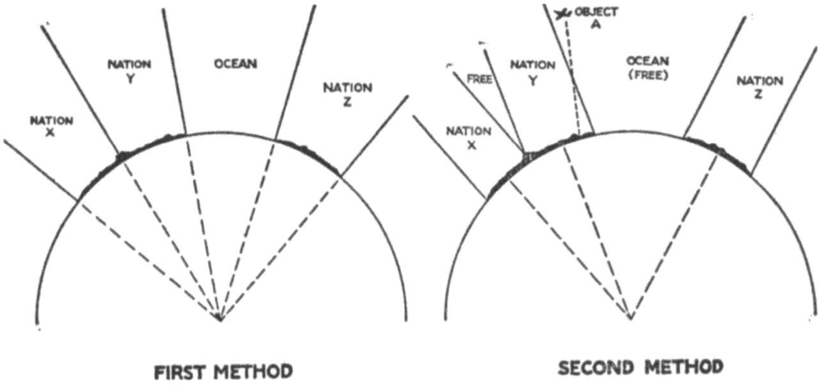

PROJECTIONS OF TERRITORIAL BOUNDARIES INTO SPACE

NOTE. The shape of the earth is shown as perfectly spherical to simplify the diagram.

In the second method an instrumentality, if far enough from the earth, could be in a "free space" and yet be "over" national territory in the sense illustrated by object "A" in the diagram.

In addition to the complexities of determining where a nation's "borders" were and just when an object was within a nation's territory as thus extended, and other problems related to the technique chosen, a basic physical difficulty is that objects in space do not necessarily rotate with the earth. Jenks has written: [58]

There are, however, more fundamental difficulties. The first is that any projection of territorial sovereignty into space beyond the atmosphere would be inconsistent with the basic astronomical facts. The revolution of the earth on its own axis, its rotation around the sun, and the motions of the sun and the planets through the galaxy all require that the relationship of particular sovereignties on the surface of the earth to space beyond the atmosphere is never constant for the smallest conceivable fraction of time. Such a projection into space of sovereignties based on particular areas of the earth's surface would give us a series of adjacent irregularly shaped cones with a constantly changing content. Celestial bodies would move in and out of these cones all the time. In these circumstances, the concept of a space cone of sovereignty is a meaningless and dangerous abstraction. The second difficulty is that missiles, space stations and space ships moving in space would be constantly changing their position in relation to the subjacent territorial sovereignties at such high speeds that whatever relationship of control might subsist between earth stations and such objects in space would have no territorial aspect analogous to the control exerted by a state in its air space or territorial waters.

While no state has as yet formally renounced all possible claims to sovereignty in outer space, the difficulties involved in expressing such claims and the presumption involved in claiming areas which thus far are outside effective reach, much less effective control, have led most writters to propose that sovereignty be limited to "airspace" or some otherwise "marked" limit above the earth's surface. Outer space would then be free of the limitations inherent in the use of the classic concepts of "territory" and "sovereignty" and would be available for shared use by all, on the analogy of the high seas, or owned by all or regulated on some basis involving cooperation among the nations on Earth. First, the problem of delimiting the area to remain within national rule must be examined briefly; further consideration will then be given to the various possibilities for a regime for space beyond national "ownership."

There have been a number of different proposals for determining the upper limit of "airspace" and hence of national sovereignty. One approach calls for the definition of airspace in terms of the "atmosphere," which in turn is defined in terms of gaseous content or of aerodynamic lift. The former would extend it perhaps to 18,000 miles or so, the limit of the exosphere, though some scientists calculate the "atmosphere" at no more than 500 miles and some commentators expressly equate the exosphere with outer space. The latter is the limit to which it is possible to fly instrumentalities deriving their support from movement of air (or gas) molecules, for example balloons and traditional aircraft.[59] Such a limit might extend no more than 25 miles above the earth, but is still well beyond the point at which current air navigation takes place.[60] It is, however, below that at which satellites can orbit for extended periods due to the insistent pull of gravity and the drag induced by the atmosphere.

Other suggestions call for the defining of "airspace" in terms of one or more combinations of physical factors, including velocity, gravitation, altitude, centrifugal force, and the like.[61] Another train of thought leads to a zonal approach with national sovereignty extending to some stated height, beyond that a zone free to all states for non-military uses, and then free outer space where "operations are not closely earth-associated but are more related to interplanetary transit." [62]

It is of course possible to suggest other tests or, indeed, to use any limit, however arbitrarily chosen, on which the nations can agree. There is not as yet any such intergovernmental agreement or even clear indication of any majority preference.

There is in addition a school of thought which suggests that it is not necessary or even desirable to draw boundaries, even if it were scientifically feasible, and that the applicable legal regime should be based on the activity undertaken—the use made of the upward reaches—"types of space craft, probable functions and potential dangers"—rather than on the area in which the act occurred.[63] Shawcross, in suggesting an international convention on outer space, asserted that the convention "should be based not upon sovereignty in the air or space but upon the permitted use of space whether for warlike projectiles, by man-made earth satellites or by pollution (*e.g.* radio-active fall-out) or dilution (*e.g.* weather control) of the atmosphere. . . ." [64] The advocates of a case-by-case school argue generally that it is premature to rush into an expanded scheme for control of or in space, since humans to this point lack sufficient scientific knowledge of the physical nature of space to draft boundaries or rules for its regulation, and that premature rules, all of whose effects cannot be foreseen, could prove dangerous in terms of national security and of international accommodation and cooperation in the future.[65] As the Chief of Staff of the United States Air Force has said: "In discussing air and space, it should be recognized that there is no division, *per se*, between the two. For all practical purposes air and space merge, forming a continuous and indivisible field of operation." [66] Thus, each problem would be considered as it arose and a "common law" of space might develop. Perhaps not surprisingly, national officials have adopted this approach in their public utterances, and it is the basis for the report of the Legal Committee of the UN *Ad Hoc* Committee on the Peaceful Uses of Outer Space in June, 1959; [67] that Committee's work will be discussed later. Application of this pragmatic approach to outer space would obviously avoid certain problems, for the moment at least, which no doubt adds to its persuasiveness.

Without any further attempt to adduce additional examples of the various opinions which have been expressed on the most satisfactory way to define the boundary between airspace and outer space, we shall assume that at some point there is a limit to the extension of terrestrial sovereignties and that in due course practical international necessities will lead to its definition. We shall now turn to a consideration of the alternatives with respect to the status in law and practice of "outer space" and the celestial bodies.

If national sovereignty is limited to some level above the earth's surface, what is the legal status of this outer area and of the heavenly bodies, including the moon? It has been argued that outer space, the moon, and other planets are in the category of *res nullius*, which would, by traditional standards, permit appropriation by national states through methods which might be those based on traditions established on Earth or by new arrangements more suitable to space. This concept has been rejected by spokesmen for several small nations who have termed the "appropriation" of space or of the heavenly bodies "impossible" or at least "improper." [68] At the other extreme are those who urge that space and the planets are in effect free for the perpetual use of all.[69] A third and by far the largest group insists that space and the heavenly bodies are not subject to appropriation or control by individual national states but argues that this *res omnium communis* or *res extra commercium* must be subjected to some international control to prevent misuse of the areas in question and danger and damage to other persons or nations.[70] Exponents of the last two positions often compare outer space with the high seas, which are said to be free for the peaceful use of all, while proponents of national sovereignty in space often use the regime of national air space as a source of their precedents.

Maritime law in general and the legal regime of the high seas in particular have been heavily drawn upon to provide analogies useful for the construction of a system of space law.[71] It is convenient to think of the vast ocean spaces on Earth, to say that they are regarded as the common property of all (*res communis omnium*), and to argue that the same regime should apply to outer space. There are indeed some useful analogies, but some parts of the history of the law of the sea should be kept in mind.

In the first place, man has always used the seas, which seemed vast open spaces even when the horizons to which men ventured were relatively near at home. Man has not until very recently used outer space. It is not true that the high seas have always been considered free and common property. Up until the seventeenth century national claims to sovereignty over vast areas of ocean were asserted. The *Mare Liberum* of Hugo Grotius was a great lawyer's eloquent and persuasive brief, but it remains more the symbol than the cause of the final adoption by the international community of the doctrine of the freedom of the seas. It proved impossible for any one state permanently to monopolize the high seas, partly because it was physically impossible to dominate them and partly because so many nations had a common interest in using them. Some day the same may be written of outer space.

It has been well said that the law of the sea is now a "checkerboard of variegated regions and legal rules." [72] It is established that each coastal state possesses a belt of territorial sea, but, as the 1958 Geneva Conference on the Law of the Sea demonstrated, the width of that belt is not agreed. Although the Conference agreed that no state may validly purport to subject any part of the high seas to its sovereignty, a number of states have reasserted off-shore claims almost as extravagant as those controverted by Grotius.[73] For centuries the phrase "freedom of the seas" covered the rights of neutral shipping in time of war, but that system has, to say the least, been greatly impaired; hopefully it will eventually be superseded by some new regime of collective security under the United Nations. The Geneva Conference listed four freedoms—of navigation, of fishing, to lay submarine cable and pipelines, to fly over the high seas—and admitted there may be others recognized by the general principles of international law.[74] There is controversy whether there is a freedom to use areas of the high seas for missile ranges and nuclear tests.[75] The appropriation there is preemptive but temporary; it may be extensive as indicated by the facts that the announced danger area around Eniwetok and Bikini amounted to 400,000 square miles, and that a missile range extends from Cape Canaveral some five thousand miles out to sea. These two cases reveal the close interrelationship of sea law and air law signalized by the Geneva Conference's fourth freedom. Of like kind are the air defense zones off the coasts of the United States and Canada, wherein foreign aircraft are required to identify themselves when not less than one hour's cruising distance from the land.[76] The defense zones in turn are supported off the coast of the United States by three "Texas towers" mounting radar which can detect approaching planes. These steel structures have been built on shoals more than a hundred miles from shore. In short, the principle of the freedom of the seas permits sovereignty over portions of adjacent waters and a variety of national uses of the still vast stretches which are truly *res communis.*

The very nature of outer space, the nonexistence of definable boundaries or subdivisions and the ability of craft to move through it at speeds a thousand or more times as great as those at which vessels can move on the seas, presents vitally different problems, especially of defense, and indicates that a mechanical extension of the law of the sea to outer space, even if the law of the sea were itself more definite and uniform, is not to be anticipated and would probably not be desirable. Having said this, however, it must be acknowledged at once that these same rules constitute an interesting precedent in the patterns of national protection already set in areas beyond the national boundaries without the complications inherent in claims to sovereignty. In addition, the practice on the high seas provides instructive precedent for operations in outer space as it did and does for use of airspace. Useful examples of international cooperation can be found in establishing rules of the road, rescue arrangements, provisions against piracy and slaving, navigational and meteorological aids, cable laying and maintenance, responsibility for collisions and other injuries, ownership of craft through registration, recognition of authority in each state to exercise jurisdiction in the high seas over its own nationals and vessels, and many other arrangements or agreed procedures indicative of a balancing of the concepts of *res communis* with the claims of states to protect their police, security, and other arrangements through reasonable exercises of authority in but not over the high seas.[77]

Similarly, in current practice of states with respect to use of airspace there are precedents for cooperation, many drawn in turn from the arrangements for use of the seas, as to:

> . . . airworthiness, registration and identification, competence of personnel, proficiency of operation, rules of the air, navigational aids, safety of life and property, rescue at sea, access to airports, routes, transit over national territory, customs, spread of disease, civil liability for damage, competition, discrimination, communications and meteorological information.[78]

It will be noted that the analogy with the regime of the seas is relevant to outer space essentially for functional apolitical problems, even as "freedom of the seas" is substantially today a peacetime concept. Furthermore, the seas are extensive enough and techniques of movement over their surface are slow enough to accommodate remote peacetime military maneuvers of an exclusionary nature without inevitably engendering conflict. Even in peacetime, outer space is likely to present a different problem on this score, so that the range of technical problems which can be solved by analogy to the regime of the seas is thereby narrowed. The perhaps crucial political and security problems are left to be solved by some other regime for space.

Practice of States with respect to High Altitude and Outer Space Activities. Thus far, only the Soviet Union and the United States have succeeded in placing objects in orbit in what is generally recognized as "outer space." Neither of these nations, nor any other, has made any definitive statements as to what it considers the upward limits of its sovereignty; nor, on the other hand, has either Soviet Russia or the United States formally claimed any part of outer space or any of the celestial bodies.[79]

Prior to the launching of the satellites, incidents in 1956 connected with meteorological balloons illustrated both national sensitivities to the presence of instruments of observation above the national territory and also the potentialities, subsequently realized, of one function which satellites can perform. In January,

1956, the United States Department of Defense published details of a meteorological survey which had been carried out over the two preceding years with the cooperation of Brazil, Japan, Panama, Turkey, and the United Kingdom. Some 4,000 balloons carrying meteorological instruments including radios and cameras had been launched, and were designed to move at altitudes above 30,000 feet. A month later Norway announced plans for a comparable balloon program involving loads of 400 pounds of instruments to be carried at 80,000 to 90,000 feet.

Shortly thereafter, the Soviet Union charged the United States with attempts to spy on Russia through aerial photography. Albania, Bulgaria, Communist China, Czechoslovakia, East Germany, Hungary, Mongolia, Poland and Rumania also protested to the United States; the Soviet Union protested to Turkey and the Federal German government; Sweden protested to Norway and the United States; and Albania, Bulgaria, and Czechoslovakia lodged complaints against the United States with the Secretary-General of the United Nations, and Czechoslovakia also protested to the European Office of ICAO. In general, the meteorological balloons were linked by the Soviet Union with propaganda balloons launched toward the Iron Curtain countries by private parties in the West (claimed to be "United States organizations"). The invasion of territorial sovereignty was stressed, but the balloons were also said to be a danger to aerial navigation and to persons and property on the ground on falling. It was stated that the balloons usually moved at altitudes of only 13,000–16,000 feet, and that many injuries due to air collision or ground explosion had already occurred.

In their replies the United States and Turkey undertook, in view of Soviet objection, to suspend provisionally the release of meteorological balloons that might cross Soviet territory. Secretary of State Dulles stressed the lack of a clear rule of international law on the subject and suggested that the cessation was not due to a recognition of a Soviet right "but as a matter of decent, friendly relations." The United States did not assert a right to fly balloons into the airspace of another state, nor did it suggest the propriety of putting "up into the air anything which could interfere with any normal use of the air by anybody else." [80]

The satellites launched by the Soviet Union and by the United States in 1957 and 1958 were, with at least one exception,[81] considered as contributions to the International Geophysical Year. No advance consent was asked of any state to the flight of a satellite over its territory [82] and no objections were made by states to the passage of any satellite included in the IGY program, though, as will be discussed later, the satellites have interfered with radio transmissions on the earth. The lack of objection to the passage of satellites launched during the IGY has been offered by several commentators and spokesmen for small nations as "proof" or at least as an indication of a principle and the setting of a precedent to the effect that outer space is free for the use of all.[83] It must also be pointed out that no state now has the technological capability of preventing the passage of a satellite. We shall consider in some detail the views of the two major powers. Here, as in all other spheres, governmental decisions will inevitably be based on various security, economic, and scientific considerations—all "freedom" of movement which involves a state's security is necessarily limited by the "necessity of guaranteeing the security of the state." [84] The question remains whether at any point the conclusion will be reached that the security of the state will be best served by entering into an international agreement for space controls, just as the United States in 1947 offered to do for the control of the use of atomic energy.

Official statements on behalf of the United States with respect to the present legal status of outer space are not to be found prior to the spring of 1958.[85] From that time a series of statements, particularly by the Legal Adviser of the Department of State, have reflected a point of view which, as the Legal Adviser himself has said, is comparable to the United States position on claims to sovereignty in Antarctica.[86] In both cases the United States denies that any other state has established a valid claim to sovereignty. In neither case does the United States make such a claim for itself, but it does assert, in effect, that if anyone has a right to claim, the position of the United States is as favorable as if not more favorable than that of any other contender. Thus he stated, as comparable to the Antarctic situation, that "in outer space the United States has already engaged in activities which, it could be asserted, have given to it certain rights as distinguished from those states which have not engaged in such activities. Up to this time the United States had made no claims of sovereignty based upon such activities." A further possible basis for the protection of rights was established by explaining that the United States had never felt the need to define the upper limits of its airspace over which, of course, it does claim sovereignty. But the Legal Adviser called attention to the suggestion which had been made "that the airspace should be defined to include 'the space' in which there is any atmosphere"; from an astronomical point of view, he said, the earth's atmosphere can be considered to extend 10,000 miles above the surface of the earth. Consequently "it would be perfectly rational . . . to maintain that under the Chicago Convention the sovereignty of the United States extends 10,000 miles from the surface of the earth, an area which would comprehend the area in which all of the satellites up to this point have entered." The Legal Adviser indicated his view that the position could be left flexible. "I do not think," he testified before a Congressional Committee, "we should be in a hurry to delimit or restrict the sovereignty of the United States unless we know that we are on the right road. . . . It is only after we have a great deal more knowledge that I feel we want to make a final decision that the boundary of the United States goes this far and no further. Because once that decision is made, it is a permanent decision." In like vein, the United States representatives in the United Nations *Ad Hoc* Committee on the

Peaceful Uses of Outer Space, took the position that there was no need to proceed at once to draft a code of space law. As the Legal Adviser said earlier, he felt that "the soundest way to progress . . . is by means of specific decisions on specific questions presented by specific fact situations." It was none the less the United States view, repeated in the UN Committee, that certain principles of law were applicable to outer space, as for example the principles of the Charter of the United Nations and the Statute of the International Court of Justice. In regard to the Charter, the emphasis was on the right of self-defense as recognized in Article 51, and the invocation of the Statute of the Court did not seem to suggest that the United States was prepared to leave to the Court, through a request for an advisory opinion or otherwise, the exposition of space law. But the United States proposed and the UN Committee agreed that the Court should be used in disputes between states as to liability for injury or damage caused by space vehicles.[87]

The Legal Adviser has also pointed out that while the arrangements for the IGY and for COSPAR were concluded between private scientific bodies and not on an intergovernmental level, they were generally supported by governments, and "no nation protested the transit of satellites launched under these auspices over its territory. . . . Up to the present the community of states appears to have been following the principle that the transit over any state of orbiting space objects or vehicles of any nation, so long as they are not equipped to inflict injury or damage, does not infringe the rights of other states and is reasonable and in the common interest of mankind. It is perhaps not too bold to suggest that we are here viewing the initial stage of development of a principle of customary international law permitting the orbiting of satellites of this nature." The United States has actually announced that it will not ask consent or necessarily give warnings of its rocket launchings, now that the International Geophysical Year has come to an end.[88] Deputy Secretary of Defense Quarles stated that the

United States would have no basis for objection if the Soviet Union put in orbit in outer space a reconnaissance satellite which would have the capability of observing the United States.[89]

The course followed by the United States after the end of the IGY in regard to the Antarctic and in regard to outer space presents interesting contrasts. It will be recalled that for the Antarctic a diplomatic conference of the twelve countries which had bases in that region was arranged after long negotiations, the suggested future basis of action proposed being essentially a continuation of the IGY with scientific cooperation and the freezing of political claims. For outer space, the United States supported the formation of the United Nations *Ad Hoc* Committee on the Peaceful Uses of Outer Space and is presumably committed to pursuing the quest for a United Nations arrangement. In the Antarctic the activities and actual presence of ten other states would make it impossible for the United States and the Soviet Union to dispose of the problem by a bilateral arrangement unless, indeed, they were prepared to do it by joint assertion of naked power, which is obviously completely at variance with political realities.[90] On the other hand, the United States and the Soviet Union are at this writing the only states in the "satellite club," and a bilateral agreement reached by them on outer space would be practically controlling, at least for the present. If it provided for a regime of general freedom rather than of appropriation to the exclusive use of the two powers, it would almost surely attract the support of all other states. So, for that matter, would a similar solution backed by the two powers in a UN committee, but the Soviet Union has so far not been prepared to cooperate on the terms proposed. Its opposition, however, seems to have been based on a current insistence upon "parity" of representation whether in a UN committee, in a meeting of foreign ministers or in COSPAR. On the substantive issue of the position in outer space the stand of the Soviet Union has not been made wholly clear.

While the Soviet system does not provide for public testimony before Congressional committees and the Soviets have not felt impelled to be as specific elsewhere as United States officials, some government statements and the writings of Soviet legal experts, implying at least some official sanction, have in recent years devoted some attention to the situation in outer space. The Soviet Union has, as noted, reserved its freedom of action with respect to claims in outer space. Soviet spokesmen and writers have urged that space be reserved for peaceful activities and, despite insistence on the absolute sanctity of airspace over the nation,[91] there is evidence of the possible acceptance of a different view for outer space. Interestingly enough, as early as 1927, a former Inspector General of Russian Civil Aviation wrote:

> In spite of the principle of unlimited liability over airspace, we should recognize the importance of the principle which is based on the Zone theory, as far as the flights of great altitude and the interplanetary communications are concerned. We hope that the considerations of military danger which have influenced the doctrine of air sovereignty will disappear with the apparition of craft circulating at a fantastic altitude and with unbelievable speed.[92]

The Soviet Union stands unquestionably for full and exclusive sovereignty over the airspace above its territory and territorial seas. The question remains as to how high this is projected. A textbook of 1957 emphasizes the extension of sovereignty to the stratosphere, since "the air territory of the State comprises the airspace above the land and waters of the State to unlimited height. In airspace is included the entire atmosphere; the lower strata (troposphere) and the upper strata (stratosphere). States as a rule do not establish any limitations on the height of their airspace." [93]

In the post-Sputnik I period, Soviet writers have argued that there is no legal regime for outer space, but that a satellite in space is like a ship on the high seas.[94] It has also been suggested that territorial air sovereignty ends at an altitude between twelve and eighteen miles above the earth's surface. Perhaps with tongue in cheek it is added that the Sputnik does not penetrate territorial airspace but rather territorial airspace passes under the orbit of the satellite.[95]

> The result at which we arrive thus reduces to the fact that the outer altitude limit of state sovereignty must be established in such a manner as to protect the state against encroachments on its territorial sovereignty, on its independence.[96]

A leading Soviet legal scholar, Korovin, writing in January, 1959,[97] observed that the Paris, Chicago, and related Conventions were inapplicable to cosmic space, that national law did not extend that far, and that analogies drawn from sea or air law were not pertinent either. Rejecting the concept of national sovereignty in cosmic space as "unscientific geocentrism, a return from Copernicus to Ptolemy," he also rejects a complete freedom, since, as with "freedom of the seas," anti-social acts equivalent to "piracy, . . . damaging ocean cables" and the like would have to be barred. While asserting that there are no agreed rules as to the status of space, Korovin insists that all universally accepted rules of international law, including the protection of foreign citizens, the ban on the use of force and intergovernmental responsibility and liability for losses due to governmental action, apply to outer space. The following passage suggests accord with the views of United States officials:

> Two groups of acts should be differentiated from the standpoint of world relations and international law: acts in the Cosmos that are acts of war and those that are not acts of war but serve in international relations as expressions of mistrust, ill will, and similar cold war consequences.
>
> Clearly one can not lump together the destruction of another country's sputniks by means of antimissile missiles with the presence of photo and TV equipment in a satellite, even if employed for reconnaissance.

It thus appears that to some extent the essential consensus does exist.

The closest approximation of an official statement of the Soviet Government's view on the subject is to be found in the draft resolution which the Soviet Delegation submitted to the First Committee in the Thirteenth Session of the United Nations General Assembly. In essence they proposed a "program for the peaceful use of cosmic space under international supervision." There was to be an agreed international program for launching intercontinental and space rockets for the purpose of studying cosmic space with research continued permanently on the same basis as in the IGY. But they went further in proposing a United Nations agency which would supervise the program, serving as a world information center and coordinating and aiding national research programs. The history of the debates in the United Nations and the work of its *Ad Hoc* Committee on the Peaceful Uses of Outer Space will be discussed in Chapter 9.

It is apparent that both the United States and the Soviet Union are sparring with the problems of outer space, waiting to see what may develop with the rapidly unfolding technological advances. It is already clear that the use of outer space can include military activities which may prove to be of very great importance. It is safe to assume that there exists in classified data information about prospective advances in "space art" of which the public is not yet cognizant. These are factors which have to be weighed against the pressures of smaller states and of sections of public opinion which call for the internationalization of space. The problem is quite comparable to that of the negotiations on disarmament. Again it may be said that as in Antarctica, long deferment of a commitment to an international solution may make that solution harder to achieve if it should later be found to be desirable. It is difficult to assert dogmatically that national security would be prejudiced by seeking to secure international agreement on the future status of outer space.

We are at the brink of what may become a new and greater age of discovery. Let us turn then to an analysis of the close-in, earth-oriented uses of outer space, leaving for Chapter 9 consideration of the problems raised by the unknown resources, strategic and material, of space and its possibly limitless potential for the creation of new centers of human population and power.

8. Problems of Controls for Space

MILITARY CONSIDERATIONS

There is a complex of problems directly connected with the security of all nations and man's ability to send vehicles into outer space which forms the critical background for consideration of all other issues. Intercontinental ballistic missiles, for example, spend at least a brief period at distances up to 600 miles above the earth. It appears too that the time may come when advances in space technology permit satellites with nuclear warheads to be launched secretly and to be maintained on distant orbits in advance of war until recalled for use against targets on Earth. They might also be used to jam attack-warning systems and to provide weather and other observations in advance of military movements on Earth. This crucial aspect of the problem—the control of such non-peaceful uses of outer space—is essentially part of the problem of world peace and disarmament rather than a peculiarity of the use of space. It is the same problem with which the world has wrestled for so many years without conspicuous success. Intercontinental missiles which pass briefly through outer space are but extensions of Napoleon's artillery; nuclear warheads descending from outer space will perhaps be more difficult to guard against but will do the same damage as those dropped from conventional aircraft.

Yet the fact that disarmament is in this sense a single overshadowing problem, whatever the arena of future conflict, raises special difficulties in the regulation of outer space for peaceful purposes. Indeed, the definition of "peaceful" remains, of necessity, inadequately specific and subject to change with time. In outer space the most peaceful uses may be suffused with military potentials. Even those satellites equipped to perform "peaceful" observations necessary for mapping, meteorological surveys, and other beneficial purposes will provide information inevitably useful for military purposes when they report what they "see" to the national state which launched them.[1] If weather can be controlled, droughts or storms may become a *casus belli* some day.[2] Without an inspection at the launching site (or a capture in space when that becomes feasible) it will not even be possible to know that a satellite is in fact destined for an announced peaceful mission. Present techniques, at least, are not satisfactory in differentiating on the ground or during the powered phase, between peaceful satellites and intercontinental missiles, all of which intensifies the danger of an accidental but devastating war.[3] Regardless of the launcher's purpose, the very existence of large numbers of objects circling the earth will cause confusion and possible disruption of radar warning systems. Short of a complete system of filing flight plans backed by an actual inspection of payload before launching or, alternatively, of a program of launching solely under the direction of an international organization, the military implications of almost any human penetration of outer space will be inescapable. The control of weapons which may pass through or operate from outer space is in this sense still an earth-associated problem—launchings will be from Earth for some time to come, though presumably not for all time; the targets are presently on Earth; and controls would be located on Earth.[4]

The question may then be considered as one of inducements to national action. A vital consideration in the history of disarmament and now in the regulation of activities in space, is whether some agreed limitation will put one or another state at a comparative disadvantage. Some of the proposals which have been made in the disarmament negotiations have been based on formulas designed to reduce total armament without shifting the existing balance of military power. It is not unrealistic to suggest that there is today a degree of balance in the scientific and technological capacities of the two rival camps. It would seem doubtful whether the momentary lead attained by the Soviets when they launched the first sputnik, or that gained by the United States in recovering the first living creatures from a passage through space, would be thought by responsible officials to represent a permanent advantage. The fact that the United States through its four years of monopoly of the atomic bomb did not use it or threaten to use it to impose its will on the Soviet Union does not suggest that the United States would refrain from reaching an agreement on space in the hope that some breakthrough would give it a new capacity to obliterate an adversary. On the other hand, neither the United States nor the Soviet Union can be expected to enter into an agreement which seems to handicap it. The history of the negotiations concerning a cessation of nuclear testing is in point and further emphasizes the always inescapable need for a system of verification or inspection. Here one can sound the hopeful note that space instrumentalities themselves might be used for international inspection as part of a system for safeguarding peace.[5] When one state perfects a system for televising from a satellite military activities in another state, and if such televising revealed threatening features, it might be assumed that their publication to all the rest of the world would be in the interest of the state which detected them and which was concerned to preserve the peace.[6] In other words, this might be a matter which could be handled on a shared international basis rather than restricted to national control for reasons of national defense. To sharpen the outlines of the picture it may be useful to notice a situation in which negotiations are already under way for an agreed international regulation.

The use of rockets to explode nuclear devices at very high altitudes has caused interference with telecommunications facilities on Earth, as well as causing auroral glows and circling the globe with a thin band of radiation. Thus when the United States exploded nuclear devices at a three-hundred-mile altitude over Johnson Island in the Pacific on August 1 and 12, 1958, and during Project Argus

SATELLITE ORBITS

Courtesy, National Aeronautics and Space Administration

Typical satellite orbits may be nearly circular or highly elliptical, and the plane of revolution may be equatorial, inclined, or polar.

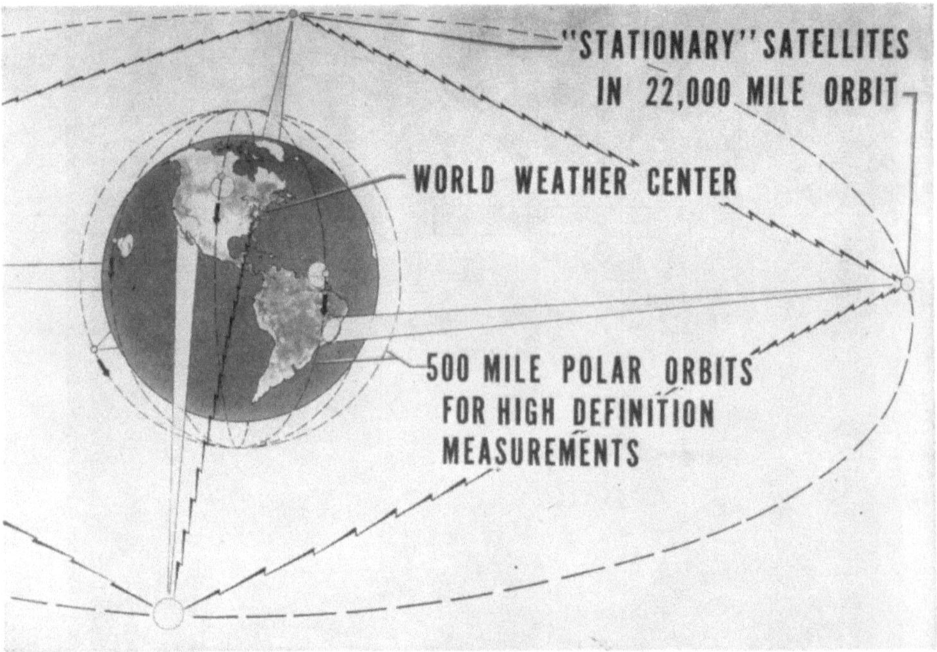

METEOROLOGICAL SATELLITES

Courtesy, National Aeronautics and Space Administration

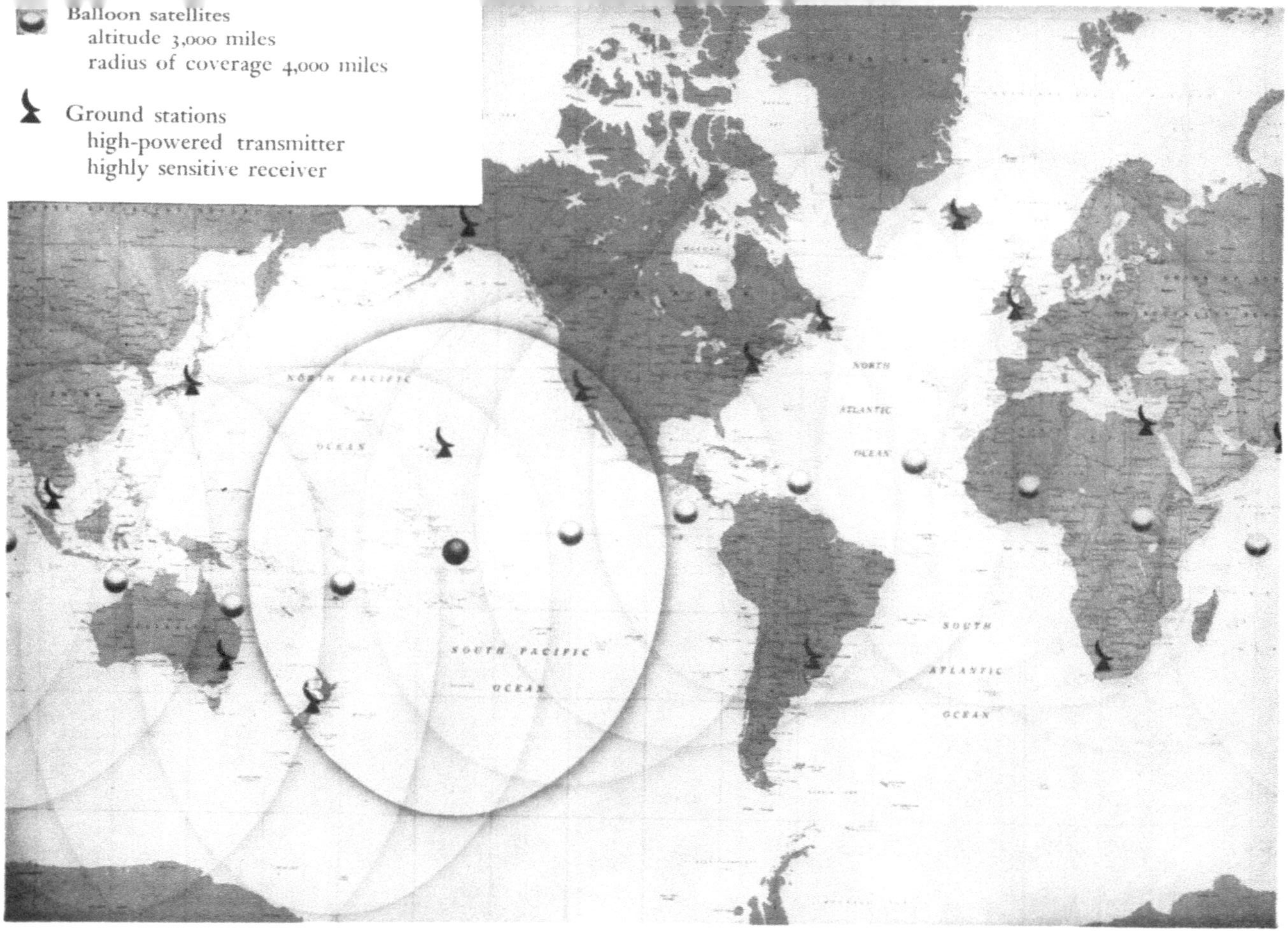

GLOBAL COMMUNICATIONS COVERAGE

Courtesy, National Aeronautics and Space Administration

in the Atlantic on August 27 and 30 and September 6, 1958, communications in the areas were knocked out for from several hours to a day; radio contact, after the first project, was cut off between the United States and Japan for several hours. The fields of radiation which were created persisted for several weeks. Radar was blurred too, leading to speculation at least, as to the possibility of the use of such a technique in wartime, since Project Argus established that certain effects of the explosions followed well-defined paths through space. An explosion over the Indian Ocean, for example, would have effects in western Russia, causing radio static which "can interfere with radio communication and . . . in principle with radar operation." [7] Banning of high-altitude nuclear explosions became an agreed subject for study by Soviet, British, and American scientists in Geneva in June, 1959, as a prelude to negotiation of an additional item in the projected treaty on the restriction of nuclear tests.[8]

The military implications of the new mastery of space can therefore be ignored only out of naiveté, blindness, or political convenience. But it is necessary to say that it is not possible for the writers to present a detailed informed military analysis. Writing in 1959 on any international problem the unofficial author is bound to remind the reader of the inescapable influence of dangers real or assumed. He is then entitled to discuss problems which will be faced if the dangers are averted. We venture to assert that the very discussion of those problems now may in some measure contribute to averting the danger. Accordingly, we shall next consider in greater detail what close-in peaceful uses of space may be available and how they may be regulated. Such uses not only confront political obstacles but also raise legal issues, and these will be analyzed.

COOPERATION IN PEACEFUL USES

While space vehicles, especially satellites, may well be performing useful "commercial" functions in the very near future (a subject discussed below), a very great value of man's entry into space is his increase of scientific knowledge, not only about space, but about the earth itself.[9] Much new information has already been obtained, for example, about the actual shape of the earth, which seems to resemble more a pear than the traditionally taught flattened orange. This knowledge permits more accurate calculation of distances on Earth and more accurate map-making. Information will be obtained on such subjects as whether or not the earth is heating up or cooling down, the nature of the atmospheres of the earth and other heavenly bodies, the nature and extent of electric, magnetic, and gravitational forces, and the like.[10] One of the most striking discoveries already made, for example, is that of a belt of high-energy radiation extending upward from a height of several hundred miles and substantially disappearing beyond 17,000 miles from Earth. The belt ranges from at least 65° N. to about 65° S., with highest intensities in the equatorial region and gaps at the geomagnetic poles. It has been named the Van Allen radiation zone after Professor James A. Van Allen, who led the group making the discovery.[11]

When it comes to learning about the universe, the possibilities of properly organized research in outer space are tremendous. Obviously, direct contact with the moon and the planets will give data that no telescope could duplicate, including details on the possibility of life as we know it. Even beyond that, most of the information that man is able to obtain about the universe comes to him in the form of electromagnetic radiations, most of which are invisible to the unaided eye. While we have developed sensors which permit us to see and measure much of the very short and very long wave length energy, only a part of the energy in space reaches the earth; blocking, deflection, absorption or screening by the earth's atmosphere and magnetic field leave us with perhaps one-twentieth of the information which is theoretically available. Indeed,

> the plight of the Earth-bound observer until now may be likened to that of a man imprisoned in a stone igloo with walls and roof 10 feet

thick. At the time of his imprisonment, a small hole in the roof directly overhead was his only connection with the outside world. Since then, through a great deal of labor, aided by ingenuity, he has been able to enlarge this roof opening slightly, and also to bore two small holes in the wall close to the ground, on opposite sides of his prison. Through these three "windows" come all the information that he is able to obtain about the world around him, and it is with this meager knowledge, coupled with his imagination, that he must construct a picture of the outside world.

Applying this idea to the radiation spectrum . . . we may say that man's knowledge of the universe has come to him through three "windows" in the spectrum. Through a radio window he "sees" a wide range of radio frequencies from different types of celestial objects; the Sun, the planets, possibly other stars, clouds of gas in our own galaxy, exploding stars, and outside universes. Through an optical window, he has been able to obtain other information about the universe with the aid of telescopes, spectroscopes, cameras, etc. And finally, there is the cosmic ray window, through which still other bits of information have come to him. Except for these apertures, however, the wall of the atmosphere shuts him in.[12]

Now, satellite-borne telescopes, spectroscopes, and other instruments will give astronomers a better chance to determine the size, age, and composition of the universe. Scientists will obtain information about the "nature" of space itself and about the radio-frequency radiation, cosmic rays, and other emanations in it.[13] Biologists and the layman as well may learn whether there are living organisms other than those on Earth.

Scientists are agreed however that, for optimum results, experiments should be conducted in a proper sequence and not be undertaken merely because the means are available, if they could contaminate or so alter the natural environment that other important experiments would no longer be possible. This might occur if a landing from Earth were made on a celestial body before observations were made to determine as closely as possible whether or not life existed there or what pre-life stage had been reached. It might "short circuit an otherwise tortuous history of evolutionary progress." Even a nuclear blast on a "dead" body, such as the moon, might be enough to foil geological studies and contaminate the area immediately surrounding the moon "for years." It is for similar purposes that scientists organized the CETEX, a program to insure that space vehicles which may reach the moon and the planets be "sterilized" to insure that no forms of life from Earth be introduced inadvertently. The United States, at least, has thus far taken precautions to see that its space probes are free of such contamination.[14]

Science has a record of international sharing and cooperation, and, in a project as vast and sensitive as the probing of the universe, coordinated efforts will prove not only useful but perhaps crucial. The long history of astronomy as an international science clearly demonstrates the efficiency and, indeed, the necessity of cooperation. Observation of natural celestial bodies, which (as viewed from the earth) are permanent and relatively slow-moving, has required the closest kind of international collaboration and the observation and tracking of man-made satellites and other space vehicles requires world-wide coordination for maximum efficiency as the earth turns on its axis.[15]

It is worth noting that the international Scientific Unions and UNESCO can contribute substantially to the organization and planning of such types of cooperation. The General Conference of UNESCO adopted a Resolution at its tenth session in 1958 which authorizes its Director General to participate in the study of scientific problems and the stimulation of research in such fields as the "exploration of extra-terrestrial space." UNESCO's viewpoint was presented in discussions at the United Nations Space Committee's sessions in May, 1959. It has also been indicated that "in this field . . . it may well prove advantageous to have the supporting authority and good will of the United Nations, particularly to assist in the resolving of international problems confronting the scientists." [16]

The IGY and COSPAR. As we have noted earlier, a joint scientific investigation of the universe has already been attempted in a limited form during the IGY. One major portion of the IGY program was aimed at an increase of man's knowledge about the atmosphere and the universe. Some six months after the passage of a resolution of November, 1954, by CSAGI, the agency established by ICSU to direct IGY activities, urging the launching of satellites, the Soviet Union formed a permanent interdepartmental Commission on Interplanetary Communications. In July, 1955, the United States announced planned launchings during the IGY, and project Vanguard, a special minimum cost satellite-launching vehicle, disassociated from military purposes but under Navy supervision, was begun. CSAGI worked out obligations to be imposed on satellite-launching countries in these terms:

It is RESOLVED that the National Committees of the countries having satellite programs be requested to provide to CSAGI or directly to any country requesting it, full technical information on optical and radio tracking equipment—and on telemetry equipment as appropriate.

It is RESOLVED that the National Committees of countries having satellite programs be requested to provide to CSAGI, or to any country requesting it, such scheduling and planning information as is essential for the preparation for and execution of optical and radio observations.

It is RECOMMENDED that for *all* IGY satellites the radio systems employed for tracking and telemetering be compatible with those which have been announced at the current CSAGI meeting [i.e., those of the United States] in order that the same ground-based receiving equipment can be used throughout.[17]

While the Soviet representative present apparently agreed to these proposals, only very limited information was received in advance of the actual Soviet launchings and no precise advance notice of launching has ever been given. Further, as we have seen, the sputniks did not broadcast on the 108-megacycles band to which the United States satellites and tracking stations were tuned. Divergencies in Soviet and Western views on the appropriate form and amount of data to be interchanged were not satisfactorily resolved.

To make the use of rockets and satellites most meaningful for all nations, Lloyd Berkner, the distinguished American scientist who was Reporter for Rockets and Satellites for CSAGI, suggested in December, 1956, that precise information on rocket launching sites and firing schedules be submitted and that World Data Centers be furnished "within a few weeks" after firing with information as to types fired, trajectories, weight, radio frequencies, and experimental results. As to satellites, launchers were to supply full tracking information, including "methods of data decoding," launching sites, time of launching, prompt data as to success of orbit attempt, precision orbital data within five months, and a "complete tabulation of the reduced, calibrated and corrected data derived from telemeter records within eight months." They were also to keep telemeter records available to other experimenters "for assurance against misinterpretations." [18] Apparently because the Soviet Union had conceived the satellite launchings as part of a military effort involving use of rockets designed as ICBMs, Soviet scientists were unwilling to make available information on such matters as launching sites, size, and weight of *all* objects in orbit (which would reveal data on the rocket launcher) and precise radio codes employed and, further, were unwilling to make their raw data available as received. As a result, no agreement on the data to be supplied was ever reached and much Soviet information is still not available to science. Lack of advance notice of such a venture as the Soviet moon-sun shot has also made it impossible or difficult for non-Soviet scientists to make useful contacts and observations, a particular loss for the periods when the vehicle is out of range of observers in the Soviet Union itself.*

The IGY demonstrated the value, in probing outer space, of co-operation among scientists at various places around the globe and of using different types of equipment, duplication of which would be expensive and largely wasteful. While it appears that a satellite

* It has been suggested that the meagerness of the data issued by the Soviet scientists is due in part to their not having it—that is, that their tracking and analytical preparations were not as good as their launching apparatus. Further, their United States counterparts have also had great difficulty, far more than was anticipated, with orbit analysis.[19]

on a true polar or equatorial orbit could pass over at least one station on every revolution, so that, by use of recording devices coupled with command control from a station at that point, it could make reports of conditions on each revolution, satellites in other orbits would require ground stations in more than one location or a much larger storage of information in order to receive the same data records. Vehicles launched toward the moon and some other celestial bodies are, due to the earth's rotation, also out of sight and contact with any single nation for part of each day. Even the United States, for example, with the aid of many observers abroad, was able to receive only about 40 percent of the available information from its lunar probe.[20]

The IGY also demonstrated that "peaceful coexistence and competition were practical realities," [21] at least to a certain extent. This led, in the field of space research, to the creation by ICSU in October, 1958, of the Committee on Space Research (COSPAR) to carry on some of the activities of the IGY.[22] COSPAR was initially given until the end of 1959

> to provide the world scientific community with the means whereby it may exploit the possibilities of satellites and space probes of all kinds for scientific purposes, and exchange the resulting data on a cooperative basis.

Further, it was to seek methods for bringing other, smaller nations into space research and to let their scientists prepare experiments to be carried out in the space vehicles of launching nations. COSPAR was also to [23]

> hold as a primary objective the maximum development of space research programs by the international community of scientists working through the ICSU and its adhering national academies and unions. Recognizing, however, the need for international regulation and control of certain aspects of satellite and space probe programs, the Committee shall keep itself fully informed on United Nations or other international activities in this field, in order to assure that maximum advantage is accorded international space science research through such regulations, and to make recommendations relative to matters of planning

and regulation that may effect the optimum program of scientific research.

COSPAR was at first composed of representatives from countries engaged in launching rockets or satellites, initially Australia, Canada, France, Japan, the Soviet Union, the United Kingdom, and the United States, together with three from countries engaged in tracking space vehicles, chosen on a rotational basis,[24] and representatives from the nine international scientific unions concerned with space research. The Committee functions through a small secretariat and an executive committee. The Committee met at London in November, 1958 and at the Hague in March, 1959, with Soviet scientists participating, despite the Soviet Union's boycott of the United Nations *Ad Hoc* Committee on the Peaceful Uses of Outer Space, created in December, 1958. At this March meeting, however, the Soviet representative suggested a revision in COSPAR's composition, and by April, the Soviet Union's representative at the United Nations was predicting a "boycott" of COSPAR as well unless the Soviet bloc was accorded "parity." It was the first political demand of this type concerning any of the IGY or post-IGY programs.[25]

The March meeting produced certain other more friendly gestures, at least on the part of the West. United States scientists, for example, reported American willingness to include experiments designed by scientists of other countries in American rockets and satellites and announced a program, sponsored by the National Aeronautics and Space Agency, under which foreign scientists from both sides of the iron curtain would be brought to the United States for extended periods as resident research associates in space-related projects.[26] Recently too a joint United States–Canadian space project was announced for the exploration of the ionosphere over the Arctic with rockets and a satellite to be furnished by the United States while the satellite's instrumentation was to be prepared by Canadians. The project was to be "strictly non-military."[27] Joint British-American experiments are also planned.

Meteorology. While the addition to man's knowledge about himself and his environment are alone perhaps worth the cost of the scientific investigation of outer space, the launching of such devices as scientifically equipped earth satellites and space probes is both a necessary forerunner of man's personal entry into the new areas and a technique through which life on Earth will be directly benefited by advances in meteorology, navigation, and communications. As pointed out earlier, the field of meteorology is particularly one in which space activities are already playing a part, though highly limited at present, and in which international cooperation is not only desirable but quite feasible despite the cold war.[28] Weather affects almost every known human activity and the weather services of the world are constantly striving both to increase their knowledge of current conditions and to make more accurate predictions. Most of the civilized nations of the world are already tied together in the World Meteorological Organization (WMO) which makes freely available to all participants the data which they collect.

Unfortunately, there are large areas of the world, such as the oceans and polar regions, where only spotty information is available through reports by ships and aircraft. Australia and New Zealand, for example, now receive very little information concerning conditions over the vast seas around them. A very large number of the less developed nations presently lack the facilities and trained personnel for making necessary observations and forecasts as well. These two factors mean that the information available on the world weather picture covers effectively only 5 to 10 percent of the globe and "lacks one quality of observation most necessary to synoptic meteorology, that of complete continuity in time and space." [29] Weather reconnaissance by means of satellites has been frequently suggested, as we have seen, for providing the necessary information about remote regions of the earth and the ability to view the earth as a whole in a short period of time. The value of more accurate forecasts in the United States alone to farming, water resource conservation, and prevention of loss of life and property has been estimated to run to several billions of dollars a year.[30]

Initially, satellites apparently will do little more than relay information on cloud patterns; however, with careful analysis this can provide "surprisingly good results in areas where no other information is available." [31] Information on wind direction, temperatures, atmospheric gas content, and water vapor content of the air will probably be available, and in such matters as forecasting for ocean areas and hurricane and typhoon warning services an improvement in current capabilities is anticipated. To be most useful, weather observations should be more or less continuous over wide areas and information must be available quickly, probably necessitating satellite weather data centers where incoming data could be processed by computers and disseminated within the hour. For this and related problems, use of the Provisional International Computation Centre (PICC), established in September, 1957, by Agreement between UNESCO and the Italian Institute of Higher Mathematics, might prove highly useful, as was several times suggested during the discussions of the UN Space Committee in May and June, 1959.

While WMO as constituted is not an operating agency, it now serves to coordinate national weather efforts and has played a direct role in obtaining weather information from whaling vessels. Should no broader international regime be developed, operation of satellites and data centers or, at the minimum, coordination of national efforts through the WMO or a new agency would appear best suited to maintain the legacy of the IGY, and, indeed, of earlier world-wide efforts in general in the field of meteorological data exchange—and the value to smaller nations of international services is potentially great. Further, an international program appears best geared to take advantage of those satellite orbits deemed most advantageous for meteorological purposes. An ultimate system to accomplish regular collection of meteorological data on a global basis might make use of six to eight satellites in 800 to 1,600 kilometer altitude polar orbits as well as several satellites in 35,000 kilometer altitude equatorial orbits.[32] The polar orbit scans the earth on each rotation and passes over the poles each time. A data station at the South Pole, for example, with several satellites in orbit reporting to it when they came overhead, each taking perhaps two hours for a circle, would receive an almost constant flow of information on conditions throughout the world which could be processed by computer and made available for tying-in with local reports and forecasts. The equatorial orbit at about 35,000 kilometers altitude results in a satellite whose period is exactly that of the earth. Thus one placed over the equator, moving eastward in its orbit, would appear to remain always at the same point in space as viewed from the earth and would be able to scan about 38 percent of the earth's surface, or 75 million square miles.[33] An internationalized program, too, would help allay fears of attempts to control the weather—a possibility which is generally felt by meteorologists to be far in the future but which has such important consequences that it cannot be ignored.[34]

At any event, meteorological satellites are already an actuality. The American Vanguard II, in orbit since February 17, 1959, is equipped with two electronic "eyes" (photocell sensors) which have observed cloud patterns and recorded their observations on a miniature tape recorder. The recorder has relayed its information on command to stations set up in the United States, Peru, Chile, Australia, Ecuador, and the British West Indies but, at this early stage, reports had to be sent back to the United States for evaluation. For what was essentially an experimental sample operation, the success achieved was gratifying.[35] Though the satellite was launched after the IGY ended, the experiment has been treated as an international one and information has been made available to all IGY participants,[36] a worthy precedent. As indicated earlier, the

United States is planning to have a number of meteorological satellites, including one with a television camera, in orbit by 1960–61, and the prospects for making great advances in meteorology are excellent.

Navigation. Another suggested use of satellites going far beyond the benefit to a launching nation is that of navigation aids. Such a satellite can "provide the basis for all-weather, long-term navigation systems to determine with accuracy geodetic position, speed, and direction of a surface vehicle or aircraft, north reference and vertical reference." [37] The satellite would radiate a continuous radio signal, but all observers would have to be provided with a table of satellite positions on which to base their own calculations. Charts can be drawn for Vanguard I, orbiting at fairly high altitudes, for about a month with reasonable accuracy, being less than five miles in error over a few days, for example. While new or improved techniques are needed, such navigational aids are in the near picture. An activity which has such great potential peacetime utility for both ship and aircraft movements round the world might well be coordinated, and indeed even operated by an international organization as in the long history of the Cape Spartel light. It might be equally feasible to deputize one nation to launch the satellite and maintain navigational charts, making them generally available, on the analogy of weather ship or ice patrol, or on the pattern of the joint facilities under ICAO. It is again an activity which will bring many direct benefits and which could be most usefully exploited through an extensive supporting organization on the ground to track and monitor the motion of the satellites and prepare and publish ephemerides. It is recognized that all this has distinct naval significance as well, particularly for long-range missile-firing submarines.

Communications. A further use of satellites, which has been touched on earlier, is as communication relays, either from one satellite to another, or, of more immediate concern, from one point on or near the earth's surface to another. Such satellites offer prospects of transmission of far greater quantities of information between widely separated points on Earth than is now possible, including overseas television, reliable overseas telephone, and cheaper long-range communications in general. The total band width of land lines, cables, and low frequency radio now in use is limited, while shortwave radio bands are crowded and unreliable due to atmospheric interference and ionospheric irregularity. Ultra-shortwave and microwave radio is usually limited to line-of-sight range. Satellites should make possible round-the-world communications by ultra-shortwave or microwave radio because the line-of-sight range at satellite altitudes is very great. Band width or channel frequencies at these wave lengths will go far toward solving foreseeable communications needs as well.[38]

Communications satellites might be placed on "24-hour" equatorial orbits and have almost a third of the earth in their line of sight. Such a hovering satellite, a prominent American scientist has predicted, might handle two billion messages a year and make possible calls to any place on the globe for as little as twenty cents a call.[39] Lower satellites would have less of a line-of-sight coverage but would need less power. Satellites would be either passive, that is, merely serve to reflect or scatter a signal from Earth, or active, in the sense of retransmitting messages. Systems using satellites would have to compete economically with other techniques for carrying messages but, as the American SCORE satellite of December, 1958, demonstrated, they are already technically feasible and the United States is experimenting with passive satellites in the establishment of a system to aid in New Jersey–California communications by 1960–61. Private companies, it has been reported, have been urged to carry out communications relay experiments with the proposed satellites.[40]

While the advent of communications satellites raises certain problems of international control directly, the first sputnik demonstrated that some aspects of the use of any space vehicle containing communications equipment for any purpose whatever might interfere with activities on Earth. The International Telecommunications Union has for years, it will be recalled, been charged with allocating frequencies among the nations of the world, and the United States obtained permission from the ITU to use the band from 107.9 to 108.1 megacycles for its proposed space vehicles. The Soviet Union, however, used for its sputniks frequencies of 20.005 and 40.002 megacycles, in violation of regulations promulgated through the ITU. Use of these wave-lengths, which was not even notified to the ITU, caused recurrent interference with broadcasts on the earth. The frequency 20.005 megacycles, for example, is in the center of a frequency band assigned by the ITU as the Standard Frequency Service for use by stations conducting "a radio-communications service for the transmission of standard and specified frequencies of known high accuracy, intended for general reception." Stations of the Netherlands and of the United States Bureau of Standards have been assigned frequencies in this area. The signals on the frequency of 40.002 megacycles are also on bands used by communications services in many parts of the world.[41] Thus, the sputniks appear to have interfered with instrument calibration and aircraft navigational aids, and they are known to have interfered with the United States Bureau of Standards Time Signals and with radio noise measurement stations. Radios in the United Kingdom also suffered from interference.[42] United States space vehicles have interfered with each other in broadcasting and in some cases have caused garbled reception of each other's messages.[43] Broadcasts from the ground and even use of radar equipment on the ground have also on occasion interfered with telemetered messages coming from the satellites. Further, as long as the batteries in these vehicles last, use of certain frequencies will be interfered with or, indeed, usurped unless a technique for silencing them is developed.[44] This is clearly important where the vehicle uses solar batteries with a possible lifetime of 1,000 years.

The problem involved in making appropriate provision for effective use of radio frequencies in connection with activities in outer space is thus many-sided. In order to avoid interference channels will have to be provided for communications systems involving satellites, for communications from and to space vehicles used for other purposes, and for such activities as radio astronomy, a growing field. Since this problem of interference affects all nations, an international regime establishing the propriety of the use of certain frequencies for space research and for space communications is essential, and in view of the speed of technological developments it is imminently necessary. ITU's regulations, for example, already provide that no avoidable interference of the type exemplified by use of satellite transmitters powered by solar batteries may be caused.[45] Indeed, consideration of this problem was stated to be of the highest immediate priority by the UN Space Committee in June, 1959.[46]

As we have seen, the ITU and its predecessors have been dealing, with at least relative success, with similar problems of the allocation of frequencies in this highly important political and commercial field for many years and the matter will be taken up at the Administrative Radio Conference of the ITU scheduled to begin in August, 1959.

The ITU is advised in its work by a scientific body, the International Radio Consultative Committee (CCIR), which meets every three years to consider technical radio questions and to make recommendations for action either by its national members or by ITU. While the CCIR does not allocate frequencies, it has the expert knowledge needed to lay out the technical pattern for allocation of frequencies for extra-terrestrial use. Indeed, at the meeting of the CCIR in April, 1959, participated in by "radio engineers and scientists" from many nations, including several Russians who were reportedly "amiable" and cooperative,[47] recommendations concerning the selection of frequencies to be allocated to transmitters on space vehicles and to radio astronomy were made. Reports were prepared on factors affecting the selection of appropriate frequencies for space communications in order to utilize to best advantage the "window" in the ionosphere which determines the range of frequencies usable for communications between the Earth and space vehicles.[48] A considerable study of the technical factors involved was also considered necessary and the CCIR set up a new Study Group to consider "the Technical Questions regarding Systems of Telecommunications with and between Locations in Space." *

If a more comprehensive organizational framework for controlling all activities in outer space is not provided, the ITU might well be able to work out and administer a reasonably satisfactory program for assuring the greatest usefulness of and the least interference by commercial communications satellites. Satellites launched for national political purposes, including propaganda attacks, obviously do not fit within any such program—without more comprehensive international controls an offended nation presumably will be left to take such action in outer space or on Earth as it can to relieve itself of the menace.

Other Uses. Briefly, satellites are already serving in the preparation of better maps of the earth itself,[49] and they offer such possibilities as the monitoring of diverse phenomena like ice movements in the oceans and forest fires on land. The delivery of mail by rockets has also been suggested as a short-run possibility, and an experimental delivery was accomplished over a hundred-mile distance by a United States Regulus missile in June, 1959.[50] Dr. Ramo, a leading American developer of rockets, has predicted that cargo rockets are imminent as well.[51] Transportation of humans, as a commercial matter, still appears to be only a long-run probability.

As one examines various international organizations and controls which may be useful in the management of man's future activities

* In addition to the studies at the international level, these problems are also receiving detailed scrutiny at the national level. In March, 1959, for example, President Eisenhower called for a study by a commission to make a thorough investigation of the federal government's role in the management of telecommunications, since "the situation is becoming no less complicated by prospective developments in satellites and space vehicles, as well as in defense weapons systems." N.Y. Times, March 4, 1959, p. 1. For studies and recommendations of United States scientists, see Int'l Astronautical Federation Doc. No. V/44-E, VI/87-E, IX/63-E.

in outer space it is obvious that man is still confronted with technological difficulties, but perhaps they are no greater than those he has already overcome. One is also aware that in several respects the political obstacles are even more serious, especially when one touches the nerves of national defense. As one turns to the legal problems, one need not minimize their complexity in recalling what Robert von Mehren has said with relation to another wonder of this age—atomic energy: ". . . once the facts of the field are mastered, the problems are for the most part similar to those with which we commonly deal although they are, of course, often presented in difficult factual environments." [52]

LEGAL PROBLEMS

Damages and Liability. A problem much mooted by the first generation of space lawyers is that of liability for damages caused to life or property on Earth, in the airspace, or in outer space by a space instrumentality through falling, collision, explosion or the like.* While it has been stated that the chance of satellites colliding is infinitesimal, portions of satellites or their carrier rockets which survive reentry into the earth's atmosphere could strike an airplane or cause damage on landing.[53] As space vehicles become larger and more numerous and are built of more durable materials, the problem of liability for injury caused by impact with persons or property will grow. The question of liability may be one of the nonpolitical subjects on which international agreement can be reached. The subject has high priority in the recommendations of the UN *Ad Hoc* Committee on the Peaceful Uses of Outer Space and in the proposals of the United States upon which those recommenda-

* Loftus Becker reported, in the *JAG* Journal for February, 1959, that: "Recently, just prior to the attempted launching of the first lunar probe, the President received a cable from a private citizen in one of the British dominions. In the cable, the writer informed the President that he had duly filed in his local registry of deeds a claim to a certain sector of one of the craters of the Moon, alluded to the proposed lunar probe, and concluded, 'I hold your government responsible for any damage to my property caused by your rocket.' One may safely predict that the new 'space age' will have its legal problems."

tions were largely based. The subject has also been described by the Soviet writer Galina as amenable to international arrangements, while Korovin has asserted that governments as the exclusive launchers, are today internationally responsible for losses occasioned.[54] In any event there are precedents which can be utilized in drafting an international arrangement concerning liability in these cases.

A comparable, but in some respects much more difficult, problem has already been faced in efforts to draft an international convention on liability for damage resulting from peaceful uses of atomic energy. A group of technical experts prepared such a draft convention on liability and insurance coverage for the European Nuclear Energy Agency of the OEEC which has been approved by representatives of seventeen countries.[55] The nuclear problem obviously becomes immensely complicated when an atomic facility is equipped by a supplier in country A, is operated in country B, and causes damage in country C. Precisely the same complications could exist in regard to a space vehicle. In the absence of a treaty, what law or laws would govern the liability of the supplier or manufacturer and of the operator? In the courts of what country or countries might suit be brought? If a judgment were secured against the manufacturer in the country where the damage was sustained, would that judgment be enforced by the courts of the country where the manufacturer has his place of business?

In the case of space vehicles used for peaceful purposes it is not to be anticipated that the damage from an accident would have the catastrophic proportions of one involving an atomic power plant, except perhaps when space vehicles are propelled by atomic power. This distinguishing fact makes it unnecessary here to discuss the insurance provisions which the OEEC draft treaty and other studies recognize as essential to spread the burden in case of nuclear catastrophe. The legal problem of liability remains.

The essential question is whether the law, presumably as embodied in a treaty, should impose absolute liability on the launcher of the space vehicle. In the present stage of the art, the launcher and the operator are the same; eventually one must anticipate the introduction of the additional factor of the fault of the pilot as in the case of aircraft today. Today the launcher-operator is likely to be a government, as Korovin says, but it might be a private company on government contract. On the other hand, a government after launching might permit private operation of a satellite, as for radio and television relays. In any case, the question of governmental liability would still arise. The instrument or vehicle itself may be constructed by a private contractor. As in the case of the atomic power facility, the accident may destroy the instrumentality itself, although this would be less certain in the case of the space vehicle. In any event it would seem to be an unfair burden to impose upon the person injured the obligation to prove a defect or negligence in manufacture or in operation. Accordingly the principle of absolute or strict liability should be accepted.

"Strict liability proceeds upon the theory that he who engages in an immensely hazardous activity must bear responsibility for the risks he thereby creates." [56] The doctrine has long been established in Anglo-American law in accordance with the leading case of *Rylands v. Fletcher*, which held that one who keeps or operates a wild or uncontrolled instrumentality is absolutely liable for any damage caused to persons or property by the instrumentality.[57] On this basis the aviation industry was at first regarded as a questionable and highly dangerous enterprise, properly subject to strict liability for damage to persons or property on the ground. Strict liability was imposed both by courts and by statute as well.[58] Continental codes in general also adopted some form of strict liability for damage caused by aircraft. Despite vigorous opposition from the aircraft industry and many legal scholars,[59] the American Restatement of Torts as late as 1939 took the position that aviation was still an "ultra-hazardous activity" on which strict liability for ground damage should be imposed.[60] As the industry developed, standards by which negligence could be judged on the basis of past experience emerged and there has been a tendency to retreat from strict liability in Anglo-American jurisdictions though the question is still unsettled—half of the states of the United States now deal with the matter by statute in one way or another.[61] It may of course also prove possible to have the type of liability imposed vary with the type of space activity engaged in.[62]

In the civil law countries, statutory developments have also moved in the direction of imposing strict liability for the operation of dangerous things. Under the Soviet Code, proof of intent or gross negligence of the victim or of *force majeure* are the only defenses allowed. These legal liabilities are those of an operator or proprietor. Different rules apply to the supplier of equipment or services and here it is American law which has taken the lead in imposing strict liability.[63]

As between the nations, an insurance principle was adopted in the Rome Convention of 1952 on Damage Caused by Foreign Aircraft to Third Parties on the Surface.[64] The Convention applies only to civil aircraft. Article 1 imposes an absolute liability for damage caused, though contributory negligence of the party injured is a defense under Article 6. The maximum liability is severely limited however, to a basic sum of about $36,850 plus certain increases based on the weight of the aircraft involved. There is no limit for the results of a deliberate act. States may require that aircraft be insured before permitting them to operate (Article 15). Actions for damages are brought before the courts of the state where the damages were occasioned (Article 20). While the Convention, like its predecessor of the 1930s, has been rejected by the United States and has received only a handful of ratifications, the concept of liability without proof of fault, coupled with compulsory insurance, is one which might prove useful in the early days of astronautics. In the opinion of the UN *Ad Hoc* Committee on the Peaceful Uses of Outer Space, the Rome "Convention and ICAO experience in relation thereto could be taken into account, *inter alia*, in any study that might be carried out in the future concerning liability for injury or damage caused by space vehicles. It was pointed out, however, that no international standards regarding safety and precautionary measures governing the launching and control of space vehicles had yet been formulated, and this fact also could be taken into account in studying analogies based on existing conventions." [65] Attention also should be called to the fact that the sum to which recovery is limited by the Rome Convention is far below what would be considered appropriate compensation in the United States. The OEEC draft convention on liability for atomic risks also seem grossly inadequate in limiting an operator's liability to $15 million which may under certain circumstances actually be reduced to $5 million, as contrasted with a possible maximum of $500 million available for indemnification in any one nuclear incident under United States statutory law.[66]

Another field regulated by international convention is that of shipowners' liability. The United States is not a party to the applicable conventions but has its own statutory law on the subject.

For damages suffered by passengers and goods within spacecraft, a more distant problem, there is the analogy of the widely accepted Convention for the Unification of Certain Rules regarding International Air Transport of 1929 (the Warsaw Convention).[67] In addition to providing for uniformity in the conditions of international carriage by air with respect to documents and the like, that Convention also established for the parties rules as to the responsibilities of carriers and their liabilities towards passengers, luggage, and freight. In exchange for establishing a *prima facie* case on behalf of anyone showing a contract of carriage plus injuries sustained, and limiting the defenses available to an aircraft operator, the Convention limited the maximum claim on behalf of a person injured or killed to 125,000 gold francs, or about $8,300 today. Recovery for injuries to property was also limited. A claim can be brought at the carrier's "domicile," principal place of business, place where the contract was made, or destination. Forty-five countries are parties, including the United States and the Soviet

Union. There has been widespread criticism in the United States of the low limit on damages recoverable in case of injury or death and of the applicability of the rules to domestic portions of international flights. A Protocol designed, among other things, to double the maximum amounts available as damages in such cases was signed by many nations at the Hague in 1957, but has in turn been subjected to vigorous attack by those who consider it still grossly inadequate.[68] The Convention does not apply to injuries to persons or property on the ground.

If strict liability is not to be the principle adopted, and negligence or intent is to be required, the Anglo-American evidentiary rule of *res ipsa loquitur* might be appropriately adopted. In brief, a complainant need only show an injury together with circumstances making it so improbable that such an accident would have happened without the negligence of the defendant that a jury of reasonable men could find without further evidence that it was so caused. Without such a rule, persons injured by falling aircraft (or spacecraft) often find it impossible to make a case—even with the rule, the burden of proof merely shifts and a defendant may still demonstrate that he was not at fault.[69] Some states have also adopted a "presumption of negligence," rule making the mere happening of an accident spell out a *prima facie* case of negligence against an airman.[70]

On whatever basis liability is assessed, it is obvious that, as Mr. Becker has put it, "The real problem in this area is one of enforceability."[71] So long as spacecraft are governmental vehicles, the responsible party would be determined by provisions for identification and registration as the UN Space Committee also suggested. The problems remain, however, as to how an injured party may bring an action against his own government if that government causes the injury, and how claims may be made by or on behalf of a national of one state against another state.

In the first case, under the domestic laws of many states, a judicial remedy is available to plaintiffs against the state only for negligent torts. This is the situation in the United States, for example, and raises again the problems of proof. There is in the statute moreover an exception for "discretionary activities" the scope of which is still not clearly fixed.[72] The tradition of sovereign immunity is much weaker in the civil law.

In the second case, there is the familiar problem of intergovernmental responsibility, which the UN Space Committee has proposed might be solved by requiring agreement on submission to the compulsory jurisdiction of the International Court of Justice in disputes between states as to the liability of states for injury or damage caused by space vehicles. The United States apparently would favor such an agreement.[73] If no comprehensive international program for control of activities in space is adopted, the use of claims commissions, particularly if an international indemnity or insurance program could be worked out, may be more satisfactory to states which have not been willing to make much use of the ICJ. In view of the well-established Soviet unwillingness to submit any question to an international judicial tribunal, consideration might be given to an agreement which would provide for the ascertainment of the facts by a mixed commission of inquiry composed of an equal number of experts from each country with no neutral participation. It might be possible to secure advance intergovernmental agreement that the amount of the damage would be paid when a majority of the commission agreed upon the facts establishing responsibility. As progress is made in the mastery of use of outer space, other solutions in keeping with institutional and technological developments in space may also become apparent.

Identification and Nationality. Another question already broached is the status of a downed spacecraft, whether fallen accidentally or through natural forces, or brought down by another state. What are the rights and duties of the state on whose territory it has landed or crashed? Need that state return the craft, its instruments, its crew? The Soviet jurist Korovin has argued that craft remain the property of the state launching them and should be returned. Mr. Becker has suggested that an international agreement, perhaps dependent on a launching state's undertaking to be liable for injury or damage caused by the landing and perhaps also on giving advance warning of the landing, if possible, may be the solution here. The UN Space Committee tentatively suggested agreements for return of property and personnel.[74] Particularly in view of the cold war attitudes of recent years with respect to balloons launched for ostensibly meteorological purposes and to off-course aircraft, the importance of the apparent accord between the views of Korovin and Becker should not be exaggerated.[75]

One other question which is at present not a matter of equal immediacy is that of jurisdiction over the spacecraft proper and acts committed on board. Here again analogies from air law and the law of the sea, both of which place primary emphasis on the "nationality" of the craft, the country of its flag or registration or possibly its actual ownership, may prove helpful. State aircraft, for example, have the nationality of the state, while civil aircraft have that of the state of "registration." It has been suggested that jurisdiction over acts aboard a civil aircraft might be taken by the state over which the craft was flying when the act occurred, by that of the last take-off, or of the first landing.[76] It should be noted that, as compared with taking jurisdiction over acts occurring on vessels at sea, some states have been slow to apply their own laws on the basis of the nationality of an aircraft. Thus, the United States made its law applicable to American planes over the high seas only in 1952, and only as to the jurisdiction of United States courts over some crimes on board.[77]

Ships "have the nationality of the state whose flag they are entitled to fly," and on the high seas the exclusive jurisdiction of the flag state is normally recognized over the ship and acts occurring thereon.[78] One problem which is still unresolved today is the regime applicable to a vessel flying the flag of an international organization, since the organization lacks a "legal system" like that of a state. The matter presumably will have to be resolved by international agreement.[79]

Nationality of a spacecraft, might easily be fixed today by assigning it that of the launching state. This will become a far more complex question in the near future as joint launchings are undertaken. If the UN Space Committee's suggestion for registration is accepted, nationality would clearly follow registration, as in the case of ships.

In many of the situations noted—avoidance of injury, liability for damages, jurisdiction over the craft, and the like—such a system of registration of spacecraft, notification of launchings, identification of launching lanes, and allocation of radio frequencies would avoid much of the difficulty otherwise to be anticipated.[80] There is an indication, as already pointed out, that the Soviet Union would be equally willing to act favorably on the questions of identifying marks, radio, and liability. When it comes to "return to earth covenants," inspection and regulation of launching sites, or exact time of launching, there is little immediate prospect of agreement.

Looking even further into the future,[81] we may find it necessary to add to our arrangements for outer space a space navigation code, analogous to the International Code of Signals and International Collision Regulations for ships at sea and the navigation code of the air constituted by the fifteen annexes to the Convention on International Civil Aviation. A space navigation code might include: a radio-communication code which would be patterned on the rules governing aeronautical telecommunications;[82] provision for certificates of qualification to be required, for their own protection and that of others, of space navigators * and other space flight and space base personnel;[83] rules governing the constructional, life saving and other requirements to be met with by spacecraft and orbital or ground stations on the moon or other planets or satel-

* The press reported in December, 1958, that the CAA had already, whether seriously proposed or not, received an application for a space pilot's license.

lites;[84] rules governing the "pollution" of space through improper discharges of waste materials, similar to those relating to the discharge of oil, and those suggested for atomic wastes today;[85] provision for the removal of derelicts or other obstructions similar to the iceberg patrol; a space rescue code, analogous to the relevant provisions of the Safety of Life at Sea Convention and the Search and Rescue and Accident Investigation annexes to the International Civil Aviation Convention;[86] and, ultimately, rules governing the carriage of passengers and goods, and possibly rules determining the law applicable to legal transactions occurring in space.[87]

As Jenks has also suggested,

> A large measure of international uniformity will clearly be necessary in respect of some or all of these matters, though it will of course be important in the early stages of development to avoid undue rigidity in technical matters and to allow considerable freedom of experiment in the use of new methods. Possibly this may be done by distinguishing, as the International Civil Aviation Organization does between standards the uniform application of which is recognized as necessary and with which states are accordingly expected to conform, and recommended practices the uniform application of which is recognized as desirable. The question will arise whether the necessary measure of uniformity should be secured by vesting jurisdiction over all activities in space directly in an appropriate international body or by relying on methods of international cooperation analogous to those which have developed in respect of shipping and aviation. In either event, provision for the continuous review of standards and practices in the light of new developments would be desirable, and close co-ordination would be necessary. . . .[88]

Eventually, too, we may need to deal with problems involving legal relations arising from regular travel by large numbers of humans in outer space, the settlement of the planets, and, still more speculatively, "relations with intelligent life encountered on other planets or in other worlds."[89]

9. *Chaos or Control?*

This book is concerned throughout with a choice of alternatives. The choice in question is presented to governments in two situations which are unique in that they are the only ones in which the very existence of any valid national or sovereign claim is still in question. The Antarctic is one; outer space is the other. One alternative is to subject the two situations to the same power struggle which has in history characterized the demarcation of national territories on the map of the world. The other alternative is to take time by the forelock and to agree that both situations will be subjected to an international rather than to a national solution or, one might better say, to a series of national solutions. Since this book is a "study in international organization," no attempt has been made here to describe the familiar pattern of the conduct of national sovereignties if their authority is recognized as extending over various sections of the Antarctic's frozen wastes. In Part II certain possible types of internationally cooperative regimes for Antarctica were described. In this chapter it seems first of all desirable to explain in some consecutive detail just what has transpired up to this time in the United Nations concerning outer space, even though the story will undoubtedly be a continuing one. The story as it has already unfolded reveals the positions and attitudes of several governments in addition to those of the United States and the Soviet Union, upon which we have concentrated hitherto.

THE ROLE OF THE UNITED NATIONS

We have seen that while neither the United States nor the Soviet Union has announced or renounced claims to outer space or to the celestial bodies, both have insisted that space be used for peaceful purposes only and both have, at different times, been instrumental in bringing problems connected with the use of outer space to the halls of the United Nations. The first steps were taken on the trail of the disarmament negotiations.

On January 10, 1957, President Eisenhower, in his State of the Union message, called attention to the dangers inherent in the development of outer space weapons and declared the willingness of the United States "to enter into any reliable agreement which would . . . mutually control the outer space missile and satellite development." [1] Four days later, Ambassador Henry Cabot Lodge submitted to the General Assembly of the United Nations a new five-point disarmament program which contained the provision that renewed negotiations should strive to insure that research and development activities concerning the propulsion of objects through outer space be devoted exclusively to scientific and peaceful purposes.

With respect to earth satellites, intercontinental missiles, long-range unmanned weapons and space platforms, Ambassador Lodge said:

> The United States proposes that the first step toward the objective of assuring that future developments in outer space would be devoted exclusively to peaceful and scientific purposes would be to bring the testing of such objects under international inspection and participation.[2]

Through that spring and summer the Disarmament Subcommittee of the United Nations met in London. In July Secretary of State Dulles summarized the United States position in those meetings regarding outer space, which was still a rather minor item on the agenda:

We are willing to cooperate in the working out of a system which would insure that outer-space missiles would be used exclusively for peaceful and scientific purposes. The use of outer space is still sufficiently experimental to make it possible to assure that future developments in this new area of knowledge and experimentation will be for the benefit of mankind and not for its destruction.[3]

This position was formalized as one item in a ten-point program submitted to the Committee by the United States, Canada, France, and the United Kingdom on August 28. The point was a modest one calling for cooperation in the establishment of a technical committee "to study the design of an inspection system which would make it possible to assure that the sending of objects through outer space will be exclusively for peaceful and scientific purposes." [4] The entire program was rejected by the Soviet Union, the outer space item playing no individual role in the question.

On October 4, 1957, Sputnik I was placed in orbit.

The scene shifted again to the General Assembly of the United Nations which in November, 1957, adopted a resolution along the line of the joint Western proposal at London; the Soviet bloc opposed.

So far, the space issue had been merely an incident in the general disagreement on disarmament. It was given special prominence in a letter from President Eisenhower to Premier Bulganin on January 13, 1958:

I propose that we agree that outer space should be used only for peaceful purposes. We face a decisive moment in history in relation to this matter. Both the Soviet Union and the United States are now using outer space for the testing of missiles designed for military purposes. The time to stop is now.

I recall to you that a decade ago, when the United States had a monopoly of atomic weapons and of atomic experience, we offered to renounce the making of atomic weapons and to make the use of atomic energy an international asset for peaceful purposes only. If only that offer had been accepted by the Soviet Union, there would not now be the danger from nuclear weapons which you describe.

The nations of the world face today another choice perhaps even more momentous than that of 1948. That relates to the use of outer space. Let us this time, and in time, make the right choice, the peaceful choice.[5]

Then on January 16, 1958, Secretary of State Dulles again proposed the formation of an international commission to insure the use of outer space exclusively for peaceful purposes.

On January 31, 1958, the United States successfully launched Explorer I.

On March 15, 1958, the Soviet Union countered with a detailed program for discussion at a summit meeting. The program lumped together the problem of "foreign" military bases with control over the use of space.[6] Simultaneously, the Soviet Union submitted its proposals to the United Nations in the form of a proposed agenda item for consideration at the Thirteenth Regular Session of the General Assembly. The "banning of the use of cosmic space for military purposes, the elimination of foreign bases on the territories of other countries, and international cooperation in the study of cosmic space" remained firmly linked. States were to undertake to launch rockets into cosmic space only under an agreed international program, and a United Nations agency for international cooperation in the study of cosmic space was proposed in order:

> To work out an agreed international programme for launching intercontinental and space rockets with the aim of studying cosmic space, and supervise the implementation of this programme;
>
> To continue on a permanent basis the cosmic space research now being carried on within the framework of the International Geophysical Year;
>
> To serve as a world center for the collection, mutual exchange and dissemination of information on cosmic research;
>
> To coordinate national research programmes for the study of cosmic space and render assistance and help in every way towards their realization.[7]

On September 2, 1958, the United States also proposed that a "programme for international cooperation in the field of outer space" be included in the Assembly's agenda.[8] On September 22 the General Assembly combined these requested items into a single "Question of Peaceful Use of Outer Space," and included the question in its agenda, referring it to the First Committee for consideration and report.

The First Committee proceeded initially on the basis of a Soviet draft resolution, which substantially followed the form of the Soviet Union's requested agenda item which continued to link the elimination of foreign military bases with a program for the peaceful use of cosmic space under international supervision.[9] On November 13 twenty nations, including the United States,[10] submitted a quite different draft resolution [11] calling only for the establishment by the General Assembly of an *ad hoc* committee on the peaceful uses of outer space to report to the Fourteenth General Assembly on:

1. (a) the activities and resources of the United Nations, its specialized agencies, and of other international bodies relating to the peaceful uses of outer space;
   (b) the area of international cooperation and programmes in the peaceful uses of outer space which could appropriately be undertaken under United Nations auspices to the benefit of states irrespective of the stage of their economic or scientific development;
   (c) the future United Nations organizational arrangements to facilitate international cooperation in this field;
   (d) the nature of legal problems which may arise in the carrying out of programmes to explore outer space.

On November 18, the Soviet Union submitted a drastically revised version of its draft resolution which dropped mention of a United Nations agency and of the elimination of military bases, and suggested instead the establishment of a United Nations committee for cooperation in the study of cosmic space and of a preparatory group, consisting of representatives of the Soviet Union, the United States, the United Kingdom, France, India, Czechoslovakia, Poland, Rumania, the United Arab Republic,

Sweden, and Argentina to draft a program for that committee.[12] The committee was to continue the spirit of cooperation engendered during the International Geophysical Year, to organize the exchange of information and to coordinate national research programs. Members of the twenty-nation group, however, objected particularly to the inclusion of so many Soviet satellites and "unfriendly" "neutral" nations on the preparatory group, and countered with a revised draft of their own resolution, which named as members of the proposed *ad hoc* committee Argentina, Australia, Belgium, Brazil, Canada, Czechoslovakia, France, India, Iran, Italy, Japan, Mexico, Poland, Sweden, the Soviet Union, the United Arab Republic, the United Kingdom, and the United States.[13]

Compromise on the states to be included proved impossible of attainment, and the Soviet Union withdrew its draft resolution, since no "unanimous" decision was in sight, and unanimity, they argued, was essential in these matters. The revised twenty-nation draft was then adopted as a whole by 54 votes to 9 (Soviet bloc) with 18 abstentions (Arab-Asian group plus Austria, Yugoslavia, Ethiopia, Finland, and Israel).[14] The Soviet Union, Poland, and Czechoslovakia immediately announced that they would not cooperate in the *ad hoc* committee's work.[15]

In addition to the "action" paragraphs already noted, the resolution recommended by the First Committee recognized "the common interest of mankind in outer space and that it is the common aim that it should be used for peaceful purposes only," and sought "to avoid the extension of present national rivalries into this new field." The *Ad Hoc* Committee was established purely as a study group to inquire into the problems of the space age and to report on areas of necessary cooperation and United Nations activities, but it marks the formal arrival of the United Nations on the space scene. Further, a perhaps surprising number of national representatives in the First Committee, in the course of discussing these draft resolutions, took stands on one or more of the "legal" and political issues involved.[16]

There was universal agreement on confining the use of space to "peaceful" purposes, a concept already expressed by the General Assembly. Several representatives felt that there were as yet no legal norms governing occurrences in outer space and that space represented a "judicial vacuum," but the Netherlander Schurmann argued that the "general principles of law recognized by civilized nations" must be applicable even now to relations between nations in space, a position not unlike that of the Soviet writer Korovin, mentioned earlier. Among those speaking to the point, there was at least general agreement that the rules of the Paris Convention of 1919 and of the Chicago Convention of 1944 related only to "air space" in the sense of the term *espace atmosphérique* as used in the Paris Convention, but only a few attempted to indicate where "outer space" began. The concept of *usque ad coelum* was, however, characterized as "absurd" with respect to "ownership" of outer space.

It was said that space, unlike the seas which are finite in nature, was "indivisible" and hence not subject to the extension of national sovereignty. Representatives of several small nations cited the lack of protests at the passage overhead of Russian and American orbiting satellites as "proof" of the nonexistence of national sovereignty at these altitudes,[17] although, as has been pointed out above, since the height of "airspace" remains undefined it cannot be said that satellites have not at various times moved through what would generally be considered "airspace." The concept that space was *res nullius* and therefore subject to acquisition was rejected by several spokesmen of smaller nations, who termed the "appropriation" of space or of heavenly bodies "impossible" or at least "improper," though the Chilean felt that the question was still open. Others seemed to insist that "space," the moon, the planets, and other heavenly bodies were "owned" or "belonged" or were the "common domain" or the "common property" of the "world" or of all nations or of all peoples.

The Canadian representative suggested that, while outer space might belong to the world as a whole, "jurisdiction" over space and its contents was properly in the United Nations. The Italian representative generously added to this the assertion that outer space "belonged" to all the states of the world, and that it was equally the property of "all other communities of thinking and organized beings living on other planets."

Representatives of several small powers, some of whom formally termed outer space as a *res communis omnium* or *res extra commercium*, stated that equality of access to and enjoyment of the benefits to be obtained from use of outer space were existent rights or at the least essential rules for man's development of space. Only a few seemed to insist on an unlimited free and equal right to "use" outer space, for most of those who discussed this point noted that rights of free use by all would be feasible only under international control, due to the danger to the rest of the world of abuse of such rights.

While both the representatives of the United States and of the Soviet Union have agreed to the need for the peaceful exploitation of man's new capabilities in outer space for the benefit of all mankind, neither has taken a position on the potential legal status of space and neither in fact has stated a position which would stop future claims from being made. Soviet representative Zorin talked of the importance of firing rockets into space only "as part of an international program," and Senator Johnson pointed out the usefulness of maintaining the current situation in which no "concessions" existed and of avoiding the mere "extension of . . . national policies" which might result from unilateral penetrations of outer space. Neither, as noted, talked in the narrower terminology of rights and obligations employed by many of the representatives of states not now having the ability to penetrate into space. Thus the lack of an agreed objectively definable law, and the many shades of national opinions, formed in the light of differing national interests and space capabilities, led to a far-ranging discussion of the implications, legal and political, for the world community of the advent of the space age. As the representatives of Canada and New Zealand correctly pointed out, however, "in the last resort, the choice between various possible legal arrangements for outer space [will be] a political decision."

When the *Ad Hoc* Committee met on May 6, 1959, not only the Soviet Union, Czechoslovakia, and Poland, but also India and the United Arab Republic were absent. The latter two states presumably stayed away in order to avoid involvement in what may have appeared to be a "cold war" dispute. The Soviet Union has recently been insistent on "parity" in both political and international scientific meetings, and probably this case was another manifestation of that policy. Actually, as in the contemplation of its proponents, the Committee's function was merely to study and define problems which it thought needed further consideration on an international scale. The nonpolitical nature of the Committee's task was repeatedly stressed by the United States delegation, which, as was to be expected, took the leading role in the first meetings.[18] The president of the Committee, Ambassador Matsudaira of Japan, emphasized that "the Committee will never be permitted to act in any sense whatsoever as an instrument of the cold war," [19] and other delegates echoed these sentiments.

After formal inaugural meetings, the *Ad Hoc* Committee formed a Technical and a Legal Committee. By mid-June these two committees had completed their Reports and the Secretariat had also prepared a Report on "the activities and resources of the United Nations, of its specialized agencies and of other international bodies related to the peaceful uses of outer space."

The members of the Technical Committee took as a basis working papers circulated by the United States and Italy on the scientific possibilities of use of outer space and on the activities and resources of the United Nations and the specialized agencies in the field of outer space.[20] The Committee also received oral comments from persons connected with such organizations as UNESCO, WMO, ITU, and ICAO.[21] There was general agreement that the exploration of space was "a task vast enough to enlist the talents of scientists of all nations." [22] Just as there was no way to limit the definition of "atmosphere" for WMO's weather purposes, there was general agreement that outer space was scientifically indivisible.[23] The usefulness of participation in space efforts by nations lacking launching capabilities, particularly through such voluntary cooperative scientific arrangements as COSPAR, was emphasized and the United States was complimented several times on its offers to permit scientists from other nations to design experiments to be carried out by U.S.-launched satellites.[24] The stress was on cooperative efforts of the COSPAR–CETEX type, though it was generally agreed that when the research stage was passed, functional intergovernmental arrangements of the WMO–ITU type were probably essential. The possibility of international launching sites was also raised.

The Technical Committee's report was approved by the *Ad Hoc* Committee on June 18 and became part of the Report to the General Assembly.[25] This report stressed that to make best use of all available talent, and in some cases due to the costs involved, "space activities, scientific and technological . . . even more than . . . astronomy . . . inherently ignore national boundaries. Space activities must to a large extent be an effort of Planet Earth as a whole." The connection between military activities and space research with its hampering effect on exchange of information was also noted, but it was concluded that the development of space vehicles had reached the point in several countries where it was a question of engineering only, not of science. Some of the potentially useful scientific studies were outlined, as were the techniques available for use and the possibilities for application of new knowledge to improvement in weather forecasting, radio communications, mapping, and navigation. International cooperation was felt to be desirable or even essential for such matters as orderly use of radio frequencies, registration of orbital elements at a central point, removal of spent satellites, termination of transmissions, reentry, recovery and return of equipment, identification of origin, and avoidance of contamination both of outer space and of the earth on return. The allocation of radio frequencies for space activities was suggested as "the first technical area in which immediate international action is required." The ITU was urged to act on the radio problem, and stress was laid on the usefulness of COSPAR, ICSU, UNESCO, the World Data Centers, and WMO in promoting international cooperation. A need was felt for a suitable center related to the United Nations to act as a focal point for cooperative efforts in outer space. It was suggested that the United Nations Secretariat might include a small section to keep cooperation under review, or a new UN body might be created to do that job. There was, however, no need yet for "an international agency for outer space."

The Legal Committee proceeded with the aid of working papers and drafts submitted by the United States and Mexico.[26] Its Report was also approved by the *Ad Hoc* Committee on June 18. The Committee observed that the provisions of the United Nations Charter and of the Statute of the International Court of Justice are, as a matter of principle, not limited in their operation to the confines of the earth.[27] It was agreed that not enough was now known about the actual and prospective uses of outer space to make a comprehensive code practicable or desirable, but that it was necessary to take "timely, constructive action and to make the law of space responsive to the facts of space." "It was unanimously recognized that the principles and procedures developed . . . to govern the use of such areas as the air space and the sea * deserved

* In a proposed draft report, the words "the sea" were followed by "and other regions of the Earth." These words were deleted at the insistence of the Argentine representative who argued that they might be taken to mean the polar regions and that "the territories of Antarctica were subject to national sovereignty, a fact that excluded any possibility of analogy with air [*sic*] space. As the general trend

attentive study for possibly fruitful analogies . . . [though] outer space activities were distinguished by many specific factual conditions . . . that would render many of its legal problems unique."

Among legal problems susceptible of priority treatment, it was suggested, is the broad one of freedom of outer space for exploration and use. Here, the Legal Committee, in mentioning the flight of space vehicles "over" countries during the IGY, suggested that "with this practice, there may have been initiated the recognition or establishment of a generally accepted rule to the effect that, in principle, outer space is, on conditions of equality, freely available for exploration and use by all in accordance with existing or future international law or agreements."

Among other priority problems included by the Committee was liability for injury or damage caused by space vehicles, including the need for machinery to determine liability and assure payment of compensation. Here the Committee suggested the compulsory submission to the International Court of Justice of disputes between states as to liability, and it considered relevant the ICAO experience with respect to the 1952 Convention on Damage Caused by Foreign Aircraft to Third Parties on the Surface. Allocation of radio frequencies, termination of transmissions, avoidance of interference between space vehicles and aircraft, identification and registration of vehicles through markings, call signs and orbit and transit characteristics, registration and coordination of launchings, and reentry and landing problems were also considered of current importance.

Problems which may be ignored for the present, as either too remote from the point of view of technological development or because activities can be conducted without their resolution, were thought to include the determination of precise limits between

---

of the report was in favor of treating outer space as *res communis omnium*, he wished to ensure that the . . . paragraph was not interpreted to mean that the same situation prevailed with respect to Antarctica." U.N. Doc. No. A/AC.98/C. 2/SR.5. (PROV).

airspace and outer space, the provision of regulations against contamination of outer space or from outer space, the promulgation of rules covering sovereignty, exploration, settlement and exploitation of celestial bodies, and rules for the avoidance of interference among space vehicles.[28] As is obvious, the Report avoids commitments on several problems which many feel are more imminent than the Committee was cautiously willing to acknowledge.

The Secretary-General's Report usefully details the activities of the international scientific organizations—the Scientific Unions, ICSU, the IGY, COSPAR, and others—in relation to the need for cooperation and coordination of research in outer space. The same treatment is then accorded to intergovernmental organizations, the United Nations itself, UNESCO (and the Provisional International Computation Centre in Rome, a UNESCO-sponsored project), WMO, ITU, and ICAO. The essentials of this report were also included in the *Ad Hoc* Committee's Report.[29]

Chairman Matsudaira's suggestions,[30] modified by Swedish proposals and some slight changes advocated during the discussions, were adopted as the conclusions of the *Ad Hoc* Committee to be transmitted to the General Assembly along with the three reports already described.[31] These conclusions may be briefly summarized. No autonomous intergovernmental agency should be created at this time, nor should any such existing agency be asked to undertake over-all responsibility for space matters. There might be a small unit in the Secretariat to serve as a focal point for cooperation and a small committee advisory to the Secretary-General. Finally, there could be a special committee of the General Assembly (although the criteria for its composition could not be agreed upon [32]) which would fulfill the following functions:

(a) to provide a focal point for facilitating international cooperation with respect to outer space activities undertaken by Governments, specialized agencies, and international scientific organizations;

(b) to study practical and feasible measures for facilitating international cooperation, including those indicated by the *Ad Hoc* Committee in its report under paragraph 1(b) of the resolution;
(c) to consider means, as appropriate, for studying and resolving legal problems which may arise in the carrying out of programmes for the exploration of outer space;
(d) to review, as appropriate, the subject-matter entrusted by the General Assembly to the *Ad Hoc* Committee in Resolution 1348 (XIII).

Thus, the Committee stressed at most a role of coordination or the promotion of cooperation for the United Nations, though the Swedish representative expressed fears that there might be an increasing gap between the great forward surge of space activities and the efforts of the United Nations to promote the use of space for the benefit of all mankind unless immediate action was taken within the United Nations.[33] Others, however, insisted on "modest proposals" to meet only the most pressing needs.

The Committee finished its work and approved its Report to the General Assembly on June 25, 1959.[34]

The *Ad Hoc* Committee was obviously very cautious. This is quite understandable in the political circumstances, since in any actual program for promoting the peaceful uses of outer space the nonparticipation of the Soviet Union would rob the effort of much of its value. It was the obvious hope that if Soviet nonparticipation were due to any misunderstanding, that difficulty would be overcome. Of course, if as a matter of national policy the Soviet does not wish to cooperate in this effort, it will find pretexts for further refusals. It is a plausible guess that in these times the Soviet government prefers to have concessions emanate from a summit meeting instead of from lower routine channels, in order that the summit meetings might seem to be the most fruitful method of reaching agreements. Although factual and scientific studies could proceed without the participation of the Soviet Union, it would seem rather futile for the United States and others to seek to reach an agreement on an outer space regime without the participation of the only other state which now has the capabilities for using outer space.

PATTERNS FOR POLITICAL ACTION IN OUTER SPACE

Putting aside the natural tendency to scoff at what still seems an imaginary future, one can delineate several possible alternative courses of action which states may follow in the treatment of the outer space problem in the years ahead.

First, they may reject all international solutions for the future of outer space and decide that it and the moon and the planets shall be left like terrestrial spaces to be acquired by the first state which develops the capacity to occupy or to exercise control. Or they may by inability to agree allow that situation to develop in practice. At the moment they are temporizing with a partial acceptance of a United Nations approach in the manner just described. So long as neither of the great "space powers" chooses to force the issue in outer space—or on Earth—and so long as they fail to achieve a general accommodation, it is not unreasonable to guess that the consideration of outer space will follow much the same course as the long-drawn disarmament negotiations. There are very few triumphs in those negotiations, but it is appropriate to note that there has been a voluntary cessation of nuclear tests during the rounds of scientific and political discussions. The powers remain poised in unstable equilibrium.

Second, a pattern may emerge which is similar to the "national" solution envisaged above but differs in that it involves a combination of states joining together to speed the acquisition of extra-terrestrial spaces. It is conceivable, however unlikely, that the two great powers possessing substantial space capabilities today might join together in controlling outer space and ruling the celestial bodies together in a condominium over cosmic space. Or they might agree to divide the heavens between them, as Spain and Portugal in the fifteenth century divided the globe. One wonders which nation now developing might in that event play the role of Elizabethan England.

More likely, considering the present inability of the United States and the Soviet Union to agree on terrestrial sharing arrangements, would be a joint national venture of states grouped on one side or the other in the cold war. The United States, Britain, and France, or all the NATO powers combined, or the Warsaw Treaty group, or perhaps, as it evolves, the European Community, might occupy or control jointly the moon or a planet. They would thus seek to be in a position to bar all outsiders, while sharing the spoils—whatever they prove to be.

To the extent that the joint sovereignty was over a relatively unpopulated place useful only for an emergency port for space craft or for celestial observation for example, the successful United States–British control over Canton and Enderbury Islands comes to mind as an encouraging precedent. To the extent that the joint control became involved with an eventual population or important economic or strategic advantages it would presumably fail, as have other condominiums of the past.

Third, a national solution for the future of outer space may be accompanied by initial or eventual nonspecific commitments by the national owners to keep their new territories demilitarized, or to permit free access, or to keep the United Nations or some other body informed as to their activities in these new additions to the national domains. Such promises have not been kept in the past where they conflicted in any way with a real or imagined national interest. There is no reason to suppose they would be better kept in the future. An analogous situation would develop if acquisition of sovereignty were generally renounced but outer space was still in fact subjected to a struggle over division into spheres of influence. With economic systems at war on Earth it is difficult to imagine a workable agreement on free development of new national areas elsewhere. Any such concept would be especially difficult for socialist and other planned economies to assimilate institutionally.

Fourth, the principal states might agree to a solution giving effect to defined and enforceable rights vested in the world community, preferably in advance of the acquisition by one or more states of capabilities permitting effective unilateral occupation of celestial bodies or control of outer space. For the first time on the international scene, it might be possible to avoid "the giddy cycle of law chasing power but never quite catching up." [35] This crucial fourth possibility will be considered at length later in this chapter.

FUNCTIONALISM AND POLITICAL PATTERNS

As in the case of the many possible national solutions for the Antarctic, international cooperation in many functional activities will be possible in the use of outer space and in fact may be predicted almost irrespective of the form of the political solution which is evolved. One of the frequently advocated approaches to the problem of controlling man's activities in space has, indeed, been a gradual one along these lines. It has been suggested, for example, that man's foreseeable needs might be met by a general rule that outer space be used only for peaceful purposes, combined with special limited cooperative arrangements for participation in "shareable" uses as they become known, following patterns similar to those discussed in Chapter 8. Some of the problems of peaceful use are, as we have seen, similar to those closer to the earth which have already been dealt with through such international arrangements as ICAO, WMO, and ITU.

Supporters of this point of view do not, of course, suggest that there be anarchy in outer space. What is suggested by those who would, wisely or unwisely, make haste slowly is that "the choice of rules . . . will represent a major policy decision for each of the various states" and that, at this time, the primary need would appear to be simply that "the activities of man on the other celestial bodies shall be peaceful. . . ." [36] Cooperation in technological and scientific matters in outer space, they suggest, can "be pursued independently of control over military uses. . . ." [37] At most, an international system of cooperation or coordination would ultimately be established, perhaps under the United Nations or, at least, with some such relation to it as that of the International Atomic Energy Agency.

What functional cooperation, however beneficial, cannot provide is assurance of the national security of the states of the world —that activities of man in outer space and on the other celestial bodies *will* be peaceful. This is a crucial omission. Further, the critical question whether peaceful and military activities in outer space can in fact readily be segregated must still be posed. If the answer is "no," the feasibility of use of functional arrangements as a substitute for an over-all political regime must again be queried. It is true that the civil uses of aviation and, to a much lesser extent, of atomic energy have come under limited international arrangements while their military uses remain largely unregulated. How to assure a real separation of peaceful from military uses of atomic energy and now of outer space is indeed a key problem in a world bristling with antagonisms, rivalries, and fears. Can it be realistically expected that the novelty and present mystery of space assure the success of techniques which have failed to give general peace on earth? In an international community which lacks both the capacity to separate neatly the peaceful uses for control by international technical agencies and the international institutions needed to guarantee national security in general, "there is no good reason to suppose that man's normal potential for good or evil would in any way be altered by his advance into space or that national struggles for supremacy would not simply be projected onto the larger screen of the cosmos unless checked at the very outset." [38] Responsible statesmen in every nation would have to echo the statements of Congressman Teller:

National space policy, like national security policy, is determined primarily by the requirements of world politics. We do not want to carry on the burden of armament, but we find that national survival and the successful pursuit of our national objectives depend upon military strength. In the absence of agreed upon and workable international programs for the control and use of outer space, the United States has little choice but to develop a national space policy as an integral part of its national security program.[39]

The line of functionalism—its relative acceptability to sovereign states, the considerable achievements in limited but useful areas of international technical cooperation which have resulted from international technical arrangements—should not blind us to its inherent limitations. Within these limitations, functionalism can be highly productive; it can never be what it is sometimes apparently intended to be, a substitute for a workable political solution.

The point is worth illustrating. If we assume that national solutions to the control of space are in fact evolved, with international cooperation substantially limited to technical matters and nations left to pursue their national security in a traditional manner (a not entirely unlikely set of assumptions), what would be some of the likely results? National security programs are apt to try to cope with many eventualities. There has been a spate of writing and discussion, for example, about the possibility of a limited war being waged. In a world which has known total war and which fears total annihilation and yet somehow cannot, for complex reasons, be brought to accept a single effective international political regime with the power to settle international political disagreements without resort to force, the concept of limited war has indeed taken on an almost comforting air. If we assume for the moment that the concept itself is meaningful and that some useful conceptual and actual dividing line between limited and total wars can be drawn, issues inherent in recent speculation—as to whether a limited war would be possible in Europe or only on some jungle frontier, whether weapons could be limited to those called "conventional," or whether one can use "small" atomic weapons without resorting to hydrogen bombs—make it obvious that keeping a war "limited" promises to be a challenging task.

In general, it appears that conflict can be kept more effectively limited when staged on the political periphery. It will be seen that this notion can be readily extended to include hostile activities in outer space and eventually around the celestial bodies. The thought has been that if the "space powers" develop the capability of maintaining an arsenal of anti-missile or anti-satellite missiles, they could destroy Sputniks and Explorers and, as time goes on, interfere with space platforms and other types of satellites. Such hostilities might not, it could be supposed, seriously harass people on Earth, especially if during this limited war the parties kept an agreement which may be made to ban nuclear explosions in the upper reaches. When satellites are manned the combat would take on an additional aspect, but on Earth it might seem quite unreal. It would be newsworthy more for its novelty than as provocative of general war. The American public, it must be said, has become somewhat calloused to reports of aerial incidents over remote lands and seas; the Soviet public does not need to know about them if the Soviet government finds such knowledge inconvenient.

These space incidents, one may suppose, would begin as measures of self-defense; it has been made clear by officials of the United States government that they hold Article 51 of the United Nations Charter which recognizes the inherent right of self-defense to be applicable in outer space. In the UN *Ad Hoc* Committee on the Peaceful Uses of Outer Space a cautious statement recognizes "the relevance" to space activities of the provisions of the Charter, but the specifications are to the Charter's principles of friendly and peaceful cooperation for the general welfare of mankind. Just as some of the aerial incidents over the Baltic and Japan Seas involve allegations that a plane has strayed into the reserved domain of airspace over the territorial sea, so one could anticipate allegations that a satellite or missile when attacked had descended into national airspace, since we have seen that the outer limit of airspace has not been defined. In other cases it might be argued that the object destroyed was identified as a hostile missile carrying a warhead.

Such arguments might be accompanied by repeated suggestions from one country that future unfortunate incidents of this kind could be avoided if the other country would only accept the proposals for the registration with an international organization of all missiles and timetables of launchings, and for a system of international inspection to verify the facts. One can see that, at least for purposes of diplomatic argument, a limited war would almost inevitably lead one party to find it advantageous to turn back to the pattern of international cooperation as the most acceptable solution.

One may carry the speculation to the time, probably not very remote, when landings are made on the moon. The first soft landing of instruments will be another technological triumph, as will be in turn the first manned landing. If a limited war in space is then being carried on, and if the capacity should exist, the instruments or the manned station might be destroyed by a counter missile, the launching of which could be denied or the impact of which could be ascribed to directional error for which regrets might be expressed. Again one can conceive of the diplomatic war being waged simultaneously in the United Nations. If State A succeeded in establishing a manned station on the moon and State B lacked the immediate capability to destroy it, a diplomatic note could be sent from B to A saying in effect that B regrets it cannot guarantee that A's installation will not be damaged or destroyed by the impact of missiles which are being launched for purely scientific purposes in the general interest of mankind; such scientific experiments, it could be argued, cannot be abandoned because of an illegal attempt to appropriate the moon which is the common property of all states. Subsequently the General Assembly of the United Nations might rather easily be induced to adopt a resolution to the effect that it deplored the wholly unwarranted and legally indefensible effort of State A to extend its territorial sovereignty over the moon. There would, after the fact, be renewed attempts to secure general agreement upon an international regime for outer space and for the moon and the planets.

Similarly, the more immediate and more dangerous problem is that of the identification of missiles or satellites which may be picked up on radar screens and then, rightly or wrongly, taken to be the launching of a hostile attack—not against an earth satellite or the moon, but against the people and territory of a rival state on Earth. After all, as has been said above, space problems are essentially earth-bound.

The problem of national security can thus be seen as one indivisible whole. Speaking in the broad terms of choices between preventive war, military alliances, and collective security, it is clear that states cannot choose one for their activities on Earth and another for their activities in space. In this sense, both peace and war are indivisible. Accordingly, a self-denying ordinance by states to limit their space activities to "peaceful" pursuits, while perhaps the maximum politically obtainable now, leaves open the usual questions of the definition of "peaceful" and of inspection to ascertain whether actual use conforms to the agreed standard. It raises anew the ghosts of earlier experiences with neutralized and demilitarized areas, as well as the unsatisfactory progress in the pursuit of atomic controls and the lethal competition in distrust we have been enduring for over a decade. For these reasons a total arrangement for outer space, designed to keep it from becoming an arena for national security problems and at least to assure governments that their defense is as secure as formerly, is appropriate.

In addition to these negative reasons, there are certain other characteristics of the space problem which indicate both the utility and inherent feasibility of an immediate broad internationalized solution. In the first place, at the present time space activities are wholly in the hands of governments. If governments agreed to abstain from some activities or to carry on others in certain ways, there would be no problem of policing lawless individuals, as has had to be done on Earth in the control of piracy or the trade in slaves, munitions, or narcotics. In the second place, paradoxically enough, governments are not yet in fact physically capable of reaching out to occupy and thus to appropriate the moon or Venus or Mars as in the history of Earth they have seized the Philippines, Madagascar, or Ceylon. (Antarctica seems in this respect to lie somewhere between the history of the past and the prospects of the future.) These characteristics may, and probably will, change and change rapidly; should the time be anticipated or awaited?

Further, while outer space and the celestial bodies have not generally received a differentiated treatment in this study, outer space is essentially just a directional or locational expression. The moon and the planets are tangible and may, as we have said, possess the potentials of sustaining a population or be the source of mineral or other wealth. Jurists have been able to talk about sovereignty in airspace because airspace at least has a fixed relationship to the land surface of the earth where sovereignty resides; outer space has no such constancy. So while it is impossible to speak of the projection of sovereignty from the earth over outer space, it is quite realistic to think in terms of the acquisition of control of outer space and even the establishment of populated centers on the moon and at least some of the planets. Even if an effective international agreement provided that national sovereignties should not be extended into outer space in order to be exercised over the heavens, and somehow eliminated national rivalries, when man develops the necessary capabilities there will arise questions of occupation, use, and exploitation of resources by human beings whether or not in government service, the control of such persons, their comings and goings, and their mutual relationships. All of that may require a regime going far beyond the type of international functional coordination or even administration which was contemplated by the United Nations *Ad Hoc* Committee on the Peaceful Uses of Outer Space. Even the suggestion of this approach is likely to appear premature and to provoke skepticism, just as have similar suggestions on the threshold of previous scientific or technological innovations. The modest report of the UN Space Committee seems almost banal today, but it would have been considered revolutionary or absurd five years ago.

We must recognize, too, that some of the problems of peaceful use of outer space—the need for vast outlays of capital, the development of radio procedures, concepts of liability for damages, identification techniques, arrangements for using scientists of all nations and sharing scientific data and for cooperation in use of weather information and navigational guides—are with us now or will be very shortly. Similarly, problems of military use, like the flight of missiles through outer space and the development of "spy" satellites, for example, are already here, despite the protestations of the major powers in favor of the peaceful use of outer space.

Major international problems that linger do not always disappear. They often grow less soluble as positions become inflexible and entrenched—vested interests grow and national pride is involved, even where "security" is only a fig leaf for rapacity. This is a lesson taught by the history of the Antarctic. As the Australian representative said in the United Nations First Committee in November, 1958:

> Experience in Antarctica may suggest how difficult it may become to consider the problems of outer space impartially and on a universal plane if decision is left until states have established themselves permanently in the field.

What might be called the "United Nations habit" exists. And we have been suggesting that even the Great Powers can be expected to appeal to an international solution at one time or another when it appears essential or convenient. Whether the Great Powers agree or not, many states will favor an international approach to preserving the use of outer space for the benefit of all mankind. There are some basic patterns for international control from which they can make their choice.[40]

PATTERNS FOR INTERNATIONAL CONTROLS

If it becomes politically possible to achieve something more than a strictly functionalist approach to the problems of outer space, a solution might well center in the United Nations system, but it need not do so. Although the dividing line between what we have termed national and what we will call international solutions is necessarily an arbitrary one, for present purposes a minimum condition of an international settlement must include the "basic rule" suggested by the Secretary-General of the United Nations, Dag Hammarskjöld, in May, 1958, "that outer space, and the celestial bodies therein, are not considered as capable of appropriation by any state and that . . . the overriding interest of the community of nations in the peaceful and beneficial use of outer space . . ." be recognized and pursued.*

Alternative methods of achieving this minimal condition exist. From the legal point of view, there could be either a universal treaty or a resolution adopted unanimously by the General Assembly which might well be considered as the equivalent of a treaty rule. Each method has advantages and disadvantages: a treaty may be adhered to without consideration of other factors bound up with a United Nations program, but if it is not universal it does not bind non-signatories. An Assembly resolution is technically only a recommendation, even to members; but, if it purports to be declaratory of law, it carries great weight.[41]

The current political acceptability of national renunciation of claims in outer space by those with the present capacity to send instrumentalities into space is another matter. It is not a political

* Mr. Hammarskjöld went on to say, in an interesting expression of his minimum immediate suggested program for the United Nations and outer space: "The General Assembly would . . . initiate steps for an international machinery to further this end. Were the General Assembly to reach this point, the governments cooperating in the United Nations would have laid what seems to me to be a valid basis for the future development, in international cooperation, of the use of outer space for the benefit of all."

impossibility however. Indeed, from a political point of view, if the temper of the times is strongly internationalist, renunciation of the possibility of making claims by those states having present space capabilities might win for them as much prestige as a claim itself. In any case, the old idea of "showing the flag" is hardly pertinent to new ventures in space. A manned landing on the moon for purely national purposes would undoubtedly arouse more resentment than admiration among the majority of states. The advocates of such a national program would, it may be suggested, have the burden of proving both to themselves and to the world that it would constitute a serious detriment to their national security to make such a landing under United Nations mandate or on behalf of the United Nations or the world community.

Although renunciation of potential sovereignty by national states is a necessity, it is not sufficient by itself to constitute a viable international solution, since such renunciation is also consistent with a political void in space. Without a political order there might well develop a state of competitive anarchy. With a political order must go the usual international requirement of verification and the usual governmental arrangements for administration. For our purposes, then, an international solution implies a renunciation of potential sovereignty by national states and an assumption of some responsibility for the maintenance of order by some general international organization.

Efforts to achieve such a general international settlement of the problems raised by the penetration of outer space might be initiated by the United Nations directly or, perhaps more appropriately, by an international conference called specially for the purpose, like the 1958 Geneva Conference on the Law of the Sea.* There

* A more limited international conference of interested states is, it will be recalled, the prospective pattern for the Antarctic. That conference has such precedents as the conferences concerning Africa held in the nineteenth century. With respect to matters above the earth's surface, it is interesting to note that a general international conference was the method used at what was considered "the time of the

are obviously several alternative approaches available to the decision makers, varying greatly in institutional details as well as in national complexion. There are what would be under strict interpretation only quasi-international solutions at one extreme, while at the other lies a general cosmic government.

One pattern for a weak international or quasi-international approach that might be followed in an international program designed primarily to demilitarize space and also to provide law and order in inhabitable areas is the familiar trusteeship pattern, particularly as currently illustrated by the Italian trusteeship in Somaliland. Under such an arrangement sovereignty would not lie in the national state trustee, but such governmental functions as are necessary would be performed by the state as Administering Authority, chosen by the Trusteeship Council or, perhaps, a new Space Council created under Article 7(2) of the Charter. The choice might be on the basis of interest in the areas in question, first exploration, or possession of the greatest number of spacecraft available for communication and transportation.

We will assume for the moment that this Council will not itself directly administer areas. Indeed, if it did—something the Trusteeship Council has never done despite the permissive language of Article 81 of the Charter—we would have quite a different type of solution which we will come to later. An agreement would be made between the Council and the trustee setting out the purposes and conditions of the trust. The trustee would presumably be legally bound therein only to assure demilitarization, the maintenance of law and order, economic access perhaps in some form, but also would probably be obligated to participate in whatever international technical and functional organizations would then have responsibilities in the area. The Council would hear reports on the fulfillment of the trust and on conditions in the area, would ask questions, send visiting missions, receive and evaluate petitions

---

first controversies between sovereignty in space and freedom in space," namely the Berlin Conference of 1906 on wireless telegraphy and the first Paris Conference of 1910 on air navigation.[48]

if a population were established, and attempt to influence and control the Administering Authorities through its only real weapon, publicity and the force of public opinion within the Authority and without. Even if additional techniques were included, such as the ability of the Council to terminate a trust for cause, political experiences suggest that they might be ineffective. No national Administering Authority would sit back and accept such international censure gracefully. Its allies would not expect it to do so.

Use of a device relying on states as Administering Authorities is subject, however, to disadvantages which are obvious in the light of history. Trusteeship in this form has been in essence a method of institutionalized political rivalry between ruler, ruled, and the rest of the world, not one of cooperation. It grew out of colonial controls and was a compromise, not an ideal solution *de novo*. Means of control over a sovereign trustee were never satisfactorily developed and probably are a political impossibility. As noted above, the relatively successful self-liquidation of the United Nations trusteeship system is resulting from extraneous forces and pressures which would not be duplicated in the hypothetical space cases. To rely on national states as administrators is an unsuitable formula for space control. It would not assure the military security of other states which is so crucial for space activities. It would prove far more sensitive to the desires of national sovereignty than to the needs of the international community.

Another pattern for an international regime for space, intermediate between a trusteeship system of the type now in use and direct international administration, would involve the reservation to the General Assembly of the United Nations or some new international body of legislative power over all technical, legal, governmental, and security matters in space but would avoid direct international administration by assigning administrative and executive power in these areas to national states or groups of states. The General Assembly itself might create the new international body or might itself carry out the job, either through or on the advice of an appropriately constituted body. Again we are assuming a renunciation of claims to sovereignty by all national states, as in the pattern previously described, but it might be well to require the administering state to renounce all claims individually and explicitly. Title to all natural resources might well be placed directly in the United Nations or the new body, and states would administer areas pursuant to the regular institutionalized legislative direction of the central authority, acting on behalf of the world community.

The tasks assigned to the trustee would presumably include the administration of the granting of concessions to groups and individuals for space resource development on terms and along policy lines specified by the General Assembly. Ownership and licensing of spacecraft within the area might also be relegated to a state or group of states or a public or private entity for purposes of resource development along approved lines and carefully restricted to eliminate military uses. Alternatively, these functions might be performed by international technical organizations set up for the purposes with the trustee left the role of coordination and supervision of the maintenance of law and order in the area, again either through use of its own police forces and courts set up specially for this purpose or, perhaps preferably, through supervision of the local activities by international forces and an international judicial system established by the international legislature. The problem of recompense or reimbursement of the trustee will also call for consideration under the proposed highly restricted regime.

One could obviously experiment endlessly with many shadings of international administration which would keep legislative control over outer space and its resources in an international organization, while using national states for the actual execution of the international will. But historical experiences suggest that such a division in essential governmental responsibilities and powers promises to be even less workable in fact than on paper when it is recalled that we are speaking of national states, rather than internationalized administrators, acting on behalf of a general international organization which itself lacks powers of enforcement. Such a solution avoids what many have always wished to avoid, direct international administration; it calls for what many have wished to create, direct international decision-making. But, in attempting such a combination, it creates the likelihood that all of the well-known problems of trusteeship will arise again, that coordination between the independent will of the trustee and the will of the international community, as expressed in its legislative decisions, will not in fact prove feasible.

On the other hand, the over-all effect on the UN system would depend largely on the exact nature of the institutions evolved. If the role of the administering states were effectively reduced by the removal of all but purely coordinating functions from the role of the trustee and by the counterbalancing weight of an international organization with legislative powers for the matters in question, it is conceivable that the United Nations would be granted enforcement powers in space through use of a space police and its own spacecraft, though it continued to lack governmental powers over Earth. In such a case the United Nations might nonetheless, through the possession of "space power," exercise more power on Earth itself.

The third major type of international solution has already been frequently alluded to. It would involve some form of direct international administration. Perhaps some totally new organization should be established outside the framework of the United Nations for the enactment of space codes as needed, the neutralization of space through ownership, operation and licensing of all spacecraft, the "government" of other spheres, and, in general, the advancement of the welfare of all men through activities in outer space. Such an agency could, alternatively, be established within the framework of the United Nations.

In this connection, past arguments against direct "ownership" or administration by the United Nations have been focused especially on the weaknesses of this organization, caused especially by the East-West split, by bloc voting, by its constitutional and actual lack of power and singleness of purpose, and (shades of the recurring past!) by its lack of "experience" as a sovereign. The political advantages of creating a new entity which would avoid the organizational defects of the United Nations in voting arrangements may, it has been frequently suggested, come to outweigh the advantages of a link with the established patterns of political cooperation. On the other hand, use of the United Nations would, it has been urged by Sir Leslie Munroe, permit "small powers . . . [to] be heard" and "public opinion" to be marshalled "throughout the world" and would follow as well from "the identity between its purposes and principles and the purposes and principles which must govern any international consideration of such problems [as] . . . peaceful use and the sharing of benefits."[43] Furthermore, by-passing the United Nations in so important a matter would be a great blow to its prestige. The simple fact is that if the states could agree to create a more effective organization, they could equally well remodel the United Nations.

Direct international administration might take any of a number of institutional forms. Suffice it to say that it might provide for an international administrative branch with considerable centralized power, thus giving the Secretariat great independence and responsibility, with the attendant problem of assuring democratic control. Or it might, at the other extreme, reserve the bulk of continuing responsibility to some organ of the General Assembly or some other appropriate legislative body with little independence or initiative left to the executive Secretariat. Again, it might call for a central administration with merely coordinating powers over a variety of technical and operating agencies of the functional type. Each of these alternative patterns would have its advantages and difficulties. Whatever the pattern of outer space administration, exploration and development might be handled through the creation of a Cosmic Development Corporation (CODEC), reflecting the interests and contributions of all nations in its composition. Indeed, in the early period where no large populations were involved such a company might even provide governmental services in outlying areas, as did the great trading companies of the age of discovery on Earth.

We have been satisfied at present to sketch in some of the various alternative types of international institutional solutions possible for outer space and some of the problems implicit in them.[44] There is no perfect solution to the organization of outer space for the benefit of mankind, but if history can serve as evidence, many of the traditionally popular approaches to such problems cannot be expected to give good results there. The occasion for a fresh approach has arrived. We do not despair that the moment will be seized. In analyzing this earth's international political problems, the realists unrealistically disdain approaches which do not promise quite proximate results. Sometimes it is useful to recall the French proverb, *c'est le premier pas qui coute.*

The experiences reviewed in this book show that through a long stretch of history states have evolved a variety of devices for cooperative and administrative activities whenever it seemed to them desirable to have a joint rather than a single nation regime. The motivations have been as various as the forms—political, economic, technical, ideological, humanitarian. In recent years a still stronger motivation—human survival—has been added. The need and the incentive have never been greater than now. Steadily the trend on the face of the earth has been toward organized multinational action in the common interest. There will be no reversal of that trend as man moves on into outer space.

NOTES

Notes

1. SHARED CONTROLS OF POLITICAL ADMINISTRATION

1. On the condominium, see generally 1 HACKWORTH, DIGEST 56–58 (1940); EL-ERIAN, CONDOMINIUM AND RELATED SITUATIONS IN INTERNATIONAL LAW *passim* (1952).

2. Cromer, *Introduction* to LOW, EGYPT IN TRANSITION xii–xiii (1914).

3. KALIJARVI, THE MEMEL STATUTE 206–7 and *passim* (1937). See also MORROW, THE PEACE SETTLEMENT IN THE GERMAN-POLISH BORDERLANDS 429 (1936).

For final arrangements, substantially confirming Lithuanian rule, see 29 L.N.T.S. 83 and LEAGUE OF NATIONS OFF. J., 5th Ass. 36, 121, 409, 539, 598 (1924). On March 22, 1939, Hitler forced the cession of Memel to Germany.

4. 2 MALLOY, TREATIES 1589–90 (1910); on Samoa, see 81 BRIT. & FOR. ST. PAP. 1058–72 (Act of June 14, 1889); HENDERSON, AMERICAN DIPLOMATIC QUESTIONS 205–86 (1901); WILLOUGHBY, TERRITORIES AND DEPENDENCIES OF THE UNITED STATES 291–94 (1905); MASTERSON, THE ORIGINS OF INTERNATIONAL RIVALRY IN SAMOA 1845–1884 (1934); American Samoa Committee, *Hearings Before the Commission Appointed by the President of the United States in Accordance with Public Resolution 89*, 70th Cong., *passim*, esp. 276–78, 308–10 (1931).

5. CMD. No. 3300 (T.S. No. 3 of 1907); CMD. No. 1681 (T.S. No. 7 of 1922); CMDS. Nos. 2829 and 2988 (T.S. Nos. 8 and 28 of 1927); Exchange of Notes of Jan. 31, 1935, CMD. No. 4852 (T.S. No. 7 of 1935); BRIT. FOR. OFF. HANDBOOK (Hist. Sec.), No. 147; 99 BRIT. & FOR. ST. PAP. 229 ff. (1910); 100 BRIT. & FOR. ST. PAP. 519 ff. (1911), and FRANCE AND ENGLAND IN THE NEW HEBRIDES: THE ANGLO-FRENCH CONDOMINIUM (monograph) (1914; Melbourne).

6. See SAYRE, EXPERIMENTS IN INTERNATIONAL ADMINISTRATION 97–104, esp. 102, and EL-ERIAN, *op. cit. supra* note 1, at 104.

7. See generally, U.N. NON-SELF-GOVERNING TERRITORIES, SUMMARIES OF INFORMATION SUBMITTED TO THE SECRETARY-GENERAL FOR 1955, 473–79 (1957).

8. BENTWICH, THE MANDATES SYSTEM 4 (1930). The population declined even further in the 1930s but had recovered to about 48,000 in 1954.

9. MANDER, SOME DEPENDENT PEOPLES OF THE SOUTH PACIFIC, 491 (1954).

10. See, generally, Reeves, *Agreement over the Canton and Enderbury Islands*, 33 AM. J. INT'L L. 521–26 (1939).

11. Agreement of April 6, 1939, Exec. Agr. Ser., State Dep't Pub. No. 145 (1939); 1 HACKWORTH, DIGEST 509–10 (1940). For President Roosevelt's Executive Order of 1938, see 3 Fed. Reg. 525 (1938).

12. Canton is mentioned in the information on Non-Self-Governing Territories transmitted to the Secretary-General by Britain (for the Gilbert and Ellice Islands), but only to the effect that the main trans-Pacific air route from Australia to the United States still passes through Canton; neither island appears to be mentioned in information submitted by the United States to the United Nations. See U.N. SUMMARIES 1955, *op. cit. supra* note 7, at 453. Today the facility is generally reserved for emergency use. Interestingly, the provisions of the *British Protectorates, Protected States and Protected Persons Order in Council*, No. 140 (1949), were made applicable to the New Hebrides and Canton Islands "as if they were protected states."

13. Apparently no food can be raised directly on the islands. Pan American World Airways experimented with hydroponics in an effort to grow fresh vegetables for its hotel. N.Y. Times, Nov. 19, 1939, § 11, p. 8.

14. On June 8, 1939, President Roosevelt, in proposing a toast to George VI, mentioned the condominium arrangement as a symbol of international understanding in these terms:

"If this illustration of the use of methods of peace, divorced from aggression, could only be universally followed, relations between all countries would rest upon a sure foundation, and men and women everywhere could once more look upon a happy, a prosperous and a peaceful world." N.Y. Times, April 7, 1939, p. 4.

15. Lord Cromer wrote: "The experiment of administrative internationalism has probably been tried in the No Man's Land [Egypt]

of which this history treats to a greater extent than in any other country. The result cannot be said to be encouraging to those who believe in the efficacy of international action in administrative matters. What has been proved is that international institutions possess admirable negative qualities. They are formidable checks to all action, and the reason why they are so is that, when any action is proposed, objections of one sort or another generally occur to some member of the international body. Any action often involves a presumed advantage accorded to some rival nation and it is a principle of internationalism, which is scornfully rejected in theory but too often recognized as a guide for practical action, that it is better to do nothing even though evil may ensue, than to allow good to be done at the expense of furthering the interests, or of exalting the reputation of an international rival." 2 CROMER, MODERN EGYPT 303–4 (1916); also 311, 312, and 149–300 *passim*. Lord Cromer in 1916 could scarcely have imagined even the currently operating system of United Nations technical assistance. On Egypt under the "Dual Control," see also NEWMAN, GREAT BRITAIN IN EGYPT (1928), and DEBIDOUR, HISTOIRE DIPLOMATIQUE DE L'EUROPE, 1878–1904, 56–59 (1916) (on divergent interpretations of instructions from Europe).

16. The Marquess of Salisbury to Lord Cromer, Aug. 2, 1898, F.O.78/4955.

17. 2 HERTSLET, THE MAP OF AFRICA BY TREATY 620–22 (3d ed. 1909); 91 BRIT. & FOR. ST. PAP. 1898–1899, 19 (1902). For Cromer's Memorandum supporting the Treaty see F.O.78/4957 (Nov. 10, 1898).

18. ROYAL INST. INTL. AFF., GREAT BRITAIN AND EGYPT 36 (1936).

19. See CMD. NO. 2269 (1924), ROYAL INST. INTL. AFF., *op. cit. supra* note 18, at 15–18; and ABBAS, THE SUDAN QUESTION 58–64 (1952).

20. THE SUDAN GOVERNMENT, THE SUDAN: RECORD OF PROGRESS 1898–1947, 133 (1947).

21. *Ibid.*

22. On later developments, see *id.* at 136–40; ABBAS, *op. cit. supra* note 19, at 115–25. The 1936 Treaty provided: "The High Contracting Parties agree that the administration of the Sudan shall continue to be that resulting from the said [1899] agreements." CMD. No. 5366 (T.S. No. 6 of 1937) Art. 11 (1).

23. See generally BEER, AFRICAN QUESTIONS AT THE PARIS PEACE CONFERENCE, 344–46 (1923); ABBAS, *op. cit. supra* note 19 *passim;* NEWMAN, *op. cit. supra* note 15, at 179 ff.; O'ROUKE, THE JURISTIC

STATUS OF EGYPT AND THE SUDAN *passim* (Johns Hopkins Univ. Studies in Historical and Political Science, Series 53, 1935); EL-ERIAN, *op. cit. supra* note 1, at 107 ff.

For the Agreement of Feb. 12, 1953, between the United Kingdom and Egypt, making the future status of the Sudan dependent on the determination of a Sudanese Constituent Assembly, see CMD. No. 8904 (T.S. No. 47 of 1953).

24. See Politis, *Condition internationale du territoire de Moresnet*, 11 REV. GÉN. DE DROIT INT'L PUB. 84 ff. (1904); 1 HACKWORTH, DIGEST 725 (1940). Interestingly enough, in *Kepp et Consorts*, the Belgian Cour de Cassation, I Pasicrisie Belge (1925) 253–55, later held that the area had been Belgian at all times, merely being subject to German claims. Other areas of similar type include the "Free State of Cracow," which was placed under the "protection" of Austria, Russia, and Prussia by the Final Act of the Congress of Vienna, June 9, 1815, with representatives of the three powers forming a control commission. 1 HERTSLET, MAP OF EUROPE BY TREATY 218 (1875). Cracow was annexed by Austria in November, 1846, and Schleswig-Holstein and Lauenburg, by the Treaty of Vienna of October 30, 1864, were ceded by Denmark to Austria and Prussia. These in turn by "condominium" agreement, divided the provinces, with Prussia taking one and Austria and Prussia each "administering" one other without decision as to sole ownership.

25. On the general rules, and for a decision rejecting the concept of a condominium over a lake, see decision of the German Criminal Court of Appeals (Div. I), Sept. 25, 1923, summarized in 1 HACKWORTH, DIGEST 615–16 (1940).

26. 55 REICHS UND PREUSSICHES VERWALTUNGSBLATT 528 (1934); LAUTERPACHT, ANNUAL DIGEST 1931–32, 50–51 (Case No. 23).

27. For the treaty, see 3 MALLOY, TREATIES 1914, 2740–42 (1923). On the decision, see also 11 AM. J. INT'L L. 674–730 (1917), and [1907] 2 FOREIGN REL. 697 (1910); [1916] FOREIGN REL. 853–62 (1925); [1917] FOREIGN REL. 1101–04 (1926); and 1 HACKWORTH, DIGEST, 702–5 (1940). The Governments of both Nicaragua and Honduras rejected the position of El Salvador on "joint" ownership. [1916] FOREIGN REL. 890–91 (1925); U.S. Dep't of State, file 817.

28. This Agreement was signed at Versailles on June 28, 1919. It was submitted to the United States Senate but laid aside by the Committee on Foreign Relations and was never "considered" by the Senate. See U.S. Dep't of State, file 763.72119/9434. A brief account of the

occupation is given in U.S. DEP'T OF STATE, THE TREATY OF VERSAILLES & AFTER 762–91 (1947) (Conference Series 92). In general, see FRAENKEL, MILITARY OCCUPATION AND THE RULE OF LAW (1944); GRABER, THE DEVELOPMENT OF THE LAW OF BELLIGERENT OCCUPATION 1863–1914 (1949).

29. The United States had desired to withdraw its forces even earlier, but this was opposed by the French on the ground that the presence of these troops minimized friction, by the British who feared an increase in the French program of annexation, and by the Germans who felt that it would be to their great detriment, probably in encouraging the French. See U.S. DEP'T OF STATE, *op. cit. supra* note 28, at 776–77. On French attempts to promote a separatist movement and thus create a buffer state in the Rhineland, see *id.* at 780.

30. ALLIED COMMISSION, A REVIEW OF ALLIED MILITARY GOVERNMENT AND OF THE ALLIED COMMISSION IN ITALY (1945).

31. 1 OPPENHEIM, INTERNATIONAL LAW 568–69 (ed. by Lauterpacht, 8th ed., 1955).

32. *Id.* at 569 n. 2 and see sources cited there. For a suggestion of a "condominium" over Germany, see Kelsen, Note, 38 AM. J. INT'L L. 689–94 (1944). The details of the special Berlin regime are not treated here.

33. The records of the Allied Control Council show that the Soviet representative vetoed proposed decisions of the other three Powers in 69 instances—nearly three times the combined number of vetoes of the others.

34. The details of the special Berlin regime and the subsequent controversies over the control of the city are beyond the scope of this study.

35. The armed forces in Germany remained under military command. Thus, the U.S. High Commissioner was not in a position to order military action but was authorized to request the U.S. Commanding General to take measures to maintain law and order and for the support of U.S. policy in Germany. An account of this period is contained in THE ALLIED HIGH COMMISSION FOR GERMANY 39 ff. (1953) (published by the Historical Division, Office of the Executive Secretary, Office of the U.S. High Commissioner for Germany).

36. Of the sixteen cases, about half revealed divergent national policies and half different interpretations of authority and responsibility of the occupants. See *id.* at 80–86, esp. 85.

37. *Id.* at 135; on the committee system generally, *id.* at 107–35.

38. Only the British-American "Bizonia" ever had an integrated operating personnel in the course of the Occupation.

39. The islands lie between 10° and 35° E. and 74° and 81° N. and comprise about 23,400 square miles of land area. Mean temperatures range from —4.5° C. in February to 40° in August. The climate is such that decay is almost unknown.

40. The best survey of the history and problems of Spitsbergen is in GRAY, SPITSBERGEN AND BEAR ISLAND (1919), published by the U.S. Government Printing Office as one of the confidential background papers for the Peace Conference. See also 1 HACKWORTH, DIGEST 465–68; [1914] FOREIGN REL. 974–81 (1922); Lansing, *A Unique International Problem,* 11 AM. J. INT'L L. 763 (1917); SAYRE, *op. cit. supra* note 6, at 92–97.

41. At one time Norwegian tourist parties visited the islands, and Swedish scientists were also active in investigating the area as well.

42. The Swedish-Norwegian Union was dissolved in 1905.

43. The countries considered interested were Belgium, Denmark, France, Germany, Great Britain, Holland, Sweden, Russia, and the United States.

44. On "claim-jumping" and related practices, and the lack of a way to obtain redress, see GRAY, *op. cit. supra* note 40, at 90 n. 9.

45. T.S. No. 18 of 1924, or 18 AM. J. INT'L L. Supp., 199–208 (1928). Russia's protest against this treaty was ignored, but she subsequently adhered in 1935.

46. In general, see VÁLI, SERVITUDES OF INTERNATIONAL LAW *passim* (2d ed. 1958).

47. See LEAGUE OF NATIONS, OFF. J. 17–19 (Spec. Supp. No. 3; Oct. 1920).

48. For the history of the islands, see LEAGUE OF NATIONS, OFF. J., Spec. Supp., No. 1, *passim* (Aug. 1923) and No. 3, *passim* (Oct. 1920). League of Nations Pub. VII. Pol., No. 1, at 2–37, and No. 2 (1921); 9 L.N.T.S. 211; RAPPARD, THE QUEST FOR PEACE 177–88 (1940). For the German-Finnish-Swedish Agreement of December 30, 1918, concerning the demolition of existing fortifications, see 113 BRIT. & FOR. ST. PAP. 993–1003 (1920).

49. 20 LEAGUE OF NATIONS OFF. J., 20th Ass. 257–60, 279–82, 284–89 (1939).

50. 39 MARTENS, NOUVEAU RECUEIL GÉNÉRAL DE TRAITÉ, 456–58 (3d ser. 1942) and U.S. DEP'T OF STATE, TREATIES OF PEACE—TREATY WITH FINLAND 3 (Pub. 2743, Eur. Series 21). For bibliography and portions

of the League's consideration of the matter, see SOHN, CASES AND MATERIALS ON WORLD LAW 87–120 (1950).

51. Convention Relating to the Regime of the Straits, 28 L.N.T.S. 117 (1924).

52. See 1 OPPENHEIM, *op. cit. supra* note 31, at 536–43; 14 DEP'T. STATE BULL. 206 (1946); 44 AM. J. INT'L L. Supp. 86–88 (1950). On Shanghai see Hudson, *The International Settlement at Shanghai*, 6 FOR. AFF. 75–88 (1927).

53. By decisions of the Berlin Congress of 1878, for example, Bosnia and Herzogovina and the island of Ada-Kalé in the Danube were left under nominal Turkish sovereignty but their full administration was turned over to Austria-Hungary.

54. See Exchange of Notes, Sept. 2, 1940, 34 AM. J. INT'L L. Supp., 184–86 (1940); Agreement of March 27, 1941, 35 AM. J. INT'L L. Supp., 134–59 (1941); Agreement concerning the Extension of Bahamas Long Range Practice Ground by Additional Sites of Jan. 15, 1952, CMD. No. 8485 (T.S. No. 10 of 1952).

55. See 1 OPPENHEIM, *op. cit. supra* note 31, at 457–58.

56. Spelar v. United States, 338 U.S. 217 (1949); Connell v. Vermilya Brown Co., 164 F. 2d 924 (1947).

57. See generally SCOTT, THE SPANISH ORIGIN OF INTERNATIONAL LAW (1934); CHOWDHURI, INTERNATIONAL MANDATES AND TRUSTEESHIP SYSTEMS 13–36 (1955); 1 BAKER, WOODROW WILSON AND WORLD SETTLEMENT 227, 262–64 (1922); Ormsby-Gore, *Indirect International Supervision*, in THE LEAGUE OF NATIONS STARTS: AN OUTLINE BY ITS ORGANIZERS *passim* (1920); Potter, *Origin of the System of Mandates under the League of Nations*, 16 AM. POL. SCI. REV. 564 ff. (1922); 1 KEITH, SELECTED SPEECHES AND DOCUMENTS ON BRITISH COLONIAL POLICY, 1763–1917 8–10 (1918).

58. 2 & 7 BURKE, WORKS 296; 16, 21–23, 110, 264–67 (1839).

59. HALL, MANDATES, DEPENDENCIES AND TRUSTEESHIP 104 (1948). Article 6 of the General Act provided, for example, that "All the Powers [with sovereignty or influence in the Conventional Basin of the Congo] bind themselves to watch over the preservation of the native tribes and to care for the improvement of the conditions of their moral and material well-being. . . ." Article 9 continued an earlier policy by indicating that the slave trade was contrary to international law.

In general, the Act "aimed at the extension of the benefits of civilization to the natives, the promotion of trade and navigation on a basis of perfect equality for all nations, and the preservation of the territories affected from the ravages of war." Keith, *The Revision of the Berlin Act*, 17 J. AFRICAN SOC'Y 249–61, at 250 (1918).

60. On the diplomatic struggle before and during the Conference, see CROWE, THE BERLIN WEST AFRICAN CONFERENCE, 1884–1885 *passim* (1942). The U.S. "recognized" the Association as a "friendly government" on April 22, 1884 (1 MALLOY, TREATIES 327). On the relationship of League Mandates to the Berlin Conference Rules (though with "external machinery" for enforcement), see remarks of Lloyd George on the Paris Peace Conference, [1919] 3 FOREIGN REL. 750 (1943). See also SADY, THE UNITED NATIONS AND DEPENDENT PEOPLES 15 (1956). Conquest and rule by private company of course was nothing new in the experience of Britain and France, but this Association was internationally sponsored and approved rather than being solely a national company.

61. See 6 TEMPERLEY, A HISTORY OF THE PEACE CONFERENCE OF PARIS 502 (1924); BEER, AFRICAN QUESTIONS AT THE PARIS PEACE CONFERENCE 78 (1923); HALL, *op. cit. supra* note 59, at 103–6, 239.

When Belgium took over the Congo area, an Act of Parliament was passed on Sept. 8, 1908 ("The Colonial Charter") which, in Article 5, set up for the Congo a detailed system of national trusteeship expressly implementing the trusteeship principle of the Berlin Act.

62. For the limitation of the "open door" policy in the Convention on the Revision of the Berlin and Brussels Acts, signed in 1919 at St. Germain-en-Laye, see 1 HUDSON, INTERNATIONAL LEGISLATION 344–52 (1931). It was retained for "B" Class Mandates in the League Covenant (Art. 22 (5)). See generally GERIG, THE OPEN DOOR AND THE MANDATES SYSTEM (1930).

63. The Times (London), Aug. 11, 1917, p. 4; Aug. 29, 1917, p. 8; Feb. 25, 1918, p. 4 (proposals of the British Independent Labour Party). See also ANTONELLI, L'AFRIQUE ET LA PAIX DE VERSAILLES 217 (1921); 1 BAKER, *op. cit. supra* note 57, at 48, 259, 268.

64. Statement prepared by Dr. Isaiah Bowman of Wilson's remarks. See 1 MILLER, THE DRAFTING OF THE COVENANT 43 (1928), and 4 SEYMOUR, THE INTIMATE PAPERS OF COL. HOUSE 281–82 (1928).

65. For the first Wilson draft, see 2 MILLER, *op. cit. supra* note 64, at 12–15, and 1 & 3 BAKER, *op. cit. supra* note 57, at 218 ff. and 88 ff. For Colonel House's draft see 2 MILLER *op. cit. supra* at 7–11. On the earlier Phillimore Plan, submitted to the British Government on March 20, 1918, with no mention of mandates, see 2 MILLER, *op. cit. supra* at 3–6. On the American drafts in particular see POTTER, *supra* note 57,

at 564–69; see also, generally, WRIGHT, MANDATES UNDER THE LEAGUE OF NATIONS 3–63 (1930), and LEAGUE OF NATIONS, THE MANDATES SYSTEM: ORIGIN, PRINCIPLES, APPLICATION *passim* (1945).

66. SMUTS, THE LEAGUE OF NATIONS: A PRACTICAL SUGGESTION 18–19 (1918). He also argued for "supervision and ultimate control" by the League with the right to remove a Mandatory, however. Pp. 17, 19, 21–22.

67. BEER, *op. cit. supra* note 61, 421–24 at 422.

68. HALL, *op. cit. supra* note 59, at 129. Emphasis added.

69. [1919] 3 FOREIGN REL., *supra* note 60, at 719, 721, 760. The Germans, hoping for some vestige of influence, were more interested in the possibilities of international administration. See STOYANOVSKY, LA THÉORIE GÉNÉRALE DES MANDATS INTERNATIONAUX *passim* (1925).

70. On other drafts considered at Paris, see 2 MILLER, *op. cit. supra* note 64, at 145–54 (Wilson's "Third Paris"), 61–64, 106–16 (Lord Robert Cecil), 658–67 ("Hurst-Miller"); 1 Miller, *op. cit. supra* at 106–8 (Smuts's revised draft, Jan. 24, 1919); *A Draft of the Composite Covenant made by the Legal Advisers of the Commission on the League*, S. Doc. No. 74, 66th Cong., 1st Sess. (1919).

71. MCDONALD, TRUSTEESHIP IN THE PACIFIC 4 (1949). *Cf.* HALL, *op. cit. supra* note 59, at 50. See also, *e.g.*, Rappard, *The Mandates and the International Trusteeship Systems*, 61 POL. SCI. Q. 410 (1946).

72. On the System, see GOODRICH & HAMBRO, CHARTER OF THE UNITED NATIONS: COMMENTARY AND DOCUMENTS (2d ed., 1949); 4 UNITED NATIONS, REPERTORY OF PRACTICE OF UNITED NATIONS ORGANS; Parry, *The Trusteeship Council*, in WORTLEY, THE UNITED NATIONS: THE FIRST TEN YEARS 47–58 (1957); U.S. DEP'T OF STATE, POST WAR FOREIGN POLICY PREPARATION, 1939–1945 (1950).

73. See Toynbee, *Peaceful Change or War*, 15 INT'L AFF. 48 (1936); U.N. GEN. ASS. OFF. REC. 4th Sess., 4th Comm., 96th Meeting, 33 (1949), U.N. Gen. Ass. Res. 325 (IV), U.N. Doc. No. A/1251 at 40 (1949); U.N. TRUSTEESHIP COUNCIL OFF. REC. 6th Sess., 608–13 (March 1950); *ibid.*, 7th Sess., 30th meeting, 266–67 (July 1950) and U.N. Doc. No. A/1856 at 23 (1951).

74. In passing on questions relating to Southwest Africa, the International Court of Justice touched on the interesting question of sovereignty which is not mentioned in the trusteeship sections of the Charter. Sir Arnold McNair, in his separate opinion, indicated that the "Mandates System (and the corresponding principles of the Trusteeship System) is a new institution, . . . a new species of international

government which does not fit into the old conception of sovereignty and which is alien to it. The doctrine of sovereignty has no application to this new system . . . What matters in considering this new institution is not where sovereignty lies, but what are the rights and duties of the Mandatory in regard to the . . . territory being administered by it. The answer to that question depends on the international agreement creating the system and the rules of law which they attract." International Status of South-West Africa, Advisory Opinion, I.C.J. Rep. 150 (1950).

75. See 4 UNITED NATIONS, REPERTORY OF PRACTICE OF UNITED NATIONS ORGANS 226–28.

76. See, generally, TOUSSAINT, THE TRUSTEESHIP SYSTEM OF THE UNITED NATIONS 208–14 (1956).

77. On the Korean case see GOODRICH, KOREA: A STUDY IN UNITED STATES POLICY IN THE UNITED NATIONS 7–71 (1956).

2. *THE ROLE OF INTERNATIONAL ORGANIZATIONS*

1. On Tangier, see the comprehensive study by STUART, THE INTERNATIONAL CITY OF TANGIER (2d ed. 1955).

2. Such taxes included those on slaughterhouses, passenger debarkation, and urban properties and license fees.

3. The Sanitary Council, which had met since 1793, was also "abolished" in 1925 but, since the United States and Italy had not accepted the International Statute, representatives of these two countries continued to meet until January, 1929, when Italy adhered to the Statute. The United States continued certain of the Council's functions until 1942 when the Council's funds were exhausted. See [1925] 2 FOREIGN REL. 594 (1940), and STUART, *op. cit. supra* note 1, at 25–26.

4. For text see STUART, THE INTERNATIONAL CITY OF TANGIER App. III, IV (1st ed. 1931).

5. A country's economic importance was calculated on a basis of the amount of local trade her nationals accounted for, the value of their local property, the amount of rent they paid, and the tonnage and number of boats entering the port flying her flag.

6. CMD. No. 2096 (1924) and CMD. No. 2203 (T.S. No. 23 of 1924).

7. On the 1923 Statute, see STUART, *op. cit. supra* note 1, at 86–87.

8. See the comprehensive reports by the London *Times* correspondent W. B. Harris. The Times (London), June 22 and July 3, 1925.

9. The calculation was based on factors similar to those agreed to in 1914.

10. STUART, *op. cit. supra* note 1, at 122.

11. See Agreement for the Reestablishment of the International Administration of Tangier, T.I.A.S. No. 2752.

12. T.I.A.S. No. 3680.

13. STUART, *op. cit. supra* note 1, at 109 and 182.

14. Treaty of Versailles, Articles 100–108, [1919] 6 FOREIGN REL. 836, 950 (1946).

15. 6 L.N.T.S. 189 (1921).

16. For comment, see U.S. DEP'T OF STATE, THE TREATY OF VERSAILLES AND AFTER 241–62 (Publication No. 2724, Conf. Series No. 92, 1947).

17. See Access to, or Anchorage in, the Port of Danzig of Polish War-vessels, P.C.I.J., ser. C, No. 55, at 96–105 (1931).

18. See *id.* at 113–20, 196.

19. *Id.* at 221. As Walters put it: "The High Commissioner was indeed an international official, responsible to an international organ; but he possessed no single attribute of government." 1 WALTERS, A HISTORY OF THE LEAGUE OF NATIONS 90 n. 1 (1952).

20. See, in general, MORROW, THE PEACE SETTLEMENT IN THE GERMAN-POLISH BORDERLANDS, 56–66 (1936); Henderson's *Report to the Council of the League*, May 22, 1931 (*q.v.*); and FRIEDRICH, DER HOHE KOMMISSAR DES VÖLKERBUNDES IN DANZIG *passim* (1932).

21. See 1 WALTERS, *op. cit. supra* note 19, at 453–55, 615–22. The League, of course, also played a role in other border and conflict areas. In Upper Silesia, for example, the Council took over the problem of creating a new German-Polish border when the Allies, having the power of decision, could not agree on a solution. On May 15, 1922, the Geneva Convention on Upper Silesia was signed, the longest treaty on record which provided for the economic unity of an area across a frontier. Minority rights were guaranteed, though the protection afforded was in fact inadequate and the League's theoretical right to intervene was not applied. One interesting point in this experience was the creation of a special court to hear nationality matters in which individuals could bring "cases" against states with the states bound by the decisions. The Court had a heavy case load and functioned reasonably well. See, *e.g.*, the report by its president, G. KAECKENBEECK, THE INTERNATIONAL EXPERIMENT OF UPPER SILESIA (1942).

22. See 1 WALTERS, *op. cit. supra* note 19, at 90 n. 1.

23. For an argument that the Saar might be under *the sovereignty of the League* and not of its Members, see WRIGHT, MANDATES UNDER THE LEAGUE OF NATIONS 302, (1930). In 1933 the French Court of Cassation (Chambre des Requètes) held that the Saar was "a German territory." Sirey, I. 92 [1934].

24. Articles 45–50 and Annex. The German representatives at the Paris Peace Conference had protested, to no avail, that: "No body representative of the people, with legislative powers, will exist. The population loses all civic rights; it is politically outlawed."

25. The inhabitants retained their German nationality.

26. The 3,300-man force represented the United Kingdom (1,500), Italy (1,300), the Netherlands (250), and Sweden (250). It was commanded by U.K. Maj. Gen. J. E. S. Brind, whose report, presented in October, 1935, was never formally published.

27. 15 LEAGUE OF NATIONS MONTHLY SUMMARY 3 (Jan. 1935).

28. In general, see 1 WALTERS, *op. cit. supra* note 19, at 90, 239–43, 586–98; Haskins, *The Saar Territory as It Is Today*, 1 FOR. AFF. 46–58 (1922); RUSSELL, THE INTERNATIONAL GOVERNMENT OF THE SAAR *passim* (1926); FLORINSKY, THE SAAR STRUGGLE *passim* (1934); U.S. DEP'T OF STATE, *op. cit. supra* note 16, at 162–82.

29. 1 WALTERS, *op. cit. supra* note 19, at 598.

30. 13 LEAGUE OF NATIONS MONTHLY SUMMARY 85–86 (March 1933). *Action by the League of Nations on the Leticia Controversy*, 67 PAN AM. U. BULL. 595–97 (1933); *The Colombia-Peruvian Protocol*, 68 PAN AM. U. BULL. 546–55 (1934); *The Colombia-Peruvian Protocol Ratified*, 69 PAN AM. U. BULL. 810–11 (1935); 2 WALTERS, *op. cit. supra* note 19, at 536–40.

31. The Commission, too, could rely in this instance on the loyal armed forces of the country whose territory was being protected.

32. See U.S. DEP'T OF STATE, THE UNITED STATES AND ITALY 1939–1946: DOCUMENTARY RECORD 173–74 (Pub. 2669, Eur. Ser. 17, 1946); and U.N. GEN. ASS. OFF. REC. 1st Sess., 2d pt., 4th Comm., Part 2, at 36 (1945).

33. See BYRNES, SPEAKING FRANKLY 76–77, 92–96 (1947), and U.N. Doc. No. A/C.1/SR.239, at 3 (1949).

On the French position and French fears of the effect on her own colonies of internationalization of the ex-Italian areas, see CATROUX, J'AI VU TOMBER LE RIDEAU DE FER, MOSCOU, 1945–1948, 123–235 (1952).

34. BYRNES, *op. cit. supra* note 33, at 96. Molotov's proposal and

comment raise another fundamental problem of setting up an international regime for a populated area, that is, what kind of society will be imposed or will the population be "educated" to accept. Mandates and trusteeships to date have assumed a capitalist or at least an individualist democratic form, which would naturally make the system less appealing to the Soviet Union as contrary to their vision of life.

This problem is closely related to others previously mentioned: whether and how democracy should be provided for, what kind of economic arrangements should be made for the area and for the rest of the world (free access?); how should the international regime balance local and nonlocal rights and the like. In populated areas, then, trusteeship seems implicitly to be only a transitional form, at least unless and until an international citizenship arises to replace provincial feelings.

35. See Bevin's statement in 414 PARL. DEB. (5th Ser.) cols. 36–37 (Oct. 9, 1945).

36. U.N. GEN. ASS. OFF. REC. 4th Sess., 1st Comm., 35–38 (1949). This was a revision of an earlier stand calling for direct trusteeship over all three areas with Libya and Somaliland becoming independent after ten years. U.N. Doc. No. A/C.1/433.

37. See U.N. Docs. Nos. A/C.1/448 and Corr. 1 and A/1285, Part II, 24–36, and 9 U.N. BULL. 697 (No. 2, 1950).

38. U.N. Doc. A/1251, Res. 289 (IV), at 10–11 (1949). On the events leading to this Resolution, see generally BECKER, THE DISPOSITION OF THE ITALIAN COLONIES: 1941–1951, 78–195 (doctoral thesis, Univ. of Geneva, 1952).

39. The Eritrean solution was not in fact reached until 1950. See U.N. Doc. No. A/1775, Res. 390 (V), 20–22 (1950).

40. See generally, *Disposal of the Former Italian Colonies*, U.N. Doc. No. ST/DP 1/SER A/70, 13–24 (1952). For the Commissioner's Reports see U.N. Docs. Nos. A/1340, A/1949, and A/1949/Adds. Administering Power Reports include U.N. Docs. Nos. A/1387 and A/1390. For other Assembly action, see U.N. Doc. No. A/1775, Res. 387 (V), 388 (V), 389 (V), 16–20 (1950), establishing a UN Tribunal authorized to give instructions and settle disputes arising from Italian assets in Libya.

41. On the need for continued UN aid to Libya to assure the existence of the state, and on aid in progress (UNESCO, FAO, WHO, TAB, etc.) see Pelt, *Report*, U.N. Doc. No. A/1949/Add. 1 and

Disposal of the Former Italian Colonies, op. cit. supra note 40, at 23–24.

42. See *supra* note 41.

43. Another proposal was for a direct UN trusteeship (Liberia). 9 U.N. BULL. 697 (No. 12, 1950).

44. The General Assembly's Resolution instructed the Trusteeship Council to "negotiate" with Italy and a drafting committee of that Council prepared a draft agreement which, after some modification, was approved by the Council on Jan. 27, 1949. See U.N. Doc. No. A/1251, Res. 289 (IV), 11–12 (1949). Ethiopia was permitted to participate in consideration of the draft but without vote and "without . . . any decision as to whether Ethiopia was, in fact, a 'State directly concerned.'" U.N. GEN. ASS. OFF. REC. 5th Sess., Supp. No. 10 (A/1294) (1950).

45. The Council's early Reports are in U.N. Docs. Nos. A/C.4/162, 178 (1948).

46. On the problems of this Council, see U.N. TRUSTEESHIP COUNCIL OFF. REC., 11th Sess., 415 Meeting (June, 1952); *Report of the Trusteeship Council*, U.N. GEN. ASS. OFF. REC. 9th Sess., Supp. No. 4, at 96–97 (A/2680) (1954); FINKELSTEIN, SOMALILAND UNDER ITALIAN ADMINISTRATION 26–29 (1955). For Reports of the Advisory Council, see U.N. Docs. Nos. T/923 (1951), T/979 (1952), T/1048 (1953), T/1116 (1954).

47. See, *e.g.*, U.N. Doc. A/C.4/178 (Nov. 9, 1950); U.N. Doc. No. T/1042 (March 16, 1953). The Trusteeship Council also obtains information through Italy's reports, petitions, and Reports of the Visiting Missions. See U.N. Docs. Nos. T/947 (1952) and T/1143 (1954). Other indications of UN interest in helping Somaliland (and sources of UN information) include the sending of missions by the Technical Assistance Board, FAO, ILO, UNESCO, and WHO.

48. Somaliland, for example, was run by an Administrative Committee consisting of the Administrator, his Secretary General, and seven to nine heads of governmental bodies. No Somali sat on this body through 1955, more than halfway through the assigned Trusteeship period. While a Territorial Council was set up in 1950 as a consultative body, it was forbidden to discuss defense or foreign affairs and none of its 51 members, including 21 regional representatives, 18 political party representatives, 8 economic group representatives, and one representative each from the Italian, Arabic, Indian, and Pakistani communities, were elected by direct suffrage through 1955. After

1955, nine seats were to be filled by direct vote. The Trusteeship Council repeatedly has urged that more Somalis be used in government. See *Report of the Trusteeship Council*, *supra* note 46, at 99–101, and U.N. Doc. No. T/1143 at 15–20 (Dec. 20, 1954).

49. See U.N. Docs. Nos. ST/DP 1/SER.A/70 at 32–34 (1952), A/C.1/522 (III) (1949) and A/1089 and Corr. 1 (1949).

50. See *Report of the U.N. Commission for Eritrea*, U.N. GEN. ASS. OFF. REC. 5th Sess., Supp. No. 8 at 24–36 (A/1285) (1950).

51. U.N. GEN. ASS. OFF. REC. 5th Sess., Supp. No. 20, Res. 390 (V) at 20–22 (A/1775) (1950).

52. U.N. Docs. Nos. A/2141, at 38 (1952) and A/2404, at 34–35 (1953).

53. 49 U.N.T.S. 3 (in force Sept. 5, 1947). On this problem, see the statement of the U.S. Representative, Johnson, 2 S.C. OFF. REC. (No. 1, 1947).

54. See, *e.g.*, *id.* at 4–19, 44–61 (Nos. 1, 3, Jan. 7 and 10, 1947).

55. The U.S. Representative added that the Statute "laid down a scheme of government, which will be as representative as practicable. The United Nations Security Council will exercise watchfulness and vigilance over the administration of that Territory, and, primarily, will ensure the human rights of the inhabitants. I think that there could be no better guarantee that the administration will be honest and in the interests of the people of the Territory, than the governing Powers are responsible to [the Security Council]" *Id.* at 12 (No. 1).

56. See CMD. No. 9288 (1954) and THE STATESMAN'S YEARBOOK 1958, 1178–79. On all of these matters, see U.N. YEARBOOK 1947–48, 352–56; 1948–49, 315–16; 1950, 6; 1951, 360; 1953, 22, 249–52; 1954, 100; 1955, 79.

57. The states members were Australia, Canada, Czechoslovakia, Guatemala, India, Iran, the Netherlands, Peru, Sweden, Uruguay, Yugoslavia. On the background and on conditions in Palestine see HUREWITZ, THE STRUGGLE FOR PALESTINE (1950).

58. See U.N. Special Committee on Palestine, *Report to the General Assembly*, 1 & 2 U.N. GEN. ASS. OFF. REC. 2d Sess., Supp. No. 11, esp. at 8–12, 42–64; and App. I (A/364) (Sept., 1947).

59. See U.N. Doc. No. A/519, Res. 181 (II) at 133 (Jan. 1948), 2 U.N. GEN. ASS. OFF. REC. 2d Sess., Plen. Meetings, 1424–25 (1947). The Jews and the United Kingdom had indicated that the plan was acceptable; the Arabs had rejected it. For the acrimonious debate in the UN's *Ad Hoc* Political Committee and in the General Assembly,

see U.N. Gen. Ass. Off. Rec. 2d *Ad Hoc* Committee on the Palestine Question 4, 6–12, 220–23, and *passim* (1947), and 2 U.N. Gen. Ass. Off. Rec. 2d Sess., Plen. Meeting, 1424 ff. (1947).

60. U.N. Doc. No. A/532 at 39 (1948).

61. Text in U.N. Trusteeship Council Off. Rec. 2d Sess., 3d pt., Annex, 4 ff. (1948).

62. On March 19, 1948, the United States, in view of the deteriorating situation, submitted to the Security Council a plan for temporary trusteeship of all Palestine under the Trusteeship Council. At the Second Special Session of the General Assembly on April 16, 1948, the United States submitted a plan for trusteeship for all Palestine based on an extended form of the Trusteeship Council's plan for Jerusalem. The Assembly rejected both this proposal and a U.S.–French plan for a temporary international regime for Jerusalem alone.

63. The General Assembly's Resolution 303 (IV) of Dec. 9, 1949, restated "its intention that Jerusalem should be placed under a permanent international regime, which should envisage appropriate guarantees for the protection of the Holy Places, both within and outside Jerusalem," and requested the Trusteeship Council to "complete the preparation of the Statute of Jerusalem, omitting the now inapplicable provisions" and, "without prejudice to the fundamental principles of the international regime for Jerusalem set forth in the General Assembly resolution 181 (II) [of 29 November, 1947], introducing therein amendments in the direction of its greater democratization, approve the Statute, and proceed immediately with its implementation." See U.N. Docs. Nos. A/1222 and A/1222/Add.1, A/1234 and A/1241 (1949).

64. See *Special Report of the Trusteeship Council*, Question of an International Regime for the Jerusalem Area and Protection of the Holy Places, U.N. Gen. Ass. Off. Rec. 5th Sess., Supp. No. 9, Annex II, 19–27 (1950).

65. U.N. Doc. No. A/427 at 9–18 (October, 1947). See U.N. Yearbook 1946–47 at 104–7, 250–251, 633; 1947–48 at 197–204.

66. The United Nations is obliged to prevent use of its territory as a refuge for those merely evading American process.

67. See U.N. Yearbook 1946–47 at 112–13, 249–50.

3. FUNCTIONAL ORGANIZATIONS

1. See, for example, the comprehensive analysis made by Jessup, Lande, and Lissitzyn in reediting the essay by Prof. Joseph P. Cham-

berlain, published by the Carnegie Endowment in 1955 under the title INTERNATIONAL ORGANIZATION [hereinafter cited as CHAMBERLAIN 1955]. The constitutional documents of over 100 multinational organizations are reprinted in PEASLEE, INTERNATIONAL GOVERNMENTAL ORGANIZATIONS (2 vols. 1956), [hereinafter cited as PEASLEE]. Many studies of individual organizations have been made, and these are cited hereinafter as appropriate. See also YEARBOOK OF INTERNATIONAL ORGANIZATIONS (annual).

2. In general, this analysis does not include the United Nations itself.

3. No special treatment is given here to organizations created primarily for purposes of mutual defense. These include NATO, SEATO, the ANZUS arrangement, the Ankara Treaty Organization, and the Warsaw Pact arrangement, despite the fact that such organizations as NATO include as designated purposes some form of economic and social cooperation, a facet which has already received some attention through study groups, particularly on the part of the European members.

4. See CHAMBERLAIN 1955, at 67–70, for a survey of "functions" performed.

5. Certain other organizations inevitably have, or may have, an interest in developments in the Antarctic and outer space, but their concern appears to merit less consideration at this point. Thus, the Universal Postal Union (UPU) may sooner or later be confronted with the need for scheduling rates for mail carried by rockets which pass through outer space. See N.Y. Times, June 9, 1959.

6. For outer space, some new political decision is essential to supplement or replace the Convention's Article 1: "The contracting States recognize that every State has complete and exclusive sovereignty over the airspace above its territory." The irrelevance of this rule to conditions in outer space is discussed in a later chapter.

7. Convention on International Civil Aviation, Article 44. ICAO has never exercised its powers in the economic field, probably because of national rivalries and the unwillingness of the larger powers to have these matters handled on a multilateral basis.

8. *Ibid.*, Article 55 (c).

9. Proposals for the internationalization of air transport services, including both the ownership and operation of such services, have been advanced at various times by such nations as France (1932), Australia, and New Zealand (1944) in order to "spread as widely as possible among all the nations of the world the beneficent effects of

this new amenity" and to help prevent war by affording "a very large degree of safety against the misuse of aircraft." See address by D. G. Sullivan, Chairman of the New Zealand delegation, 2d Plenary Session, Chicago Conference, Nov. 2, 1944; U.S. DEP'T OF STATE, 1 ICAO PROC. 77–80 at 80 (1944) and, generally, VAN ZANDT, CIVIL AVIATION AND PEACE (1944). The proposals have always been rejected as undesirable. The language is reminiscent of suggestions for use of outer space, however.

On the very important role played by private and nationalized air companies and by the nongovernmental International Air Transport Association (IATA), made up of some one hundred scheduled airlines of over 50 countries and territories, in the work of ICAO and in the field of air transport generally, see CHAMBERLAIN 1955, at 30–31.

10. Article 54 (1) permits the Council to adopt "international standards and recommended practices." Such "Annexes" are submitted to the States Members and become effective within three months unless a majority of Members disapprove them. Under Article 38, however, a State finding it impracticable to comply merely so notifies the Organization. Where the Convention itself is amended, through ratification by two-thirds of the Members, a State which fails to ratify within a specified period may be dropped from the Organization if the Assembly so provides. (Art. 94).

11. See REIFF, THE UNITED STATES AND THE TREATY LAW OF THE SEA 205 ff. (1958). The 1954 agreement was the latest in a series of arrangements of this type; the text is in T.I.A.S. No. 3186.

12. ICAO, MEMORANDUM ON ICAO (1958); REIFF, *op. cit. supra* note 11; 20 DEP'T STATE BULL. 164–66 (1949); N.Y. Times, Nov. 25, 1958, p. 58M.

13. Convention, Article 3. See in general CODDING, THE INTERNATIONAL TELECOMMUNICATION UNION: AN EXPERIMENT IN INTERNATIONAL COOPERATION (1952) and U.N. Doc. No. A/AC.98/4, at 41–45 (16 June 1959).

14. Convention, Article VI, 5 (1).

15. The importance of commercial enterprises in this field is apparent from the composition of the organs of the Union. While only States are members, under the International Telecommunications Convention of 1952 national delegations may include representatives of private organizations as delegates or advisers (Annex 3, Gen. Regs., Ch. 1, par. 8 (a) and Ch. 2, par. 3(1)(a); representatives of operating companies may participate in revision of the Regulations, if authorized by

their Governments, but not of the Convention (Arts. 10(2)(1)(a) and 9(1)(f)); recognized private agencies can with governmental approval be *members* of the Consultative Committees (Art. 7(3)(b)); and Administrative, but not Plenipotentiary, Conferences also call on international nongovernmental organizations such as the International Broadcasting Union, the International Conference on Large Electric Systems, and the International Chamber of Commerce to aid in discussions, though they are denied a vote. Under predecessor conventions, such as the International Telegraph Convention of 1875, private companies participated even more directly in the debates and international relations between private companies were also regulated. For the Telegraph Convention of 1875, see 66 BRIT. FOR. ST. PAP. 19 (1882). For that of 1891, see LE BUREAU INTERNATIONAL DES ADMINISTRATIONS TELEGRAPHIQUES, DOCUMENTS DE LA CONFERENCE TELEGRAPHIQUE INTERNATIONALE DE PARIS (1891).

It must be kept in mind, too, that the "commercial" companies involved in the ITU are not ordinary commercial companies (as is largely true of the ICAO too)—they are public utilities in most cases, either regulated or nationalized for the same reason that an international division of rights and control is needed, that is, they are "natural" monopolies, even international "natural" monopolies, in which a few companies, or even one, are much more efficient than many. This is due to the large efficient size of operation and distribution and, in this case, the physical limitation on available "raw materials." In these cases, the companies are granted special privileges in return for performing a public function under government control.

16. General information on WMO is found in its Bulletins and the Annual Reports of the Secretary-General and of the Congresses. See also WMO, The Sea that Unites Us (mimeographed), and U.N. Doc. No. A/AC.98/4, 35–40 (16 June, 1959).

17. *Final Report of the Commission for Maritime Meteorology of the WMO*, London, 14–29 July, 1952 (WM)—No. 10.RP.2; Res. of the Exec. Comm. Res. 24 (EC-III), Annex.

18. Under Art. 3, an amendment becomes effective 90 days after notification by the Commission to the Parties. An objection delays the entry into force by an additional 90 days. Thereafter the amendment enters into force for all nonobjecting Parties. In general see Kellogg, *The International Whaling Commission*, U.N. Doc. No. A/Conf. 10/7, p. 256 (1956); REIFF, *op. cit. supra* note 11, at 293 ff.

19. See Protocol to the International Convention for the Regulation

of Whaling, 85th Cong., 1st Sess., EX:E at 4 (1957); and REIFF, *op. cit. supra* note 11 at 293–97.

20. Art. 9. Parties are to transmit details of infractions and punishments to the Commission. (Art. 9(4)) Bonuses may not be paid for whales taken in contravention of regulations. (Art. 9(2)).

21. See Walter Sullivan in N.Y. Times, May 18, 1959, p. 1, col. 4; *cf.* Tokyo dispatch *ibid.*, May 22, 1959, p. 2, on the difficulties of setting new quotas. In June, 1959, the Netherlands and Norway withdrew from the International Whaling Convention. Apparently neither country hereafter will abide by the catch limit, but Norway will respect the duration of the whaling season; N.Y. Times, July 2, 1959.

22. 3 MALLOY, TREATIES 1914, 2966 (1923).

23. There was an earlier treaty in 1952, T.I.A.S. No. 2521. The 1957 Convention is in T.I.A.S. No. 3948. See also REIFF, *op. cit. supra* note 11, at 285. For United States provisions on punishment of nationals, seizure of foreign nationals, and maintenance of a naval squadron for enforcement of the treaty rules under an Interim Treaty of 1944, see 16 U.S.C. 631, a, j, k, m, n.

24. U.S.T.S. No. 917.

25. Articles II, III, VII, T.I.A.S. No. 2786.

26. T.I.A.S. No. 2089. Members include Canada, Denmark, France, Germany, Iceland, Italy, Norway, Portugal, Spain, the United Kingdom, the United States, and, since 1958, the Soviet Union.

27. Doc. No. FAO/51/8/1847, Agreements, Art. 3. See 1 PEASLEE 582, 588.

28. The members are the United States, Panama, and Costa Rica. The Convention entered into force in 1950. See 1 PEASLEE 681. Pending the deposit of ratifications to the conventions adopted at the Geneva Conference on the Law of the Sea in 1958, it is too soon to tell whether they will succeed in introducing further progress in the steady course of the efforts to conserve the riches of the sea.

On the Geneva Conference generally see Sørensen, *The Law of the Sea*, INTERNATIONAL CONCILIATION No. 520 (1958).

For earlier studies see LEONARD, INTERNATIONAL REGULATION OF FISHERIES (1944), and Jessup, *L'Exploitation des Richesses de la Mer*, 4 Hague Academy of International Law, 1929 RECUEIL DES COURS 405–24 (1930).

29. Articles 22, 23, and 7 (a)(7) of the Statute, 2 PEASLEE 190 ff.

30. International Commission for the Scientific Exploration of the Mediterranean Sea. For Statute, see 2 PEASLEE 96. The UN has recom-

mended its termination (U.N. ECOSOC COUNCIL OFF. REC. 10th Sess. Supp. No. 1, Res. 286 (X), 21 (1950)), but it appears on recent lists of organizations published by ECOSOC.

31. International Council for the Exploration of the Sea. The Statutes are published by the Council.

32. See U.S. Dep't of State, *International Organizations in which the United States Participates*, 8 *International Organization and Conference Series I*, 117–18 (Pub. No. 3655, 1950). 20 *Statutes at Large* 709; U.S.T.S. No. 673. Also the Central Bureau of International Map of the World on the Millionth Scale provides liaison between the governments actually doing the work. See 46 *Statutes at Large* (22 U.S.C. 269a). The work of the map bureau is now under the UN Secretariat.

33. For conventions, constitutions, etc., of the Organizations, see 1 & 2 PEASLEE 673; 616, 645.

34. The New Scientist, Feb. 19, 1959, p. 418.

35. The FAO, for example, is itself charged with promoting and recommending national action with respect to research and conservation, but it has many other functions as well and is therefore not appropriately considered here. See generally HAMBRIDGE, THE STORY OF FAO (1955).

36. For Convention see 1 PEASLEE 702, Art. 2. At the opening session in January, 1959, the Chairman of the United States Delegation stressed that the United States was "committed to a limited program covering only those technical activities urgently required." N.Y. Herald Tribune, Jan. 7, 1959. For description of the legal issues arising at the first meeting see Jessup, *The United Nations Conference on the Law of the Sea*, 59 COLUM. L. REV. 234, 255 (1959).

The problem of safety at sea has been handled through treaties apart from any international organization. See REIFF, *op. cit. supra* note 11, *passim*, for descriptions of the rules of the road, regulations as to construction, safety devices, radio, and the like. The United States acts as "monitor" of the Atlantic sea lanes, reporting to the flag state ships which do not use the proper "tracks"—any corrective action is left to the flag state.

37. Convention, Article 1.

There is in existence today an International Convention for the Safety of Life at Sea, which, among other things, sets out the type of equipment appropriately carried by vessels, safety procedures, and the like. These standards are left for application to member States.

Presumably IMCO's Maritime Safety Committee will function in this field and make studies and recommendations to improve safety facilities at sea.

38. See CMD No. 9065 (1952); 1 PEASLEE 183 ff., esp. Art. 57 of each Convention. On earlier arrangements, see Jessup *et al.*, in CHAMBERLAIN 1955 at 144–46.

39. See 2 PEASLEE 127.

40. See, *e.g.*, The Paris Motor Traffic Convention, 1909, 102 BRIT. FOR. ST. PAP. 64; The Motor Traffic Convention 1926 (superseding that of 1909), 108 L.N.T.S. 123; Pan-American Motor Traffic Convention, 1930 and 1943; 5 & 9 HUDSON, INTERNATIONAL LEGISLATION 786; 91; The United Nations Convention on Road Traffic 1949 (U.N. Pub. Sales No. 1950. VIII.2); The European Agreement of Sept. 1950 and The Protocol on Road Signs and Signals 1949, U.N. Doc. No. E/ECE/TRANS/228.

41. The principle of freedom of navigation on "international" rivers was proclaimed by the Executive Council of the French Republic in 1792 and Articles 108–116 of the treaty produced by the Congress of Vienna in 1815 set out guiding ideas for later arrangements. The Barcelona Convention of 1921 and the Statute on the Regime of Navigable Waterways of International Concern of April 20, 1921, and an Additional Protocol of the same date, with twenty Parties plus Germany, Austria, Hungary, and Bulgaria, as a result of provisions in the peace treaties formalized the principles of equality of use and charges, non-discrimination among flags, control on an equitable basis by the riparians, etc. See 7 L.N.T.S. 36 ff., 66. On a proposal for an international commission to run the Panama Canal see Travis and Watkins, *Control of the Panama Canal: an Obsolete Shibboleth?* 37 FOR. AFF. 407, 417–18 (1959). After the Boxer Rebellion settlement of 1901, a mixed group of Chinese officials and representatives of the powers with extraterritorial rights in China was established as the Whangpoo Conservancy with the task of regulating, policing, and dredging the river at Shanghai. Financing the international operation proved difficult, and control was increasingly left to the Chinese. The joint effort substantially ended in 1941 and was actually terminated in 1949; see REIFF, *op. cit. supra* note 11, at 101.

42. See SAYRE, EXPERIMENTS IN INTERNATIONAL ADMINISTRATION 131–41 (1919); CHAMBERLAIN 1955 at 123–24, 134.

43. By the time of the First World War the members were England, France, Austria-Hungary, Germany, Italy, Rumania, Russia, and Turkey.

44. It may be noted that the original plan for the Danube, envisaged in the 1856 settlement, called for the Danube Commission to supervise the engineering program and for a different *riparian* commission to manage the works and navigation. See note 45 *infra.*

45. The Parties are Bulgaria, Czechoslovakia, Hungary, Rumania, Ukrainian SSR, USSR, and Yugoslavia. As noted, a "Riparian Commission" was also tried for the lower Danube under the original Treaty of Paris of 1856 but was soon opposed by Britain and France when it proposed to raise tolls above expenses and attempted to exclude non-riparian shipping. It really never got under way, and its proposed functions were handled by the general Commission. See generally SAYRE, *op. cit. supra* note 42, at 38–47.

46. See earlier section on Tangier.

47. Gumpert's salary was apparently paid him throughout the period while he resided in Spain, and he was reinstated at the end of the war.

48. When the question was raised in 1929, it is interesting to note that M. Marchegiano, the judicial counselor of the International Zone of Tangier, held that the Commission had achieved a juridical position and personality like that of the Danube Commission. In general see STUART, THE INTERNATIONAL CITY OF TANGIER 26–34 (1955), and *The International Lighthouse at Cape Spartel*, 24 AM. J. INT'L L. 770–76 (1930). The venture was formally terminated by a protocol of March 31, 1958, 38 DEP'T STATE BULL. 749 (1958).

49. See, for example, T.I.A.S. No. 2495 and No. 2507 (International Convention for the Safety of Life at Sea, 1948, Chap. V, Regs. 5, 6); N.Y. Times, Jan. 31, 1959, p. 2.

50. See, for example, T.I.A.S. No. 2589 (entered into force May 28, 1952).

51. The Commission is an outgrowth of a joint body established by the United States and the United Kingdom in March, 1942. It publishes an Annual Report to the Governments concerned. See also CMD. No. 6972 (1946) and T.I.A.S. No. 1799.

52. A Central Secretariat is maintained at Port of Spain, B.W.I. Assessments are based one-third equally, one-third on population in the area, and one-third on national income. See, e.g., *U.S. Relations with International Organizations*, S. REP. No. 1757, 80th Cong., 2d Sess., p. 25.

53. See Public Law 403, approved Jan. 28, 1948 (62 *Statutes at Large* 15), *Report on the South Seas Conference*, 16 DEP'T STATE BULL. 459–65 (1947).

54. See CMD. No. 9066 (1954).

Among the subsidiary organizations are the Inter-African Bureau for Epizootic Diseases, the Inter-African Permanent Bureau for Tsetse and Trypanosomiasis, the Inter-African Bureau for Soils and Rural Economy, the Inter-African Pedological Service, and the Inter-African Labor Institute.

Members include France, Belgium, Portugal, Rhodesia and Nyasaland, the Union of South Africa, and the United Kingdom.

55. The OAS is a complex and multidimensional entity, the prime purpose of which is hemisphere security (Charter, Art. 4). Functioning through an Inter-American Conference which meets every five years, an Advisory Defense Committee, a Security Council, Specialized Conferences, Specialized Organizations (dealt with under their fields of specialization herein), the Pan American Union (which coordinates cultural affairs and provides a Secretariat), and a Council which has as subordinate agencies, an Inter-American ECOSOC, Council of Jurists, and a Cultural Council, the OAS presents multiple opportunities for discussion, consultation, study, and cooperation. In its non-defense activities, it is limited to these.

56. The Charter of this organization observes that the Members are "separate parts of one and the same nation." See 2 PEASLEE 562 and Fenwick, *The Organization of Central American States*, 46 AM. J. INT'L L. 509 (1952).

57. Members of the Council of Europe are Belgium, Denmark, France, the Federal Republic of Germany, Greece, Iceland, Ireland, Italy, Luxembourg, Netherlands, Norway, Sweden, Turkey, and the United Kingdom. See COUNCIL OF EUROPE, THE COUNCIL OF EUROPE (1957).

58. Members include Austria, Belgium, Denmark, France, the Federal Republic of Germany, Greece, Iceland, Ireland, Italy, Luxembourg, The Netherlands, Norway, Portugal, Sweden, Switzerland, Turkey, and the United Kingdom. The United States and Canada send observers. The European Payments Union (EPU) was established in 1950 essentially for clearing operations between these countries. On the OEEC, see CAMPS, THE EUROPEAN COMMON MARKET AND AMERICAN POLICY (1956), and BROWN AND OPIE, AMERICAN FOREIGN ASSISTANCE (1953).

In other parts of the world there are such organs for cooperation as the International Islamic Economic Organization, designed to stimulate economic development in Muslim lands and to foster cooperation, prepare plans, and the like, but conducting no programs itself (see 2

PEASLEE 224); and especially the U.N. Economic Commissions for Europe, Asia, Latin America and Africa.

59. See Convention of Sept. 5, 1944, and Protocols, 1 PEASLEE 107, and generally, COUNCIL OF EUROPE, THE PRESENT STATE OF ECONOMIC INTEGRATION IN WESTERN EUROPE (1955), esp. at 52. See YEARBOOK OF INTERNATIONAL ORGANIZATIONS, 1958–1959, 122. Less significant is the Council for Mutual Economic Aid formed in January, 1949, by the Soviet bloc in Eastern Europe to exchange economic experience and raw materials, to render mutual technical aid, and to do large scale planning.

60. In force July 25, 1952. For general discussion, see DIEBOLD, THE SCHUMAN PLAN (1959); MASON, THE EUROPEAN COAL AND STEEL COMMUNITY (1955); and BOK, THE FIRST THREE YEARS OF THE SCHUMAN PLAN (1955).

61. The first steps were made effective on Jan. 1, 1959. On the Treaty, see The European Commission, First General Report on the Activities of the Community (Sept., 1958). See also, e.g., Diebold, *The Relevance of Federalism to Western European Economic Integration*, in MACMAHON, FEDERALISM, MATURE AND EMERGENT (1955); same author, THE SCHUMAN PLAN, A STUDY IN ECONOMIC COOPERATION 1950–1959 (1959).

62. There have been some attempts to organize a rational world trading system. Thus, it was hoped in United States circles at least that the proposed charter of an International Trade Organization (ITO), which sought to protect consumers (Art. 60) as well as producers, would be, together with the IBRD and the IMF, a third support for a non-discriminatory multilateral post-war world trading system. The more recently proposed Organization for Trade Cooperation (OTC) has been designed to provide the permanent organizational framework for the administration of the General Agreement on Tariffs and Trade (GATT). Even though the OTC would not be permitted to impose obligations on members beyond those formally undertaken through ratification of GATT, important nations have been unwilling to commit themselves to a system involving an overseer of performance under the principles of freer and non-discriminatory trade and neither the ITO nor the OTC is in existence at this time. See Gorter, *GATT after Six Years*, 8 INT'L ORG. 1–18 (1954).

63. See AUBOIN, BANK FOR INTERNATIONAL SETTLEMENTS, 1930–1955 (1955) and ANNUAL REPORTS of the Bank.

64. On the IBRD, see THE WORLD BANK, POLICIES AND OPERATIONS

and ANNUAL REPORTS. On IMF see its ANNUAL REPORTS. On the IFC, see Snavely, *The International Finance Corporation: A New International Investment Agency*, AM. J. ECON. & SOCIOLOGY 341–52 (July, 1958). See also N.Y. Times, Aug. 16, 1959, p. 1.

65. Article XII (C) and (A) (6) (7). A member in financial arrears may lose its vote and one persistently violating the Statute may be suspended, but only by two-thirds vote of the General Conference. Art. XIX.

In general, see Annual Reports of the Board of Governors to the General Conference (First Report, July, 1958) and Stoessinger, *The International Atomic Energy Agency: The First Phase*, INT'L ORG. (Summer, 1959).

66. See generally, A TARGET FOR EURATOM (1957); Euratom, Premier Rapport Général sur l'activité de la Communauté (Sept., 1958); COUNCIL OF EUROPE, EUROPEAN COOPERATION IN 1958, Part I, 35–39; KNORR, NUCLEAR ENERGY IN WESTERN EUROPE AND UNITED STATES POLICY (1956). On British cooperation with Euratom, see N.Y. Times, Feb. 5, 1959, p. 8.

67. See Annual Reports, and AMALDI, THE SCOPE AND ACTIVITIES OF CERN, 1950–1954.

68. An International Convention on Security Control was signed by the OEEC members in December, 1957, as well but was not yet in force in July, 1959.

On ENEA, see ENEA, First Report on the Activities of the Agency, OEEC, Sept., 1958 and Council of Europe, *op. cit. supra* note 66, at 23–26.

69. The countries are Austria, Belgium, Denmark, France, Italy, Norway, the Netherlands, Portugal, Sweden, Switzerland, Turkey, and the Federal Republic of Germany. See Chapter 4, *infra*.

70. In 1956 the Soviet Union and eleven other states of the Communist bloc established a Joint Institute for Nuclear Research with its seat in Moscow. Its avowed purpose is to construct joint laboratories and generally to coordinate nuclear research; see YEARBOOK OF INTERNATIONAL ORGANIZATIONS 1958–59, 188.

71. For accounts of the IGY, see Sullivan, *The International Geophysical Year*, INT'L CONCILIATION NO. 521 (Jan. 1959); Atwood, *The International Geophysical Year in Retrospect*, 40 DEP'T STATE BULL. 682 (1959), and U.N. Doc. No. A/AC.98/4, at 11–17 (16 June 1959). For the astronautical accomplishments in particular, see also *U.S. Aeronautics and Space Activities, Jan. 1 to Dec. 31, 1958*, H.R. Doc.

No. 71, 86th Cong., 1st Sess. 1–8 (1959). See also Odishaw, "The IGY and World Politics," 13 AM. J. INT'L AFF. 47–56 (1959).

72. For stress on the nongovernmental nature of the IGY by national officials, see pp. 215–17 *infra*.

73. Argentina, Australia, Austria, Belgium, Bolivia, Brazil, Bulgaria, Burma, Canada, Ceylon, Republic of China, Colombia, Cuba, Czechoslovakia, Denmark, Dominican Republic, East Africa, Ecuador, Egypt, Ethiopia, Finland, France, German Democratic Republic, German Federal Republic, Ghana, Greece, Guatemala, Hungary, Iceland, India, Indonesia, Iran, Ireland, Israel, Italy, Japan, Democratic People's Republic of Korea, Malaya, Mexico, Mongolian People's Republic, Morocco, Netherlands, New Zealand, Norway, Pakistan, Panama, Peru, Philippines, Poland, Portugal, Rhodesia and Nyasaland, Rumania, Spain, Sweden, Switzerland, Tunisia, Union of South Africa, USSR, United Kingdom, United States, Uruguay, Venezuela, Democratic Republic of Viet Nam, Republic of Viet Nam, Yugoslavia.

74. Sullivan, *supra* note 71, at 268.

75. The unions are:

GENERAL UNIONS

International Astronomical Union (IAU)
International Union of Geodesy and Geophysics (IUGG)
International Union of Pure and Applied Chemistry (IUPAC)
International Union of Pure and Applied Physics (IUPAP)
International Union of Biological Sciences (IUBS)
International Mathematical Union (IMU)

SPECIALIZED UNIONS

International Scientific Radio Union (URSI)
International Geographical Union (IGU)
International Union of Crystallography (ICUCr)
International Union of Theoretical and Applied Mechanics (IUTAM)
International Union of History and Philosophy of Science (IUHPS)
International Union of Physiological Sciences (IUPS)
International Union of Biochemistry (IUB)

National academies of science or comparable bodies representing 45 nations also participate.

76. On ICSU, see ICSU, A BRIEF OUTLINE (1958).

77. See Sullivan, *supra* note 71, at 267.

78. CSAGI, BULL. D'INFORMATION (NO. 4, 1955).

79. CSAGI, BULL. D'INFORMATION 11 (NO. 6, 1956).

80. See Sullivan, *supra* note 71, at 279.

81. See *id.* at 294. On this problem generally, see *id.* at 284–94.

It might be added, however, that a CSAGI meeting proposed for the United States was shifted to Canada to avoid having delegations from North Korea, North Viet Nam, and Outer Mongolia, all IGY participants, set foot in the United States, and a Chinese Nationalist delegation somehow failed to get visas in time to attend a CSAGI meeting in Moscow in the summer of 1958. *Id.* at 328–31.

82. *Id.* at 321–28.

83. Atwood, *supra* note 71, at 688–89.

4. PATTERNS FOR THE FUTURE

1. CHAMBERLAIN 1955, at 60.

2. For the 1902 Convention, see 23 HERTSLET, TREATIES AND CONVENTIONS BETWEEN GREAT BRITAIN AND FOREIGN POWERS 579. See generally SAYRE, EXPERIMENTS IN INTERNATIONAL ADMINISTRATION 117, 131 (1919), and CHAMBERLAIN 1955, at 130–32.

3. There are also the International Cotton Advisory Committee, the International Rice Commission, and the Rubber and Wool Study Groups, which are consultative and advisory only. The International Wine Office is also a cartel-like institution and investigates such matters as violations of price agreements, but it is essentially an information agency and probably a means for dividing the market informally.

4. The International Tin Agreement of 1953 has similar provisions in Article 17 (7).

5. See U.S.T.S. 970. Of 36 votes the United States had 12, Brazil 9, Colombia 3, and each other producing nation 1.

6. See, *e.g.*, International Whaling Commission: regulations changed by three-fourths vote, other decisions by majority vote (Art. 3(2)); WMO: generally two-thirds (Art. 10(b)).

7. For example, ILO, WHO, ICAO, IMCO, IBRD, IMF, International Sugar Council, International Wheat Council, United Nations Commission on Narcotic Drugs.

8. Metzger, *Settlement of International Disputes by Non-Judicial Methods*, 48 AM. J. INT'L L. 408 (1954). See generally CHAMBERLAIN 1955, at 45–52.

9. International Office of Public Health, 2 MALLOY, TREATIES 2214 (T.S. No. 511); International Institute of Refrigeration (Art. 9).

10. Under the older International Sugar Agreement of 1937, the Council was composed of all Members while the Executive Committee consisted of three representatives each of the sugar-importing, cane-

sugar producing, and beet-sugar producing countries, and the United Kingdom, the United States, Cuba, and the Netherlands had to be included.

Under the Rubber Agreement of 1934, neither the Malayan rubber interests nor the Netherlands Indies could be outvoted on any matter of importance.

11. See 75 REV. GÉN. DES CHEMINS DE FER 3, 4, 6 (Jan. 1956) and see generally, YEARBOOK OF INT'L ORG. 1958–59 (7th ed.). See also the European Conference of Ministers of Transport, *First Report*, paras. 27, 28 (1955); *Second Report*, paras. 3, 19, 39 (1956); *Fourth Report*, paras. 54, 55, 86–94, Annex I (1958). On earlier problems of European railroads, see Masters, *International Organization of European Rail Transport*, INT'L CONCILIATION No. 330 (May, 1937).

12. See Ambassade de France, Note d'Information, Mar. 8, 1956; Barron's, Aug. 13, 1956, p. 9; L'Économie, Mar. 12, 1959, p. 19.

13. See ENEA AND THE EUROCHEMIC COMPANY, FIRST REPORT OF THE STEERING COMMITTEE FOR NUCLEAR ENERGY TO THE *O.E.E.C.* (1958); ENEA, FIRST REPORT TO THE CONSULTATIVE ASSEMBLY OF THE COUNCIL OF EUROPE (1958); British Information Service, British Record, 1959, Feb. 20, 1959, p. 2.

14. Convention, Articles 17, 18, 28, 60. On the controversy over the meaning of "ship-owning nations," see Jessup, *The United Nations Conference on the Law of the Sea*, 59 COLUM. L. REV. 234, 255–57 (1959).

15. ICAO CONVENTION Art. 50; UPU, Art. 15; WHO, Art. 24 and UNESCO CONSTITUTION Art. 5; ILO CONSTITUTION Art. 7 (representatives of workers and employers participate as well as those from governments); ILO, Art. 36; IAEA, Art. 6; Narcotic Drugs, ECOSOC Res. 9 (I), Feb. 16, 1946; IMF, Art. 12 (3); IBRD, Art. 5 (4).

5. THE ANTARCTIC

1. The United Kingdom, for example, treats such possessions as South Georgia, which is north of the 60th parallel, as at most sub-Antarctic but, on the other hand, bases her claims to an Antarctic "sector" (see *infra*) in part on activities on this island. See Hayton, *The "American" Antarctic*, 50 AM. J. INT'L L. 583, 597 n. 67 (1956), hereinafter cited as Hayton, *American Antarctic*.

2. See generally GOULD, ANTARCTICA IN WORLD AFFAIRS (For. Pol. Assoc., Headline Series, No. 128, 1958), hereinafter cited as GOULD, and

SULLIVAN, QUEST FOR A CONTINENT (1957), hereinafter cited as SULLIVAN, QUEST.

The Antarctic is here treated as a "continent" despite speculation that it may in fact be an archipelago. See *infra.*

3. GOULD 3.

4. While such speculation is interesting from the point of view of problems of freedom of the seas, claims to portions of the "high seas," and the like, it is of little practical significance since the Antarctic is expected to remain frozen for the foreseeable future, despite the gradual warming in progress. Further, the findings of recent expeditions tend to make this theory less tenable. On recent geological findings, and for speculation on potential legal problems, see Hayton, *Polar Problems and International Law*, 52 AM. J. INT'L L. 746, 760–61 (1958), hereinafter cited as Hayton, *Polar Problems.*

5. See SULLIVAN, QUEST 210 ff., 256 ff. Vincennes Bay and the hills around Prydy Bay are ice-free.

6. GOULD 7.

7. GOULD, 8–9; Fleming, 23 INT'L AFF. 551 (1947).

8. See Hayton, *Polar Problems* 762; Sullivan, *Antarctica in a Two-Power World*, 36 FOR. AFF. 164–65 (1957), hereinafter cited as Sullivan, *Antarctica.* On the use of compacted ice for airstrips, see SULLIVAN, QUEST 244.

9. See GOULD 11–12; American Geographical Society, The Geographical Review, Vol. XLVII, No. 1 (1957), 1–28; CHRISTIE, THE ANTARCTIC PROBLEM (1951), hereinafter cited as CHRISTIE; SULLIVAN, QUEST 21–75.

10. Hayton, *American Antarctic* 583, 597–99 (1956).

11. GOULD 18, referring to Stackpole, *A First Recognition of Antarctica*, BOSTON PUBLIC LIBRARY QUARTERLY (Jan. 1952).

12. On the legal status of the Antarctic, see generally Dollot, *Les espaces polaires de l'Antarctique*, 75 HAGUE RECUEIL DES COURS, II, 173–91 (1949); SMEDAL, ACQUISITION OF SOVEREIGNTY OVER POLAR AREAS (Oslo, 1931); Jenks, *An International Regime for Antarctica?*, 32 INT'L AFF. 414 (1956) (appears also in THE COMMON LAW OF MANKIND 366 ff. [1958]); Waldock, *Disputed Sovereignty in the Falkland Islands Dependencies*, 25 BRIT. YB. INT'L L. 311–53 (1948); Jessup, *Sovereignty in Antarctica*, 41 AM. J. INT'L L., 117–19 (1947); GIDEL, ASPECTS JURIDIQUES DE LA LUTTE POUR L'ANTARCTIQUE (1948); 1 HACKWORTH, DIGEST, 449–65 (1940); MINISTERIO DE RELACIONES EXTERIORES Y CULTO [Argentina], SOBERANIA ARGENTINA EN LA ANTARTIDA (1948); MADARIAGA, LA ANTARTIDA SUDAMERICANA (1945); PINOCHET DE LA BARRA, LA ANTAR-

TICA CHILENA: ESTUDIO DE NUESTROS DERECHOS (1948); United States Naval War College, *Declarations Concerning Antarctic Territories*, INT'L LAW DOCS. 1948–49, 217–45 (1950); ROBERTS *et al*, ANTARCTICA, A SELECTED BIBLIOGRAPHY (U.N. Library, 1956).

For excellent maps of the claims, see Heron, *Antarctic Claims*, 32 FOR. AFF., 662 (1954); Sullivan, *Antarctica* 157, and Hanessian, *Antarctica*, PROC. AM. SOC'Y INT'L L., 1958, 146.

13. See Simsarian, *The Acquisition of Legal Title to Terra Nullius*, 53 POL. SCI. Q. 111–28 (1938); KELLAR, LISSITZYN, & MANN, CREATION OF RIGHTS OF SOVEREIGNTY THROUGH SYMBOLIC ACTS, 1400–1800 (1938); 1 OPPENHEIM, INTERNATIONAL LAW 558 (ed. Lauterpacht, 8th ed., 1955); 1 HACKWORTH, DIGEST 393–409, 449–65, 465 ff.; SMEDAL, *op. cit. supra* note 12; 1 HYDE, INTERNATIONAL LAW CHIEFLY AS INTERPRETED AND APPLIED BY THE UNITED STATES 347–55; Lakhtine, *Rights Over the Arctic*, 24 AM. J. INT'L L. 703–17 (1930); Jessup, *supra* note 12, at 117–19.

14. HILL, CLAIMS TO TERRITORY IN INTERNATIONAL LAW AND RELATIONS 146–58 (1945).

15. [1924] 2 FOREIGN REL. 519–20 (1939).

16. This matter is discussed *infra* at 153–56.

17. 2 U.N. Rep. Int'l Arb. Trib. 840 (1949), 22 AM. J. INT'L L. 877 (1928). On the Palmas Island Case, see Jessup, *The Palmas Island Arbitration*, 22 AM. J. INT'L L. 735–52 (1928). Huber also pointed out that "inchoate rights," if they exist, are worthy of note only if "completed eventually by actual and durable taking of possession within a reasonable time."

18. 26 AM. J. INT'L L. 390 (1932).

19. He added that "mere constructive occupation is kept within bounds by the doctrine of contiguity."

20. P.C.I.J., Ser. A/B, No. 53, 45–46, 52, 63 (1933); See 1 HYDE, *op. cit. supra* note 13, at 336.

21. Chile had four stations, at Greenwich Island, Deception Island and Palmer Peninsula (2). Argentina had nine, on Laurie, Gamma, Persson, Deception, and Livingston Islands, Hope Bay, Bismark Strait, Marguerite Bay, and Coats Land. The British had eight, at Anvers, Horseshow, Signy, Argentine, and Deception Islands, Port Lockroy, and Hope Bay.

22. See, for example, Jessup, *supra* note 12, at 119. See generally SMEDAL, *op. cit. supra* note 12, at 54–76; Heron, *supra* note 12, at 663; Lakhtine, *supra* note 13, at 703–17; Reeves, *Antarctic Sectors*, 33 AM. J. INT'L L. 521 (1939).

23. The Hon. Paschal Poirier first advanced the principle on Feb.

20, 1907. Speaking in the Canadian Senate, he said: "A country whose possession today goes up to the Arctic regions will have a right, or should have a right, or has a right to all the lands that are to be found in the waters between a line extending from its eastern extremity north and another line extending from the western extremity north. All the lands between the two lines up to the North Pole should belong and do belong to the country whose territory abuts up there." See SMEDAL, *op. cit. supra* note 12, at 54, 64–67.

24. See, *e.g.*, Toma, *Soviet Attitude Towards the Acquisition of Territorial Sovereignty in the Antarctic*, 50 AM. J. INT'L L. 611–26 (1956). The Soviet Union has tended to reject a sector theory for the Antarctic as somehow being a cover for an alleged surreptitious onslaught by United States "imperialists." See Kulski, *Soviet Comments on International Law*, 45 AM. J. INT'L L. 766–69 (1951), and Toma, *supra*. On Soviet and Canadian claims in the Arctic, see also PROC. AM. SOC'Y INT'L L. 1958, 138–40.

25. See Hayton, *American Antarctic* 603–7.

Britain generally accepts the 60th parallel but pushes its sector northward to the 50th parallel between longitudes 20° W. and 50° W. to include several islands.

26. See, for example, *Report of the International Law Commission, 1951*, U.N. Doc. No. A/1858 at 17–20 (1951); U.N. Doc. No. A/2456 at 12–19 (1953); U.N. Doc. No. A/2693, 12–21 (1954) and U.N. Doc. No. A/2934 at 12–21, 42–72 (1955); Lauterpacht, *Sovereignty over Submarine Areas*, 27 BRIT. YB. INT'L L. 376–433 (1950). The doctrine of contiguity at least was rejected by Huber in the *Palmas Island Case* as having "no foundation in international law" as a basis for sovereignty. Scott, Hague Court Reports (2d Ser.) 84, 128 (1932).

There have been assertions, at least for the Arctic, that each Polar State has sovereignty over the aerial space above its whole sector as well. See Lakhtine, *supra* note 13, at 703 ff. See generally Svarlien, *The Legal Status of the Arctic*, PROC. AM. SOC'Y INT'L L. 1958, 136 ff., and Plischke, *Trans-Polar Aviation and Jurisdiction over Arctic Airspace*, 37 AM. POL. SCI. REV. 999 (1943).

27. On opposition of the Soviet Union to the sector theory in the Antarctic, see also Toma, *supra* note 24, at 619–21. On United States rejection of "sectors," see Reeves, *supra* note 22, at 519–21.

28. The original Letters Patent had to be amended because they included, apparently through inadvertence, portions of the South American mainland (Patagonia and Tierra del Fuego). See 101 & 111 BRIT.

& FOR. ST. PAP. 76–77 (1912); 16–17 (1921). No protests appear to have been made by other nations at the time.

29. On British claims, see *The British Title to Sovereignty in the Falkland Islands Dependencies*, 8 POLAR RECORD 125–51 (1956); Hayton, *American Antarctic* 583–619; Waldock, *supra* note 12, at 321–53 CHRISTIE *passim*.

30. See Letters Patent of June 23, 1843; April 28, 1876; Feb. 25, 1892; and Dec. 13, 1948 (the latter in 150 BRIT. & FOR. ST. PAP. 608–13 (pt. I, 1956); GOEBEL, THE STRUGGLE FOR THE FALKLAND ISLANDS *passim* (1927).

31. See CHRISTIE 206–19. A Chilean company was given a license for mining and grazing privileges on South Georgia by the Governor of the Falkland Islands at about this time as well.

32. Falkland Islands Ordinance No. 3 of 1906 (Oct. 5, 1906).

33. *Statutory Rules and Orders 1908*, 1042–1044.

34. See *supra* and CHRISTIE 206–19.

35. See CHRISTIE 247–51.

36. SULLIVAN, QUEST 268.

37. See, *e.g.*, Hayton, *American Antarctic* 583 ff. CHRISTIE 263–88. On conflicts *between* Chile and Argentina, see Hayton, *American Antarctic* 601–3, and sources cited.

38. See GOEBEL, *op. cit. supra* note 30, at 47–216, 261–76, 361–63, 412–32.

39. On Argentine protests of British claims in the Falkland Islands, dating from as early as 1834, see GOEBEL, *op. cit. supra passim.*

40. It thus overlaps the Chilean claim between 53° and 70° W. For bibliography concerning the Argentine claim, see Hayton, *American Antarctic* 587 n. 22.

41. Argentine Note to Britain of Feb. 20, 1953, La Prensa (Buenos Aires), Feb. 21, 1953.

42. The Laurie Island Post Office and a meteorological station date from 1904.

43. See Hayton, *American Antarctic* 590, and sources cited.

44. Boletín Oficial, June 30, 1955.

45. Decree-Law No. 2191, Boletín Oficial, March 19, 1957. See 9 POLAR RECORD 52–53 (1958). Included in this new territory are Tierra del Fuego, Isla de los Estados, Isla Ano Nuevo, Islas Malvinas (the Falkland Islands), South Georgia Island, South Sandwich Islands, and the Argentine-claimed Antarctic sector.

The Instituto Antártico Argentino was recently reorganized and now issues a twice-yearly *Boletín*. Volume 1, No. 1 was issued in May, 1957.

46. Hayton, *American Antarctic* 557–58, and sources cited. The departure of Peron has been reported as having had a moderating effect but only to a limited degree.

47. Boletín Oficial, Nov. 6, 1940. Britain, Argentina, Japan and the United States expressed their reservations.

48. See PINOCHET DE LA BARRA, CHILEAN SOVEREIGNTY IN ANTARCTICA (1955), for a detailed account of the development of the Chilean claim, beginning with the Papal divisions. See also CHRISTIE 277–85.

49. See Hayton, *American Antarctic* 585, for an account of these claims.

50. *Ibid.;* see also sources cited there. See also N.Y. Times, Feb. 25, 1948, p. 22 (letter to the Editor from the Chilean Ambassador to the United States).

51. SULLIVAN, QUEST 282–84.

52. See Hayton, *Polar Problems* 759 n. 40.

53. See generally Hayton, *American Antarctic* 583 ff. The only other overlap which has existed was that of the German claim from 17° E. to 5° W., which was within the Norwegian claim—it is no longer considered active. See Martin, *The Antarctic Sphere of Interest,* in WEIGERT *et al* (eds.), NEW COMPASS OF THE WORLD 61–79 (1949).

54. See CHRISTIE 247–51; SULLIVAN, QUEST 266–67; Hayton, *American Antarctic* 590–97.

55. See N.Y. Times, June 10, 1950, p. 2.

56. Chile, Ministry of Foreign Affairs, MEMORIA, 1948, 245–46, 353–56. On possible solutions to the Chilean-Argentine claims, and on theories that the Palmer Peninsula is a continuation of South America, see Hayton, *American Antarctic* 595–97, and sources cited.

57. See, *e.g.*, 31 DEP'T STATE BULL. 817 (1954). The United States has observed this agreement and originally "congratulated" the powers on reaching it.

58. See N.Y. Times, Feb. 4, 1952, p. 6; Feb. 5, 1952, p. 16; Feb. 6, 1952, p. 9. The Notes exchanged are reprinted in 6 POLAR RECORD 413–18 (Jan. 1952); see also SULLIVAN, QUEST 269–70.

59. SULLIVAN, QUEST 285.

60. GOULD 23, 21. See also SULLIVAN, QUEST 281.

61. Since the "sector" principle has never been subject to formal judicial scrutiny, these nations may fear that *a court* would not accord the weight they consider proper to their claims. For an earlier sugges-

tion as to the usefulness of a Court ruling or opinion on Antarctic claims, see Jessup, *supra* note 12, at 119.

62. QUARANTA, EL SEXTO CONTINENTE 130 (monograph, 1950).

63. Applications Instituting Proceedings filed in the Registry of the Court on May 4, 1955, Antarctica Case, *United Kingdom v. Argentina, United Kingdom v. Chile;* Orders of the Court of March 16, 1956, [1956], I.C.J. REP. 12, 15; N.Y. Times, May 7 and Aug. 4, 1955 (for Chilean and Argentine rejections).

64. Hayton, *American Antarctic* 607–10; SULLIVAN, QUEST 285, 326.

65. See Hayton, *American Antarctic*, for consideration of alternative solutions.

66. *Statutory Rules and Orders, 1923*, 712–13. On New Zealand, see Hanessian, *supra* note 12, at 155–56.

67. On the United States–New Zealand correspondence, see 1 HACKWORTH, DIGEST 456–59 (1940).

68. SULLIVAN, QUEST 356–57.

69. Journal Officiel, March 29, 1940. See generally, CHRISTIE *passim*. The French claim aroused some distress in the United States, where it was felt that Wilkes's squadron had discovered this area.

70. Journal Officiel, April 6, 1938. The United States reserved all rights. See 1 HACKWORTH, *op. cit. supra* note 67, at 460.

71. See CMD. No. 5900 (T.S. No. 73 of 1938); 1 HACKWORTH, DIGEST 459; SULLIVAN, QUEST 286.

72. See SULLIVAN, QUEST 286–96.

73. *Statutory Rules and Orders, 1933*, 2089–90.

74. See Charteris, *The Commonwealth of Australia and Antarctica*, 18 BRIT. YB. INT'L L. 177–79 (1937), and, see generally, SULLIVAN, QUEST 114–23.

75. SULLIVAN, QUEST 119.

76. *Id.* at 123. On Australian "concern" over Russian IGY bases in the sector claimed by Australia, and, in particular, over the raising of the Soviet flag at an IGY base, see Hanessian, *Antarctica*, PROC. AM. SOC'Y INT'L L. 1958, 152–53; The Times (London), Feb. 6, 1957; and *infra* p. 162.

77. See 143 BRIT. & FOR. ST. PAP. 663 (1939). In 1911 Amundsen reached the Pole and placed the Norwegian flag there. In 1929 Captain Riiser-Larsen photographed what is now Princess Martha Coast from the air, and Norwegian expeditions explored portions of this region in 1930–31 and 1935. See SULLIVAN, QUEST 109–13. The United States

(1 HACKWORTH, DIGEST 460–61) and Chile (MEMORIA 1939, 271) reserved all rights.

78. The United States, in effect, reserved its rights. [1929] 3 FOREIGN REL. 717–19 (1944) and 1 HACKWORTH, DIGEST 468–70.

79. See 34 AM. J. INT'L L. Supp. 83 (1940); 1 HACKWORTH, DIGEST 463; CMD. No. 3875 at 2 (T.S. No. 25 of 1931).

80. See N.Y. Times, May 29, 1948, p. 2.

81. See, *e.g.*, N.Y. Times, Jan. 4, 1948, p. 12; Jan. 9, 1948, p. 17; Jan. 27, 1948, p. 17; and CHRISTIE 290.

82. [1924] 2 FOREIGN REL. 519–20 (1939).

83. 1 HACKWORTH, DIGEST 454.

84. GOULD 26.

85. See, *e.g.*, Reeves, *Antarctic Sectors*, 33 AM. J. INT'L L. 521 (1939).

86. 72 CONG. REC., S. Res. 310–12, Part II, 12179.

87. Act of June 16, 1936, 49 *Statutes at Large*, 2324.

88. See Sullivan, *Antarctica in a Two-Power World*, 36 FOR. AFF. 156 (1957).

89. SULLIVAN, QUEST 138.

90. U.S. National Archives, *Preliminary Inventory of the Records of the United States Antarctic Service*, PRELIMINARY INVENTORIES No. 90, 15–18 (1955). For comment, see Hayton, *Polar Problems* 746, 762–63.

91. See Sullivan, *supra* note 88, at 157–58.

92. The operation was a training exercise in polar combat set in the Antarctic to avoid any charge of saber-rattling in the more sensitive Arctic. Some 13 ships and 4,700 men participated. For a first-hand account of Highjump, see SULLIVAN, QUEST 173–248.

93. See *id.* at 249–61. A private United States expedition led by Finn Ronne was also in the Antarctic in 1947. Ronne raised an American flag on Stonington Island, the scene of American explorations in 1940, but in 1947 the site of a British base. The British commander protested the flag-raising and asked its meaning. Ronne answered in perfect lawyerese that it was as follows: "As an American expedition re-occupying this base on Stonington Island, we have reflown the American flag on the American-built flagpole at the American camp." He did not reveal that he had also been appointed United States Postmaster for Stonington Island. See SULLIVAN, QUEST 271–79; 16 DEP'T STATE BULL. 30 (1947); N.Y. Times, March 25, 1947, p. 3.

94. Operation Plan No. 155, Commander, U.S. Naval Support Force, Antarctic, p. 2, for Deepfreeze I noted that the action was to establish "permanent stations in the Antarctic . . . in support of United States rights in the area." On Deepfreeze I and II, see also, Committee on Interstate and Foreign Commerce, *IGY: The Arctic and Antarctic*, H. R. REP. No. 1348, 85th Cong., 2d Sess., 31–34 (1958).

95. See SULLIVAN, QUEST 346.

96. See generally, Sullivan, *supra* note 88, at 154–66; Time, Dec. 31, 1956, pp. 12–17. Note however, as pointed out by Sullivan (QUEST 344), that in January, 1956, the United States group in the Antarctic, which had completed an aerial survey of Wilkes Land, sent a message to the Soviet group that was moving in there on the ground in what was taken by the United States press to be a "we got there first" move: "Welcome to Wilkes Land. Hope you are having good luck finding your IGY base site. We recently flew over interior in vicinity of your planned inland bases. . . ."

97. 16 DEP'T STATE BULL. 30 (1947).

98. See, *e.g.*, Hanessian, *supra* note 76, at 159–63. It has been reported, too, that a U.S. Air Force map with United States sectors is on file in the Chilean Foreign Office. Hayton, *American Antarctic* 584 n. 5.

One Congressional suggestion in 1957 called for the creation of an autonomous Antarctic Commission similar to the Atomic Energy Agency to maintain an information depository, conduct laboratory and field work, assist or advise in the establishment of United States territorial claims, supervise all expeditions and activities in the Antarctic under United States auspices, and issue needed publications. 103 CONG. REC. 8130–35 (May 1957). (S. 2189, introduced on a bipartisan basis by Senator Wiley of Wisconsin and 22 co-sponsors). A similar bill was introduced in the House on Aug. 7, 1957, by Representative Clair Engle. The Bills, however, made slow progress. In its latest form the proposal names the Commission after Admiral Byrd, 105 CONG. REC. June 5, 1959 (S. 764).

Wiley listed as "vital factors" requiring attention a decision on territorial rights, the prevention of a seizure of strategic areas by Russia and "capitalizing" on mineral deposits and the like in the Antarctic. The threat of closure of the Panama Canal was mentioned. 104 CONG. REC. 1032–34 (Jan. 1958).

99. H.J. Res. 353, 83d Cong., 2d Sess. (Jan. 18, 1954). The Resolu-

tion based its claims on exploration and discovery in the nineteenth and twentieth centuries. It was referred to the House Committee on Foreign Affairs and apparently died there.

See generally, PROC. AM. SOC'Y INT'L L. 1958, 161–63, for description of possible United States action.

100. *Supra* note 94, at 46. A recently prepared list indicates that over a dozen major United States departments or agencies are concerned with the Antarctic. These include the Departments of Defense, State, Interior, and Commerce, the National Science Foundation, the National Academy of Sciences, the Central Intelligence Agency, the AEC, the Departments of Health, Education, and Welfare, the National Archives, the Library of Congress, the Smithsonian Institution, and the Board on Geographical Names. See list: U.S. Government Departments and Agencies Participating in or Interested in the Antarctic, compiled by Dr. H. M. Dater, Office of U.S. Antarctic Projects (mimeo.).

101. SULLIVAN, QUEST 124–27. German explorers had conducted expeditions in 1874, 1902, and 1912, but no assertions of sovereignty were made. See also Fleming, 23 INT'L AFF. 552 (1947), and N.Y. Times, April 12, 1939, p. 25.

102. For a thorough examination of the Soviet position, see Toma, *Soviet Attitude Towards the Acquisition of Territorial Sovereignty in the Antarctic*, 50 AM. J. INT'L L. 611–26 (1956). In 1946, the Soviet Union became a party to the International Whaling Convention and began to send whaling fleets into Antarctic waters.

103. See Orlov, *Russian Antarctic Discoveries of 1821 are Basis of Soviet Claim*, 9 USSR INFO. BULL. 296–97 (May 13, 1949); Toma, *supra* note 102, at 625–26.

104. The theory of "effective occupation" is rejected in the form defined at the Berlin Conference of 1885 as a technique designed to plunder Africa. See Toma, *supra* at 617.

105. See *infra*, pp. 172–73.

106. 10 USSR INFO. BULL. 380 (June 23, 1950). See also Toma, *supra* note 102, at 624–25. Toma points out that the Soviet Union has also used the term "states that have the historical right" to participate in a solution (at 612).

107. Kostritsin, *Vopros o Rezhime Antarktiki*, 42 SOVETSKOE GOSUDARSTVO I PRAVO (March, 1951), cited by Toma, *supra* note 102, at 613 n. 12.

108. See, *e.g.*, N.Y. Times, Oct. 24, 1949, p. 39; and June 16, 1950,

p. 51; Toma, *supra* note 102, at 613 n. 12; and Section on the IGY, *infra.*

109. Belgium, U.S. Antarctic Programs Officer, Aug. 20, 1957 (mimeo.), cited in PROC. AM. SOC'Y INT'L L. 1958, 153 n. 23. See also N.Y. Times, Feb. 27, 1949, p. 4; and June 22, 1947, § 2, p. 25.

110. See Hayton, *American Antarctic* 759; and, *e.g.*, articles in *El Día* of Montevideo on the Uruguayan position (May 13, p. 9; May 14, p. 9; May 15, p. 10 [1958]).

6. COOPERATION IN THE ANTARCTIC

1. See Sullivan, *Antarctica in a Two-Power World,* 36 FOR. AFF. 158–59 (1957).

2. 104 CONG. REC. 1032–34 at 1032 (Jan. 27, 1958).

3. SULLIVAN, QUEST FOR A CONTINENT 349–50 (1957). All expeditions have flown their own flags at their own stations—in view of the IGY "gentleman's agreement," it cannot be said that any "claim" was thus made.

4. GOULD, ANTARCTICA IN WORLD AFFAIRS 34 (1958). See also CHRISTIE, THE ANTARCTIC PROBLEM 292–93 (1951), and section on Argentina and Chile, *supra.*

5. CHRISTIE, *op. cit. supra* note 4, at 297.

6. See SULLIVAN, *op. cit. supra* note 3, at 353–54.

7. Report of the Committee on Interstate and Foreign Commerce, *International Geophysical Year: The Arctic, Antarctica* H.R. REP. No. 1348, 85th Cong. 2d Sess., 20–21 (1958), hereinafter cited as *House Report IGY.*

8. Such a vast change is not to be anticipated momentarily, but equally great changes are known to have occurred in the past. For example, the sea level rose some 220 feet at the time the ice sheets vanished from North America some 10,000 years ago.

9. The cost of an air facility comparable to the one at Thule is estimated as high as $300,000,000 over a six-year period. A more modest, nonmilitary base might cost substantially less.

10. See T.I.A.S. No. 3880. See also agreement with Brazil, T.I.A.S. No. 4143. About the same mileage (13,000 plus) is involved, for example in the following routes from London to Christchurch: via New York, San Francisco, Honolulu; via Middle East, India, Australia; via Rio de Janeiro, Buenos Aires, Antarctica.

11. *House Report IGY* 41, 45. Pan American World Airways sent

the first commercial airliner, complete with stewardesses, to McMurdo Sound, Antarctica, on October 15, 1957, presumably as a stunt.

12. *House Report IGY* 40.

13. For a glowing account of the Antarctic's mineral and other riches and ability to sustain a population, see remarks of Paul A. Siple, scientific adviser to Chief of Army Research and an old Antarctic hand, N.Y. Times, March 3, 1959, p. 3.

14. See N.Y. Times, June 24, 1959, p. 7; and SULLIVAN, *op. cit. supra* note 3, at 352.

15. One recent example of a newly developed potential use came with the discovery through use of American satellites of the so-called Van Allen radiation belt which proved to be "thinnest" at the Poles. While firing rockets from polar stations was suggested as a possible way to take advantage of this escape hatch, the difficulties of establishing a polar facility, as compared with launching elsewhere and "steering" the rocket through the radiation's thin spot, make the latter the probable choice. For deep space probes, however, polar tracking stations have distinct advantages.

The Antarctic has also been suggested as a possible site for atomic and nuclear tests, because of its desolation and isolation. It has also been suggested that the germ-free nature of the area would make it ideal as a vast storehouse for foodstuffs. It is true that spoilage and decay are relatively unknown, so the possibility does exist; but, under foreseeable conditions, the long haulage necessary to the Antarctic and the lack of facilities for transporting goods there and protecting them from Antarctic winds make the project prohibitively expensive.

16. While the IGY is technically nongovernmental, much official support has been given to the studies undertaken. The United States efforts in the Antarctic, for example, were carried out under the aegis of the United States Antarctic Projects Office, with Rear Admiral George Dufek as Projects Officer, and have been transported, supported, and largely staffed by members of the United States armed forces.

For information on the IGY in the Antarctic, see Hanessian, *Antarctica: Current National Interests and Legal Realities, A.S.I.L. Proceedings* 145–66 (1958); SULLIVAN, *op. cit. supra* note 3, at 299 ff.; Sullivan, *The International Geophysical Year*, INT'L CONCILIATION NO. 521 (Jan. 1959) and *House Report IGY*.

17. See CSAGI, BULLETIN D'INFORMATION NO. 7, at 17. The ap-

pearance of delegations from Chile and Argentina at IGY meetings headed by their Ambassadors rather than by scientists caused some initial consternation, but these diplomats refrained from injecting political considerations into the deliberations. See Sullivan, *supra* note 16, at 320.

18. *E.g.*, the United States' Byrd and Amundsen-Scott South Pole bases. See *House Report IGY* 16–17, and map therein opposite p. 19. In 1934 Admiral Byrd spent several months alone at a base 123 miles south of Little America.

19. The Soviet Union had 175, the United States 340, and New Zealand, Australia, Norway, the United Kingdom, Belgium, Japan, Argentina, and Chile 200 all told. Figures are approximate.

20. See ICSU (SCAR), Minutes of the Meetings at the Hague, Feb. 3–5, 1958 (CIR. 446 17-2-58 [100 RV]); at Moscow, 4 and 11 Aug., 1958; at Canberra, March, 1959 (SCAR CIRC. No. 27). See generally Hanessian, *supra* note 16, at 147–60 (on SCAR and post-IGY national programs); GOULD, *op. cit. supra* note 4, at 44 ff.; Hayton, *Polar Problems and International Law*, 52 AM. J. INT'L L. 746–65 (1958).

21. See comments by Gen. G. R. Laclavere of France, president of SCAR, in UNESCO FEATURES No. 330, at 3 (1959), and, generally, see Minutes of the Third Meeting of SCAR, SCAR CIRC. No. 27 (mimeo).

22. N.Y. Times, Feb. 21, 1958, and Hayton, *supra* note 20, at 755 n. 31.

23. See N.Y. Herald Tribune, Jan. 11, 1959, p. 5; N.Y. Times, Jan. 11, 1959, p. 17. Walter Sullivan suggested in the Times that the reason for the Soviet refusal was "bureaucratic."

24. 38 DEP'T STATE BULL. 912 (1958). On 1959 plans for all nations see Minutes of the SCAR Meeting, Aug. 4, 1958 (mimeo.); on 1960 plans, see Minutes of the SCAR Meeting, March 2, 1959 (SCAR CIRC. No. 27).

25. See U.N. Doc. No. T/PET/GENERAL 15, at 4 (Oct. 4, 1947).

26. *Report*, p. 207. See also pp. 6–7, 213–216.

27. See 19 DEP'T STATE BULL. 301 (1948); 10 DOC. AM. FOREIGN REL., 1948, 544 (1950). Chile replied with a proposal to "freeze" the status of the Antarctic for a number of years; 456 PARL. DEB. (5th ser.) cols. 10–11 (1948) (written answers to question); N.Y. Times, Jan. 19 and 20, 1949. It will be recalled too, that, in 1939, President Roosevelt, faced with the Axis threat, asked the Department of State to consider the advisability of a joint claim "in behalf of and in trust for, the

American Republics as a whole." See 1 HULL, MEMOIRS 758–59 (1948).

28. N.Y. Times, Feb. 21, 1958. A joint Norwegian-British-Swedish exploration party operated in Antarctica in 1949–52. See SULLIVAN, *op. cit. supra* note 3, at 128–34; and N.Y. Times, Jan. 20, 1952, p. 16.

29. Sydney Morning Herald, Feb. 12, 1958. See also *British Seek Pact on the Antarctic,* N.Y. Times, Feb. 13, 1958.

30. The Dominion (Wellington), Feb. 20, 1958, cited by Hanessian, *supra* note 16, at 163. See also his earlier remarks, suggesting a UN trusteeship, in The Times (London), Jan. 25, 1956, p. 8, and the favorable comments of Admiral Byrd and Shackleton in The Times (London), Feb. 17, 1956, p. 9; and Feb. 17, 1956, p. 6.

31. Several notes of acceptance, including that of the Soviet Union, made general reservations regarding territorial claims and other rights without, however, going beyond what would be implied by the United States' proposal's suggestion of the preservation of the status quo.

For Latin American comment, see, *e.g.*, article by Julio Escudero G., *La próxima conferencia internacional antártica,* El Mercurio (Santiago, Chile), May 31, 1958, cited by Hayton, *supra* note 20, at 759 n. 38.

32. See U.N. Doc. No. A/3852 (July 15, 1958). For an unofficial Japanese suggestion along similar lines, see N.Y. Times, Jan. 12, 1958.

33. U.N. Doc. No. A/3118 (Feb. 21, 1956).

34. Chile, Ministry of Foreign Affairs, Administrative Bureau, Foreign Information and Cultural Relations Branch, *Circular No. 21,* Santiago (Feb. 18, 1958).

35. See JENKS, THE COMMON LAW OF MANKIND 366 ff. (1958).

36. 39 DEP'T STATE BULL. 452, 460 (1958).

37. On possible alternatives, see *A.S.I.L. Proceedings,* 1958, 164–74. As Hayton has somewhat optimistically written: "an institutional framework for the treatment of the problems of . . . the Antarctic would be . . . a major landmark in the history of international relations. A *successful* formula would yield priceless precedent in international law and organization for possible broader application at some future date." Hayton, *supra* note 20, at 764.

38. It may be recalled that under the Treaty of Lausanne of 1923 an International Straits Commission which checked on passage of warships and military aircraft through the Straits was established. The

Commission was only a supervisor of transit, responsible for seeing that warships would pass through the Straits without hindrance and for reports on the numbers and types of warships using the waterway and present on the Black Sea. The regime ended in 1936. See 28 L.N.T.S. 117 (1924).

39. The United States suggested a system under the Security Council. The proposal recommended that:

"there be promptly established the Northern zone of international inspection against surprise attack, comprising the area north of the Arctic Circle with certain exceptions and additions, that was considered by the United Nations Disarmament Subcommittee of Canada, France, the U.S.S.R., the United Kingdom and the United States during August, 1957.

The proposal, further:

"*Calls upon* the five states mentioned, together with Denmark, and Norway, and any other States having territory north of the Arctic Circle which desire to have such territory included in the zone of international inspection, at once to designate representatives to participate in immediate discussions with a view to agreeing on the technical arrangements required; . . ." U.N. Doc. No. S/3995 (April 28, 1958).

The proposal was supported by the Secretary-General. Ten Members of the Security Council were in favor, but the Soviet Union vetoed it.

40. The theory of the substitution of an open door and free trade for unilateral colonial rule is that a free and joint development would eliminate most bases for rivalry since the possession of a colony would no longer pay, or at least not pay as much. In any system of trusteeship or of international control, the same problem has to be faced—should there be a free sharing of the economic benefits available in the territory.

There are several modern drawbacks to this apparently "democratic" concept of the open door, certainly for populated areas, since the emerging nations in the territories want protective tariffs for development and presumably would refuse to be kept as a storehouse of raw materials, open to exploitation by all. This, however, is a late problem in the course of the cycle of colonialism. Even in a relatively unpopulated area, the open door still gives a governing power advantages in jobs, prestige, use of his language and laws in doing business, wartime control and monopoly and, today, in a divided up currency system, membership in his currency bloc. This currency point is so important in the modern world that it tends to make even an ostensible open door relatively meaningless.

Throughout the early part of this century, however, and even in the 1940s, many economists felt that the open door was the answer to colonialism and made "imperialism" an absurd and expensive pleasure. Based on this equality of opportunity posed against costs of administration, they "proved" that colonies did not pay. Without a population, currency and tariff problems may remain unimportant—though even in this case, the presence of uranium or other strategic materials in a "national" zone might limit the possibility of establishing a shared program.

41. U.N. YEARBOOK, 1952, 387–90 (1953).

42. On the virtues of such an arrangement, see GOULD, *op. cit. supra* note 4, at 47–49.

43. On one of Byrd's flights over the South Pole he dropped flags of all the Members of the United Nations to represent "the ideal of brotherhood among peoples." SULLIVAN, *op. cit. supra* note 3, at 234.

44. Report, *op. cit. supra* note 26.

45. On the feasibility of international administration, see JENKS, *op. cit. supra* note 35.

For a suggestion of the advantages of placing both the Arctic and the Antarctic under a single international regime, *e.g.*, the seasonal nature of activities in these areas, permitting the shifting of trained personnel for the summer seasons, the need for coordination of scientific research at the two Poles, the difficulty presented for the Soviet Union with respect to the Arctic if military inspection is accepted for the Antarctic by the nations having a predominant interest there, and so forth, see Hayton, *supra* note 20, at 764–65.

The Trusteeship Council, it will be recalled, in 1947 refused to discuss the possibility of its own potential role in the Antarctic.

46. See Jessup, *Sovereignty in Antarctica*, 41 AM. J. INT'L L. 119 (1947); on the Soviet attitude see Toma, *Soviet Attitudes Towards the Acquisition of Territorial Sovereignty in the Antarctic*, 50 AM. J. INT'L L. 661–62 (1956).

47. See, *e.g.*, the Soviet comments in 1946 on the meaning of the term "States directly concerned" in the UN Charter. In practice, and as the United States and the United Kingdom originally insisted, the term is limited to states with clearly cognizable political interests. See, *e.g.*, Informal Minutes of the Preliminary Consultations on Trusteeship by the Representatives of Five Powers, 3–7, 10; U.N. Secretary

General, *The Question of "States Directly Concerned,"* U.N. Doc. No. A/C 4/36, *passim*, esp. 1–6 (Oct. 16, 1946); Wolfe, *The States Directly Concerned: Article 79 of the United Nations Charter*, 42 AM. J. INT'L L. 368–88 (1948); GOODRICH AND HAMBRO, CHARTER OF THE UNITED NATIONS 437–45 (2d rev. ed. 1949).

As the Peruvian Ulloa stated in another context, when such a problem arises, "All States whichever they are, are directly concerned in the matter . . . because it has not only a political aspect but also economic, social and humanitarian aspects." U.N. GEN. ASS. OFF. J. No. 28, XXVII Plen. Meeting, 490 (Feb. 9, 1946).

48. As IMCO's history indicates, no criterion is assured of automatic application.

The Organization's Maritime Safety Committee of fourteen members is to include at least the eight "largest ship-owning nations," a provision which led to bitter controversy in 1959 as Panama and Liberia, backed by the United States, insisted on inclusion on that Committee, citing their ranks as third and eighth in Lloyd's Registry, while other nations insisted that ships flying "flags of convenience" should not be counted in calculating "largest ship-owning nations." The question was referred to the International Court of Justice for an Advisory opinion. See Jessup, *The United Nations Conference on the Law of the Sea*, 59 COLUM. L. REV. 234, 255–57 (1959).

49. What the Agency would decide to do is another matter; see Von Mehren, *The International Atomic Energy Agency in World Politics*, 13 J. INT'L AFF. 57 (1959).

50. For a technique of dealing with minerals under an international regime through licensing, concessions, etc., and on the methods of obtaining "title" thereto, see Jenks, *supra* note 35, at 366 ff., and the Spitsbergen proposals. Title to fissionable materials might, Jenks suggests, be placed in the IAEA.

51. 2 PEASLEE, INTERNATIONAL GOVERNMENTAL ORGANIZATIONS 51–70 at 65–66. See also Jenks, *op. cit.*

7. *OUTER SPACE*

1. While the sun is medium-small as stars go, it has a diameter 108 times that of the earth. Surface temperatures are estimated at 11,000° F. For recent surveys of astronomical knowledge, see Staff Report of the Select Committee on Astronautics and Space Exploration, *Space Handbook: Astronautics and its Applications*, H.R. Doc. No. 86, 85th Cong., 2d Sess. (1959) *passim,* hereinafter cited as *Space Handbook;*

Time, Jan. 19, 1959, pp. 54–60; NASA, THE CHALLENGE OF SPACE EXPLORATION (1959).

2. Light is usually considered as traveling 186,300 miles per second.

3. *Space Handbook* 13. On the pros and cons of the possibility of life, see also N.Y. Times, June 19, 1958, p. 20, and Nov. 13, 1958, p. 11, and for Dr. de Vaucouleurs's assertion at the meeting of the American Physical Society in April, 1959, that the existence of life on Mars has been established almost beyond question, see report of Walter Sullivan, N.Y. Times, May 1, 1959, p. 9.

4. *Space Handbook* 23.

5. Jeans, *Life on Other Worlds*, in SHAPLEY, ED., A TREASURY OF SCIENCE (1954); HALDANE, GENESIS OF LIFE, THE EARTH AND ITS ATMOSPHERES (ed. Bates, 1957); N.Y. Times, April 10, 1959, p. 31.

6. *Astronautics and Space Exploration; Hearings Before the Select Committee on Astronautics and Space Exploration on H.R. 11881*, 85th Cong., 2d Sess., 44 (1958), testimony of Von Braun, hereinafter cited as *Hearings on H.R. 11881*. See also N.Y. Times, March 29, 1958, p. 8.

7. See, for example, Hogan, *Legal Terminology for the Upper Regions of the Atmosphere and for the Space Beyond the Atmosphere*, 51 AM. J. INT'L L. 362 (1957). See generally *Hearings Before the NASA Authorization Subcommittee of the Committee on Aeronautical and Space Sciences on S. 1582*, U.S. Senate, 86th Cong., 1st Sess., Part I, 127–53 (April 7–10, 1959), hereinafter cited as *Hearings on S. 1582*.

8. *Hearings on H.R. 11881* at 109, testimony of Dr. Hugh Dryden.

9. Hogan, *supra* note 7, at 371.

10. *Ibid.* See generally KALLMANN, A STUDY OF THE IONOSPHERE 638 (RAND Corp.).

11. *Hearings on H.R. 11881* at 777, testimony of DuBridge.

12. Kaplan, *The Earth's Atmosphere*, 41 AM. SCIENTIST 49–65, esp. chart facing p. 49 (1953).

13. Hogan, *supra* note 7, at 374–75.

14. See Gladwin Hill, *Explorer of the X of Space*, New York Times, April 26, 1959 (Magazine), p. 52; and *Hearings on S. 1582* at 581–98.

15. See British Information Service, British Record, May, 1959, p. 4, and New York Times, Mar. 20, 1959, p. 1.

16. See *Hearings on H.R. 11881* at 277, testimony of Hayward and Fulton; and New York Times, Aug. 30, 1958, p. 4. See also *Hearings on S. 1582* at 6.

17. The successful efforts are listed in the accompanying table. Two

Name	*Date Launched*	*Weight with Payload (in pounds)*	*Orbit Time (in minutes)*	*Maximum Altitude (in statute miles)*	*Minimum Altitude (in statute miles)*	*Angle to Equatorial Plane*	*Payload*	*Life (actual or predicted)*
Sputnik I	10/4/57	184	96.2	588	142	65°	Batteries radio	3 months
Sputnik II	11/3/57	1120	103.7	1038	140	65°	dog and instruments	5½ months
Explorer I	1/31/58	30.8	114.5	1573	224	34°	11 lbs. instruments	*c.*3–5 years
Vanguard I	3/17/58	3.25	134	2453	409	33.34°	Batteries radio	several thousand years
Explorer III	3/26/58	18.56	118	1746	121	33.4°	11 lbs. instruments	3 months
Sputnik III	5/15/58	2925	106	1167	135	65.3°	2,129 lbs. instruments	*c.*15 months
Explorer IV	7/26/58	25.8	110	1380	163	50°	18.26 lbs. instruments	*c.*one year
SCORE (Atlas)	12/18/58	150	101	920	110	32.3°	communication instruments	1 month
Vanguard II	2/17/59	20.74	126	2064	347	32.9°	weather sensors	ten years or more
Discoverer I (?)	2/28/59	245	95.9	605	99	3° off earth's N-S axis		6 days
Discoverer II	4/13/59	440	90.5	220	142	.2° off earth's N-S axis		2 weeks

American space probes, Pioneer I (Oct. 11–12, 1958) and Pioneer III (Dec. 6–7, 1958), attained "heights" of 71,300 and 63,500 miles respectively, and Soviet and American "moon shots" Mechta (Jan. 2, 1959) and Pioneer IV (March 3, 1959) finally broke the grip of the earth's gravity and sent probes off into space and, presumably, into perpetual orbits around the sun. See, *e.g.*, *Hearings on S. 1582* at 661–67 (Appendix).

18. Clark, *Programming for Space Defense*, JAG J. 20, 21 (Feb. 1959).

19. N.Y. Times, April 14, 1959, p. 1. The payload appears to have fallen in the Arctic or possibly on Spitsbergen.

On Soviet and East German expressions of alarm and threats of retaliation in space, in the air and on the ground in the face of potential "spying," see N.Y. Times, Mar. 6, 1959, p. 4, and Korovin in INT'L AFF. (Moscow), No. 1, p. 56 (Jan., 1959).

20. See N.Y. Times, May 29, 1959, and July 7, 1959 (Soviet recoveries).

21. *Space Handbook* 5. See also *Space Flight: A Look Ahead*, ASTRONAUTICS 24–28 (Nov. 1958).

22. *Space Handbook* 6; see also *ibid.* 74–76. The American Pioneer IV was tracked some 400,000 miles in March, 1959, and it is predicted that by 1962 communications at a range of 4 *billion* miles will be possible. N.Y. Times, March 4, 1959, p. 1.

23. See the remarks on this by Glennan, N.Y. Times, Jan. 25, 1959, p. 1.

24. See N.Y. Times, April 21, 1959, p. 19, and section on meteorology *infra*.

25. *Missile and Space Activities, Joint Hearings Before the Preparedness Investigating Subcommittee of the Committee on Armed Services and the Committee on Aeronautics and Space Sciences*, U.S. Senate, 86th Cong., 1st Sess. (Jan. 29–30, 1959). On Dr. Glennan's estimate that a 6-million-pound-thrust vehicle would be available by 1965, capable of placing 30,000 pounds in orbit, see p. 170. See also N.Y. Times, April 9, 1959, p. 1, col. 5, and Feb. 3, 1959, p. 1; also NASA, SOME THOUGHTS ON THE NEXT DECADE OF SPACE EXPLORATION (1958).

26. On this United States "Project Mercury," see *Hearings on S. 1582*, Part I, 408–15.

27. On the rocket to Mars, see *Hearings on S. 1582*, Part I, 120. Von

Braun has guessed that there may be a man on the moon by 1963. N.Y. Times, Aug. 29, 1958, p. 7. Gen. Schriever estimates a moon landing by 1966 and a moon base by 1970, at great expense. See *Hearings on H.R. 11881* at 653.

28. San Francisco Chronicle, Mar. 29, 1959, § 1, p. 1.

29. Radioteknika, Jan. 1959. See also report by Harry Schwartz, N.Y. Times, April 26, 1959.

30. DE JURE BELLI AC PACIS (trans.) II.ii.2 § 3, p. 190 (Carnegie Endowment for International Peace, *The Classics of International Law*, Series No. 3, 1925).

31. The First Hague Conference of 1899 adopted a measure prohibiting the discharge of projectiles from balloons "or other new methods of a similar nature." U.S. Dep't of State: *Freedom of the Air*, 1 DOCS. AND STATE PAPERS No. 5, 303 (Aug. 1948). *Survey of Space Law, Staff Report of the Select Committee on Astronautics and Space Exploration*, 85th Cong., 2d Sess., 16–18, hereinafter cited as *Survey of Space Law.*

32. See, for example, Fauchille, *Le Domain aérien et le régime juridique des aerostats*, 8 REV. GÉN. DE DROIT INT'L PUB. 414 (1901). He recognized state sovereignty for security purposes up to 330 meters, however. See generally SHAWCROSS & BEAUMONT, AIR LAW 3–9, (2d ed. 1951). Kislov & Krylov, *State Sovereignty in Airspace*, INT'L AFF. 35–44 (Moscow), No. 3 (March 1956).

33. See Goedhuis, *Civil Aviation after the War*, 36 AM. J. INT'L L. 596, 598–99 (1942). See too the resolution of 1906 of the Institute of International Law, 21 ANNUAIRE DE L'INSTITUT DE DROIT INTERNATIONAL 293 (1906), and see generally Young, *The Aerial Inspection Plan and Air Space Sovereignty*, 24 GEO. WASH. L. REV., 565–89 (1956).

34. Even during the war, neutral nations insisted on the right to keep foreign aircraft out of their airspace, even by use of force, if necessary. See Swiss Declaration of Neutrality, Aug. 4, 1914, § 17(b). The same was true in the Second World War. On Dutch and Belgian rejection in 1940 of German claims that it could fly its planes above their territory as long as they kept *above* a *three-mile* limit, see Kuhn, 34 AM. J. INT'L L. 104 (1940); and, more generally, SPAIGHT, AIRCRAFT IN PEACE AND THE LAW 203–15 (1919).

35. 11 L.N.T.S. 173 (1922). On British proposals, see Cooper *Some Historic Phases of British International Civil Aviation Policy*, 23 INT'L AFF. 189, 191 ff. (1947). See also LISSITZYN, INTERNATIONAL

AIR TRANSPORT AND NATIONAL POLICY (1942), and Goedhuis, *Sovereignty and Freedom in the Air Space*, 41 TRANSACT. GROT. SOC'Y 137–52 (1956).

The United States and the Soviet Union were not Parties to this Convention though some thirty states had ratified it by 1939.

36. "*Art. I.* The High Contracting Parties recognize that every Power has complete and exclusive sovereignty over the air space [*espace atmosphérique, spazio atmosferico*] above its territory.

"For the purpose of the present Convention, the territory of a State shall be understood as including the national territory, both that of the mother country and of the colonies, and of the territorial waters adjacent thereto.

"*Art. II.* Each contracting State undertakes in time of peace to accord freedom of innocent passage above its territory to the aircraft of the other contracting States, provided that the conditions laid down in the present Convention are observed."

37. For example, the British Air Navigation Act and Orders in Council of 1920 stated Britain's "full and absolute sovereignty and rightful jurisdiction . . . over the air superincumbent on its territory." See also AERIAL NAVIGATION ACTS OF 1911 AND 1913. See too U.S. Air Commerce Act of 1926 (44 *Statutes at Large* 568, 49 U.S.C. 171, 174–77, 179–84) and Civil Aeronautics Act of 1938 (52 *Statutes at Large* 973, 980; 49 U.S.C. § 401(33)); Air Code of the U.S.S.R., Art. 1, 1932, and 1935 in *Collection of Laws, U.S.S.R.*, 1935, No. 43, p. 359b ("To the Union of Soviet Socialist Republics belongs complete and exclusive sovereignty in the airspace above the Union . . ."). See Kislov and Krylov, *supra* note 32, at 35–44.

38. On Italian demands for virtual subsidies to permit other national craft to fly over her territory; Turkey's refusal to let craft headed for Asia to fly over her territory; the U.S. refusal to let the Dutch fly from Batavia to Manila or from the West Indies to Miami; Australia's refusal to let Pan American, a U.S. company, fly from Noumea (New Caledonia) to Brisbane; England's refusal to give a U.S. company landing rights at Hong Kong; and so forth, see VAN ZANDT, CIVIL AVIATION AND PEACE, esp. 57–59 (Brookings Inst., 1944). On treatment by neutrals of belligerent aircraft in the Second World War, see SPAIGHT, AIR POWER AND WAR RIGHTS 424 ff. (3d ed. 1947).

39. U.S. DEP'T OF STATE, INTERNATIONAL CIVIL AVIATION CONFERENCE: FINAL ACT AND RELATED DOCUMENTS 4–5, Conference Series No. 64, Pub. No. 2282 (1945).

40. 61 *Statutes at Large,* 1180 (1944); T.I.A.S. No. 1591; 15 U.&.T.S. p. 295. For Parties it replaces the Paris and Havana Conventions. The Soviet Union is not a Party to this Convention but 74 nations are, as of June, 1959. "China" is a Party, but this has not as yet brought in the Peking Government.

41. Annexes to the Convention have defined "aircraft," for purposes of the Annexes only, in language derived from the Paris Convention of 1919 as "any machine which can derive support in the atmosphere from the reactions of the air." Annexes 6, 7, 8. This definition is literally not applicable to satellites or other space craft. National legislation has also generally failed to define such terms. The U.S. legislation defines "aircraft" in the Federal Aviation Act of 1958 (49 U.S.C. 1301 [5]) however, as "any contrivance now known or hereafter invented; used, or designed for navigation of or flight in the air."

42. "Art. 3(a): This Convention shall be applicable only to civil aircraft, and shall not be applicable to State [i.e., military, customs and police] aircraft."

43. At the Disarmament Conference of 1932, similar proposals for internationalizing air transport were rejected as economically undesirable and militarily ineffective. See VAN ZANDT, *op. cit. supra* note 38, at 41–49. For a suggestion in 1946 that the disarmament of ex-enemy states should include placing their airspace under UN trusteeship, see COOPER, *Air Power and the Coming Peace Treaties,* 24 FOR. AFF. 451–52 (1946).

44. See generally U.S. DEP'T OF STATE, PROCEEDINGS OF THE INTERNATIONAL CIVIL AVIATION CONFERENCE *passim* (Pub. No. 2820, 1950); Colclaser, *The New International Civil Aviation Organization,* 31 VA. L. REV. 457 (1945); Sullivan, *The Case for International Ownership of Air Transport,* 8 FREE WORLD 503 (1944).

In 1944 two additional conventions were prepared, the International Air Services Transit Agreement ("Two Freedoms") and the International Air Transport Agreement ("Five Freedoms"). The Transit Agreement gives to scheduled services only the right to fly over without landing and to land for non-traffic reasons. It was accepted, as of January, 1959, by 50 states. The Transport Agreement gives more commercially valuable rights with respect to mail, cargo, and passengers and was in force (as of January 1959) for 11 states, not including the United States.

45. See Beresford, *The Legal Control of Outer Space,* ABA, Sec-

tion of Int'l Law, Aug., 1958, reprinted in *Space Law, A Symposium, Prepared by the Special Committee on Space and Aeronautics*, U.S. Senate, 85th Cong., 2d Sess., 410 ff. hereinafter cited as *Space Law, A Symposium;* Feldman, *An American View of Jurisdiction in Outer Space*, paper delivered at the I.A.F. meeting, the Hague, August, 1958, reprinted *ibid.* 428 ff.

46. See Goedhuis, *supra* note 33, at 596 ff.; Goedhuis, *supra* note 35, at 137 ff.; LISSITZYN, *op. cit. supra* note 35.

47. On rights of self-defense, even without claims of sovereignty, see Craig, *National Sovereignty at High Altitudes*, 24 J. AIR. L. AND COMM. 384, 388 (1957). On the possible effects of acceptance of an air inspection scheme as part of a disarmament arrangement, see Young, *supra* note 33.

48. *Survey of Space Law*, 18.

49. See General Communications Regulations attached to the International Telecommunications Convention, Madrid, Dec. 9, 1932, and Revisions of Feb. 1 and Apr. 9, 1938. European Broadcasting Conventions, June 19, 1933, and Sept. 15, 1948, CMD. NO. 7946 (T.S. No. 30 of 1950); Aaronson, *Space Law*, INT'L REL. 423 (April, 1958).

50. 1 OPPENHEIM, INTERNATIONAL LAW 517 (ed. Lauterpacht, 8th ed. 1955).

51. The laws of Brazil refer, perhaps wisely, only to "space" above its territory, and the 1950 Constitution of Nicaragua includes "atmospheric space" and the "stratosphere" above the nation as national territory.

52. Westlake, as early as 1906, justified an unlimited extension of sovereignty upward with the following analysis:

"In the air the higher one ascends, the more damage the fall of objects will cause on the earth. If there exists a limit as to the sovereignty of the state over the oceanic space, none exists for the sovereignty of the state over the airspace. The right of the subjacent state remains the same whatever may be the distance." Cited by Cooper, *High Altitude Flight and National Sovereignty*, 4 INT'L L.Q. 411 ff. at 412 (1951).

53. United States v. Causby, 328 U.S. 256, 260–61, 66 S. Ct. 1062 (1946). Lord McNair has condemned the maxim in these terms: "Like most maxims and slogans, [it] has merely been used either to darken counsel or to afford a shortcut and an excuse for not thinking the matter out upon a basis of principle." THE LAW OF THE AIR 297 (ed. Kerr & MacCrindle, 2d ed. 1953). See also Cooper, *Roman Law*

and the Maxim 'Cuius Est Solum' in International Law, 1 McGILL L.J. 23 ff. (1952).

54. See, for example, Peng, *Le Vol à haute altitude et l'article I de la Convention de Chicago, 1944*, 12 REV. DU BARREAU 277, 292 (1952). The aims of ICAO, while stressing "air" transport, do not necessarily foreclose a role in space development. The ICAO deals only with civil aviation, of course. See Cooper, *Flight-Space and the Satellites*, 7 INT'L & COMP. L.Q. 82 ff., esp. p. 85 (1958); Meyer, PROC. AM. SOC'Y INT'L L. 97 (1950); HALEY, SPACE LAW—THE DEVELOPMENT OF JURISDICTIONAL CONCEPTS (reprinted by the Amer. Rocket Soc'y 1957).

55. This was an earlier view of Cooper. See *supra* note 52, at 418; see also remarks of McDougal, PROC. AM. SOC'Y INT'L L. 109 (1956).

56. See, for example, Hingorani, *La Souveraineté sur L'espace Exo-atmosphérique*, 20 REV. GÉN. DE L'AIR 248 (1957).

57. See FREEDOM OF THE AIR 32, 33 (Project No. Au 1–55 ESAWC, Air University, 1955). See also Schofield, *Control of Outer Space*, AIR U.Q. REV. 93–104 (1958), reprinted in *Space Law, A Symposium* 355–66.

58. *International Law and Activities in Space*, 5 INT'L & COMP. L.Q. 99, 103–4 (1956). In a strict sense, this same observation could be made about *space* within the atmosphere though not to *air*. See also Welf Heinrich, Prince of Hanover, *Luftrecht und Weltraum* (dissertation, Göttingen, 1953) translated in *Space Law, A Symposium* 64–66.

59. See Roy, PROC. AM. SOC'Y INT'L L. 94–95 (1956); Cheng, *Recent Developments in Air Law*, 9 CURRENT LEGAL PROB. 208 (1956); Schachter, *Legal Aspects of Space Travel*, 11 BRIT. INTER-PLANETARY SOC'Y J. 14 (1952); Cooper, *Flight-Space and the Satellites*, 7 INT'L & COMP. L.Q. 82, 89 (1958).

60. Other related proposed locations range from 10 miles, the biological limit for man without breathing apparatus, to 650 miles, a different estimate of the "end" of the atmosphere. See Haley, *The Law of Space. . .*, 4 N.Y. L. FORUM 262, 264–65 (1958), and Danier, *Les Voyages Interplanétaires et le Droit*, 15 REV. GÉN. DE L'AIR 422 (1952).

61. See, for example, Kroell, *Elements Createurs d'un Droit Astronautique*, 16 REV. GÉN. DE L'AIR 222, 245 (1953); Boehme, *Lufthoheit und Weltraumflug*, 5 ZEITSCHR. F. LUFTRECHT 184 (1956); Cooper, *High Altitude Flight and National Sovereignty*, 4 INT'L COMP. L.Q. 416 (1951); Simpson, *Into Deep Space*, 32 L.A. BAR BULL. 355, 360 n. 9 (1957); Pépin, *Legal Problems Created by the Sputnik*, 4 McGILL L.J.

66, 68 (1957), and Haley, *Space Law and Metalaw—Jurisdiction Defined*, 24 J. AIR L. & COMM. 286, 297–98 (1957), *Hearings on H.R. 11881* 1435–37, and *Law and the Age of Space*, 5 ST. LOUIS U.L.J. 1 (1958).

62. One writer explains the basis for a threefold division as follows: As to "national air space" (up to 50 nautical miles): "The figure . . . was arrived at as the useful altitude at which aircraft may operate that depend on reaction of the air for lift and control. . . . Also by this limit a portion of atmospheric density above national air space is available in which free-fall vehicles can decelerate and assume a glide path comparable to that of powered aircraft before re-entry into the national air space of a sovereign state. State sovereignty is implicit in the term 'national air space.' All air space above international waters would remain international as now recognized by the International Civil Aviation Organization. [Within] . . . international space [50–2,000 miles] . . . will fall the great number of vehicular and orbital trajectories. Ballistic missiles aimed halfway around the earth need not exceed an altitude of 2,000 miles. This height is sufficient for trajectories incident to the launching of orbital vehicles of a permanent nature. Powered space vehicles could establish orbits or flight paths within international space and depart outward or return to earth as desired." Schofield, *supra* note 57, at 93, 104 (1958), reprinted in *Space Law, A Symposium* at 365. See also Cooper, *Legal Problems of Upper Space*, PROC. AM. SOC'Y INT'L L. 1956, 85, 91, and letter to The Times (London), Sept. 2, 1957. For comments by others on this concept, see Cooper, *supra* at 94 ff.

63. The difficulties in attempting definitions, which this approach might avoid, are exemplified by the repeatedly unsuccessful attempts to define an important related concept, aggression, on some rational basis which have again been put off, this time until 1962. See N.Y. Times, Apr. 18, 1959, p. 2.

64. Letter to The Times (London), Sept. 5, 1957.

65. See McDougal and Lipson, *Perspectives for a Law of Outer Space*, 52 AM. J. INT'L L. 407 ff. (1958).

66. White, *Air and Space are Indivisible*, Air Force Magazine, Mar. 1958, p. 40 at 41.

67. See U.N. Doc. No. A/AC.98/2. For views of U.S. Officials to this effect, see testimony of Loftus Becker, Legal Adviser, Dep't of State, *Hearings on H.R. 11881* 1273, and *U.S. Foreign Policy and the Development of Law for Outer Space*, JAG J. 4 ff. (Feb. 1959); Ward,

Projecting the Law of the Sea Into the Law of Space, JAG J. 3–8 (March, 1957), and *Space Law as a Way to World Peace*, JAG J. 10 ff (Feb. 1959); Keating, *Reaching for the Stars*, 45 ABA J. 54, 56 (1959). Becker suggested too, for example, that taxation of U.S. citizens in a satellite could be covered by existing tax laws; that there is sufficient domestic and international law to cover an object from outer space which reaches the earth; and that any infringement of airspace by a satellite or missile would be covered by existing law as equivalent to infringement by an airplane. *Hearings on H.R. 11881* at 1297–1303. Would this not require a prior definition of "airspace" however?

68. See U.N. Docs. Nos. A/C.1/SR 986, at 9; 991, at 6; 992, at 3.

69. See, for example, Kroell, *supra* note 61, at 245.

70. For discussion of these points at the United Nations in the fall of 1958, see Taubenfeld, *Consideration at the United Nations of the Status of Outer Space*, 53 AM. J. INT'L L. 400, 402–4 (1959). See also Jenks, *International Law and Activities in Space*, 5 INT'L & COMP. L.Q. 99, 103 (1956); Schachter, in PROC. AM. SOC'Y INT'L L. 105 (1956); Smirnoff, *La Réglementation internationale des vols dans l'éspace supra-atmosphérique*, 20 REV. GÉN. DE L'AIR 348 (1957); Bendiner, *Who Owns Outer Space*, 18 The Reporter, June 12, 1958, pp. 17–20.

71. See, for example, Aaronson, *supra* note 49, at 416 ff. Sec'y-Gen. Hammarskjöld, N.Y. Times, Aug. 15, 1958, p. 10; Jacobini, in 6 *West. P.Q.* 680 (1953); Jenks, *supra* note 70, at 99, 118.

72. *Survey of Space Law* 15. See also Ward, *supra* note 67, at 3.

73. See U.N. Conference on the Law of the Sea, OFF. REC. DOC. No. A/Conf. 13/37–43; Convention on the High Seas (1958), Arts. 8, 9, and Convention on the Continental Shelf (1958).

Compare, however, the following statement of the Soviet lawyer N. Vishnepolski, quoted in 1952, 41 TRANSACT. GROT. SOC'Y 149 (1955): "Historical, political, and legal facts give us a claim to full sovereignty over the Arctic seas. The international rules governing the open seas cannot be applied in the Arctic. The Arctic Seas are our national waters whose legal status must rest on unconditional recognition of the U.S.S.R.'s sovereignty."

74. See Art. 2, Convention on the High Seas (1958).

75. For argument that this is a lawful use of the seas for security purposes, see McDougal & Schlei, *The Hydrogen Bomb Tests in Perspective: Lawful Measures for Security*, 64 YALE L.J. 648 (1955), and McDougal, *The Hydrogen Bomb Tests and the International Law of the Sea*, 49 AM. J. INT'L L. 356 (1955). *Contra*, see Margolis, *The*

Hydrogen Bomb Experiments and International Law, 64 YALE L.J. 629 (1955), and REIFF, THE UNITED STATES AND THE TREATY LAW OF THE SEA 363 ff. (1959).

76. See, for example, Civil Aeronautics Act of 1938, § 1201, as amended Sept. 9, 1950, 64 *Statutes at Large* 825, 49 U.S.C. §§ 701, 703; see also 15 F.R. 9180, 20 F.R. 8184, 14 C.F.R. 620, 21–23. For the U.S. Regulations of 1955 and those of Canada as well, see MURCHISON, THE CONTIGUOUS AIR SPACE ZONE IN INTERNATIONAL LAW (Canadian Dep't of Nat'l Defense, 1956) 79–94, Appendixes I and II. U.S. NAVAL WAR COLLEGE, INTERNATIONAL LAW SITUATION AND DOCUMENTS 1956, 577 ff. (1957). See generally Cooper, *Space Above the Seas*, JAG J. 8 ff. (Feb. 1959), esp. 31; REIFF, *op. cit. supra* note 75, at 365–68.

77. See, for example, Schachter, *Who Owns the Universe*, in RYAN, ACROSS THE SPACE FRONTIER (1952), reprinted in *Space Law, A Symposium* 8 ff. On the combination of freedom to use the seas with state responsibility for national users, see "*Decatur's Doctrine*"—*A Code for Outer Space*, U.S. NAVAL INST. PROC. 931–37 (September 1957). See also the 1958 Convention on the High Seas, esp. Arts. 5 ff.

78. See REIFF, *op. cit. supra* note 75, at 34–35. On maritime analogies in air law, see MCNAIR, THE LAW OF THE AIR 233–62 (ed. by Kerr and MacCrindle, 2d ed. 1953).

79. See Becker, *United States Foreign Policy and the Development of Law for Outer Space*, JAG J. 7 (Feb. 1959). The Russian "moon shot" in January, 1959, carried a stainless-steel sphere made up of segments each of which bore the Soviet coat of arms and the inscription "U.S.S.R. January 1959." The rocket did not touch the moon. See N.Y. Times, Jan. 13, 1959, p. 1. No claims were made. On the wisdom of not claiming the moon too early, see remarks of Loftus Becker on Mar. 6, 1959, in N.Y. Times, Mar. 7, 1959, p. 3, col. 1.

80. See Cheng, *International Law and High Altitude Flights: Balloons, Rockets and Man-Made Satellites*, 6 INT'L & COMP. L.Q. 487–505 (1957); Kislov & Krylov, *State Sovereignty in Airspace*, INT'L AFF. 35–44 (Moscow), No. 3 (March 1956); Quigg, *Open Skies and Open Space*, 37 FOR. AFF. 95–106 (1958) N.Y. Times, Feb. 6, Feb. 8, Feb. 9, 1956; 34 DEP'T STATE BULL. 293, 426–27 (1956); ICAO DOCS. Nos. A10-WP/150, EX/16; A10-WP/87, EX/24.

81. The U.S. Atlas communication satellite launched in December, 1958, was "strictly a national experiment designed to develop information for the Defense Department's Advanced Research Projects Agency." See N.Y. Times, Dec. 20, 1958, p. 1.

82. A right to fly over could not be claimed under the International Civil Aviation Convention since, if the Convention is applicable to the areas in which the satellites orbit, even disregarding the fact that certain states, the USSR among them, are not parties to it, it provides that pilotless craft will not be flown over the territory of contracting states without special authorization (Article 8).

83. Schachter, *The Law of Outer Space*, Proceedings and Committee Reports of the American Branch, Int'l Law Assoc., 1957–58, pp. 37 ff. cited in *Survey of Space Law* at 12. See also the remarks of several statesmen at the United Nations reported in U.N. Docs. Nos. A/C.1/SR.982, at 8–10; A/C.1/SR.983, at 6–8; A/C.1/SR.984, at 2; A/C.1/SR.987 at 2; A/C.1/SR.988, at 6; A/C.1/SR.990, at 5; and A/C.1/SR.991, at 6.

On the possibility of acquisition of a "right" through continued use, it is interesting to note that when the United States began to fly planes at altitudes above 10,000 feet in the air corridors to West Berlin in 1959, the Soviet Union protested that flights had not been made above that altitude for all the years of joint control, and that a "kind of prescriptive right" had arisen and the U.S. was violating the "established order of air communication." The protests and warnings of "incidents" were rejected by the U.S., but the flights were discontinued to avoid "incidents." See N.Y. Times, Apr. 4, 1959, p. 9 (Soviet warning); Apr. 5, 1959, p. 1 (U.S. rejection); Apr. 6, 1959, p. 3 (Soviet note); Apr. 14, 1959, p. 10 (U.S. note); Apr. 16, 1959, p. 1.

84. Galina, *On the Question of Interplanetary Law*, SOVIET STATE AND LAW 52–58, No. 7 (1958), reprinted in *Space Law: A Symposium* 508 ff.

85. See Lissitzyn, *The American Position on Outer Space and Antarctica*, 53 AM. J. INT'L L. 126 ff. (1959).

86. For Becker's statements, see *Hearings on H.R. 11881* at 1269 ff.; Hearings on S.3609, U.S. Senate, 85th Cong., 2d Sess., May 6–15, 1958, 315 ff. See further, Becker, *The Control of Space*, 39 DEP'T STATE BULL. 416 (1958); Becker, *United States Foreign Policy . . .* , JAG J. 4 ff. (Feb. 1959).

87. Report of the Legal Committee, U.N. Doc. No. A/AC.98/2 (June 12, 1959).

88. N.Y. Times, Dec. 24, 1958, p. 1.

89. *Hearings on H.R. 11881* at 1107.

90. On the Antarctic-outer space analogy, see Lissitzyn, *supra* note

85, at 131, and Quigg, *supra* note 80, at 95–106 (1958). The Soviet writer Korovin "rejects" the analogy on the grounds that all states, communist and non-communist, have rejected sovereignty in outer space as incompatible with the facts of astronomy. INT'L AFF. 5 (Moscow) No. 1 (Jan. 1959). This is not, of course, an official Soviet renunciation of sovereignty.

91. See, for example, Sternfeld, *To Whom Does Outer Space Belong?* in ARTIFICIAL EARTH SATELLITES, 174–77 (Moscow, 1956), and Kislov & Krylov, *supra* note 80.

92. Cited in Pépin, *supra* note 61, at 66–67.

93. Translation from AKADEMIYA NAUK SSSR, INSTITUT PRAVA, MEZHDUNARODNOYE PRAVO 187 (1957).

94. Galina, *supra* note 84; Zadorozhnyi, *The Artificial Satellite and International Law*, Soviet Russia, Oct. 17, 1957, p. 3, reprinted in *Space Law: A Symposium* 504 ff. See generally Neumann, *The Legal Status of Outer Space and the Soviet Union*, in *Space Law: A Symposium* 495 ff.

95. Zadorozhnyi, *supra:* "The Soviet artificial earth satellite does not violate the air sovereignty of any state, if only because it does not fly into the space over other states. Instead, the territories of these states, by dint of the earth's rotation, pass so to speak under the satellite's orbit, which is fixed in relation to the earth and the stars. Disputing the legality of the appearance of the satellite over the territory of one or another state would be just as absurd and ridiculous as disputing the appearance over a given territory of the moon, the sun, or any other heavenly body."

96. Galina, *supra* note 84, at 513–14.

97. *International Status of Cosmic Space*, INT'L AFF. 53–59 (Moscow) No. 1 (Jan. 1959).

8. PROBLEMS OF CONTROLS FOR SPACE

1. On "observation" from a satellite and its implications and possible uses, see Staff Report of the Committee on Astronautics and Space Exploration, *Space Handbook: Astronautics and Its Applications*, 85th Cong., 2d Sess., 172–81 (1959), hereinafter cited as *Space Handbook*.

2. On weather control generally, see LOEBSACK, OUR ATMOSPHERE (1959).

3. See, for example, testimony of Doctors Hagen and Stever, *Hearings Before the Select Committee on Astronautics and Space Explora-*

tion, on H.R. 11881 85th Cong., 2d Sess., 323, 395 (1958), hereinafter cited as *Hearings on H.R. 11881*. See also *Survey of Space Law, Staff Report of the Select Committee on Astronautics and Space Exploration*, 85th Cong., 2d Sess., hereinafter cited as *Survey of Space Law*. On the "cluttering up" of space, which would also affect astronomical observations, see Quigg, *Open Skies and Open Space*, 37 For. Aff. 95–106 (1958).

4. See, for example, testimony of Dryden and Dubridge on the control of space through ground sites and on the relative short-range unimportance of the Moon as a potential military base for use against Earth at this stage of technology, *Hearings on H.R. 11881* at 109, 781. Cf. Von Braun, *Space Travel*, 35 For. Serv. J. 20–21 (April, 1958).

5. Testimony of Dr. Hans A. Bethe, reported in N.Y. Times, Feb. 20, 1959, p. 6. See also suggestions by the scientists assembled at Geneva in July, 1958, N.Y. Times, July 29, 1958, p. 1, and generally *Space Handbook* at 183.

6. See, *e.g.*, *Space Handbook* 171–91.

7. See testimony of Dr. Herbert York, reported in N.Y. Times, June 21, 1959, p. 39, and N.Y. Times, March 19, 1959, p. 1 (articles by Sullivan and Baldwin); March 20, 1959, pp. 1 and 10, and March 25, 1959, p. 16 (Dep't of State comment). At least part of the data was collected by the Explorer IV satellite. See also *Space Handbook* 134.

8. On April 13, 1959, the United States proposed as a first step that atomic explosions in the "atmosphere" (and under water) be banned. The Soviet Union insisted on a ban of *all* testing. At almost the same time, Dr. Teller commented with interest on the possibility of exploding a nuclear device 100 million miles from the earth to test Einstein's theory of relativity and the nature and completeness of the vacuum in space. Fallout on the earth was expected to be nonexistent or infinitesimal. This type of testing has also been backed by Commissioner Libby of the Atomic Energy Commission.

9. See generally *Space Handbook* 209–16.

10. United Nations *Ad Hoc* Committee on the Peaceful Uses of Outer Space, *Draft Report on Paragraph 1(b)*, U.N. Doc. No. A/AC.-98/3, *passim* (11 June 1959), hereinafter cited as *UN Draft Report*.

11. See *IGY and Space Research, Staff Report of the Select Committee on Astronautics and Space Exploration*, 85th Cong., 2d Sess., 29–30, and *Space Handbook* 16.

12. *Space Handbook* 211.

13. On the various experiments which rockets and satellites can perform, see *U.N. Draft Report*, *passim*, and *Space Handbook* 215–16. A series of lectures on the advantages of astronomical observation from extra-terrestrial stations formed part of the program of the American Physical Society, meeting at Washington, D.C., on April 30, 1959. For an early report, see N.Y. Times, May 1, 1959, p. 11.

14. See *U.N. Draft Report*, 23–25, and N.Y. Times, July 6, 1958, p. 17 and Sept. 30, 1958, p. 13. The scientists' committee was known as CETEX (Committee on Contamination in Extra-Terrestrial Exploration). Its functions are being performed under COSPAR. On U.S. observance of precautions, particularly with respect to "moon shots," see N.Y. Times, Sept. 30, 1958, p. 13, and Oct. 12, 1958, p. 56. The fate of the native peoples of the world when exposed to conquerors from distant lands gives a warning of the need for caution. Even the Antarctic penguins have suffered because of transference of human diseases. See SULLIVAN, QUEST FOR A CONTINENT 295 (1957).

15. *Space Handbook* 3–4. See also the remarks of Schachter, PROC. AM. SOC'Y INT'L L., 1958, 247.

16. *U.N. Draft Report* 25; *Report of the Secretary-General*, U.N. Doc. No. A/AC.98/4, 32–35 (16 June 1959), hereinafter cited as *Report Sec'y-Gen.*

17. CSAGI Rocket and Satellite Conference (Washington, D.C., 30 September–5 October 1957), Doc. 5 (mimeo.), 25 Sept. 1957, p. 7. See also *Report Sec'y-Gen.* 12–16.

18. See Sullivan, *The International Geophysical Year*, INT'L CONCILIATION No. 521, 307–8, 310–17 (Jan., 1959).

19. *Ibid.* 301–17; N.Y. Times, Aug. 1, 1958, p. 23; Aug. 6, 1958, p. 11; Aug. 10, 1958, p. 41. For post-IGY problems of exchange of scientists see N.Y. Times, April 20, 1959, p. 18.

20. See *U.N. Draft Report* 17–19; N.Y. Times, March 3, 1959; and *Space Handbook* 83–84.

21. Sullivan, *supra* note 18, at 327. Cf., however, his report of certain censorship difficulties at the Moscow meeting in Moscow in July–August, 1958. *Ibid.*, 330–31. See also Science, Nov. 14, 1958, pp. 1197–98.

22. See *Report Sec'y-Gen.* 18–22.

23. Resolutions, Eighth General Assembly, ICSU, Res. VI. published provisionally by the National Academy of Sciences, Washington, D.C. (mimeo.).

24. Initially, the Union of South Africa (three-year term), India (two-year term) and Peru (one-year term). The terms indicate that COSPAR is in fact expected to continue beyond the end of 1959.

25. For accounts of attempts to work out an acceptable formula, and on Sobolev's remarks, see articles in the N.Y. Times, April 28, 1959, p. 8 (Hamilton), and p. 28 (Sullivan).

26. See N.Y. Times, Mar. 15, 1959, p. 32.

27. N.Y. Times, April 22, 1959, p. 1, col. 7. For Senator Jackson's suggestions on the appropriateness of NATO scientific satellites, see N.Y. Times, Nov. 18, 1958, p. 11. As a precedent, NATO is already embarked on a joint study of the oceans, using the Italian oceanographic center at La Spezia, Italy, as its base. N.Y. Times, March 30, 1959, p. 1.

28. See *Report Sec'y-Gen.* 35–40, and Report of Dr. H. Wexler to WMO, reprinted as Annex I thereto. See also *Hearings Before the NASA Authorization Subcommittee of the Committee on Aeronautical and Space Sciences on S. 1582,* U.S. Senate, 86th Cong., 1st Sess., Part I, 228–51 (April 7–10, 1959).

See generally *Space Handbook* 192–98. On all "applied" areas, see Report of the Scientific Advisory Committee, of which Dr. Killian was the chairman, to President Eisenhower, March 26, 1958. For an estimate of the real monetary value of such research, see testimony of Dr. Lloyd Berkner, *Hearings on H.R. 11881* at 1064.

29. *Space Handbook* 192.

30. See Widger & Touart, *Utilization of Satellite Observations in Weather Analysis,* 38 BULL. AM. METEOR. SOC'Y 531–33 (1957); Wexler, *Observing the Weather from a Satellite Vehicle,* 13 BRIT. INTER-PLANETARY SOC'Y J. 269–76 (1954); testimony of Dr. F. W. Reichelderfer, Chief, Weather Bureau, *Hearings on H.R. 11881* at 910–11, 919. See also N.Y. Times, January 11, 1959, p. 5, for a Congressional estimate that savings in the United States might run to $4 billion annually.

31. *Space Handbook* 193.

32. *U.N. Draft Report* 10.

33. *Space Handbook* 187.

34. See *Space Handbook* 198; testimony of Reichelderfer, *Hearings on H.R. 11881* at 915; Ball, *Shaping the Law of Weather Control,* 58 YALE L.J. 213–44 (1949); LOEBSACK, OUR ATMOSPHERE (1959).

35. See N.Y. Times, Feb. 18, 1959, p. 1, col. 8, and p. 15; Feb. 19,

1959, p. 11, col. 2; Feb. 26, 1959, p. 2, col. 4. Many of the "pictures" have apparently been difficult to evaluate due to a "wobble" in the satellite.

36. N.Y. Times, Feb. 18, 1959, p. 14, col. 3.

37. *Space Handbook* 199. On the anticipated substantial benefits to navigation, see N.Y. Times, Dec. 31, 1958, p. 5.

38. See *Space Handbook* 202 ff; Haviland, *The Communications Satellite,* paper presented at the Eighth Int'l Astronautical Cong., Barcelona, Oct. 1–12, 1957; NASA, SOME THOUGHTS ON THE NEXT DECADE OF SPACE EXPLORATION 5–6 (1958); *Hearings on S. 1582, supra* note 28, at 251–65.

39. Dr. Lloyd Berkner, address as President of the International Scientific Union, N.Y. Times, May 7, 1959.

40. N.Y. Times, June 1, 1959, p. 1.

41. HALEY, LAW OF OUTER SPACE—AN IMMEDIATE PROBLEM 4–5. See his footnote reference to ITU Radio Regulations, Chap. I, Art. 1, p. 4-E; Chap. III, Art. 5, p. 42-E, and to the *Liste des Fréquences,* ITU Bureau, 1947. See also Sullivan, *supra* note 18, at 305, and Haley, *Law of Outer Space—Practical Legal Rules,* paper presented to the Institute on World Organization, Washington, D.C., Oct. 23, 1958.

42. Aaronson, *Space Law,* INT'L REL. 416, 423 (1958).

43. *Survey of Space Law* 26; Haley, *supra* note 41, at 8–11.

44. Satellites at present cannot be shot down and have not been equipped with devices to turn themselves off. *U.N. Draft Report* and N.Y. Times, March 18, 1959, p. 4.

45. On the ITU and its advisory organs, see *Report Sec'y-Gen.* 41–45.

46. *U.N. Draft Report* 22.

47. N.Y. Times, May 3, 1959, p. 27.

48. See CCIR documents 437, 530, 531, 538, 662. Documents 437, 531, and 538 are reprinted as Annexes II–V to *Report Sec'y-Gen.*

49. See *Space Handbook* 182–83.

50. N.Y. Times, June 9, 1959, p. 12.

51. *Hearings on H.R. 11881* at 496. For an opinion that this would be inefficient and too expensive, see remarks of Gen. Boushey, at 585.

52. *The Development and Use of Nuclear Power . . . ,* 13 RECORD OF N.Y.C.B.A. 350, 362 (1958).

53. See *Hearings on H.R. 11881* at 376 (Dr. Whipple) and *Survey of Space Law,* 22 ff.

54. Galina, *On the Question of Interplanetary Law,* SOVIET STATE

AND LAW 52–58 (No. 7, 1958); Korovin, *International Status of Cosmic Space*, INT'L AFF. (Moscow) 56 (No. 1, 1959).

55. N.Y. Times, June 19, 1959. The draft text of the convention is reproduced in the valuable report, prepared under the auspices of Harvard Law School and Atomic Industrial Forum, entitled *International Problems of Financial Protection against Nuclear Risk* (1959), hereinafter cited as Harvard Study.

56. Harvard Study 10.

57. 1865, 3 H. & C. 774, 159 Eng. Rep. 737 and 1868, L.R. 3, H.L. 330.

58. See generally McNAIR, THE LAW OF THE AIR 53–77 (Kerr and MacCrindle, eds., 2d ed. 1953); RHYNE, AVIATION ACCIDENT LAW 64 ff. (1947); PROSSER, TORTS 203, 345–46 (2d ed. 1955). Section 9 of the British Air Navigation Act of 1920 imposed an absolute liability for damage caused by a plane in taking off, landing, or dropping a part or article. This was somewhat modified by § 15 of the 1936 Act.

In the United States the Commissioners on Uniform State Laws incorporated the doctrine into § 5 of the Uniform Aeronautics Act in 1922. Twelve American states adopted this rule without limitation, and some five others have modifications of the rule. See Eubank, *Land Damage Liability in Aircraft Cases*, 57 DICK. L. REV. 188, 193 (1953). The Uniform Act was withdrawn in 1943 for further study and has not been reissued. For an early case, see Guille v. Swan, 19 Johns., N.Y., 381, 10 Am. Dec. 234 (1822).

59. See Cooper, *Aircraft Liability to Persons and Property on Ground*, 17 ABA J. 435 (1931); Ewing, *The Ground Rule of Torts by Aircraft at the American Law Institute*, 5 AIR L. REV. 323 (1934); *Report of A.B.A. Standing Committee on Aeronautical Law* (1931).

60. Section 520, Comment b. See, upholding this position, Vold, *Strict Liability for Aircraft Crashes and Forced Landings on Ground Victims Outside of Established Landing Areas*, 5 HASTINGS L.J. 1 (1953); Bohlen, *Aviation under the Common Law*, 48 HARV. L. REV. 216 (1934).

61. See PROSSER, *op. cit. supra* note 58, at 346.

62. See Schachter, PROC. AM. SOC'Y INT'L L. 1958, at 247.

63. Harvard Study 24, 25.

64. See McNAIR, *op. cit. supra* note 58, at 263–69; Latchford, *Bearing of International Air Navigation Conventions on the Use of Outer Space*, 53 AM. J. INT'L L. 405, 410–11 (1959).

65. United Nations *Ad Hoc* Committee on the Peaceful Uses of

Outer Space, *Report of the Legal Committee*, U.N. Doc. No. A/AC.98/2, 5 (12 June 1959).

66. Harvard Study 17; see also § 170 of the U.S. Price-Anderson Act of 1957.

67. 137 L.N.T.S. 11; 5 HUDSON, INTERNATIONAL LEGISLATION 100. See SHAWCROSS & BEAUMONT, AIR LAW §§ 321–30 (2d ed. 1951); RHYNE, *op. cit. supra* note 58, at 254–74.

68. A limitation on amounts recoverable for injuries caused to persons is contrary to the concepts of American tort law, certainly where negligence can be shown. Thirteen states limit amounts recoverable for wrongful death, however, and of course in such matters as Workmen's Compensation an insurance principle has been substituted for tort suits in most cases.

The limitations imposed by the Warsaw Convention have been defended on the basis of a need to protect an infant industry against threat of catastrophic losses which would make it impossible to raise capital, uniformity of law, the availability of insurance to passengers —arguments that may be heard when commercial space vehicles for transport purposes become feasible. Critics point out that the domestic experience of U.S. airlines does not bear this theory out; that the limitation on a carrier's defenses is no bargain since the civil law presumes a carrier liable anyway where a contract of carriage plus no safe arrival are shown (unless *force majeure* or the passenger's sole negligence is shown); and that in Anglo-American jurisdictions which do not use rules of strict liability the doctrine of *res ipsa loquitur* is often available; that purely domestic cases are affected, and so forth. In general, see DRION, LIMITATION OF LIABILITIES IN INTERNATIONAL AIR LAW (1954); Wright, *The Warsaw Convention's Damages Limitations*, CLEV.-MAR. L. REV. (1957); ASS'N OF THE BAR OF THE CITY OF NEW YORK, REPORT OF THE COMMITTEE ON AERONAUTICS ON THE WARSAW CONVENTION AS AMENDED BY THE HAGUE PROTOCOL (1959).

69. See MCNAIR, *op. cit. supra* note 58, at 50–53; RHYNE, *op. cit. supra* note 58, at 121–39. For application of *res ipsa loquitur* in air law, see Smith v. Penn. Central Airlines, 76 F. Supp. 940 (1948); Northwest Airlines v. Rowe, 226 F.2d 365 (1955); Sappetux v. U.S., 153 F. Supp. 496 (1957); Trikey v. Transocean Airlines, 255 F.2d 824 (1958).

70. Georgia, Nevada, and Maryland.

71. 40 DEP'T STATE BULL. 889 (1959).

72. On problems of the U.S. Tort Claims Act, see Dalehite v. United States, 346 U.S. 15 (1953).

73. See Press Release No. 3179, at 6. See also De Rode-Verschoor, *The Responsibility of the States for the Damage Caused by the Launched Space-Bodies*, paper presented to the I.A.F., Aug., 1958, reprinted in *Space Law, A Symposium, Prepared by the Special Committee on Space and Aeronautics*, U.S. Senate, 85th Cong., 2d Sess., 434–435; and McLaughlin, *The International Law of Outer Space*, in NATIONAL SECURITY IN THE NUCLEAR AGE, 55–56 (proceedings of a conference held at the U. of Minn., Feb. 17–21, 1958, mimeo).

74. *Report of the Legal Committee, supra* note 65, at 7.

75. See Korovin, *supra* note 54, at 56; see *Survey of Space Law*, 26–27. Off-course or damaged civil aircraft and ships are usually returned by friendly nations but this is often said to be a matter for specific agreements or of comity. The United States has urged with respect to craft downed by the Communist bloc countries that there is an *obligation* to return planes forced off their path in distress. There is also a general policy of return for craft stolen in another nation, seized by pirates or mutineers, and the like. See generally Lissitzyn, *Treatment of Aerial Intruders in Recent Practice and International Law*, 47 AM. J. INT'L L. 559 ff. (1953). For practice with respect to *ships* in distress, see JESSUP, THE LAW OF TERRITORIAL WATERS AND MARITIME JURISDICTION, 194–208, 220–21, 254–55, 258–63, 450, 466 (1927).

76. See generally Fenston and De Saussure, 1 MCGILL L.J. 66 (1952).

77. See *Draft of a Convention on the Legal Status of Aircraft and of Crimes Committed on Board of Aircraft*, 25 J. AIR L. & COMM. 455 ff. (1958).

78. Convention on the High Seas (1958), Articles 5 and 6; Jacobini, 6 WEST. P.Q. 680 (1953); Jenks, 5 INT'L COMP. L.Q. 99, 108 (1956); REIFF, THE UNITED STATES AND THE TREATY LAW OF THE SEA 34–35, 76–80 (1959); 1 OPPENHEIM INTERNATIONAL LAW 541 (ed. Lauterpacht, 8th ed. 1955).

On piracy, see Convention on the High Seas, Arts. 14–22; *Piracy Laws of Various Countries*, 26 AM. J. INT'L L. Supp. 893–902; REIFF, *supra* at 76.

On other problems and analogies, see Convention, Arts. 14–22; Ward *Projecting the Law of the Sea into the Law of Space*, JAG J. 3–8 (March 1957); Korovin, *supra* note 54, at 54–55.

79. Article 7 of the Convention on the High Seas of 1958 provides that: "The provisions of the preceding articles do not prejudice the question of ships employed on the official service of an intergovernmental organization flying the flag of the organization."

See also Report by François, Special Rapporteur for the I.L.C., *The Right of International Organizations to Sail Vessels under Their Flags*, U.N. Doc. No. A/CN.4/103 (May 8, 1956). Some trawlers built with the aid of UNKRA flew the UN and Korean flags in 1955. 1 U.N. REV. 15 (1954).

80. On identification through use of visual markings, call signs, orbits, or orbital characteristics and registration, see *Report of the Legal Committee*, *supra* note 65, at 6. See also McDougal, *Artificial Satellites: A Modest Proposal*, 51 AM. J. INT'L L. 74 (1957).

81. *Survey of Space Law* 29 suggests that some of the problems to be resolved at a later date include:

> Use of substances and forces found in space, such as properties which may be used for power or propulsion purposes as basic advances occur in engineering techniques.
> Emigration and customs controls.
> Franchise of commercial carriers.
> Recognition, in law, of the effects of time differentials, not only in regard to lengthy space travel but in regard to the peculiarities of the tempo of life caused by significantly high speeds.
> Adjustment of the affairs of space travelers as to wills, abandoned property, desertion, presumption of death, domicile, etc.
> Regulation of space-station orbits and functions.
> Extension of earth-made law to other planets.

On who may leave the earth and return thereto, see Haley, *Space Law and Metalaw . . .* , VII INT'L ASTRO. CONF. PROC. 1956, 12–13.

82. See the International Collision Regulations annexed, for example, to the International Convention for the Safety of Life at Sea of 1948; ICAO, Int'l Standards, Rules of the Air: Annex 2 to the Convention on International Civil Aviation and Annex 10 to Aeronautical Telecommunications. See also REIFF, *op. cit. supra* note 78, at 100 ff.; COLOMBOS, INTERNATIONAL LAW OF THE SEA 252–55 (3d ed. 1954); KNAUTH, COLLECTED MARITIME CONVENTIONS (1957); Ward, *supra* note 78, at 3–8. On sea law analogies in air law, see MCNAIR, *op. cit. supra* note 58, at 233–62. On the "rules of the road" and "customary" international law, see also *The Scotia*, 14 Wall 170 (1871).

It has also been suggested that, to the extent spacecraft can be assimilated to civil aircraft, they ought to follow ICAO safety standards and recommended practices while in the airspace, though these are not strictly binding even as to aircraft. See remarks of Colclaser, PROC. AM. SOC'Y INT'L L. 1956, 100–1.

83. Cf. ICAO, Personnel Licensing, Annex 1 to the Convention; Officers' Competency Certificates Convention, 1936, 1 INTERNATIONAL LABOUR CODE, Articles 976–981 (1951); Certification of Able Seamen Convention, 1946, Articles 982–986, *ibid.*

84. Cf. ICAO, Airworthiness of Aircraft, Annex 8 to the Convention; International Convention for the Safety of Life at Sea, 1948 G.B. T.S. 302–423. Cf. the International Load Lines Convention of 1930 (T.S. 858 and T.S. 942).

85. On oil: Convention on the High Seas, Art. 24; Convention on Oil Pollution (1954); REIFF, *op. cit. supra* note 78, at 225.

On nuclear wastes: Convention on the High Seas, Art. 24. The Resolution of the Geneva Conference on Pollution of the High Seas by Radioactive Materials, April 27, 1958, recommends that the IAEA aid in establishing standards, drawing regulations, and the like to control this pollution.

86. Cf. ICAO International Standards and Recommended Practices, Search and Rescue, Convention Annexes 12 and 13 (Aircraft Accident Inquiry).

87. See, for example, Warsaw Convention for the Unification of Certain Rules Regarding International Air Transport, 1929, 137 L.N.T.S. 11–59, as amended, and IATO, General Conditions of Carriage, MCNAIR, *op. cit. supra* note 58, at 435–68, 146–232. For maritime analogies see Brussels Convention for the Unification of Rules relating to Certain Bills of Lading, 120 L.N.T.S. 155–85; SCRUTTON, CHARTER PARTIES AND BILLS OF LADING (16th ed. 1955); CARVER, CARRIAGE OF GOODS BY SEA (8th ed. 1938). See also generally JENKS, *supra* note 78.

88. JENKS, THE COMMON LAW OF MANKIND 392–93 (1958). It should be noted that *neither* the "standards" nor the "recommended practices" of ICAO are, strictly speaking, binding.

89. See statement of Becker, 40 DEP'T STATE BULL. 890 (1959).

9. CHAOS OR CONTROL?

1. 36 DEP'T STATE BULL. 124 (1957).
2. *Id.* at 227.
3. 37 DEP'T STATE BULL. 271 (1957).
4. *Id.* at 453.

5. 38 DEP'T STATE BULL. 126 (1958).

6. Text in N.Y. Times, March 16, 1958, p. 34. See also p. 1. There is a remarkable similarity between the Soviet program and proposals made by Senator Wiley on December 24, 1957, in an address at Georgetown University titled *Challenges Old and New in the Space Age: The Need for an International Space Organization* (mimeo.).

7. U.N. Doc. No. A/3818 (March 17, 1958). On events at the United Nations through December, 1958, see Taubenfeld, *Consideration at the United Nations of the Status of Outer Space*, 53 AM. J. INT'L L. 400–405 (1959).

8. U.N. Doc. No. A/3902 (September 2, 1958).

9. See U.N. Doc. No. A/C.1/L.219 (November 7, 1958), and, for the supporting reasoning, the statement by Mr. Zorin, U.N. Doc. No. A/C.1/SR.982, 2–5 (November 15, 1958). Curbs on the use of space were also proposed by the United States at about this time in the "surprise attack" talks then in progress. N.Y. Times, November 5, 1958, p. 5, col. 1.

10. Others were Australia, Belgium, Bolivia, Canada, Denmark, France, Guatemala, Ireland, Italy, Japan, Nepal, the Netherlands, New Zealand, Sweden, Turkey, the Union of South Africa, the United Kingdom, Uruguay, and Venezuela.

11. U.N. Doc. No. A/C.1/L.220 (Nov. 13, 1958).

12. U.N. Doc. No. A/C.1/L.219/Rev. 1 (Nov. 18, 1958).

13. U.N. Doc. No. A/C.1/L.220/Rev. 1 (Nov. 21, 1958).

14. See, generally, *Report of the First Committee*, U.N. Doc. No. A/4009 (Nov. 28, 1958).

15. See U.N. Doc. No. A/C.1/SR.995, 15 (Nov. 24, 1958).

16. For further details and citations to U.N. documents see Taubenfeld, *supra* note 7, at 402–5.

17. See, for example, statement by the representatives of Austria, Chile, Iran, the Netherlands, Peru, the Philippines, and Sweden. U.N. Docs. Nos. A/C.1/SR.990, 5–6; 982, 8–10; 988, 5–7; 987, 2–3; 983, 6–8; 991, 5–7; 984, p. 2. Some, but not all, noted that launching of satellites, up to the time of the Committee's sessions, had occurred under the network of international arrangements constituting the International Geophysical Year and might be unobjectionable on that account alone.

18. See *Summary Records*, U.N. Docs. Nos. A/AC.98/SRs 1–3, esp. Speeches of Ambassador Lodge, Dr. Hugh L. Dryden (Deputy Administrator of NASA) and Loftus E. Becker (Legal Adviser to the State Department), SR.1, pp. 4–6; SR.2, pp. 4–6; SR.3, pp. 3–7.

19. U.N. Press Release PM/3728 (May 6, 1959).

20. See U.N. Docs. Nos. A/AC.98/L.1 and Rev. 1; L.2; L.4–6 (Italy).

21. See, for example, *ibid.*, SR.2, 3 ff.

22. Dr. Hugh Dryden, *ibid.*, SR.2, 4–6. See also comments of the Iranian representative, *ibid.*, SR.2, 3–4.

23. Comment of the Canadian representative, *ibid.*, SR.2, 6–7.

24. See remarks of the Japanese and Italian representatives, U.N. Doc. No. A/AC.98/TECH/SR.1.

25. The Technical Committee's Report is U.N. Doc. No. A/AC.-98/3.

26. U.N. Docs. Nos. A/AC.98/L.7 and L.8.

27. The Legal Committee's Report is U.N. Doc. No. A/AC.98/2.

28. The United States has also suggested that the problem of relations with extra-terrestrial life has a very low priority. U.N. Doc. No. A/AC.98/L.7.

29. See U.N. Doc. No. A/AC.98/4 and, as approved by the Committee, U.N. Doc. No. A/AC.98/L.13.

30. U.N. Doc. No. A/AC.98/L.10.

31. See, U.N. Docs. Nos. A/AC.98/L.11, SR.4 (PROV.), and SR.5 (PROV.).

32. The Australian representative suggested that not only geographical distribution but the present distribution of capabilities and active interest in outer space also be considered. U.N. Doc. No. A/AC.98/SR.5 (PROV), 4. On the difficulties with this idea, see U.N. Press Release OS/26 (June 25, 1959).

33. U.N. Doc. No. A/AC.98/SR.4 (PROV), p. 6.

34. See *ibid.*, SR.5 (PROV). The Report is U.N. Doc. No. A/4141.

35. Editorial, 101 SOLICITORS J. 965 (1957). And see the remarks by Keating, Ninth Annual Congress of the International Astronautical Federation, Aug. 29, 1958, printed in 45 ABA J. See also Schofield, 10 AIR U. Q. REV. 101 (1958).

36. Becker, JAG J., Feb. 1959, p. 6.

37. Becker, 38 DEP'T STATE BULL. 962 (1958).

38. Maxwell Cohen, quoted in The Reporter, June 12, 1958, p. 19.

39. Cited by Ward, Am. Bar Ass'n, *Report of the Section on International Law, 1959*, p. 27.

40. For various suggestions as to regimes for outer space, see Commission to Study the Organization of Peace, *Strengthening the United Nations, Report* (1957); JENKS, THE COMMON LAW OF MANKIND

(1958); Sir Leslie Munro, 4 U.N. REV. 7–10 (Feb. 1958); former President Truman, N.Y. Times, April 10, 1959, p. 1; KNAUTH, LEGAL PROBLEMS OF OUTER SPACE IN RELATION TO THE UNITED NATIONS (1958); Cox, *International Control of Outer Space*, Missiles and Rockets, June, 1957, p. 71 (on a U.N. Space Police organization); Wiley, *Challenges, Old and New, in the Space Age; The Need for an International Space Organization*, address at Georgetown U., Feb. 24, 1958 (mimeo.); Horsford, *The Law of Space*, 14 J. BRIT. INTERPLANETARY SOC'Y 144–50 (1955); and the proposals of Haley for an "Independent and Sovereign Authority" in *Space Law and Metalaw*, Harvard Law Record 1–2 (Nov. 1, 1956).

41. See Johnson, *The Effect of Resolutions of the General Assembly of the United Nations*, 32 BRIT. YB. INT'L L. 97 (1957).

42. See Pépin, *Space Penetration*, PROC. AM. SOC'Y INT'L L. 1958, 229–35.

43. Sir Leslie Munro, speech on Nov. 22, 1957, reprinted in *Space Law, A Symposium* at 377.

For a study of organs and agencies established by treaty within the framework of the United Nations (the Permanent Central Opium Board and the Drug Supervisory Body, the International Bureau for Declarations of Death, and the International Atomic Energy Agency), see *Conference on the Elimination or Reduction of Future Statelessness*, U.N. Doc. No. A/CONF.9/8 (7 April 1959).

44. Adequate treatment of all the possible complexities would require us to duplicate the bold and comprehensive studies of CLARK & SOHN in WORLD PEACE THROUGH WORLD LAW (1958), a task we have not pretended to perform.

Index

Bei Fragen zur Produktsicherheit wenden Sie sich bitte an:
If you have any questions regarding product safety,
please contact:

Walter de Gruyter GmbH
Genthiner Straße 13
10785 Berlin
productsafety@degruyterbrill.com